SHOWDOWN

SHOWDOWN

THURGOOD MARSHALL AND THE
SUPREME COURT NOMINATION
THAT CHANGED AMERICA

Wil Haygood

ALFRED A. KNOPF · NEW YORK · 2015

THIS IS A BORZOI BOOK
PUBLISHED BY ALFRED A. KNOPF

www.aaknopf.com

Knopf, Borzoi Books, and the colophon are registered trademarks
of Penguin Random House LLC.

Library of Congress Cataloging-in-Publication Data
Haygood, Wil, author.
Showdown : Thurgood Marshall and the supreme court nomination
that changed America / by Wil Haygood.
pages cm
Includes bibliographical references.
ISBN 978-0-307-95719-1 (hardcover)—ISBN 978-0-385-35316-8 (eBook)
1. Marshall, Thurgood, 1908–1993.   2. United States. Supreme Court—Officials and
employees—Selection and appointment—History—20th century.   3. Judges—Selection
and appointment—United States—History—20th century.   I. Title.
KF8745.M34H394 2015
347.73'2634—dc23   2014044440

Jacket photograph: Thurgood Marshall in his New York residence,
September 11, 1962, after the Senate confirmation of his year-old nomination
to the Second U.S. Court of Appeals. AP Photo.
Back-of-jacket photograph: On June 29, 1991, Thurgood Marshall informs the nation
he is stepping down from the U.S. Supreme Court. © 1999, *The Washington Post.*
Reprinted with permission.
Jacket design by Abby Weintraub

Manufactured in the United States of America
First Edition

For Michael B. Coleman, and for Larry James

CONTENTS

SHOWDOWN

Johnson and Marshall prepare to meet the press on the day
of the historic nomination.

Bound for Room 2228

THE HUNGER FOR NEGRO FREEDOM began as soon as the first slave ships from West Africa and Brazil landed on America's shores. The desire to be free constituted a fierce, undying impulse. All through the seventeenth and eighteenth centuries, however, the ships kept coming. While Great Britain ended its participation in the international slave trade in 1807, America, which relied on cheap labor for its cotton production, did not. In time, there would be uprisings and bloody insurrections, led by the likes of Denmark Vesey in South Carolina, John Brown in Kansas, and Nat Turner in Virginia. Abolitionists bolted from horse-driven carriages into statehouses, railing against slavery while displaying pictures of men, women, and children in chains. Slavery, the abolitionists were constantly reminded, was intertwined with American law. "Let the South have her negroes to her heart's content, and in her own way—and let us go on getting rich and powerful by feeding and clothing them," *The Chicago Times* advised.

President Abraham Lincoln's threat to end slavery ignited the Civil War. On New Year's Day 1863, Lincoln issued his Emancipation Proclamation. Three and a half million Negroes were to be set free. The bold decision stunned members of the president's cabinet. As Secretary of the Navy Gideon Welles would put it, the decision was "fraught with consequences, immediate and remote, such as human foresight could not penetrate." Battered into submission in the intervening months, the Confederate general Robert E. Lee finally surrendered at Appomattox on April 9, 1865. Days later—April 14, 1865—Lincoln was assassinated by a lunatic gunman in a theater in Washington.

Beyond Reconstruction, and the dawning of the twentieth century, the question lingered: How free was the Negro? Not very. The answer was all too obvious: Racial murders haunted the land. White vigilante militias rose in power. There existed entire communities in the South where the Negro could not vote. The tenets drawn out in the Declaration of Independence and the U.S. Constitution were beautiful and declarative, but in practice they often seemed beyond the reach of the Negro.

In 1909, to address disparity and inequality, an eclectic group— among them James Weldon Johnson, W. E. B. DuBois, Mary White Ovington, and Joel Spingarn—organized the NAACP, the National Association for the Advancement of Colored People. The group's aim was to protect Negroes from abuse while fighting for their rights and elevating their standing nationwide. Members paid dues; progressive whites joined up. With limited resources, it was expected that executives of the organization would, out of necessity, use their imaginations when it came to strategizing.

IN 1940, Thurgood Marshall—who had joined the NAACP as a lawyer four years earlier after working at a barely-making-it law practice in his native Baltimore—came up with an idea to form a permanent legal arm of the NAACP. It was known as the NAACP Legal Defense and Educational Fund, and its mission was clear: to assault discrimination and legal segregation in America's courtrooms. Marshall was its architect; he utilized the services of plenty of other lawyers, but he quickly became its marquee performer. He roamed the country—when he wasn't in the courtroom, he packed lecture halls and churches—and amassed a stunning array of landmark court victories. There was *Smith v. Allwright* in 1944, a case that outlawed the all-white Democratic primary in Texas. *Shelley v. Kraemer* made front-page news in 1948, in which the high court ruled it was illegal to bar Negroes and other minorities from purchasing property even if the homeowner had written it into a clause of the deed. Two years later—in another case rooted in Texas—came the *Sweatt v. Painter* victory, in which the high court ordered the University of Texas to admit a Negro it had previously barred from its law school. (It was while in Texas during the primary court battle that Thurgood Marshall first began hearing of a young U.S. Senate candidate by the name of Lyndon Johnson. Johnson did not win his 1941 Senate campaign, but Marshall was very much aware that as labor forces abandoned Johnson's candidacy, "the Negro support stuck with him.") Then, in 1954, came the Marshall-led titanic achievement of *Brown v. Board of Education*, which outlawed the separate-but-equal doctrine that had been the law of the land and ordered the desegregation of public schools. That decision tore at the spiritual heart of all who believed that separate was equal in any facet of American society. There was not another lawyer in America whose constitutional victories could match Thurgood Marshall's in the arena of equal rights. It was as if Marshall had rethreaded parts of the Constitution itself, stitching the Negro, at long last, into the fabric of the nation.

The NAACP legal victories were both wonderful and newsworthy, but because they were rarely respected by federal willpower or muscle, they were often ignored and went unenforced. Municipalities worked tirelessly to devise tricky and malevolent ways to get around the high court decisions.

The Negro was still not free.

Then came the early 1960s newsreel footage of Negroes being beaten and bitten by dogs held by law enforcement officers, all because of the quest for freedom. Following President Kennedy's assassination, Lyndon Johnson assumed the presidency. American presidents were bewitched by race. Johnson, however, understood that when three civil rights workers—Andrew Goodman, Michael Schwerner, and James Chaney—went missing and were found murdered in Mississippi in 1964, a new era had begun.

On March 7, 1965, nine months after the Mississippi murders, civil rights activists gathered in an attempt to cross the Edmund Pettus Bridge in Selma, Alabama, in a quest for voting rights. A nation saw scores of marchers being viciously beaten. Northern cities were soon torched in widespread rioting. Johnson knew the time had come, that Negroes would not retreat. He had signed the landmark Civil Rights Act of 1964. Finally, the 1965 Voting Rights Act was signed into law.

Now he had signed two of the most powerful pieces of presidential legislation since the Civil War and the Emancipation Proclamation. It mattered not at all to him that the South vowed to rebel in the midst of all the civil rights legislation and melodrama taking place. And it mattered not at all that southern senators were castigating him in their home districts. Some refused his invitations to the White House for coffee. But Lyndon Johnson was not yet finished.

The U.S. Supreme Court, since its founding, had always featured white justices. A Negro had never even been seriously considered. Even as Johnson was fighting a war in Vietnam and battling poverty, it was race that truly haunted and tore at the fabric—and fragility—of a nation. "The nastiest mail we got was over race—not Vietnam," says the LBJ aide Joseph Califano.

On the morning of June 13, 1967, LBJ gathered some key members of his staff in the Oval Office. Among them were the aides Marvin Watson and Clifford Alexander. Also there was Thurgood Marshall— who had been a federal appeals court judge and was the current solicitor general—and Louis Martin, a White House political adviser. Martin, a Negro, was also a high-ranking member of the Democratic National Committee. He had known Marshall for years and looked upon him with an enormous amount of reverence. A Negro butler served light refreshments to the small gathering. There was a feeling around the room of heightened emotion mixed with swooning, especially by all the Negroes present.

The president was going to nominate a Negro to the U.S. Supreme Court. He aimed to emancipate the nation's legal system by aiming for the very top of it. He told no one save a very few close aides; he was not going to be talked out of it. "I want to do this job that Abraham Lincoln started," Johnson had confided to a few aides about his plans.

Thurgood Marshall had been considered Public Enemy No. 1 in the South because of his court victories upending many of the laws of segregation. With Johnson's looming nomination of Marshall, it was as if the president were hammering the final nail into the coffin of white supremacy. "Thurgood," LBJ said to Marshall, "I'm nominating you because you're a lot like me: bigger than life, and we come from the same kind of people." Marshall smiled widely.

There had never been a president with the kind of ease around

Negroes that Lyndon Johnson possessed. Johnson knew how much it meant to Louis Martin to be in the White House on this momentous day. "He really had power, and he deserved it," Marshall would later say—not of Johnson, but of Louis Martin. "He was a great guy. He knew his way around. I doubt that any meaningful Negro in this country would exist without Louis knowing about it."

President Johnson finally rose from the sofa after ordering Marshall to phone his wife, Cissy, and inform her of what was about to happen. Johnson began to lead the group outside. Louis Martin was an emotional sort. He had desperately wanted to get a job on a major newspaper after taking a journalism degree from the University of Michigan in 1934, but major newspapers were not hiring Negroes. He wound up in Cuba, writing freelance articles before returning to America and editing a Negro newspaper. Whenever he'd run into Marshall—airports, train stations, Chicago or Harlem barrooms—they'd get to reminiscing about all the things they'd seen: Negro chain gangs, segregated movie theaters, all-white police departments; they'd get to recalling those restaurants that made them go around the back just to get a sandwich. Now this—a Supreme Court nomination. Louis Martin was so sentimental that he would often cry when there was some kind of exalted Negro achievement to celebrate, big tears welling up in his eyes. As President Johnson began to walk alongside Thurgood Marshall out of the Oval Office, Martin began sobbing, quietly—for two reasons. The first was sheer joy and how happy he was for Marshall.

The second reason was worry and fear. He knew how difficult the looming battle for confirmation was going to be.

When Johnson and Marshall emerged from the White House, walking toward the Rose Garden and the bank of microphones, members of the press suddenly looked up. Some squinted to see more clearly against the glare of sunlight as the hum of whispering began. When Marshall himself was unmistakably spotted—just over the president's left shoulder—the air filled with heightened curiosity. Reporters started jockeying for better positions. Photographers raised their cameras. There was a feeling something profound was about to happen.

DAY ONE

1

The Ghosts of Little Rock

Please, sir, no nigger on the Supreme Court bench.
                    —*an Arkansas family in a letter to Senator John McClellan*
                                    about the Marshall nomination

The Supreme Court in 1966. It had been composed of only white men since
President George Washington's first appointees in 1789.

JOHN MCCLELLAN was going to stop Thurgood Marshall.
     He simply could not imagine the likes of Marshall on the U.S.
Supreme Court, so he convinced himself he could prevent it. He was
Senator John McClellan, and he was powerful, and people feared
him. He had a hard face—a dead ringer for the comic Jack Benny if
Benny had been dipped in plaster—and a hard, scratchy voice. He
wore horn-rimmed glasses from which, time and again during previous hearings while sitting in judgment of others, he peered down on
witnesses with menacing glares. He combed his hair straight back, in

a severe manner. McClellan was one of the Senate barons—men who had served for years and seemed to have grown out of the very building that housed the U.S. Senate. He loathed small talk and abhorred social teas and the like, which many senators and their wives seemed to enjoy. Even when his Arkansas constituents visited his Washington office, he seemed impatient, as if he wished they could state their business as fast as possible and be on their way. He'd shoot an aide *that* look and then the aide would begin motioning toward the door and McClellan would toss final words at his guests: thanks for coming by, say hi to the folks back home, don't forget to take a souvenir.

He had been sent to Washington by Arkansas voters, first as a congressman in 1934 and then, in 1942, as a U.S. senator. And now he found himself with a coveted seat on the powerful Senate Judiciary Committee. He told his aides to start digging. He wanted as much information on Thurgood Marshall as he could get, and he wanted it as fast as he could get it. John McClellan looked upon himself as a force for good, standing between Thurgood Marshall and the Supreme Court of the United States of America.

In Washington, McClellan prided himself on his activities, his constant motion. At one time, he sat on fourteen subcommittees. In 1954, he found himself on a committee with the Wisconsin senator Joseph McCarthy, who was galloping around the nation's capital on a one-man witch hunt for Communists. McCarthy had charged the State Department with having dozens of Communists in its employ. At a time when Americans were fearful of Communism, McCarthy's charges landed him on the front pages. Many were riled up. All of this intrigued McClellan, as ready as anyone to corral a Communist. But McCarthy, who was a shambling and reckless figure, soon made McClellan nervous. It was McCarthy's lack of discipline and some of his aides who were so utterly unprofessional. "I'm fond of Joe McCarthy," McClellan allowed, "but he's getting out of hand, and we have to do something to control him." McClellan quit the McCarthy-led committee he was on. He escaped the shadow of McCarthy with prescient timing, as the Army-McCarthy hearings, nationally televised, exposed McCarthy as a mean-spirited liar. The Senate eventually censured him.

In 1957, McClellan led the celebrated Senate Labor Rackets Committee, which took on mobsters and their henchmen and eventually exposed the criminal underworld in America. That was the moment that John McClellan's profile rose in America. Because of disclosures exposed by his committee, two teamsters, Jimmy Hoffa and Dave Beck, had been sent to prison. Another round of hearings in 1963 offered up Joseph Valachi, a mobster who seemed to thrill television viewers with his insider's account of cold-blooded doings in the Mafia. The *Omaha World-Herald* had once said of McClellan that he possessed a "steely mask of Old Testament righteousness." If John McClellan had stopped gangsters, he figured he could certainly thwart LBJ's new Supreme Court nominee.

In Washington, they didn't bother to refer to him as Senator McClellan; they called him "the Chairman," because he had been chairman of the Senate Permanent Subcommittee on Investigations, as well as chairman of the Senate Select Committee on Improper Activities in the Labor or Management Field, which was the committee that provided him with the tools to go after the mobsters. Because those racketeering hearings were nationally televised, everyone knew Senator John McClellan. The young aides in the Johnson White House knew well how dangerous McClellan could be to their efforts in getting Thurgood Marshall onto the U.S. Supreme Court. "Virtually every speech he made inscribed a rising curve from the prudent statement of fact to polemical rage, his powerful voice quavering with indignation," is how the Johnson aide Harry McPherson put it.

The Johnson administration had drawn a battle line. Thurgood Marshall was the lawyer who had won the *Brown v. Board of Education* ruling, a ruling that led to utter embarrassment in McClellan's home state in the fall of 1957, when nine Negro schoolchildren had tried to desegregate Little Rock Central High School and been stopped by whites hurling epithets, spit, and large rocks. (It was also the year that *Time* magazine named McClellan its Man of the Year.) Reporters on the scene to cover the story were chased and bloodied by the mobs. This had forced President Dwight Eisenhower to go into military mode and dispatch troops to protect the children. The troops had to remain at the school watching over the Negro children for an entire year. Little Rock was thus seared into the nation's psyche as mean and bigoted. And on his trips back home to Arkansas at the time, to attend all those social events and grand openings and visit family as all politicians do, John McClellan had to endure all the chatter about Little Rock, about how the government was attacking states' rights, how Negroes were trying to take over the schools. And all he could do was assure his constituents that he was doing everything he could to protect their way of life, the southern way of life. It made McClellan angry, though, how he had to take up all of this time defending himself and how hard he was working in Washington to keep Arkansas as it had always been. Thurgood Marshall, if he made it to the Supreme Court, was not going to keep Arkansas as it had always been.

But first, before McClellan could do anything about Marshall, he had to clear his throat. He did not like it one bit that President Johnson had stunned him with the suddenness of the Marshall nomination. After all, he was a southern Democrat like Johnson himself! John McClellan so prided himself on having the pulse of government, of government at the highest levels, of what they were doing over at the White House, that this series of events—a justice departing, then, in a flash, a new nomination—only gnawed at his sense of propriety and even decorum. McClellan couldn't figure out how all of this had transpired, had been put into motion without any hints falling his way. And he did not like any of it at all.

IT WAS OFTEN SAID around the Johnson White House that what LBJ wanted, LBJ got. And in the summer of 1967, LBJ wanted to put Thurgood Marshall, a Negro, on the Supreme Court. There was a small problem: there was no vacancy nor had a single sitting justice been talking about stepping down from his lifetime appointment. Johnson looked to his Texas roots and saw clearly how he could solve the problem.

Lyndon Johnson had first met the associate justice Tom Clark back in Texas in 1938, when Johnson was a young congressman. The Johnson and Clark families went on outings together, their little children romping across wide lawns. "A friendship developed that included the whole family; it was much more than a professional relationship between the two men," Tom Clark's daughter, Mimi Clark Gronlund, would recall. When Johnson's daughters, Lynda and Luci, became engaged, the Clarks threw parties for them. (There was something interesting about Texas men who had more amenable attitudes toward Negroes than others in the state. "I knew him when he first came to Washington," Thurgood Marshall would come to recall of Tom Clark. "I knew his mother. And his brother in Dallas . . . His mother, way back—this will go back to the late thirties—her housekeeper, a Negro, ate dinner with her. They ate right at the same table together. Now, back in the thirties, you didn't do that in Texas.") Clark had originally been encouraged to come to Washington in 1937 by the House majority leader, Sam Rayburn, who was Johnson's mentor. Clark joined the Justice Department as a special assistant. After the death of Franklin D. Roosevelt, President Truman appointed Clark attorney general. And when the Supreme Court justice Frank Murphy died in 1949, Truman nominated Clark to the court. Court openings were created, often, by grave and declining health, or death. But in 1967, as Justice Clark's family knew, he was in good health and had not at all talked of resigning from the court. In order to nominate Marshall, Johnson had to make some fast chess-like moves.

First, Johnson encouraged Attorney General Nicholas Katzenbach to resign, then appointed Katzenbach undersecretary of state. Johnson intended to appoint Ramsey Clark—the deputy attorney general, who happened to be Tom Clark's son—to the position permanently. But Johnson knew others—inside the legal profession and out—would wonder about a perceived conflict of interest because Clark's father sat on the high court. But Lyndon Johnson knew people; he knew the dynamics of fathers and sons, how a rising son could make a father swoon with pride, and how a father, if called upon to make a sacrifice for his one and only son, might do it almost as reflex, without giving it a second thought. "He talked to Tom Clark to tell him he wanted to appoint Ramsey attorney general," Johnson's aide Joseph Califano would recall. "Johnson needed a vacancy to put Thurgood Marshall on the court. So Tom Clark had to retire, and Johnson got the vacancy." Decades later, recalling the Johnson maneuverings, Califano could still beam with amazement: "It was a classic Johnson move."

So grateful was Johnson for Tom Clark's resignation that he sent Clark and his wife on a once-in-a-lifetime trip around the world. Ostensibly, it was a goodwill mission sponsored by the Department of State with Clark expected to exchange ideas with foreign officials about their respective judiciaries, but it really was a gift to the Clarks for Tom Clark's stepping down. The couple set foot in more than a dozen exotic locales, among them Honk Kong, New Zealand, Jordan, Indonesia, Greece, Turkey, Tokyo, and finally Rome—where they dined in style and saw the ruins. Mrs. Clark called it their "great adventure."

The Johnson White House aimed to use surprise as a weapon in its strategic rollout of the Clark-Marshall announcements. And it worked, because some of the Senate Judiciary Committee members—especially the southerners—complained bitterly about the swiftness of the move, which had caught them off guard. "He'd just call Senator Eastland, Senator Thurmond, and say, 'Senator, I'm nominating Thurgood Marshall to the Supreme Court,' and before they could say anything," says Califano, "he'd hang the phone up and call the next senator." McClellan, James Eastland, Strom Thurmond, and all the other Judiciary Committee members were treated with similarly fast phone calls.

The Marshall announcement unleashed waves of pride within the Johnson White House, a pride that bubbled especially among Negroes nationwide.

The White House, at 1600 Pennsylvania Avenue, had a peculiar and vexing relationship with blacks throughout history. In 1901, President Theodore Roosevelt had the educator—and onetime slave—Booker T. Washington to the White House to dine. The engagement was private, unannounced. But word quickly seeped out. The southern newspapers let the epithets fly: "Roosevelt Dines a Darkey." "A Rank Negrophilist." "Our Coon-Flavored President." "Roosevelt Proposes to Coddle the Son of Ham." "At one stroke, and by one act," *The Richmond News* opined of Teddy Roosevelt, "he has destroyed the kindly, warm regard and personal affection for him which were growing up fast in the South. Hereafter . . . it will be impossible to feel, as we were beginning to feel, that he is one of us." Not many years later, in 1915, the D. W. Griffith movie *The Birth of a Nation* opened in theaters. It was based on Thomas Dixon's novel *The Clansman*, a vile piece of fiction that painted blacks with evil stereotypes. They were thieves and sexual marauders lusting after white women. The NAACP condemned the movie, but not President Woodrow Wilson, who hosted a screening at the White House, then heaped praise on the movie. Wilson also went on to segregate the federal workforce in the nation's capital. A

Negro was not appointed to an executive White House position until President Eisenhower's first term, and even that move was fraught with pain. E. Frederic Morrow—a Bowdoin College grad, a CBS public relations executive, a man of steely resolve and great dignity—had done campaign work for candidate Eisenhower. Members of Eisenhower's team were so impressed with his work they promised a White House position. When Ike won, Morrow's phone did not ring. He complained. He was finally given a job at the Commerce Department. But it did not sit well with him; he had been promised a White House position. Republican allies of Morrow's in New York City put pressure on the White House to deliver on its promise, and Morrow finally became a White House staff member in 1955.

Little wonder Negro newspapers around the nation proudly trumpeted the Marshall nomination.

But with pride aside, the Johnson White House knew the first stop was the Senate Judiciary Committee. It was a historic committee and one of the original standing committees in the Senate, first authorized in 1816. Throughout its history, the committee took on a wide range of assignments, from bankruptcies, to state boundaries, to contested Senate elections. The committee even played a role in the aftermath of Reconstruction, settling matters when it came to Confederate states and their restoration to the Union. It had long been a committee steeped in thorny challenges and national urgency. "There was clear knowledge that there would be a fight," remembers the Johnson aide Clifford Alexander of the Marshall nomination. "Johnson knew because he came out of the leadership of the Senate. It was key to get the nomination out of the Judiciary Committee. The Democrats were the segregationists."

It was the job of the senators on the Judiciary Committee to grill the president's judicial nominee and, depending on where they stood philosophically on the choice, search for and expose either weaknesses or strengths. Because a position on the Supreme Court was a lifetime appointment, the hearings were considered gravely important, the highest mission for judiciary members. Questions were developed and shaped in advance, then honed and studied by senators and their staffers. Those questions would be fashioned from investigations that the senators launched in the wake of a nominee's being announced. When the hearings were over, a report would be issued from the Judiciary Committee—from its minority and majority members—to the full Senate. The full Senate would study the report. And then it would vote. It was expected of senators that their votes would, in some way, reflect the mood of their voters back home. Those voters could weigh in on the nominee by letter writing, phone calls, or even making personal visits to the senator's in-state offices. The beauty about the Senate, of course, was that senators served six-year terms. These senators were like ambassadors from their states. The length of their terms sometimes gave them immunity against unchecked emotions from the citizenry. They could dig in on a certain position, the position that was expected of them, or be bold and buck the desires of the people back home.

A part of any president's legacy is judged by his Supreme Court appointments. Some presidents are luckier than others in their opportunities at nominations. Thomas Jefferson had three high court nominations; Abraham Lincoln, five; William Howard Taft, six; Calvin Coolidge, just one; Harry Truman, four; John F. Kennedy, two. Abe Fortas had been President Lyndon Johnson's first Supreme Court nominee in 1965. Fortas—a protégé of the liberal justice William O. Douglas's—and Johnson had known each other for years. Fortas had made a reputation for himself by opposing the internment of Japanese-Americans in World War II and later defending victims of McCarthyism. He also had defended Johnson in a contested 1948 primary election in Texas. Judging by President Johnson's first high court selection, he valued the kind of lawyer who stood up for the rights of the aggrieved. Thurgood Marshall simply affirmed the type of nominee Johnson admired, while also attacking a racial barrier.

THE WHITE HOUSE BEGAN INQUIRING when the Judiciary chairman, James Eastland, would schedule hearings. Through back channels, he sent word he'd schedule them when he was damn ready. Days and days passed. Eastland was going to make them stay around Washington and endure the hot, sticky summer heat. And to hell with their planned summer vacations.

Finally, the Senate Judiciary Committee announced that the hearings for Thurgood Marshall's nomination to the Supreme Court would take place beginning July 13, 1967. In explaining the delay, Eastland claimed he had to return to Mississippi to investigate allegations of hunger in his state. It was a wisecrack lost on few: Eastland loathed the antipoverty workers who were exposing the hunger problem in Mississippi and used their probing as reason to delay the hearings.

In 1967, there were sixteen members of the Senate Judiciary Committee. Eleven were Democrats, members of President Johnson's own political party: John McClellan of Arkansas; Sam Ervin of North Carolina; Thomas Dodd of Connecticut; Phil Hart of Michigan; Edward Long of Missouri; Edward Kennedy of Massachusetts; Birch Bayh of Indiana; Quentin Burdick of North Dakota; Joseph Tydings of Maryland; George Smathers of Florida; and James Eastland of Mississippi. The five Republicans were Everett Dirksen of Illinois; Roman Hruska of Nebraska; Hiram Fong of Hawaii; Hugh Scott of Pennsylvania; and Strom Thurmond of South Carolina.

It would seem, on the surface, because Democrats outnumbered Republicans on the committee, that President Johnson had the numbers in his favor. But the mathematical equation had to be tabulated against the fact that seven members—and, most important, the committee chairman himself, Eastland of Mississippi—were southerners. "Marshall," the committee member Joseph Tydings would recall decades later, "was considered a public enemy of the South."

Johnson's White House aides were far from naive. They were fully prepared to lobby behind-the-scenes support for Marshall. White House operators had a potent array of contacts in the legal community. Even though the White House was contending with the Vietnam War, racial issues forced themselves almost daily upon LBJ's agenda.

Karen Hastie Williams was the daughter of William Hastie, Marshall's former law professor at Howard University Law School. Marshall considered her to be as close as family. She followed the Marshall nominating dynamics with a keen interest. "Marshall had no idea if he would be confirmed," she recalled. "You had the white southerners at the time saying, 'Oh, you can't put a black man on the Supreme Court!' And of course black people thought the nomination was like something from heaven."

Some Senate staffers thought, given the drama and interest in the nomination, that Eastland might move the hearings to a larger room to accommodate more people, among them reporters. "Eastland didn't care for the press," says Jim Flug, a Kennedy staff aide. "Eastland wasn't eager to begin hearings in which people already knew where he stood."

THE JOHNSON WHITE HOUSE was so nervous in the interval between the Marshall announcement and the start of hearings that it ordered the nominee not to utter a word to the press—lest he say something that could be used against him. Always a voluble sort and a raconteur, Marshall complained to friends about the necessity to keep quiet—and away from reporters.

Finally, the Marshall hearings got under way inside room 2228 of the New Senate Office Building on July 13. Marshall arrived with his wife, Cecilia. The pop of camera flashes pinged all around. Marshall—as big as a heavyweight prizefighter—glided to his seat with many eyes following his every step. The seats, as expected, had all quickly filled. It was customary that a nominee's home state senators would introduce him, and the Johnson White House had no problem in getting the New York senators, Jacob Javits, a Republican, and Robert F. Kennedy, a Democrat, to introduce Marshall. The White House hoped the presence of Kennedy might help them with McClellan. Kennedy had first made a name for himself by serving as chief counsel on the McClellan Rackets Committee (1955–1958), and McClellan had praised young Kennedy's performance. Furthermore, Robert Kennedy's brother President Kennedy had nominated enough segregationist judges to have kept the likes of John McClellan and James Eastland mollified. (Robert F. Kennedy wanted to be on the Judiciary Committee, but Eastland would not have two Kennedys; Robert relinquished the quest in favor of his brother Edward.) Javits was a Republican, and his presence was a nod toward bipartisanship.

But in the minds of some of the southern Democrats, who controlled the committee, Javits was actually the worst kind of Republican: he was an easterner, a liberal, and a Jew. (Eastland himself had openly cracked crude jokes about both Negroes and Jews.) "He is one of the most distinguished lawyers in the land," Javits said to committee members in introducing Marshall. "He has fought very hard to vindicate every aspect of the Constitution, and with remarkable success, especially in the difficult fields in which it has developed since the early 1950s." Javits continued, "I think it is a great thing for our nation that the president has now named him to one of the highest offices in the land, the cherished dream of every lawyer, which he richly deserves, through a lifetime of dedication and the sharpening and acquisition of professional skill."

Then it was Senator Kennedy's turn. Kennedy referred to Marshall as "a man whose work has symbolized and spearheaded the struggle of millions of Americans before the law." He mentioned his brother President Kennedy, who had appointed Marshall to the U.S. Court of Appeals for the Second Circuit. Kennedy also reminded the committee that Marshall had been a familiar presence at the Supreme Court, "arguing case after case of petitioners seeking vindication of their constitutional rights."

Committee members listened dutifully. But John McClellan was eager to get started. The chairman banged his gavel.

It might have been expected by those inside room 2228 that James Eastland, the chairman, would open the hearings by questioning Thurgood Marshall. But he did not. Such was the respect in which John McClellan was held by his colleagues—and his longevity as a senator—that the honor was given to him.

McClellan had been talking about the riots sweeping urban areas, about rising crime, for months. These were, of course, the spasms of violence erupting from the decades of black disenfranchisement. Some days, McClellan just ached to be a prosecutor again; he told acquaintances he wished he could cuff the rioters and put them behind bars himself. He couldn't stop from telling stories to staffers about blacks' having attacked whites while walking in the vicinity of the Capitol. Sometimes he told these stories at dinner parties, other times at legal gatherings. In 1962, McClellan appeared before the American Bar Association in Little Rock. Shortly into his remarks, he told a story about a woman who had been assaulted inside a Washington church. "While thus engaged in reverent worship she was brutally assaulted by a Negro man, stabbed nine times, robbed, and very nearly murdered." Some of his tales appeared apocryphal; others were bolstered by news clippings that he would produce out of a coat pocket. (On the day the Marshall nomination appeared at the very top of page 1 of *The Wash-*

ington Post, there was another story, inches below, with a Tampa dateline. "The scene was becoming familiar to American cities," the story began. "It was a morning-after-the-riot frieze on the three blocks of Central ave. The fires had been put out, but the glass had not been swept up yet. Policemen with automatic rifles patrolled the sealed-off street.") But something else about McClellan heightened the respect many of his colleagues granted the senator and explained the rather soft spot they had for him even if he was far from being a warm personality. The Arkansas senator had suffered profound tragedies in his personal life. McClellan's mother had died when he was just an infant. His first wife divorced him; spinal meningitis killed his second wife. He had three sons, and each of them died, forcing their father to endure unbearable grief. One had been killed in World War II, another had died in a car crash, and a third in an airplane accident. Some had wondered how McClellan, a veteran of World War I who had risen from being a small-town Arkansas prosecutor, had even held on through the years. But he held on and asked for no one's sympathy.

JOHN LITTLE MCCLELLAN was born in another century, in 1896, a mere thirty-three years after slavery's end. His grandfather had fought for the Confederacy. John McClellan himself had been so precocious that he had gotten admitted to the Arkansas Bar at the age of seventeen. His father, Isaac McClellan, had implored the legislature to pass a special bill that would waive the accepted age requirement to get his son admitted to the bar. Isaac McClellan's sense of politics began with his telling his son about the day President Theodore Roosevelt had invited the Negro educator Booker T. Washington to the White House—under the cover of darkness—to dine. Isaac McClellan was outraged that a black man had been invited to eat at the White House, and he was proud when his son wrote a school paper deploring the invitation. Young McClellan got a good grade on that paper and felt so proud of himself that he would carry it around and show it off to politicians his father introduced him to.

As he worked his way through small-town politics, the law soon became everything to John McClellan. He forged a reputation in Washington. In 1959, he received the George Washington Award from the American Good Government Society. In 1962, he was given the Freedom Award from the Order of Lafayette. In 1963, the Law Enforcement Intelligence Unit presented him with a certificate of appreciation. The honors never let up. It wasn't long after his arrival in Washington that law enforcement agencies across America began to revere him. In time, John McClellan could get the FBI director, J. Edgar Hoover, on the phone anytime he desired, because Hoover found much to like about McClellan's political conservatism.

Leading up to and during the Marshall hearings, McClellan's aides let him know the sentiments expressed in the letters pouring into the office about the nomination. Many of the letters came from Arkansas, but because of McClellan's national reputation, they came from around the country as well. "Please do not confirm the Negro to the Supreme Court," wrote Carrie Stevenson from Amarillo, Texas. "Isn't [William] Douglas and Earl Warren enough for you! And you from Arkansas where the great Eisenhower sent the Army with bayonets poked in the back of the white—to let a nigger pass." Linton Cook, a retired American consul living in Anniston, Alabama, weighed in by telegram: "Marshall Appointment Must Not Repeat Not Be Confirmed." The letter from Dorothy Kohlars came by way of Oceanside, California. "No amount of Federal intervention is going to mix black and white," she said. "It is about time our policy makers in Washington realized and accepted that fact." The letter from Calhoun Road in Magnolia, Arkansas, was written on behalf of the entire family: "Please, sir, no nigger on the Supreme Court bench—with looting and burning and riots all over the country, and Mr. Johnson conscious only of votes, again please don't confirm. So many feel as we do here. Sincerely, and Best Wishes—The Harshaws."

McClellan received another letter—also about the Marshall nomination—from the tiny town of Texarkana, Arkansas. The letter writer identified herself as "a Negro, an American." She wrote, "It has been made quite clear which side you are on. We all know why you and the other southern senators don't want him to be in the Supreme Court and it's not because of the Constitution . . . You don't want him because he's black and that is the only reason." It was a neatly typed one-and-a-half-page letter. "Chances are that the nomination will be turned down . . . Color doesn't make the person, Senator, character makes the man." The letter writer's name was Barbara Ross. Beyond her small hometown, she was unknown to the outside world. Ross concluded her 1967 letter with words that can only be described as powerfully prescient: "One of these days the President of the United States will be a Negro." John McClellan never replied to Barbara Ross's letter.

THURGOOD MARSHALL had reshaped American law, which had freed the Negro. And now the Negro was rioting. Black Panthers such as Eldridge Cleaver—joined by activists led by Stokely Carmichael—were advocating an armed revolution: blacks versus whites. Sit-ins began to turn violent. Much of white society was uneasy and downright fearful because of spreading black rage. The southern Democrats on the Judiciary Committee figured there was no one better, not even Chairman Eastland, to open the Thurgood Marshall hearings than the crime fighter John McClellan. Before the hearings began, McClellan and Eastland had plotted a line of opening day strategy. They believed that all the newsreel footage and those front-page and above-the-fold headlines about urban rioting would bolster their strategy of proclaiming Marshall's judicial philosophy as being soft on crime.

As the hearings got under way, John McClellan wasted little time with niceties. He announced he wished to avoid questions about Marshall's "legal ability or training or character," because he had something else on his mind. It was crime, with its powerful racial undercurrents in American society.

> MCCLELLAN: Now back to the line of questioning that I was pursuing. Is my understanding correct that as of now, you do not think that the crime rate in this country has reached proportions where it endangers and jeopardizes our internal security?
> MARSHALL: Endangers internal security. I would understand that to mean that there was going to be a revolution or something, and I certainly don't see that . . . I just don't understand your question.

McClellan didn't like Marshall's retort. Gangsters had certainly heard him well enough to understand exactly what he had been saying from his chair. McClellan bore in.

MCCLELLAN: Do you think it is reaching proportions where we will have a reign of lawlessness and chaos?

MARSHALL: I would say that I have great faith in the ability of our country to meet any emergency, and I—

The senator, perturbed, cut Marshall off.

MCCLELLAN: I am not asking what the country can meet . . . I am trying to determine your attitude or sense, realization, of the danger confronting this country with respect to this enemy of our security.

Now it was out in the open: "this enemy." This is what Chairman Eastland wanted to hear; this is what he liked. The black kids—Negro, colored, whatever they were being called—along with the radical essayists and the hippies roaming around the big plantations down south talking about unionizing and such, were behind this mayhem. This is what was tearing his country—especially his beloved South!—apart.

But beneath the root of McClellan's exchanges with Marshall, of course, lay the pain of the black man in America, and those in room 2228 had to sense it. In 1964 alone, more than twenty thousand citizens had been arrested in the South following their protests for racial equality. In McClellan's eyes, those citizens had committed crimes. The following year, 1965, more than three dozen churches had been firebombed by segregationists in Mississippi. There had been recent racial outbursts in northern cities, right up to the time of the beginning of the Marshall hearings. In 1963, in a prelude to all of this—to all the words cascading around room 2228—the great political thinker and essayist James Baldwin wrote *The Fire Next Time*. It was a thin volume of prose and quite powerful. "If we—and now I mean the relatively conscious whites and the relatively conscious blacks, who must, like lovers, insist on, or create, the consciousness of the others—do not falter in our duty now, we may be able, handful that we are, to end the racial nightmare, and achieve our country, and change the history of the world. If we do not now dare everything, the fulfillment of that prophecy, re-created from the Bible in song by a slave, is upon us: *God gave Noah the rainbow sign, No more water, the fire next time!*"

This is what Senator John McClellan was sensing—in fact

knew—while sitting before Thurgood Marshall: the fire had come. It was right out the windows. And he seemed to loop those fires around both internal and external security. And he wanted to know the depth of Marshall's commitment, his beliefs, in putting out those fires.

MARSHALL: I say in answer, Senator, that I am as alarmed, I am sure, as you are. But I am equally alarmed that whatever is to be done by governmental agencies to meet this situation has to be done within the framework of the U.S. Constitution. That is my only position.

The two men, Marshall and McClellan, had a different approach to justice and safeguarding the rights of American citizens. McClellan was not happy with Marshall's answers, but he bore on, because he was already wading into another arena.

In 1966, the Supreme Court issued a landmark ruling, *Miranda v. Arizona*. That 5–4 high court decision had come down on the side of Ernesto Miranda, a ninth-grade dropout in Arizona who had been arrested on a rape and kidnapping charge. Prosecutors would later admit that Miranda had answered questions without an attorney present, opening him—or any suspect, as expressed in the 5–4 ruling—to self-incrimination. The historic high court decision, establishing a suspect's right to have counsel present, was lauded by those who believed that suspects had rights also. Others would claim it undermined the ability of law enforcement to do its job. McClellan was clearly referring to *Miranda* when he brought up other 5–4 decisions, which, in his mind, gave a single justice the ability to alter law. Marshall decided to offer a bit of tutelage to McClellan regarding one-vote decisions.

MARSHALL: The nine men meet in a conference, and there is considerable give and take in the conference room. And where the vote ends up by one, nobody knows how it started off.

There was a gentle stirring in seats.

As the morning went on, Senator McClellan began to grow more and more agitated. He wanted more direct answers from Marshall about the dreaded *Miranda* ruling.

MCCLELLAN: Do you subscribe to the philosophy that the fifth amendment right to assistance of counsel requires that the counsel be present at a police lineup?

MARSHALL: My answer would have to be the same. That is a part of the *Miranda* case.

Marshall's answer hardly satisfied John McClellan.

MCCLELLAN: I do not care who it is that comes before this committee hereafter for the Supreme Court; I am going to try to find out something about their philosophy and not take the chances I have taken in the past. I mean that. This is a fundamental principle and an issue here that I think I have a grave duty to perform.

I have asked these questions in all good faith. I thank you for your attention. I regret I have not been able to get an answer that would disclose to me your viewpoint on these vital issues.

In Chairman Eastland's mind, the first day's hearings could not have gone better. His fellow senator, one of the most highly praised senators in law-and-order circles, had seemingly painted Thurgood Marshall as being sympathetic to criminals. With rioting and bloodshed fresh in the public's mind, this had been a strategy that they both had considered potent.

Eastland readied to bring the first day's hearings to a close, believing momentum lay with his forces. But Senator Ted Kennedy did not wish to end on such a note. He aimed to end the hearings with a dose of unvarnished present-day reality. The Massachusetts senator asked Chairman Eastland for permission to speak.

Kennedy secretly referred to the southern elders on the committee as "reliable Old Bulls." He resented so many of their ways. "They controlled Judiciary as a sort of fiefdom," he felt. Not long after he arrived in the Senate, Kennedy found himself invited over to Eastland's spacious office to talk about committee assignments. Some drinks were poured, ice cubes tinkling in glasses. "You Kennedys always care about the Negras," the powerful chairman said to him that day, the vulgarity commonly used in the South tossed about in Eastland's conversation like a casino chip. "Always hearing about you caring about those."

The Old Bulls had been dealing with "Negras" since young Ted Kennedy had been a schoolboy. They allowed him onto the committee because of their begrudging affection for his slain brother. Eastland allowed Kennedy to speak.

> KENNEDY: Just yesterday . . . in Boston, the NAACP announced its plans to file suit in 11 cities because Negro workers are still being denied access to employment opportunities in construction industries. Certainly one of the most important tasks of the 90th Congress will be to close the gap between these two disparate phenomena.

Kennedy and the others on the committee soon heard the voice of Senator Birch Bayh, who, until now, had been quiet. Bayh had been elected to the Senate from Indiana in 1962. He and Kennedy—both young civil rights supporters who had gotten choice Judiciary Committee assignments—had found many reasons to bond, none more dramatic than the plane crash they had been in together on June 19, 1964. They'd been flying in a small private plane to Springfield, Massachusetts, to attend the state's annual Democratic convention. They were flying at night, and the plane went down, falling through fog and darkness right into an apple orchard. Two on board died. Bayh and his wife survived and were able to wrest themselves from the wreckage. Bayh pulled Kennedy to safety. Kennedy had suffered broken vertebrae, broken ribs, and a punctured lung. In the days leading up to the hearings, Bayh worried about what plots might be hatched by southern committee members. He decided now was the time to challenge—however gently—McClellan.

> BAYH: Just let me say very quickly that I followed with a great deal of interest the penetrating interrogation or questioning, searching analysis, of my distinguished colleague from Arkansas, knowing very well that he had a loud voice in the Congress in this area of crime prevention . . . However, I must say that I differ slightly with my friend from Arkansas, inasmuch as I am

also appreciative of the deep quandary described by Senator Kennedy and Senator Hart facing the nominee. Without at all being critical of my friend from Arkansas, let me say that my analysis of the background of the nominee and the record of his accomplishments persuades me that the President has been wise indeed, and the country would be well served by a man of his competence.

It was nearing noon, and Chairman Eastland called the day's hearings to a close. They would reconvene in the morning at 10:30.

The Eastland-McClellan strategy had been to keep the hearings short, and the first day's hearings lasted less than ninety minutes. Marshall allies on the committee who had told the chairman they could well appear at an afternoon session were rebuffed. Eastland or McClellan did not want an episodic recitation of Marshall's legal victories and accomplishments. "Marshall Grilled by Senate Critics," the next day's *Washington Post* headlined, pointing to the barrage of testy questions directed to Marshall. White House officials monitoring the morning session were not caught off guard. They expected the grilling to continue and told Marshall he must expect it and must be prepared. They had repeatedly cautioned him to not lose his temper. Marshall seemed disappointed that the hearings had ended so suddenly. Accustomed to debating, he had thought he would have more time.

Aides to conservatives and southern Democrats began sharing a column that had been written by the celebrated Washington columnist Joseph Kraft. Before the hearings had begun, Kraft concluded that Marshall "will not bring to the Court penetrating analysis or distinction of mind."

JOHN MCCLELLAN told his aides he felt very good about the first day's proceedings. He had done just what he aimed to do: put Thurgood Marshall in the crosshairs of the civil unrest taking place on American streets and at city halls and on all those college campuses. And he also knew there were bigger weapons—Chairman Eastland, the revered attorney Sam Ervin, Senator Strom Thurmond—lying in wait for Marshall.

Those who departed the confines of the hearing room at the conclusion of that first day had now seen Thurgood Marshall up close. They had arrived early and filled every one of the seats. Now they couldn't help but wonder about his fate.

To the general public—which hardly paid much attention to the accomplishments of Negroes beyond sports and music—he was a man of great mysteries. Many were curious how Thurgood Marshall reached room 2228, where he was now caught squarely in the axis of churning history, race, and politics.

2

Willie and Norma Marshall's
Brave Son

At Lincoln University in Pennsylvania, Thurgood Marshall
(middle row, second from right) distinguished himself as a debater,
a skill he utilized to upend decades-long discrimination laws.

MANY FAMILIES IN BALTIMORE at the turn of the twentieth century were suffering from financial woes and barely putting food
on the table. But the family at 1632 Division Street, on the city's west
side, was not one of them. Willie Marshall and his wife, Norma—they
had married in the spring of 1905—had elevated themselves above the
Negro misery that was obvious in various sections of Baltimore. They
had moved around, given Willie Marshall's sometimes itinerant work,
and even at one time had relocated to Harlem for a few years before
returning to Baltimore. They were not too comfortable, however, to

ignore that custom of extended living practiced by many Negro families as a way to survive: this piece of furniture might be passed on to relatives; those gabardines bound for the trash heap could certainly be worn by other family kin or close friends.

WILLIE MARSHALL was constantly lifting himself up by his bootstraps: He worked as a porter for the railroad, pocketing tips—occasionally someone with deep pockets would flip him a fifty-cent piece—and holding his head high. He later worked in an exclusive country club. He was a handsome man, and his skin so light that sometimes he caught the curious glances of white women. He could only offer smiles in return. Willie knew he and Norma would never go hungry: his family owned a local grocery store. Willie also knew he owed his admirable family reputation to his father, Thorney Good Marshall.

Thorney Good had distinguished credentials, and they stretched back to the Indian Wars that claimed much of the nation's attention following the Civil War. Those wars involved the effort of the American military to relocate Indians in the West. American officials employed black soldiers to aid the effort; the Indians were so impressed with these black soldiers that they called them buffalo soldiers—owing to their skin color being the color of buffalo. Thorney Good was one of those buffalo soldiers, making $13 a month and acquiring countless stories to tell his grandchildren who sat listening at his knee on the living room floor. In Baltimore, Thorney Good had the biggest Negro grocery store—T. G. Marshall's. The store would be in the Marshall family—serving as a beehive of community conversation as well as commerce—until 1930, the year that one of Thorney Good's grandsons, Thurgood, ventured off to Howard Law School. (When Thorney Good died, at the age of sixty-five, a local newspaper paid tribute to him by saying that "his career in trade should inspire those who believe that racial enterprises merit support of the thousands of colored people here.")

Norma Williams hailed from a local family that was intent on seeing her get a good education. She made them happy when she began studies in Baltimore at Coppin State, a respected teachers college. But then there was disenchantment when she became pregnant by Willie Marshall. Norma was resolute about wanting to finish college. She did, in 1905, the same year she married Willie Marshall. Norma gave birth on September 15 to William Aubrey, the couple's first child, whom everyone called Aubrey. The young couple began to budget as never before.

Baltimore might not have experienced the kinds of racial convulsions at the turn of the century that many other southern cities did, but Maryland certainly was a state that knew well the haunting specter of the Civil War and slavery. Just hours after John Wilkes Booth had fatally wounded President Lincoln in Washington, he was galloping through the wilds of Maryland, cavalry units on his trail. A Maryland doctor, Samuel Mudd, tended to Booth's fractured leg. Mudd was a Confederate sympathizer: he cursed Lincoln upon losing all eleven of his slaves after emancipation. "The escape of . . . Booth, and his confederates can only be for a few days or hours," believed the *Chicago Tribune*. "Millions of eyes are in vigilant search of them, and soon they will be in the hands of justice . . . no place on this side of perdition can shelter them." Booth was traveling with David Herold, a co-conspirator. Hiding in the woods of Charles County, Maryland, the duo suffered from menacing insects that tore into them. The nights grew damp. Booth's ego, however, remained in flight. He carried a date book. Between April 17 and April 22—speaking of the shooting—he wrote, "I struck boldly and not as the papers say. I walked with a firm step through a thousand of his friends . . . Our country owed all her troubles to him, and God simply made me the instrument."

Secretary of War Edwin M. Stanton had been particularly close to Lincoln. In one "Wanted" poster, he appealed directly to those whom Lincoln had freed. "To the colored people of the District of Columbia and of Maryland, of Alexandria and the border counties of Virginia: Your President has been murdered! He has fallen by the assassin and without a moment's warning, simply and solely because he was your friend and the friend of our country. Had he been unfaithful to you and to the great cause of freedom he might have lived. The pistol from which he met his death, though held by Booth, was fired by the hands of treason and slavery." Stanton mentioned reward money, then seemed to realize it likely held no additional power of persuasion in service of the man who had freed the Negro: "But I feel that you need no such stimulus as this. You will hunt down this cowardly assassin of your best friend, as you would the murderer of your own father. Do this, and God, whose servant has been slain, and the country which has given you freedom, will bless you for this noble act of duty." Riders on horseback distributed the posters and handbills among black communities throughout Washington, Maryland, and Virginia. Freed slaves who couldn't read the handbills gave them to those who could. Federal troops by way of New York soon cornered Booth and Herold inside a Virginia farmhouse. Herold surrendered. Booth preferred battle and was shot dead.

The assassin who had slain the president who freed the Negro was buried in his family's plot in the city of Baltimore.

Forty-three years later, on July 2, 1908, in that same city, Norma Marshall gave birth to her second son. Of course no one knew at the time, nor could have imagined, that this son would come to devote his life to Lincolnesque goals in the service of those millions of Negroes who, like him, were born unto a scarred and bruised land.

HE HAD THE SHOWSTOPPING FIRST NAME Thoroughgood, given to him because an uncle shared the name. The boy grew tiresome of snickers—not to mention teachers having difficulty with the spelling—and persuaded his parents to shorten it to Thurgood. He was big for his age and grew to become willful. It was expected that young boys who had size would gravitate to some kind of sport. But Thurgood Marshall did not. He instead managed to charm friends with his intellect, giving analysis of sporting events—Negro baseball and football games especially—with the assuredness of a bon vivant. The confines of a grocery store did not appeal to young Thurgood's father, Willie Marshall, as they had to Willie's own father. Ignoring the grocery store, Willie took the kinds of jobs available to well-mannered Negro men of the time: dining car waiter on the Baltimore & Ohio Railroad for a while. Then there was a better job: a steward at the Gibson Island Club, twenty miles outside Baltimore on the Chesapeake Bay. This was the job, when it came to remembering his father's life, that would scar young Thurgood's memory. He would eat at many fine hotels and restaurants and spend an enormous amount of time on trains. The waiters and Pullman porters on the trains were often

Negro, and he saw the visage of his father in them—the long hours they worked, the low pay, the disrespect accorded them by some.

The Negro men who worked the Gibson Island Club catered to business barons, politicians, tobacco plantation owners, and corporate executives. The club members could be seen in summertime wearing seersucker suits and swinging walking sticks. Their daughters were married on Gibson Island in lavish ceremonies as white doves flew overhead. On lovely weekends, the wives of the country club members sat under umbrella shades, sipped martinis, played gin rummy, and plucked cigarettes from silver cigarette cases while Negro waiters soundlessly glided by. Sailboats bobbed on the blue water. Rolls-Royces and Bentleys sat gleaming in the parking lot like metal trophies. An employee would remember a stark road sign on the way to Gibson Island that doubled as a warning: "No Niggers and Dogs Allowed."

By all accounts, Norma Marshall doted on her two sons, Aubrey and Thurgood. The boys, so close in age, were quite different. Aubrey seemed self-centered, prone to illnesses, a bit effete, and a clothes-horse. Thurgood was loud, silent when touched by illness, and, some thought, a bit reckless in his wanderings. He couldn't care less how he looked in his dress. When outside the home, the boys did not hang together. It was as if each were determined to forge distinctive and separate identities. "In Baltimore," Thurgood Marshall would come to recall, "where I was brought up, we lived on a respectable street, but behind us there were back alleys where the roughnecks and the tough kids hung out. When it was time for dinner, my mother used to go to the front door and call my older brother. Then she'd go to the back door and call me." Norma Marshall refused to play favorites. "I can see her now," a family friend would remark, "sitting in the yard, talking about her two boys." The assortment of Marshall family relatives in Baltimore heaped attention on the two Marshall boys. There were uncles who imparted wisdom, sometimes veering between true and apocryphal tales about life farther down south. And there were aunts who talked to them about civility, current affairs, and which Negro girls came from the most respectable families. Norma Marshall had a strong effect on Thurgood regarding industriousness and loyalty. "She worked like just all get out," Thurgood would recall. "And her only fault was that she was with you, if you were in the family, she was with you, right or wrong. I mean, she would just defend you." Literacy was valued in the Marshall neighborhood. Everyone seemed to always be reading *The Baltimore Sun* or the *Baltimore Afro-American*, delivery boys scooting about tossing the latest edition onto porches. Willie Marshall enjoyed digesting the news of the day at the dinner table. The conversations with his two boys were animated and lively; his learned wife, Norma, seemed to delight in the back-and-forth jousting. The conversations often rolled into debates; positions had to be staked out and defended. The debates would sometimes grow so noisy that neighbors—especially in the spring and summertime—could hear the conversations through the raised windows. It was the usual cacophony from the Marshalls, neighbors would say. Sometimes Willie would lean back and stare at his two boys. And a prideful smile would creep upon his face. This is what he and Norma had given the world, two boys who he just knew would become strivers.

As Thurgood Marshall began to show a keen interest in inequality and the ways it seemed anchored in Negro life—where a Negro could and couldn't go—his father took notice. He started taking his son downtown with him. They'd visit the courthouse, where they would watch the motions of justice. It was so clear to see—for father as well as son—that the wheels of justice so often churned differently for blacks and whites. That reality didn't keep Willie Marshall from telling his son, "Anyone calls you a nigger, you not only got my permission to fight him—you got my orders to fight him."

Young Thurgood Marshall attended segregated elementary, junior high, and high schools. Many of his classmates would continue with him from one school to the next. Carrie Jackson was one of Marshall's classmates. She would remember him as nice, thin, and angular, with good hair. "Thurgood was restless, inquisitive, and a bit untidy," she would recall. "He would drive his mother crazy. The boys wore shirts outside their pants. Thurgood's shirt was always coming out. His mother was the epitome of neatness. She would be so disgusted with him. I guess until we reached the eighth grade, Thurgood didn't care about his personal appearance. He wasn't dirty, just sloppy."

In school—he completed junior high in 1921 and shortly thereafter began high school—Marshall loved the sound of his own voice, which was stentorian, deep. Gough McDaniels, one of his high school teachers, became enamored of the young student, watching as Marshall seemed to take over the classroom with yet another summation of that day's homework assignment. But McDaniels had a breaking point and would interrupt the voluble Thurgood. Marshall's fellow students got a kick out of all of it. Marshall himself couldn't wait to pop back up, to showcase his intellectual prowess once again. "It was taken for granted that we had to make something of ourselves," Marshall would come to recall. "Not much was said about it; it was just in the atmosphere of the home." Marshall's high school was called, simply, the Colored High and Training School.

Marshall quickly learned the bylaws of being a Negro in a segregated southern city. "In the department stores downtown," he would remember, "a Negro was not allowed to buy anything off the counters. As you went in the store, you were told to get the hell out." There was something else about downtown Baltimore that he did not like: there were no toilet facilities for Negroes. "I remember one day, I had to go, and the only thing I could do was get on a trolley car and try to get home. And I did get almost to the house, when I ruined the front doorsteps." He roughhoused with neighborhood boys, appeared both talkative and inquisitive, stood out because he was tall for his age, eschewed sports but was not mocked for it because he had that gift of gab. That gift really began to shine in high school, where Marshall became one of the star debaters. Debaters had to be voracious readers. They were forced to keep up on national and international events. It all harked back to those dinner debates inside the Marshall household, Mom and Dad turning from one son to the next. At school, the jocks were sometimes intimidated by the wily smarts of those on the debate team.

As a debater, Thurgood Marshall's talents were so obvious that he was soon made a varsity captain. Even in class, when called upon, Marshall was prone to talk beyond the normal limits. "Once a week, every Monday, we had to give a current history report," Essie Hughes, one of Marshall's classmates, would recall. "Well, of course we read the papers. Some read and digested it and some just read it. Thurgood always chewed and digested his news, and he'd get up there and Mr. McDaniels [the teacher] would always have to say, 'All right, Thurgood, your time is up.'" Another classmate, Charlotte Shervington, had similar feelings about Thurgood Marshall. "He could outtalk and out-argue anybody."

Marshall enjoyed rising in front of classmates. Where others might have wilted, he appeared energized. He would recall his third year of high school: "Many times during the term, I gave short talks before the student body on certain requirements of school life and also talks on the activities of the student council of which I was a representative."

But young Thurgood—his brother, Aubrey, had left home to attend Lincoln University—also proved quite industrious outside the class-room. After school, he'd get down to Charles Street, one of the city's bustling byways with expensive and well-appointed shops. He'd gotten himself a job as a delivery boy in a dress shop owned by Mr. Schoen. The dresses were beautiful, made of silk and cotton; the hats were the envy of any woman in Baltimore. The men and women who came into Mr. Schoen's shop were the same men and women who summered out on Gibson Island, where the elder Marshall worked. Thurgood would scan his delivery addresses and plot his movements across the city with his packages—which trolley car to catch and where—then begin deci-phering an estimation of what time to catch the trolley back to the shop so he could begin another round of deliveries. There were kind white people, who handed over generous tips. And there were other kinds of white people.

Marshall would never forget one particular day: "I was getting in a trolley car, and joined the people getting on; a man grabbed me and pulled me back and said, 'Nigger, don't you push in front of white people!'" Marshall rebuffed the man, just as his daddy had told him to do. Voices were raised, trolley car riders stood on their feet amid the commotion, hat boxes tumbled onto the floor of the trolley car, white ladies appeared to be gasping for air with their hands at their mouths. Soon enough, the police arrived. Thurgood Marshall was arrested, taken to the police station. He fretted not about himself but about the hats; they were now quite possibly ruined. Perhaps Mr. Schoen would take it out of his pay, but they were expensive hats; he'd have to work at the shop forever, he feared, to pay for the damaged goods. Furthermore—the thought finally crossed his mind—there was the issue of bail. It was Mr. Schoen, feeling for his young employee, who quickly bailed young Marshall out. Still, he could not stop worrying about those hats.

"Forget about them, what about you?" Mr. Schoen asked, wanting to know if Marshall was okay. The question and concern heartened Marshall. As did the lawyer Schoen hired, who got the case dropped.

Norma and Willie Marshall knew that their younger son must go to college. It seemed preordained. He graduated with high marks from high school; his brother, Aubrey, was already in college. Thurgood himself was admitted to Lincoln. The Marshalls would now have to scrape money together, but they were determined that Thurgood not be denied. They began counting their savings. What few luxuries they indulged in would have to be curtailed. There were several questions for prospective students on the Lincoln college application. "What do you plan as your life's work?" To which Thurgood Marshall—debater, raconteur, sympathizer with the downtrodden—answered, "Lawyer."

THERE WERE MORE than a dozen public funerals for Abraham Lincoln spread across thirteen cities. Millions in those cities—among them Buffalo, Cleveland, Columbus, Indianapolis, Chicago, and Baltimore—would see his train chug by. In the aftermath, a great many institutions and civic organizations across the country rushed to name things in Lincoln's honor. The Lincoln Institute, in Jefferson City, Missouri, was the dream of colored soldiers from the Sixty-Second and Sixty-Fifth Infantries. It opened in 1866. Nevadans named Lincoln County after the president in 1866; Minnesotans named the town of Lincoln after him in their state the same year. Also in 1866, the Ashmun Institute, in Chester County, Pennsylvania, renamed its school Lincoln University in honor of the Great Emancipator. The school had been founded during slavery—in 1854—with an intention of educating young males of African descent. The school proudly proclaimed itself as "The Oldest Institution in the United States for the Collegiate and Theological Education of Colored Youth."

One more colored youth, Thurgood Marshall, walked onto the campus in the fall of 1925. He had no idea—because they dared not tell him—how much his parents were already worrying about keeping up the tuition payments for both him and his brother, Aubrey.

Seventy-five students made up Lincoln's freshman class that year. It was a small but lively Negro campus—the all-white faculty would not integrate for several years—and those students who were enrolled appeared eager to learn. They were also quite worldly, as the small campus boasted Africans, Asians, and students from all over America. Prideful alums referred to the school as the black Princeton; there were, in fact, Princetonians on its faculty. Thurgood, always gregarious, made friends quickly. He joined in the familiar campus pastimes: mangling the school fight song while sitting around bonfires before football games; giving other students nicknames following some bit of quirky and unforgettable behavior on their part; hitching rides to nearby Philadelphia or Wilmington and dining in the eateries that specialized in southern cuisine. He joined the Alpha Phi Alpha fraternity—more high jinks. Monroe Dowling became one of Thurgood's best friends. Dowling hailed from Atlantic City, was interested in social work, and was quick to lend a buck: "Money" was his nickname.

As in life, as in growing up, Thurgood and his older brother, Aubrey, did not hang around each other much on the Lincoln campus. Each still seemed intent on continuing to forge his own identity rather than displaying acts of brotherly affection.

Thurgood's booming laugh on the Lincoln campus signaled his presence from around corners. His pranks were ribald; he became an expert in the art of tossing water balloons in the direction of the unsuspecting. He had a cool demeanor in the face of imminent exams—"do good enough to pass" is how he humbly put it—and came away with grades good enough to make honor roll lists. He became the envy of others.

One of the more arresting figures who would often be seen walking the campus alongside Thurgood was Langston Hughes, already admired as a published poet. Hughes had transferred to Lincoln from Columbia University. He wore his hair pomaded—a slicked-back fashion that was popular and gave one's hair a noticeable sheen—and dressed stylishly enough to draw stares. He appeared mature for his age. Little wonder, inasmuch as Hughes, born in 1902, was at least six years older than most Lincoln freshmen. He had published a remarkable book of verse, *The Negro Speaks of Rivers*, before his arrival at the college. Langston Hughes was also a hepcat who knew the gin joints and speakeasies of Paris before setting foot in rural Chester County. "I like the school out here immensely," Hughes would write to his friend Carl Van Vechten, a Harlem bon vivant. "We're a community in ourselves. Rolling hills and trees and plenty of room. Life is crude, the dorms like barns but comfortable, food plain and solid, first bell at six-thirty, and nobody dresses up—except Sunday . . . I room with the campus bootlegger." The young men of Lincoln tagged Hughes with a nickname: "Lank." His celebrity could hardly have gone unnoticed. "February of our Freshman year a poet came into our midst . . . He is a product of Central High School of Cleveland," a fellow student would come to write for a campus publication at the time. "One who travels extensively acquires a certain amount of education just from contacts and so Lank came to us with many stories of the South Sea Islands, northern borders of Africa."

Hughes had quite a gift in sizing people up; it was not unexpected given his worldly wanderings. The poet thought young Thurgood Marshall keen of mind but a bit randy, remembering the Baltimorean as "rough and ready, loud and wrong, good natured and uncouth."

Willie and Norma Marshall were quite proud to have two sons in college. But the financial strain quickly took a toll. It was heartbreaking for Willie to watch his wife bent over pen and paper, writing letters to campus administrators, explaining the tardiness of yet another tuition payment. "My first payment will be on the 8th of March when I receive my check," she wrote to the school during Marshall's sophomore year. "I had thought of sending Mr. Marshall's check which he was to have received Tuesday, but because he has been at home for the past two weeks sick with the grippe . . ." Another letter from Norma Marshall a year later, in 1927, sounded a similar plea: "Enclosed find a check for $100 on Thurgood Marshall's bill. I will send balance just as soon as possible."

One day, the Marshall boys phoned home about an upcoming away football game, which featured Howard University and Lincoln. It was a popular contest, much discussed on campus, for its athletic rivalry as well as for the exuberant socializing that would surely take place. Norma was forced to tell her sons the family simply did not have the extra money for the outing. But for days it bothered Willie Marshall that he couldn't afford to get money to his sons to go to the game.

"Norma," Willie Marshall asked his wife, days before the game, "how much money do we have, total?"

"Six dollars," she told her husband.

"Give it to me," he said. The tone of his voice worried her, and she hesitated. "Just give it to me," he demanded, and she finally did.

Willie Marshall was gone for hours that evening, and Norma worried what he was up to. Stress had often driven him to drink more than he should, and she prayed he wasn't dousing his miseries in a bottle, throwing away what little money they had. Actually, he was gambling, trying to turn $6 into a grander sum so his boys could attend a football game. And when Willie Marshall returned home that night, he had the strut of a king: through his gambling prowess, he had amassed $150. Norma smiled. Their boys went to the football game.

Something about attending football games always lit a spark in Thurgood Marshall. It wasn't just the action on the field; it was the ready-made crowd around him. It was in these settings that Thurgood Marshall was often prone to practice the debating skills he had first honed in high school. With a captive audience, he could debate anyone in his crowd who disagreed with him, and he'd talk from game to dorm room to until the lights were flicked off. And then came his deep mellifluous voice through the darkness of the dorm room.

Thurgood proved a natural for the Lincoln University varsity debate team, which he had first joined during his sophomore year. Marshall—tall, deep-voiced, and a quick thinker—earned kudos, despite an overall losing effort for the team, following a February 26, 1927, debate performance. The debate title was "Resolved, That the Volstead Act Should Be Modified to Permit the Manufacture and Sale of Light Wine and Beer." (The Volstead Act was otherwise known as the National Prohibition Act.) Much was made of the debate, which took place in Philadelphia, because it pitted a white school, Penn State, against a Negro school. Marshall's hometown *Baltimore Afro-American* newspaper took note. "Penn State . . . has been the first institution to stretch its hands across the color line and ask for a debate with a sister college of color," it said in an editorial. "At the present time we cannot think of a better way to banish snobbery and Ku Klux fallacies from college halls." *The Philadelphia Tribune* took particular note of the performance by Thurgood Marshall, believing that "with possibly a little more experience, Thurgood should stand preeminently above most of the debaters of color in collegiate competitions in the country."

Willie Marshall's boy was utilizing all the skills he had used around the family dinner table: staking out a position, rubbing and massaging it, defending it against attacks. Gales of laughter would erupt from his heaving chest when he would tell dorm mates about which opposing debaters he had ripped apart.

By Marshall's junior year, the Lincoln University debate team had started garnering a national reputation. (Norma Marshall kept the newspaper clippings, proudly sharing them with relatives.) Debates were scheduled up and down the East Coast. Lincoln graduates sent word out on the school grapevine telling about debate team appearances, encouraging high turnouts. Before the Christmas holiday in 1927, Lincoln's debate team glided into the Mother African Methodist Episcopal Zion Church in Harlem. They would square off against teams under the umbrella of England's National Union of Students. The Lincoln debaters—now facing foreign challengers—had grown accustomed to having full-throttled questions to debate onstage. At the church in Harlem, the debate topic garnered wide interest: "Resolved, That the Attitude of the Anglo-Saxon Race Toward the Colored Races Under Its Control Is Unethical and Prejudicial to Progress." Marshall, one of three members of the debate team, was forceful in assailing colonialism, arguing that "the history of the Anglo-Saxon races has been one of imperialistic oppression for the sake of business advantages." The debaters from England tiptoed around colonialism while suggesting that Britain had helped its colonies by offering economic assistance. Both teams, appearing before nearly three thousand attendees, drew generous applause, although the judges could not decide on a winner and none was declared.

For drama, however, the Harlem-set debate paled against the debate that later took place at Harvard University. When Harvard announced it would host a debate featuring its own Liberal Club against Lincoln—the topic being "Resolved: That Further Intermixing of Races in the United States Is Desirable"—the Ku Klux Klan began to howl. It resented that such a topic was even being debated. Harvard would not cancel the event but did increase security. After all, debate organizers prided themselves on creating challenges for debaters. Marshall was disappointed when given the task of arguing against interracial mixing. Such assignments, of course, were what distinguished debaters from one another. Marshall and his debate teammate were forced to argue, in essence, against racial advancement. It is little wonder Marshall did not consider the evening to be one of his better debate performances. Perhaps the commotion leading up to it had rattled him. What made news about the event back at Lincoln University was the fact that Klansmen had thrown bricks through the window of the Liberal Club before the event took place. "The fact that Marshall and I stayed in Klaverly Hall, one of the dormitories, was in part the cause of the trouble," Marshall's debate mate, Richard Hill, would tell a reporter. The hooligans who attacked the dorm were unnerved not only that a discussion of racial matters and thoughts had taken place but that Negroes were staying there. While the dormitory was not off-limits to Negro students, their appearance there was so rare that it became noteworthy.

Certain athletes leave a playing field with a reputation marked by a particular skill set; colorful adjectives become attached to their names. Thurgood Marshall—for his relentless debating skills, for his ferocious concentration on a point he had to prove on a stage—would become known as "the Wrathful Marshall." It was all in jest, part mockery, part admiration, but he liked the sound of it.

Thurgood Marshall spent his first summers during college in Baltimore working on the B&O Railroad, a job he got through his father's contacts. It was a paltry salary, $55 a month. "So the only money you made was tips, and it was not a good living," he would remember. He got a better job, with much better tips even, during the summer of his final year in college, when he worked alongside his father at Gibson Island. At Gibson Island, Thurgood saw all the things his father saw: old money on display; the stark color line; the class distinctions of America; and how those at the top lived. It was not beyond the Gibson Island Negro waiters to sample the beverages now and then. It was at Gibson where Thurgood began to acquire his taste for alcohol. The young Marshall came to love the taste of it; "a forty-year-old hogshead of old Pikesville bourbon" was one treat that delighted his taste buds.

Marshall's gift of gab, however, manifested itself in more places than on debate stages up and down the East Coast. During his undergraduate years, he talked his way into the heart of Vivian "Buster" Burey, a University of Pennsylvania student. She came from a middle-class Negro family of means, with her parents working as caterers. She was vivacious, lively, and lovely in appearance. "Thurgood," she would recall, "was the funniest looking man. When I met him, he was six foot one and weighed 141 pounds—nothing but skin and bones." He charmed her with his knowledge and his voracious reading appetite, because just as athletes had to run, run, and run, debaters had to read, read, and read. He had a touch of the rough-hewn poet about him. No matter that both sets of parents warned about the challenges of married life at such a young age, the couple were determined to go their own way. A Baltimore newspaper took note of the planned nuptials. There was a picture of Marshall with the headline "To Wed Philly Belle," followed by a brief announcement: "Son of Mr. and Mrs. William Marshall of 1836 Druid Hill avenue to wed Miss Vivian Burey, formerly of Philadelphia." In the photograph, Marshall sports a thin mustache. There are slight waves in his hair.

They were married on September 4, 1929, at a Philadelphia church. Then it was back to Lincoln and their own apartment. They were kids facing a coming Depression, and they were Negroes, and life would be challenging going forward. Both realized as much.

Thurgood Marshall was forced to graduate a semester late, with the class of 1930, because an injury—he had slipped while trying to hop aboard a moving vehicle—had kept him out of school for a while. But his spirit lay with his classmates from the class of 1929. And those classmates—Marshall's original classmates—had, in ribald fashion and often veering between sarcasm and dead-on assessments, took time to sum up the keenest attributes of their fellow seniors. The honor of "Most Popular" went to Langston Hughes; Bill Hill was thought to have the "Best Physique"; John Robinson was the "Most Vivacious"; Frank Norris was the "Most Henpecked"; Mark Parks was the "Luckiest in Love"; and the humorous honor of "Quietest" went to one of the campus's loudest and most vocal students—Thurgood Marshall. (It was a credit to Norma Marshall's relentlessness that her two sons—with tuition bills yearly for them both—got through college. When she had to, she borrowed money; sometimes she sold clothing or jewelry. She gently harangued her husband that the tuition bills had to be paid.)

All of Marshall's classmates had one thing in common: They were, for the most part, emancipation's children; so many were the grandsons and great-grandsons of slaves. Their parents had so strongly desired that they enter the workforce using brains and not brawn. They represented fervent hope. "The time has come when our paths must divide," a fellow senior classmate of Marshall's would write of that final year. "Each must choose his own field and I trust that each man will go forward into life with the same idea that has prevailed while we have lived here together and then when our ten years are up we can all return to our 'dear old orange and blue' and celebrate the first reunion of the Class of '29."

Thurgood Marshall had spent his undergraduate college years honing a particular skill. That skill—being a debater—required smarts, instinct, and flexibility. Being a debater, actually, was not unlike being an actor: Minds had to be bent in the audience; a stage had to become friendly terrain. Actors had to convince directors; debaters had to convince judges. Many of the renowned abolitionists had themselves been great debaters. And Thurgood Marshall, who possessed a confidence in his own intellect that many found endearing, needed a place to further hone this particular skill. Not only hone it, but shape and mold it into something powerful.

Marshall might have convinced others he was a bit reckless and too boisterous for academic honors, but he managed to graduate cum laude. It was a trait that would mark his entire life—the hidden smarts, the riveting proof when most needed of his concentration and focus. He was also powerfully determined.

IN 1930, thirty-six incoming Negro law students walked up the steps of a small and undistinguished-looking brownstone at 420 Fifth Street in the northwest section of Washington, D.C. It was the Howard University Law School. Norma Marshall had hocked her engagement ring and wedding band to help with her son's law school expenses. Aubrey had proved his smarts as well. He was off to medical school.

Howard held its law classes at night, prompting many to snicker and even wonder about the seriousness of its mission. It had a shoddy, ill-equipped library and an undistinguished faculty. Its past graduates scuffled along in the often grubby world of their clients' rent disputes and marital and criminal woes. The American Bar Association had yet to grant the school accreditation. It was sometimes called—to the horror of its graduates—"Dummies' Retreat." And as a graduate of those times would come to remember, "That was one of the nicest names."

But the school did have a new dean in Charles Hamilton Houston, who had arrived a year earlier. Houston had degrees from Amherst and Harvard Law School, credentials considered downright eccentric for a Negro in early twentieth-century America. Houston was handsome, coldly severe, and a World War I veteran who was bent on changing the perception of the school. He set about doing so with a vengeance. He hired new faculty and fired those who did not measure up to his standards. He sought donations, vastly increasing the law library's holdings. He invited distinguished legal scholars to visit the campus. Houston was just what the struggling school needed.

One of the courses Marshall took in his final semester at Lincoln had a rather explosive title. It was called Race Problems. Thurgood Marshall had arrived at Howard Law School in the giddy aftermath of the victory the National Association for the Advancement of Colored People had recently won in stopping the appointment of a southern federal judge to the U.S. Supreme Court. The whole affair could be singularly pointed to the "race problem." On March 8, 1930, Edward Terry Sanford, a U.S. Supreme Court justice, died in Washington. President Herbert Hoover chose the federal judge John J. Parker, a North Carolina native, as his replacement. The NAACP—formed twenty-one years earlier and since then blissfully ignored by powerful segregationist politicians—decided to do some probing of Parker's past. The investigation was led by Walter White, acting NAACP secretary—a position that in effect had him running the civil rights organization. White got in touch with NAACP officials in North Carolina, Parker's home state, and they revealed to him disturbing information: in his 1920 campaign for governor, Parker was quoted as saying that "the participation of the Negro in politics is a source of evil and danger to both races and is not desired by wise men in either race or by the Republican Party of North Carolina." Victory was not a problem for Parker, because he lost, but the words he left behind certainly were. The NAACP gnawed hard on those words. Parker refused to answer any of the organization's queries. NAACP officials decided to oppose the Parker nomination and flexed its muscle coast-to-coast. There were community meetings, anti-Parker editorials in the Negro press. Letters poured into the White House and the offices of many senators. Whites across the country who had never paid much attention to the NAACP beyond slight curiosity now did so.

The NAACP's effectiveness was proven when the Senate Judiciary Committee invited Walter White to appear before it to voice his opinion of the Parker nomination. White told committee members that Parker's views were a "shameless flouting of the Fourteenth and Fifteenth amendments of the federal constitution" that amounted to disrespect of the Negro. The North Carolina senator Lee S. Overman was incensed at White's charges, telling him during hearings that "niggras vote freely" in his state. White House officials scrambled for Negroes who might support Parker. It was a fruitless search. Robert R. Moton, who headed the Tuskegee Institute (Booker T. Washington's school) and had campaigned for Hoover, confided to the White House that he "could have nothing less than an uncompromising and everlasting hostility" toward Parker. Influential news outlets—*The Washington Post*, *The Nation*, the Scripps Howard newspaper chain—denounced the Parker nomination. W. E. B. DuBois, the Harvard-educated editor of *The Crisis*, the NAACP magazine, felt that the anti-Parker campaign had been "conducted with a snap, determination and intelligence never surpassed in colored America and seldom in white."

Parker's nomination could not be saved. He was defeated by a 41–39 vote. Although it was by a mere two votes, it was a profound victory for the NAACP. *The Christian Science Monitor* felt that Parker's defeat was "the first national demonstration of the Negro's power since Reconstruction days." (The White House went on to nominate Owen J. Roberts to the seat. He had been named a special U.S. attorney during the Teapot Dome scandal, which came to light when a cabinet officer in the Harding administration was convicted of having taken bribes and sent to prison. NAACP officials had good things to say about Roberts. They particularly liked that he was a trustee of the all-black Lincoln University—the very school the new Howard law student Thurgood Marshall had recently graduated from.)

As soon as he entered law school, Thurgood Marshall was introduced to some of the faculty members who had helped in the defeat of the Supreme Court nominee John Parker. Marshall now knew that with the right coalition, and the right forces in alignment, a lot could be accomplished within the system to advance the cause of racial equality.

Charlie Houston, the dean, had studied the plight of the Negro lawyer in America, studied it and gathered statistics, and those statistics were stark and indisputable. He would constantly remind his students of the crisis confronting the Negro lawyer. Houston discovered that "there are not more than 100 Negro lawyers in the South devoting fulltime to practice: 100 Negro lawyers to care for the rights and interests of 9,000,000 Southern Negroes or approximately one Negro lawyer to every 90,000 Negroes." Drawing from the 1930 census, Houston's findings revealed, for instance, that there were nearly 1 million Negro residents of the state of Alabama and just 4 Negro lawyers; Mississippi had more than 1 million Negroes and 6 Negro lawyers. Houston—because the fraternity was so small—was aware of the older Negro lawyers working in the South and the fact that most, to succeed, had been forced to limit their practice to nonthreatening areas such as civil law and the administrative tasks their clients required. There was constant backlash against the Negro lawyer: "In many instances, they are the victim of subtle propaganda spread by the lower-class white lawyer to the effect that a Negro throws away his case in getting a Negro lawyer because a Negro lawyer has no influence with the court."

Thurgood Marshall—walking hallways, sitting in class, poring over his thick law books, listening to Houston—found the Howard environment heady and intoxicating. "This was what I wanted to do for as long as I lived," he had felt within a week's time of his arrival.

Within a year, Charles Houston—constantly challenging faculty and students alike—had achieved one of his main goals: the American Bar Association granted the law school accreditation. The proud Houston shared the news within legal circles as often as he could. The workaholic dean had guest lecturers—among them Clarence Darrow, that crafty lawyer for the damned, and Arthur Garfield Hays of the American Civil Liberties Union (ACLU)—come to the school. Marshall and his classmates peppered the guest lecturers with questions. Houston sensed his charges breathing the law in like fresh air to the lungs. He took them to visit the city's jails and from there to the intimidating surroundings of the U.S. Supreme Court. The once-mocked law school was on the move.

Among the courses that Marshall and his fellow classmates took were Legal Bibliography and Argumentation; History of Law; Evidence; Criminal Law Laboratory; Common Law Pleading; and Conflict of Laws and Municipal Corporations. The law school that Charles Houston had remade with warp and grinding speed was not a place that tolerated inattention or foolishness. Attrition was severe. One year, Houston instituted what he called "the cutback system," an arrangement that granted any faculty member the right to cut five points from a student's passing grade. In effect, every student was operating with a five-point deficit; it was the old rhubarb of a Negro student's having to be twice as good as—or at least five points better than—a future white adversary. But the rattled students thought there was no rhyme to it because professors could use it on whomever they wished. Students, of course, thought the tactic wicked and capricious. They came to call Houston "Iron Pants" behind his back. "I'll never be satisfied," Iron Pants told those students who had arrived in 1930, "until I go to one of the dances up on the hill on the campus and see everybody having fun with all my law school students sitting around the sides reading law books. Then I'll be happy, and not before."

Houston had warned students early that a third of them were likely to flunk out. Classmates began judging other classmates, doing their own arithmetic. "He had come down here from Lincoln with the reputation as something of a playboy," Oliver Hill would recall of his classmate Thurgood Marshall. But Hill and others, even as they witnessed Marshall gulp back beers and jawbone a little too long during social outings, were fascinated by one thing: his ability to study long and hard, and retain what he had studied, was becoming legendary. He had the look of a scuffler. "I got through simply by overwhelming the job," Marshall would remember. He bragged to friends that he studied seven days a week—even with a commute, a young bride to keep happy, and an assortment of part-time jobs he held during law school study. The schedule, however, would come to take a toll on young Marshall: tall and stout of build, his weight went from 170 pounds to 130 pounds; his mother, Norma, worried and sat heaps of food in front of him, but it seemed to do little good as he was always out the door, burning off the calories.

On campus, because he now stood six feet three inches tall—and seemed even taller, angling around in long, loping strides—Marshall was impossible to miss. His absences would have been quickly noticed as well (the cutback system!), so he dared not miss class.

By year two, Marshall had risen to the top spot in his class. The harder the course work, the more he seemed to shine. William Hastie, one of the gifted young new faculty members Houston had recruited, taught Marshall and Oliver Hill in a course about preparing appellate briefs. "Their brief," Hastie would later remember of one Marshall-Hill collaboration, "was better than many I've seen since by practicing lawyers."

One of the consistencies of youth is that men and women will often gravitate toward their contemporaries for sustenance. But the young Thurgood Marshall was different: he bonded with older Negro men who had a love of the law. He wanted to impress them; he wanted to confide in them; most important, he wanted them to see him as a striver.

Marshall's high law school marks attracted much attention at Howard. He got a job in the law library as an assistant. It was an enviable job and also allowed Marshall to hang around when Houston hosted meetings in the library with visiting lawyers who were working on important civil rights cases. Walter White of the NAACP was one such visitor, working on a Virginia rape case. White took note of the "lanky, brash young senior law student who was always present" during his visit to the school. Marshall, according to White, did "everything he was asked, from research on obscure legal opinions to foraging for coffee and sandwiches." It became easy for these visiting legal scholars to see that TM—as he had begun signing some of his correspondence—possessed a sharp legal mind, a mind that could envision bending the law in directions the law itself had not yet been bent. Young TM was the kind of student who made these men rock their heads a little in affirmation of his potential and prowess. They chatted among themselves—the cigar smoke wafting about them—that he was someone who possessed special talents.

By his final year of law school—at a school that had undergone a profound metamorphosis during his time there—Thurgood Marshall remained at the top of his class.

But what, in reality, could Negro law students, graduating in 1933—in the Depression's grip—expect to do? Firms on Wall Street did not want them, nor did fancy law firms anyplace else. So where could TM find an opportunity that might challenge him or any of his classmates? The dilemma weighed on the mind of Houston, the law school dean: "It would follow that in those communities where sentiment and tradition are strongest against the Negro taking part in governmental activity, one would expect to find the greatest scarcity of Negro lawyers." To his young charges, Houston appeared to be laying down the gauntlet. The South was dangerous, but that was where the work happened to be, the biggest challenges for the Negro. Houston knew that Negro lawyers with grandiose plans of filing lawsuits on behalf of Negro equality would hardly be welcome in the South. "Yet," in Houston's mind, "it is where the pressure is greatest and racial antagonisms most acute that the services of the Negro lawyer as a social engineer are needed." To the bravest of his young Negro charges studying the law, Houston had a challenge, fraught as it was with danger and uncertainty. "The great work of the Negro lawyer in the next generation must be in the South and the law schools must send their graduates there and stand squarely behind them as they wage their fight for true equality before the law."

So they would have to cross the Rubicon if they wished to keep measuring up to the challenges of the great and demanding Charlie Houston. Houston knew that Thurgood Marshall was of the next generation. The ruthless dropout rate from Marshall's entering law school class, among other things, certainly told him so. Only five of Marshall's classmates remained from his incoming class as the 1933 school year drew to a close. Houston knew well what TM had accomplished: He had endured a daily commute without complaint. He had dazzled academically. He seemed at ease in courtrooms he had visited—including the Supreme Court, which might have heightened the heartbeat of any law student. He had met the nationally known and well-connected Walter White. The law entranced Thurgood Marshall. He had come to realize that there were passions behind laws and that the best lawyers were not only smart but also cagey and resourceful. What limited rights the Negro had in American society had been won, for the most part, through the American legal system. Thurgood Marshall became convinced, just as Charles Houston knew, that the greatest challenges for any Negro lawyer truly lay in the American South, in those courtrooms with the segregated balconies. The South, as Houston knew, was dangerous, unpredictable, and murderous. But if that dynamic and equation could be turned and altered, it might mean salvation, freedom, and equality for the Negro people.

As Marshall and his classmates strode through the hallways of Howard University in those last weeks of law school, they had already been made aware, in a powerful way, of just what the Supreme Court could do in the name of justice. The high court had issued a ruling that the so-called Scottsboro Boys—eight of nine Negro youths in Alabama sentenced to death over charges of raping two white women in a case that had become an international cause célèbre—deserved a new trial. For two years, the case, buzzed about on the Howard campus—Dean Houston had helped raise money for the defense—gripped the nation, and especially Negroes, for what they saw as injustice. The nine youths, aged from thirteen to twenty, were taken off a train in rural Alabama after a scuffle that involved whites. Two white women were on the train, traveling as itinerants. In court, the women, with a lynch mob hovering outside the courtroom, said they'd been raped by the Negroes. In Alabama, such an accusation doomed them. Eight of the accused were sentenced to death. The *Birmingham Age-Herald* proclaimed that the collection of meted-out death sentences were "without parallel in the history of the nation." In Houston's mind, the case had touched the conscience of "every Negro in the country." (The death sentences were eventually vacated in a Supreme Court case decided in November 1932, but the defendants, even as the women recanted, received long prison terms.)

Marshall and his classmates could not ignore the fact that the times were quite worrisome as graduation day approached. There were breadlines across the country; weary souls were sleeping in alleyways and city parks in Washington, blocks from the Howard Law School. President Roosevelt had been in office for only three months and was readying his New Deal program, but its hoped-for effect would not be felt right away.

Marshall was proud of himself and the approaching end to his law school studies. Some folks back in his Baltimore neighborhood seemed surprised to hear from his parents that he had done so well in law school. "I'd got the horsin' around out of my system and I'd heard law books were to dig in," he would say. "So I dug, way deep."

So it was that as Thurgood Marshall finished his law school studies in 1933 (cum laude, the sole law school student to earn such an honor), he walked out into a world of deep pain—and with a vague dream he might be able to change it. He was quite aware of how high the stakes were with what lay ahead. He would come to remember his law school years with a blunt clarity: "Charlie Houston was training lawyers to go out and go in the courts and fight and die for their people."

Marshall—unlike his fellow law school graduates—had an intriguing offer upon graduation. Harvard University was dangling a fellowship. So he could continue his studies or, with Houston's admonition echoing in his ears, travel the South—prepared to die. From the White House to every Negro street corner and plantation field, from Los Angeles to Baltimore, the challenges facing the Negro below the Mason-Dixon Line were no mystery. "Unfortunately," President Theodore Roosevelt had written in 1903 to a friend as he contemplated the Negro and the South, "there is in the South a very large element . . . which hates and despises the Negro but is bent upon his continuing in the land."

IT WAS CHARLIE HOUSTON—unable to forget his prized law school pupil—who would provide a restless and young Thurgood Marshall with his first notable trip to the American South.

Houston had begun forming strong alliances with the NAACP while at Howard, offering legal counsel. The New York–based organization was always short of funding, jeopardizing its ambitions. Fortune came like a bolt of lightning: In 1922, Charles Garland, a Harvard dropout, received $800,000 from an estate left by his father. He agonized over how to spend the money. Garland finally decided the money should go to help social causes. The American Civil Liberties Union and the NAACP were among the lucky recipients of the Garland Fund. NAACP officials announced a plan for their donation: the money would be used to finance "a large-scale, widespread, dramatic campaign to give the Southern Negro his constitutional rights, his political and civil equality, and therewith a self-consciousness and self-respect which would inevitably tend to effect a revolution in the economic life of the country." It was tantamount to drawing a line in the sand of the South—while using a Yankee sword to do so. Roger Baldwin of the ACLU became a Garland Fund adviser. Baldwin's heart was with the Negro cause, but he had reservations that such a strategy would work across the South "because the forces that keep the Negro under subjection will find some way of accomplishing their purposes, law or no law."

The Garland Fund team, at the insistence of Charlie Houston, brought Nathan Margold aboard. Margold—a onetime assistant U.S. attorney—had been on the *Harvard Law Review* with Houston. Houston wanted Margold—Jewish, intense, socially conscious—to prepare a report analyzing the fund's best strategic approach to tackling the South. Margold concluded he admired what the fund aimed to do with its money regarding the plight of Negroes, but he felt the legal mission should be streamlined. The Supreme Court, as he reminded his readers, had repeatedly upheld the separate-but-equal doctrine. Margold told the fund's advisers—Thurgood Marshall was in the loop now because of Houston—that the Supreme Court needed to be pressured into deciding if segregation was a principled law; his reasoning was that if presented with a comprehensive enough ultimatum, the court would back down. As Margold put it, "If we boldly challenge the constitutional validity of segregation if and when accompanied irremediably by discrimination, we can strike directly at the most prolific sources of discrimination." Margold knew states had been hiding behind the fallacy of separate being equal, a supposition that on its face opened the door for many states to keep insisting that when it came to education, they were providing the same amounts of money to Negro schools as to white schools, which made the Negro schools equal. It was a falsehood but would have to be legally proven.

Margold also made mention of another legal case long decided. In 1886, the Supreme Court ruled, in *Yick Wo v. Hopkins*, that San Francisco could not discriminate against Chinese laundry owners. The case began a year earlier when one of the Chinese merchants, Yick Wo, was told that because his business structure was made of wood—and not brick, favored by the white merchants—his license would not be renewed unless he rebuilt. Yick refused to rebuild and was subsequently fined and even arrested. He believed his Fourteenth Amendment rights were violated, took his case all the way to the Supreme Court, and won. In the high court's mind, when a law "applied and administered by public authority with an evil eye and an unequal hand, so as practically to make unjust and illegal discrimination between persons in similar circumstances" was being practiced, it was tantamount to the denial of the equal protection clause of the Constitution. The Yick Wo ruling would be remembered by those, like Thurgood Marshall in the years to come, who planned to launch a legal assault on the separate-but-equal doctrine in American society.

In the late summer of 1933, Charlie Houston had some time on his hands, and he knew what he planned to do with it. He was going to go south. He was going to start—thanks to money from the Garland Fund—amassing documentation about and analyzing some of those all-Negro schools in the region. He hoped the evidence he gathered would eventually help the legal assault on school segregation. Houston—who already had a penchant for going on fact-finding missions—owned a Graham-Paige automobile with a dependable six-cylinder engine. Still, he knew traveling Negroes rarely poked about the South alone, especially those with Yankee accents. There was safety in numbers, as the Negro Leagues baseball players knew, as the jazz musicians surely knew. Houston needed a road companion, someone who might be as interested in such work as he was. He needed someone to ride shotgun. Houston thought of his prized Howard Law School pupil. Thurgood Marshall all but jumped at the opportunity.

Before the two departed, they were forced to listen to warnings from relatives and friends regarding their safety. They were given scraps of paper with phone numbers deemed important, and on the other end of those phone numbers, they were told, would be people who would come to their aid in case of emergency. These were names of preachers, funeral home directors, NAACP officials spread across various southern states. Houston and Marshall packed cool clothing in anticipation of the heat. They packed a typewriter, notebooks, pencils, pens. They were going south to document.

And off they rolled.

They went through the Carolinas, passing the turpentine camps and clumps of workers. They went into Mississippi, where the cotton fields stretched before their eyes. They sat with the Negro educational officials who were not too afraid to be seen with them. They listened as teachers told them about the low pay and decrepit schoolhouses. They were told everything was separate all right—but hardly equal. Marshall and Houston were quite a sight, two tall, refined Negroes with straight hair arriving out of the blue behind the wheel of a Graham-Paige automobile. Many of those they met had never laid eyes on a Negro lawyer, let alone two at the same time. Children scampered around them while their parents chatted with Marshall and Houston. Both were appalled at the conditions of the schoolrooms they were shown, particularly the toilet facilities, which were often just a covered shed out back of the schoolhouse. On occasion, they had to bend their ears because of the thick southern accents, but Marshall had a gift, if Houston didn't, of putting strangers at ease. Houston stood amazed at a particular talent of Marshall's: He would adopt a pronounced southern accent in the presence of white southerners, a verbal tactic that seemed to put them at ease. "Yes, sir" became "yessuh"; "no" became "naw"; "sure enough" became "shonuff." Such verbal mimicry was beneath the erudite Houston but not Marshall.

They kept moving and writing. They were writing down the size of classrooms, the number of children enrolled, the size of the staff. They'd walk by the white schools and could clearly see the difference: how much better the white schools looked; how solid, sometimes new, those buses for the white children looked. Sometimes, exhausted, they'd roll onto the campus of a Negro college and introduce themselves and get a meal. At night, they'd look over their notes and talk about all the information they had compiled and how they hoped it would help the NAACP and the Garland Fund folks up in New York City. They rolled on, through Alabama and Louisiana. When their stomachs growled, they didn't even bother looking in the direction of white dining establishments. "That's why we carried bags of fruit in the car, most of the time we'd just eat the fruit," Marshall would recall of the journey.

At the end of their sojourn, Houston and Marshall easily concluded that Negro education lagged woefully behind the educational opportunities for whites. The Negro children were cut off from white America and any kind of intellectual discourse with it. It was as if they had been snapped off from America itself. And if they were cut off—particularly from the Constitution—how were they going to rise and get ahead in the world? If there was an eye upon them, it indeed seemed to be evil. In one stark discovery—gleaned from 1932–1933 documentation—it would be revealed that South Carolina "spent $331,932.00 transporting 29,624 white children to elementary school, but only $628.00 transporting 87 Negroes to elementary school."

· · ·

WILLIE AND NORMA MARSHALL were quite happy to see their son return home from his trip with Houston. Norma constantly worried while he was away, and all those news stories she read in the Baltimore newspapers about mistreatment of the Negro only deepened her agonizing. Then she would have to listen to the worry from Vivian, Marshall's wife. He confided to them how awful the conditions in the Deep South were, how threadbare the educational opportunities for Negroes. Marshall couldn't forget what he had seen. He was not going to fear the American South. He'd study the photographs they had taken, of the run-down schools, of the desperate looks on the faces of the school-age children. He'd seen how magical the word "education" was to the Negro parents, even as they grasped how elusive it was for their children to obtain a decent education. Thurgood Marshall was now determined to better the lot of the Negro in American society. He was equally determined to lean on the U.S. Constitution to help him do so.

Marshall passed his Maryland bar examination on the first try and formally became a lawyer on October 11, 1933. In Baltimore, he set about finding office space. It was not easy. "I have had quite a job getting offices here and have been refused almost every place because of being colored," Marshall confided to his onetime law school dean. He finally landed on Redwood Street in east Baltimore, sharing an office suite with Warner T. McGuinn and William Alfred Carroll Hughes Jr., two other Negro attorneys.

That first year, Marshall scuffled to get by, taking on misdemeanor cases, divorces. Some of the clients had been recommended by acquaintances of his father and mother: Negro waiters, schoolteachers, Pullman porters who might need legal assistance of some kind. He had two secretaries, Lucille Ward and Sue Tilgman, whom he barely paid. But he was so personable, so bighearted, and so full of life barreling into the office in the mornings that they understood he was trying to forge a reputation, to make a name for himself. "He had a genius for ignoring cases that might earn him some money," one of the secretaries would recall. "Sometimes we'd get our $7.50 a week, sometimes we'd just get carfare, other times we were out-of-pocket at the end of the week. But we loved that man." Now and then the Colored Funeral Directors Association would toss some work his way. His first-year compensation amounted to less than $1,000. But he was voluble, and he possessed the skills of a winning debater, and so he barreled into conversations and small gatherings. The talk often turned to politics and ills that were constantly upsetting the daily lives of Negroes. In restaurants and bootleg joints, Thurgood Marshall would regale listeners with stories about the long trip he'd made with Charlie Houston throughout the South. He'd show up on picket lines, his wife, mother, and father beginning to worry about him because those lines could get raucous. But TM did not shy away from the spotlight. "Old-timers had the feeling that here finally was a leader," A. Briscoe Koger, who had graduated from Howard Law School in the 1920s, would recall of Marshall. "Everybody was in his corner. Others had none of the assurance and power that whites are accustomed to, but Thurgood Marshall had that."

Marshall began doing legal work for the NAACP. Charlie Houston always kept a close eye on his onetime star pupil. "There's never a dull or lazy moment, except when I have to travel with him," Alice Stovall, another one of Marshall's earliest secretaries, would come to recall. "Then I'm always left on the train while he spends his time in the dining car, gossiping with the crew . . . If we have a layover, changing trains, I sit by myself in the station, by preference, while he goes off to see one of those they-went-that-a-way pictures; any one will do, even singing cowboys."

In late 1934, Houston and Marshall joined forces on a case that young Marshall went after like a feeding shark.

It had been an ambition of Norma Marshall's that her son go to the University of Maryland Law School. But the school did not accept Negroes, so Howard Law School became the default choice. Even with the meager real-life lawyerly experience he had, Thurgood Marshall never forgot about the Maryland school and the pain it caused his mother. He went out and found Donald Murray, a recent graduate of Amherst College, and encouraged him to apply to Maryland's law school. Marshall knew they would turn him down, and as soon as they did, he launched his lawsuit. The lawsuit was filed April 20, 1935. Marshall was eager to "get even with Maryland for not letting me go to its law school." The lawyers argued that the school, in denying Murray admission, was in violation of the Fourteenth Amendment. Judge

Eugene O'Dunne saw great merit in the Houston-Marshall argument and ruled in Murray's favor. The law school at the University of Maryland would have to desegregate. Marshall had cracked the color bar in a law school in his home state. H. L. Mencken, the cigar-chomping *Baltimore Sun* columnist, opined that "there will be an Ethiop among the Aryans when the larval Blackstones assemble next Wednesday." To those who couldn't decipher those words, it meant that the cast of the lily-white law school was in for an awakening.

Following the Murray victory, drinks were raised in Marshall's honor at some watering holes around Baltimore. The old-timers truly began looking upon him as something of a local legend, even at his young age. Walter White, who had become executive secretary of the NAACP in 1929, was duly impressed with Marshall's role in the lawsuit. "I have never sent a check to anyone accompanied by such sincere congratulations as this one," White wrote to Marshall from New York City. "The victory in the University of Maryland case is epoch making and all of us here join in sending our warmest congratulations."

Both Marshall and Houston ignored the threatening letters that were sent to them by the Ku Klux Klan. Once Murray began classes, Marshall was so bold as to sometimes accompany him to the law school, as if he dared confrontation. Like a shark, Thurgood Marshall had now tasted the blood of freedom. More than ever, he was sure of his direction.

By 1935, Charlie Houston had taken a job in New York City as the first full-time counsel to the NAACP. Within a year—and because there was simply too much work for a single lawyer—Houston was proposing to the executive director, Walter White, that they add another full-time lawyer to the staff. He had only one lawyer in mind for the job. "I don't know of anybody I would rather have in the office than you or anybody who can do a better job of research and preparation of cases," Houston wrote to Marshall in the fall of 1936. Marshall, constantly low on money and struggling to support a household, did not need long to ponder and accept a job as first assistant counsel to the NAACP. And in 1936 he moved with his wife to New York City, uptown into Harlem.

·　　·　　·

THE NAACP HEADQUARTERS were located downtown at 69 Fifth Avenue, on the high floor of one of those sturdy structures overlooking the city. Some days the location was easily identified by a flag that had been placed in a holder that jutted from a windowsill. The flag was like a just-arrived telegram from below the Mason-Dixon Line. Five large words were on it: A MAN WAS LYNCHED YESTERDAY. The man could have been anywhere—Georgia, Alabama, Mississippi, Arkansas—when he met his demise. And as the flag flapped, the world knew.

Thurgood Marshall, hired at an annual salary of $2,400, might now have been sitting in "tush-tush" surroundings, as he chirped upon laying eyes on the Fifth Avenue offices, but he hardly intended to become anyone's deskbound attorney. He had the barnstormer's juice in his veins.

In October 1937, he found himself rolling, alone, through Virginia and, after that, on to North Carolina. From North Carolina, he wrote, "School situation is terrible. Principal of elementary school is gardener and janitor for the county superintendent of schools and is a typical uncle tom . . . Elementary schools terrible." ("Uncle Tom" was a derisive term, culled from Harriet Beecher Stowe's novel, used to identify blacks who lacked spine and did not support the best interests of fellow blacks. Such individuals greatly unnerved Marshall.) In Dallas, Texas, while Marshall was probing why Negroes were excluded from juries, the police chief pulled a gun on him. Another officer intervened and kept Marshall from being shot.

By mid-1938, Charlie Houston had left the NAACP to return to Washington and the law firm he ran with his father. "Charlie Houston passed through here and left a lot of sparks," the NAACP official Roy Wilkins would say. When the search began for a successor, it began and ended with Thurgood Marshall. Bigger sparks were on the horizon.

AS AN ATTORNEY, Thurgood Marshall had begun thinking of ways to make the NAACP more potent in the fight for equal rights. His own job, as it were, found him entering all areas of complaints for justice as he dealt with southern sheriffs, weary NAACP officials around the country, politicians of various ideological stripes, parents whose sons

had been beaten or killed in dank southern prisons, plantation workers who were not given time off to vote. He was an all-purpose trou-
bleshooter. And he often complained to NAACP officials that there
was too little money to fund the kind of work he wished to do. So, in
1940 Marshall wrote out a charter, which would establish the NAACP
Legal Defense and Educational Fund Inc. Its mission was to "render
legal aid gratuitously to such Negroes as may appear to be worthy"
of immediate help, Negroes who were actually in danger without any
legitimate avenue of help. Marshall was boldly creating another legal
unit within the offices of the NAACP. The attorneys Marshall gathered would cast a wide net across the nation when it came to battling
for Negro rights.

The Marshall style was informal. He'd call meetings, the fish sandwiches in cellophane would be unwrapped, and the long debates about
the Fourteenth Amendment—equal rights—would commence. The
environment became looser; ideas began to fly about. "I changed
things," Marshall would relate, "and I think I've done a pretty good job
of busting up the formality. Now I can operate in my own natural-born
way." Marshall's stewardship of the legal fund only raised his profile
more. He accepted a good many of the speaking invitations that came
his way. Many were from Baptist churches and lodge halls. Trying to
raise money for the fund, he sat around dining room tables all over the
country with those sympathetic to the NAACP's cause. Elmer Carter,
a member of the New York State Commission Against Discrimination,
saw Marshall up close at work. "It's very important that we Negroes
have a man who is at home in the Supreme Court and equally at home
with the man on the street," Carter said of Marshall. "Thurgood can
talk on terms of equality with a social scientist like Sweden's Gunnar
Myrdal, but he talks the argot of Harlem with the man on the street
corner. He creates confidence on all levels of Negro life."

In morning darkness, Marshall would bolt from his Harlem home
to Idlewild Airport, just outside Manhattan, and hours later be in
some southern town quite aware of the dangers around him. Sometimes, before leaving a southern town—he knew the art of conviviality
even in hostile surroundings—he'd leave a bottle of good liquor for
the sheriff himself. Who knew when he'd be through there again, and
a good impression left behind might be remembered. "He was a very

courageous figure," Herbert Hill, an NAACP official, would recall of Marshall. "He would travel to the courthouses of the South, and folks would come for miles, some of them on muleback or horseback, to see 'the nigger lawyer' who stood up in white men's courtrooms."

The first black funeral home in Blakely, Georgia, was founded by Walter Sullivan in the 1940s. Sullivan had dressed and prepared the bodies of his share of black men who had been lynched, their family members wailing and collapsing right in front of him. As a business-man and local NAACP president, Sullivan had cachet. Sullivan's son Louis—who would become secretary of health and human services under President George H. W. Bush—remembers, as a young boy, Marshall's arrival in Blakely. "When Marshall would come, my father would have his other friends there. His friends were prepared for the Klan, or even someone who might show up, trying to arrest Marshall." Young Louis would stare as Marshall and his father, joined by others from the community, would take over the dining room, discussing NAACP strategy as the food in the oven cast off delicious aromas. "The attitude toward Marshall was that he was brave," says Sullivan. "He was a hero in the community. He provided sophistication about the law." He goes on: "The people in the community were living day to day, and they needed someone to show them how to leverage and change things."

Once, in Hugo, Alabama, Marshall stood in court to defend a black man accused of murdering a family of five. The NAACP thought the suspect might have been framed. Local Negroes insisted Marshall sleep in a different home every night for his safety. Whites crowded the small courtroom and stared with wonder at the sight of the lawyer all the way from up north. The attention grew so heavy that the super-intendent of schools declared a half holiday so that students could go over to the courthouse "and hear that cullud lawyer."

Marshall, even as he relished decision making, cast his net wider still for assistance. He was sometimes presiding over more than five hundred cases per year. He was quick to call upon any number of vol-unteer lawyers whose hearts and minds dovetailed with the work of the NAACP. Among their ranks were Morris Ernst, Arthur Garfield Hays, Bartley Crum, and Samuel I. Rosenman. They were some of the keenest minds in the country when it came to constitutional law.

Marshall credited himself with the important ability to "get expert advice, then follow it."

WHEN IT CAME TO PATRIOTISM, American Negroes were eager to join the cause of wartime service. They had been proud of their contributions from the Civil War onward. But there were always segregation woes and frustration. "Honey," a black corporal wrote to his girlfriend from the South during World War II after he had been thrown off a bus because of his color, "I am so hurt inside, so much that I don't really know what to do . . . Just think I may have to fight some day, but honey what will I be fighting for, surely not the rotten conditions we have to bear down here."

Of all the military branches during World War II, the navy had the worst record when it came to its treatment of Negroes. It wasn't until 1942 that the navy allowed Negroes to join, and even with that they were mostly assigned to cleanup duties—or the dangerous work of handling ammunition and explosives. In May 1944, however, the new navy secretary, James Forrestal, announced a series of measures to treat Negroes more fairly, starting with allowing them to undertake sea duty.

During the war, many ships sailed back across the Pacific to Suisun Bay and the Port Chicago Naval Magazine there. The ships were to be reloaded with ammunition and other weaponry to fight the war. There were 1,431 Negroes stationed at Port Chicago in the summer of 1944, and it took them little time to realize they were the only ones—and not the white sailors—doing the dangerous work of loading ammunition. On any given day, they were required to load up to seven tons of bombs. The Negroes fretted to one another that they were not given adequate training to perform these duties. Some of the ammunition was referred to as "hot cargo"—meaning fuses were attached to it. The white officers worked them around the clock, in three shifts.

At 10:00 p.m. on July 17, the men would have heard a familiar utterance over the loudspeakers: "Lights out, quiet about the deck." Then, minutes later, it came—a thunderous and deafening explosion that woke the men in a startled fright. They knew something was wrong; they feared a foreign attack. Glass flew everywhere; the sky lit up with colors from the explosion; blood squirted from men who had been badly cut by flying glass or the large pieces of metal that were zooming about; bunks flew upward; the entire sick bay exploded. Suddenly fire was circling boxcars, which were loaded with ammunition. "Fellows were cut and bleeding all over the place," one Negro sailor would recall. "One fellow's feet were bleeding and I gave him my shoes. Another fellow had a cut all the way down his arm, and I put a tourniquet on it to try to stop the bleeding. There were no medics around—it was chaos." Ships anchored in the bay vanished in the explosion; the pier, all one thousand feet of it, was gone, blown to pieces. Screams pierced the night. Arms and legs were strewn about, ripped from bodies. Men cried while pulling bodies from the bay.

The death toll was staggering: 320 sailors were dead; more than 200 of those were Negro. Hundreds were injured. Those who lived in nearby San Francisco imagined an earthquake had struck.

The worst fears of the Negro sailors—that something awful would happen with the furious handling of the ammunition—had come to pass. No one could figure what caused the ammunition and bombs to ignite. "As was to be expected," Admiral Carleton Wright would say, "Negro personnel attached to the Naval Magazine Port Chicago performed bravely and efficiently in the emergency. As real Navy men, they simply carried on in the crisis attendant on the explosion in accordance with our Service's highest traditions."

The navy transferred the surviving Negro men to Camp Shoemaker, which was nearby. And soon the Negro men heard something that greatly upset them: that white officers were blaming them for the two explosions, intimating they had been faulty in their loading of the bombs and ammunition. The men decided, as soon as they had recovered from their injuries, that they would refute that allegation.

Congress considered giving the families of those who died $5,000 each. But the Mississippi congressman John Rankin raised a fuss, arguing that Negro families should not receive that much money. The figure was reduced to $3,000.

But the navy, within a month, had decided to send the Negro sailors who survived the Port Chicago explosion back to work—loading ammunition. On August 4, the men, now at a base on San Pablo Bay, in Vallejo, California, were marched toward a waiting ship, the USS

Sangay, which was an ammunition ship they were supposed to load. White officers led them in formation. The soldiers marched. Then, as if on some kind of internal cue, stopped en masse. Their commanding officer was befuddled. He repeated the marching orders. The sailors would not move. The marine guards looked at them quizzically. The rebellion was under way. The Negro sailors announced they would do any other task the navy asked of them, but they were not loading an ammunition ship, because they felt it was not safe. The men were told the consequences of their actions. Navy officers stared at them, stunned. Finally, about 100 of the men agreed to load the ship, but 258 refused.

The sailors who refused were taken to the prison barge. "Now, the slightest provocation, we will shoot," they were warned by a marine guarding them. A navy admiral came and visited the rebellious men, informing them mutiny was punishable by death. That threat forced a group of the men to return to work. Fifty remained steadfast.

News of the Negro sailors, now charged with mutiny, spread throughout black America. The lives of the sailors hung in the balance. They needed help. Thurgood Marshall was summoned.

Marshall immediately asked Secretary of the Navy James Forrestal if he could attend the trial and offer any assistance to the defense he deemed necessary. Forrestal granted the unusual request, and Marshall flew to California in early October. Marshall firmly believed the sailors were being tried "solely because of their race."

Marshall's presence helped bring media attention to the case. "As a matter of fact his presence," said a local NAACP official of Marshall's arrival on Treasure Island, "caused the San Francisco Chronicle to give the hearings about three or four times as much space this morning as they have been giving it before."

James Coakley, the navy prosecutor, argued that the Negro men had plotted and schemed to mutiny, claiming that it was well orchestrated. Gerald Veltmann, the navy officer defending the sailors, argued that it was not mutiny, that the sailors were simply afraid of losing their lives loading ammunition and saw no other way out than a work stoppage. Sitting in on the trial convinced Marshall the Negro sailors had staged nothing less than a heroic protest. "Negroes in the Navy don't mind loading ammunition," Marshall told an NAACP audience in the area. "They just want to know why they were the only ones doing the loading! They want to know why they are segregated, why they don't get promoted!"

During the trial, Marshall demanded naval authorities launch a full-scale investigation into the explosion. "I want to know," he said, "why commissioned officers at Port Chicago were allowed to race their men. I want to know why bets ranging from five dollars up were made between division officers as to whose crew would load more ammunition."

All fifty men were found guilty. They were sentenced to fifteen years of hard labor. Their mothers wept. Marshall proclaimed the sentence and trial "one of the worst frame-ups we have come across in a long time." He promised the families of the sailors he would appeal. He did not want the sailors getting in more trouble in prison. "Play it cool," he told them. "I'm working."

The war ended. Marshall pushed the Port Chicago appeal. Secretary of the Navy Forrestal rejected their appeal. Negroes across the country continued to be outraged and protested to Congress and to First Lady Eleanor Roosevelt, who let her displeasure be known to both Forrestal and President Roosevelt.

In early January 1946—with his conscience getting the better of him—Forrestal changed his mind and reduced the sentences of the Port Chicago 50, ordering many of them back to duty. They shipped out to sea aboard a navy ship.

In 1948, President Truman signed an order desegregating the American military. The Port Chicago sailors were discharged "under honorable conditions." They were eligible for veterans' benefits but were forbidden to receive benefits of the GI Bill, such as educational opportunities.

The men of the Port Chicago 50, who rose as brave civil rights heroes in the eyes of many, never forgot the attorney who had flown across the country to take up their cause. They sent him letters, notes, postcards, thanking him. They considered Thurgood Marshall their savior.

MARSHALL'S PHOTOGRAPH began showing up in periodicals and Negro newspapers around the country. He'd be seen getting on a train or an airplane, carrying a leather briefcase, wearing a fedora and long tweed coat. He walked in long, loping strides, like a man in a practiced rush. He scribbled his phone number and passed it along to any number of people—deputies, FBI agents, southern hotel clerks—who might need to contact him in an emergency. It didn't seem to matter where Marshall was. Those in dire need always seemed to find him. He took care to establish a rapport with J. Edgar Hoover, convincing Hoover of his mission to fight his cases inside the courtroom, not outside it. It was a tactic that paid off: Hoover never maligned Marshall as he would, in years to come, Martin Luther King Jr. and others who had taken the nonviolent protests to the streets. (Marshall utilized a carrot-and-stick approach in dealing with Hoover. He would constantly remind the FBI director of his anti-Communist stance and that of the NAACP. That, of course, appealed to Hoover's own fears about the spread of Communism. Marshall, who knew of Hoover's disdain for renegade groups trying to thwart federal law, took extra efforts to point out to Hoover the dangers of the Ku Klux Klan. Hoover loathed the Klan, referring to it as "a group of sadistic, vicious white trash." Marshall—in another tactic—would compliment Hoover's agents, allowing in missives to Hoover that he doubted if his agents were prejudiced but informing Hoover that some of the law enforcement officers in the South certainly were and that FBI agents should be careful in dealing with them. Hoover and Marshall would intermittently exchange letters—Marshall was worried enough about escalating death threats to sometimes inform the bureau when he was going South—and Hoover seemed to foster an abiding respect for Marshall.)

Marshall received plenty of those dire phone calls seeking his help. Once he had been tracked down at a poker game in Washington. The caller, in a southern state, told him about a lynching party just then forming. Marshall had to think fast. He reached a white politician in the town by phone. "Look," Marshall told the politician, "just two sets of people can't afford a lynching at this time—us Negroes and you people. You're right in the midst of a Dixiecrat political campaign and a lynching's going to make your people look awful bad." The politician took Marshall's number, told him he'd dash to the scene and call him back as soon as he could. Twenty minutes later, the phone rang. Marshall answered. "The state troopers made it in time," he was told. "Call this number in a few minutes; your man will be there, unharmed." Marshall verified the man's safety and went back to his poker game.

At a 1947 news conference, Marshall reiterated his legal ambitions: "There can be no equality as long as there is segregation, regardless of the so-called 'dollar-and-cent equality argument' that any persons have raised in the past. The only way to attack racial segregation is to attack racial segregation." In 1940, the NAACP could count 50,000 dues-paying members. Six years later, the figure had increased nearly tenfold, to 450,000 members. Few could deny that Thurgood Marshall's presence inside the organization had reaped benefits beyond the courtroom. The NAACP clearly had a marquee performer.

Some constantly worried not only about Marshall's safety but about his health. "I can testify there are times," Marshall admitted, "when you're scared to death. But you can't admit it; you just have to lie like hell to yourself. Otherwise, you'll start looking under the bed." The work was grinding. But he kept going. Sometimes, before gatherings—a good many church groups would invite him to speak—he would start reciting the U.S. Constitution. And he'd be pointing his fingers out over them and he would be perspiring, and they would be up on their feet and stomping their feet. The applause would be thunderous as he left the stage. He'd get something to eat and be gone again.

In the early part of the twentieth century, the state of Tennessee—birthplace of the Ku Klux Klan—practiced a code of justice without fear when it came to Negroes. In 1946, the Negro citizens of Columbia sent word they needed Thurgood Marshall.

Marshall soon arrived, intent on helping a mother and son who had been jailed.

It was February 25, 1946, when Jim Stephenson, a local Negro, accompanied his mother, Gladys, to a store in town. She had earlier dropped off her radio to be fixed, later retrieved it, turned it on at home, and realized it was still not working. Thus her return visit. Billy Fleming, the repairman and son of the store owner, told Gladys Stephenson he believed she had broken the radio anew after he had fixed it, and now she was trying to get him to repair it again—for free. She said she did no such thing; Fleming didn't like the tone of her voice and slapped her in the face, at which point her son, just back from the military and fighting Hitler, coldcocked Fleming, who tumbled through a glass window. There was blood, and gasps from onlookers. Police quickly arrived and arrested Gladys Stephenson and her son. Ominous-sounding conversations went on about an uppity black man and his mother and the bleeding and hurt Billy Fleming. There were plots about revenge. By nightfall, a lynch mob had formed. The local sheriff did an admirable thing: with the assistance of a couple of local Negroes, he spirited the Stephensons out of town. Shooting nevertheless erupted on the Negro side of town that evening when residents—among them Negro military vets—saw white police-men coming in their direction. The Negroes fired on the policemen, believing they were just the first arrivals of a forming lynch mob. Four policemen were hit, though all survived. Pleas for help were quickly sent by whites over telephone wires. National guardsmen descended on the Negro community the next day. Businesses and homes were ransacked; children wailed. A Negro funeral home was destroyed. "The hate-ridden orgy was topped off with a huge KKK scrawled in white chalk across one of the caskets," a report would later divulge.

By week's end, upwards of a hundred Negroes had been arrested. An editorial appeared in the Columbia *Daily Herald* that read, in part, "The white people of the South . . . will not tolerate any racial distur-bances without resenting it, which means bloodshed. The Negro has not a chance of gaining supremacy over a sovereign people and the sooner the better element of the Negro race realize this, the better off the race will be."

Days after the arrests, two Negro suspects, while under question-ing, were shot dead inside the interrogation room of the police station. Police said they were trying to escape. Not many believed it. The news spread throughout the country. While in the intervening days many of those arrested would be released, twenty-five suspects remained jailed. They were charged with, among other things, attempted murder and assault. Those sympathetic to the plight of the Negroes staged rallies from Washington; Eleanor Roosevelt was among those demanding justice. Those who remained jailed needed a good lawyer, which is why—three months after the glass shattered, and the salesman Flem-ing flew through that window, and the Negroes armed themselves, and the policemen were shot, and the suspects were shot dead at the police station—Thurgood Marshall arrived in Columbia. Signs on the road leading into Columbia would have been hard for anyone to miss: NIGGER, READ AND RUN. DON'T LET THE SUN GO DOWN ON YOU HERE. IF YOU CAN'T READ, RUN ANYWAY.

Many Negro citizens in the town proceeded to tell Marshall about ill-treatment and brusque tactics from FBI agents. Marshall fired off a letter to the FBI Director, Hoover, who responded by asking Marshall to provide the names of FBI agents who had violated the rights of Negroes during the investigation. It was a demand the jittery and frightened Negroes of Columbia could hardly meet because they dared not offend an FBI agent by requesting his name, imagining such a request might in turn lead to their own arrest.

A federal grand jury was convened, but no indictments were brought against any whites. The FBI itself refused to bring charges against any white police officers. Marshall believed this was the "best example of what happens" when all-white law enforcement runs a state. A jury, however, did indict twenty-six Negroes for attempted murder. Marshall, their attorney, made a motion for a change of venue, arguing that no Negro had ever served on a jury in Maury County. Surprisingly, the trial was indeed moved to Lawrenceburg, about thirty miles away. On trial's eve, Marshall became sick and wound up back in New York City. "Mr. Marshall's condition is due solely to the fact that he has worked himself almost to death without any thought of self," Walter White informed the NAACP board.

Even ailing, Marshall continued to offer advice to the lawyers while recuperating. When the trial got under way, Alex Looby, Maurice Weaver, and Leon Ransom were now the defendants' attorneys. Weaver was white and was greeted with the same coarse epithet the Negro attorneys heard daily. The lawyers couldn't help worrying about their own safety, in addition to that of those they were defending. "Open threats," Walter White of the NAACP would recall of the trial, "were made by the unshaven, overall-clad spectators that the lawyers who dared defend Negroes would wind up in the Duck River." The Duck River was a notorious spot for public lynchings near the town.

The strategy of Marshall and the other attorneys—to have the trial moved—reaped rewards as a flush look appeared on the face of the judge when he looked at the verdict rendered by the all-white jury: twenty-three of the defendants were acquitted. Any celebration, however, was muted, because two of the defendants, William Pillow and Lloyd Kennedy, still faced attempted murder charges.

With the timing of a great actor appearing for the all-important final act, Thurgood Marshall rallied and returned to Tennessee to defend Pillow and Kennedy. Some of the Negroes who spotted Marshall upon his return rushed up to him as if he'd just dropped from the sky.

Soon Marshall found himself standing before an all-white jury trying to make a case for the two defendants, Pillow and Kennedy. He told the jury the defendants, in a night of violence, were only trying to defend themselves, given that a lynch mob had formed earlier in the day, prior to the gunfire. In the end, the jury partially agreed with Marshall: Pillow was acquitted; Kennedy was sentenced to five years. (The sentence would later be reduced, and he would serve just ten months.)

In the world of southern justice, the outcome was considered a near miracle. Thirty minutes after the verdicts were announced, Marshall and his passengers—Looby, Weaver, and Harry Raymond, a reporter for the *Daily Worker*, the Communist newspaper, who had been covering the trial—were on the road, heading to Nashville, where they had been sleeping because of safety concerns. It was dark. Marshall was behind the wheel and soon heard a siren. A group of men—wearing civilian clothes and twirling a lit flashlight—pulled alongside Marshall, yelling for him to stop. Marshall pulled over. Everyone tensed up. They were told to get out of the car, and when they stepped into the darkness, they noticed a couple of state trooper cars nearby. The men told Marshall they had a search warrant, that they believed whiskey was in the car, and that they were breaking the law because it was a dry county. The police did a careful search of the car. There was no whiskey. They were allowed to drive off. However, now Marshall wanted Looby to drive, and he did. Moments later, their car was stopped again—flashlights twirling. They were told again to get out of the car. Marshall was asked why he was no longer driving. His explanation seemed to suffice, because they were let go. Then they were stopped a final time minutes later. "We have got to arrest you for drunken driving," one of the men said to Marshall, who quickly protested that he had not been drinking. Nevertheless, he was arrested and placed inside a sheriff's car with four armed men. Marshall's cohorts were told to drive on to Nashville. Looby, Weaver, and Raymond stood in shock as the car with Marshall inside vanished. When they saw it turn off the main road onto a side road, they gave pursuit: they imagined Thurgood Marshall was going to be lynched. The brazen pursuit seems to have startled the law officers, because they finally turned around from the darkened road and took Marshall on to Columbia.

In Columbia, standing on a dark street across from the police station, Marshall was told to proceed to the station—alone. He knew better: a bullet to the back, a charge of trying to escape. "I told them that if we went over there we were all going over there together since I wasn't going by myself inasmuch as I was under arrest." The magistrate administered a breath test and announced that Marshall was not drunk. He was released. They all breathed relief, but everyone remained shaken from the ordeal. The Marshall group decided it wise not to go to Nashville in the same car, which could easily be spotted, so they ventured over to the Negro section of town, lay low for a while, then borrowed another car, finally making it to Nashville without further incident. Marshall filed a complaint with the Justice Department, asking for an investigation into his arrest. "Had Looby and Weaver obeyed the order to drive to Nashville—which they had no intention of doing—and failed to follow the car into which Thurgood had been put down the dark road toward the Duck River," Walter White felt, "there is little doubt that he would have never been seen again."

It pained Marshall that southern politicians would blame local unrest on northern "agitators"—such as himself—for brewing discord. Marshall felt such finger-pointing only ignored the bravery of southern Negroes. "Thurgood Marshall's supposed to be masterminding this whole campaign," Marshall himself said, "somehow, against the wishes of Southern Negroes, those millions of childlike, happy, easygoing colored folk—that's the way segregationists talk about Negroes when they're not describing them as vicious, immoral and diseased—who would be as contented as pie if agitators didn't come along and stir them up." Marshall—fond of retelling stories to prove a point—went on: "It reminds me of the story of the crowd that was rushing at top speed down the street. A man standing on the sidewalk saw them go by and naturally got curious. He went out on the road and grabbed a guy huffin' and puffin' along at the tail end of the crowd and said, 'What's goin' on here?' The other guy pulled loose and cried, 'Don't hold me back, man! Don't you know I'm the leader of that crowd? And if I don't run like hell they'll get away from me altogether.'"

. . .

THE NEGRO COMMUNITY was now always talking about Thurgood Marshall.

They talked about him in pool halls, and they talked about him in gin joints. They talked about him in jazz clubs and also in the small business establishments that Negroes owned. A Negro—Thurgood Marshall—was constantly standing up to white terror in courtrooms, and many Negroes could not have imagined such a thing. They talked about him at backyard barbecues and on front porches where old Negro men and women, many the grandchildren of slaves, sat dreaming of real freedom. They talked about him in and around courthouses throughout the country. "Thurgood was this young lawyer making headway," recalls Virginia-born Billie Allen, who would become a renowned dancer and grande dame of the arts in Harlem and who first saw Marshall in the late 1940s. "My mother took me to some of his trials to hear him speak. She wanted me to be well-grounded. My mother was so enamored of him. He knew his onions. He was so sure-footed." Negro sailors out at sea talked about him; so too did Negro soldiers far from the home front. Jazzmen and Negro singers and Negro ballplayers talked about him. The Negro newspaper reporters on the Negro newspapers—the white papers wouldn't hire them—wrote about him and sipped beer with him when they could track him down. The Negro college kids talked about him and especially the paltry number of Negroes going to law schools. They not only talked about Thurgood Marshall; they wrote him letters, plenty of letters. He once received a letter from Levi G. Byrd, who headed the NAACP branch in Cheraw, South Carolina. It didn't matter that Byrd's letter was riddled with misspellings and bad grammar; it was passionate and beautiful in its own way, so beautiful that Marshall sometimes carried it around in his coat pocket and showed it to people.

Dear Mr. Marshall:

Just a few words to let you know how things is going around Cheraw. People is not making Much Fuss hear in Chesterfield County. But I am obayen just what the Bible says, I am watching First and Prayen with my Eyes Open at all times . . . VERY SORRY

THAT I LIVE IN A STATE LIKE THIS BUT WE ARE
DETERMINED TO MAKE IT A DECEN PLACE TO LIVE
FOR OUR CHILDREN ALL THAT COMES AFTER US.
BY ABAYEN THE LAW OF OUR GREAT AMERICA AS A
WHOLE.

The papers, The State has just Published about the Thugs shooting in Rev. Hintons Home Monday Night . . . We will see just what The Gov. of S.C. Will do about this. Nothing of course.

Trust that your Office will I know look after this matter in the right way.

AS LONG AS I AND SOME OTHERS THAT HAVE NINE
LIVES THE N.A.A.C.P. WILL NEVER DIE IN S.C. RIGHT
WILL WIN.

Trusting that you is injoyin your Married life. I wish you much success and a long life.

> *Very truly yours,*
> *Levi G. Byrd—Secretary-Treas.*

Somewhere, they were always writing Thurgood Marshall letters, always talking about him. He had entered the dreams of the oppressed.

· · ·

THURGOOD MARSHALL realized he could not be everywhere. He often had to dispatch members of his staff into the Deep South to file or appeal cases. He had to ponder, like a chess master, where he might want to send a white staffer as opposed to a Negro staffer, or vice versa. The jurisdictions could be downright hostile, and Marshall knew anyone stepping into a southern town with an NAACP calling card would be watched carefully—and even threatened. So he made calls ahead, setting up houses of host families where his staff members could stay, and he often asked the male members of those households if they had their shotguns ready for protection. Marshall had befriended a reverend named Lucas in Houston. Lucas knew well the ways of the South. "In the glove compartment of his car," Marshall would recall of Lucas, "he had two items—a Bible and a .45."

IN THE LIFE OF Thurgood Marshall, few days were like the early afternoon of May 17, 1954. And from that day onward, Marshall would be credited with lifting the dreams of the downtrodden by virtue of a Supreme Court victory that was as powerful in its own way as Lincoln's Emancipation Proclamation.

Few things in the South haunted Negro parents more than their inability to provide decent educations for their children. Plantation owners revered the bottom line: more hands picking cotton in the field meant more cotton production. So children were often put to work, without regard to their futures, and their hours inside a classroom greatly sacrificed. Sometimes, however, parents passed on ingenious ideas to their children. William Henry Holtzclaw had a little brother who picked cotton just like him. "One day I plowed and he went to school, the next day he plowed and I went to school; what he learned on his school day he taught me at night and I did the same thing for him. In this way we each got a month of schooling during the year."

It became clear to Negroes who worked on plantations in the South at slavery's end and on into the twentieth century that the only hope of delivering their children from the life of servitude they led was to deliver them to a schoolhouse door. And it was clear to those same Negroes that even when they did, the schools for their children were often decrepit, ill-equipped, and mostly ignored by whites who held power. It was rare in Clarendon County, South Carolina, for Negroes to get beyond the fourth grade. By that age, they were strong enough to pick cotton, so they went to work, with little regard for their future. And yes, there were buses for students in Clarendon County, but those buses were for white students. The Negro children had to walk, or hop on a mule, or climb in the back of a horse-drawn wagon. Rain would pelt them in the springtime, and they'd get back home with coughs and colds. And worse, picking cotton was often easier than going to school. To the white owners of the plantations, that was more productive and valuable. "Yessir, we got good nigras in this county," is how Charles Plowden, a successful banker and cotton farmer in the area, felt about the disenfranchised blacks.

On March 16, 1948, the Negroes of Clarendon filed a lawsuit in U.S. district court against the bus policy. They got two Howard Law School graduates—Harold Boulware, who lived in the state capital of

Columbia, and Thurgood Marshall—to be their attorneys. Marshall initially went into the case over the awful gap in bus systems for Negro and white, but he began to turn it into a thrust for equality involving salaries, buildings, school materials—all the things any civilized community would expect for its children. In the weeks leading up to the initial arguments, Marshall implored the residents of Clarendon County to not give up. Many had received death threats, and some had fled the county after those threats. Their bravery had a profound effect on Marshall when he saw them in the courtroom hanging on his every word: "A very few got seats, a few more stood shoulder to shoulder for hours in the courtroom, which was so crowded that they could not even move. The others stood outside the door and in the hallway." The case went through its permutations, becoming known finally as *Briggs v. Elliott:* Harry Briggs was a local gas station attendant with children in the school system, and Roderick W. Elliott was chairman of the local school district.

The decision in South Carolina came down in a 2–1 ruling upholding segregation in Clarendon County, and while it seemed odd to conclude that the NAACP had somehow "won" in a 2–1 defeat, the dissenting voice of Judge J. Waties Waring could be seen as encouragement. The case—looped with four other legal assaults upon school segregation—eventually made its way to the U.S. Supreme Court.

In a 9–0 decision on that day of May 17, 1954, the Warren Court ruled that the legal tenets of separate but equal as espoused in the *Plessy v. Ferguson* decision were unconstitutional. The bulwark of Jim Crow America—separate facilities and accommodations for the Negro—had been stunningly overturned. The penultimate school desegregation decision had its roots in legal assaults—*Shelley v. Kraemer, McLaurin v. Oklahoma State Regents, Sweatt v. Painter, Smith v. Allwright*—that had been spearheaded by the chief counsel for the plaintiffs, Thurgood Marshall, and the NAACP over the past two decades. In the decision, *Brown v. Board of Education of Topeka, Kansas,* Chief Justice Warren cited a finding by the Kansas court leading up to the high court's ruling:

Segregation of white and colored children in public schools has a detrimental effect upon the colored children. The impact is

greater when it has the sanction of the law, for the policy of sepa-
rating the races is usually interpreted as denoting the inferiority
of the negro group. A sense of inferiority affects the motivation of
a child to learn. Segregation with the sanction of law, therefore,
has a tendency to [retard] the educational and mental development of negro children and to deprive them of some of the benefits they would receive in a racial[ly] integrated school system.

Warren anticipated fallout and even backlash given the scope of the
decision. "Because these are class actions, because of the wide applica-
bility of this decision, and because of the great variety of local conditions," he wrote, "the formulation of decrees in these cases presents
problems of considerable complexity."

There would indeed be re-arguments in the months ahead, but the
nation-shaking *Brown* ruling—the result of federal lawsuits from several states which upended school segregation in a landmark decision—
had been issued and would be unaltered. It would be ground into the
psyche of the American populace: separate was separate; it was not
equal in any manifestation. And while the decision focused on education, psychologically its tentacles reached much further. It seemed to
say to the nation—even if Negroes knew it all along—that the daily
activities of the country were propped up on immoralities. That segregated classrooms, fire stations, hospitals, summer camps for children,
were all wrong. That segregated neighborhoods and graduate schools
and law schools were all wrong. That America had been operating in
violation of its own constitutional safeguards. That American society
had blessed this way—this conditioning—in its day-to-day existence.
The court had said, in essence, that a society could no longer afford to
look itself in the mirror every morning under such a practice, because
now, with this ruling, the mirror had cracked, and not just in the
American South but everywhere: separate was not equal in Cincinnati,
or Buffalo, or Sacramento, or Flint, Michigan.

America was a powerhouse of a locomotive, zooming down the
tracks of the twentieth century. It was the envy of the world. Marshall
had called that big locomotive to a halt. Now the train had to back
up. Now civil rights—the idea of them had seemed so foreign to so
many for so long—would be boarding that train. (The news of the

court ruling went global, announced all over the world by the Voice of America.) Thurgood Marshall had not only stopped the train but reconfigured the tracks. When the May 17, 1954, ruling came down, the young Martin Luther King Jr. was not yet a national figure. (He had actually delivered his first sermon as the new minister at Dexter Avenue Baptist Church in Atlanta just two weeks before the decision.)

Few expected southern communities to adopt the court's recommendation of enacting *Brown* in a timely manner. James Reston, the respected *New York Times* columnist, didn't approve of the court's decision at all, allowing that "the Court insisted on equality of the mind and heart rather than on equal school facilities."

Marshall was hardly naive himself and imagined challenges going forward. "You can say all you want," he told his friend, the Baltimore newspaper publisher Carl Murphy, "but those white crackers are going to get tired of having Negro lawyers beating [them] every day in court. They're going to get tired of it."

SOMETIMES MARSHALL COULDN'T WAIT to return to his Harlem apartment. His wife, Buster, would invite friends over. She'd cook: chitterlings, pot roast, yams, collard greens, a feast. Media Dodson, one of Thurgood's aunts, would recall one celebration: "Thurgood's wonderful to behold when he comes back from a hard case and gets together . . . There he is, singing—though he can't turn a tune any more than an alligator—dancing, telling funny jokes and things. Everyone just says, 'This is Thurgood's night; look at him go.'"

But Buster Marshall couldn't help wondering how long her husband could keep up this hectic pace. "He's aged so in the past five years; his disposition's changed, he's nervous where he used to be calm—this work is taking its toll of him," she had confided in 1952 about her forty-four-year-old husband. "You know, it's a discouraging job he's set himself."

Still, he was seen again and again, and he kept being seen out there on the road, in those small southern towns. In July 1950, Marshall had snuck quietly into Baton Rouge, Louisiana. The mainstream white press did not routinely cover the comings and goings of Thurgood Marshall. And rarely did its reporters cultivate Negro contacts in communities on any constant basis. But that summer, Warren Rogers, a writer for *Look* magazine, got a tip that Thurgood Marshall was hanging out over in Scotlandville, a Negro section of Baton Rouge. "Brother Rogers," the caller mysteriously said to him, "I think I've got a story for you. If you go right now, you'll get the story . . . Go to the back room. You'll find Thurgood Marshall and some others there." Rogers asked the caller, whom he recognized as being a Negro, about Marshall's presence in town. "They're going to register 12 of our boys in the LSU graduate school in the morning!" Rogers grabbed notebook and pen and rushed out to Scotlandville, checking the scribbled address as he drove. He wasn't used to being on the Negro side of town. The sights and sounds—little Negro children playing, dogs barking, adults on porches and eyeing his slow-moving car—were so different. "I felt like an intruder," he would remember. The address was actually a home, and he was directed around to the backyard, where there was a makeshift fish-fry shack. He could smell the aromas of fish and sizzling grease. He walked up to the screen door and knocked.

"Who's that?" came a voice from inside.

Rogers identified himself. A. P. Tureaud, a lawyer for the NAACP—short and serious-looking—came to the door. He looked Rogers up and down, asked him what he wanted.

"I want to talk to Thurgood Marshall," he said. Tureaud and others, mindful of Marshall's notoriety, were always protective about him. There was just no telling who was looking to do harm to Thurgood Marshall.

"What about?" Tureaud wanted to know.

"About those students you're going to register at LSU tomorrow."

Then came a voice from inside. "Let him in." It was Marshall.

Rogers stepped inside, looking around at the gathered Negroes. He could tell he had intruded upon a secret-like meeting. Marshall broke the silence with roaring laughter. "Now," he said, "we'll talk if you promise not to write anything in advance. We need the surprise, OK?" The young reporter, suddenly happy, now relaxing, agreed. Marshall told Rogers about the Negro students they would be accompanying to the school. A few days later, the twelve students—"frightened but determined," as Rogers would remember—filed into the registrar's office at LSU and filled out their registration forms. The white administrators took their forms and they left. On July 28, 1950—mere days later—LSU issued its all but foregone conclusion: "Be it resolved that pursuant to the laws of Louisiana and the policies of this Board the administrative officers are hereby directed to deny admission to the following applicants: Nephus Jefferson; Dan Columbus Simon; Willie Cleveland Patterson; Charles Edward Coney; Joseph H. Miller Jr.; Roy Samuel Wilson; Lloyd E. Milburn; Lawrence Alvin Smith Jr.; James Leo Perkins; Edison George Hogan; Henry A. Wilson; Anderson Williams."

Then Marshall and Tureaud went to court, filed suit against LSU, and won. The first Negro students would enter the school in 1953.

THURGOOD MARSHALL'S momentum awed many. But the absences from home would have taken a toll on the sturdiest of marriages. Buster Marshall knew her husband was apt to socialize on the road after long and challenging courtroom days. She heard rumors of his womanizing. Marshall thought he could stifle her worries with gifts—pearls, a fur coat, pretty dresses.

Buster had been ailing before and during the legal arguments surrounding the *Brown* court case. She went back and forth to visit doctors. A battery of tests were taken. Some mornings she could barely rise from bed. She minimized her illness to her husband, implying to him it wasn't all that serious. She imagined if she revealed to him her own health worries, it might somehow derail his mission and focus. It was a twenty-five-year marriage, and it had a routine: Thurgood would fight for the rights of Negroes; she would support him at all costs. So she worried more about his health than he did about hers. But finally Buster Marshall had to confide to her husband that she had lung cancer. Marshall hurried home. Buster's family members in Pennsylvania also arrived at the Marshall home. Latent furies began to rise. Maude Jones, Marshall's mother-in-law, thought he had been an inattentive husband through the years, and she told him so. Marshall felt her bitterness on an almost daily basis as she watched her daughter's situation become more and more grave. The 1954 Christmas holidays were a grim time for Marshall and his terminally ill wife. "He stayed by her bedside constantly," a friend of Marshall's would remember. The New

Year came in; January rolled into February. Buster Marshall's birthday was looming. It came on February 11, and that was the very day she died. "I have wanted most, all these years, to help him make good," Buster Marshall had once said of her husband.

There was a well-attended funeral in Harlem at the fabled St. Philip's Episcopal Church. Marshall accompanied his wife's casket on a train back to Philadelphia, where she was buried. In the days that spooled forward, Marshall's health quickly began to deteriorate. He lost his appetite; he began drinking in his lonely Harlem apartment. Friends worried about him. He did not care to commiserate with them on the telephone. "During this period," the NAACP attorney Jack Greenberg would recall, "he lost so much weight that he became cadaverous in appearance." NAACP Legal Defense Fund board members met secretly to discuss Marshall, fearing he would have a mental collapse. They decided a vacation would help and voted to present him with a $600 cash gift—"for the purpose of a short cruise." Marshall traveled to Mexico City and was shown the sights by a cousin of Jack Greenberg's. Then, to escape the bustling of that city, Marshall ventured onward to a spa in San José Purua, Mexico.

MARSHALL, NOW A WIDOWER, seesawed between New York City and Washington in the aftermath of Busters death. In Washington, there were still arguments to be made relating to the *Brown* decision before the justices. There was much work to catch up on as he tried to find his bearings after losing Buster.

While he had been away, however, there was much intrigue about what the future might hold for Thurgood Marshall's romantic life. Harlem was rife with gossip: one of the most accomplished Negro men in the country was now single. Marshall continued to live in the Sugar Hill apartment where he and Buster had resided for years.

In Harlem, Sugar Hill was known for its sophistication and high-achieving residents. Among the Marshalls' neighbors were W. E. B. DuBois, the folksinger Josh White, the poet William Stanley Braithwaite, the NAACP head, Walter White, the musician Mercer Ellington, and the psychologists Kenneth Clark and his wife, Mamie. Walter White's well-appointed Sugar Hill apartment on Edgecombe Avenue became so popular for soirees it was called the White House of Harlem, and on any given night there the loud and energetic voices of Thurgood and Buster could be heard bouncing amid the cacophony.

So there were many Negro women—some egged on by their mothers—who made inquiries about when Thurgood Marshall might begin to socialize again. Some of the single women interested in him stopped by the legal fund office, feigning interest in the foundation's work, really there to see if they could make an impression on Marshall.

It was not obvious until it blatantly became so: Marshall had begun inching closer and closer to an NAACP secretary by the name of Cecilia Suyat, whom everyone called Cissy. At NAACP affairs—which Buster had refrained from attending because of her worsening illness in the late winter of 1954—Cissy and Marshall would be seen leaving together. On a few occasions, they were even spotted dining in Harlem eateries.

Cecilia Suyat was a native of Hawaii; her Filipino parents had immigrated to the island in search of work. (The first wave of Filipinos to immigrate to Hawaii had come to work on the sugar plantations, which was a piece of cultural history that made Suyat sensitive to the plight and history of American Negroes.) Relatives in New York City who were studying at Columbia University had encouraged Suyat to come to the city. She studied stenography and found work at the NAACP as a typist. And one day, there she was, on a picket line with others because a local theater was showing *The Birth of a Nation*, the racially inflammatory movie that had caused protests by blacks years earlier. In 1948, Cissy was promoted to private secretary to Gloster B. Current, head of all NAACP branches.

Marshall now began assiduously courting the petite, attractive Cissy Suyat. She had a round face and bright eyes. But when he started talking about marriage, she rebuffed him, worrying about the negative reaction to an interracial marriage.

Cissy Suyat had reason to worry. She wasn't particularly concerned about her family, as they were still in Hawaii. And it wasn't exactly the nosiness she knew would be felt from others; that could be sensed simply by walking down the street with Marshall. (Not to mention the gossipy stories that sometimes appeared to jump off the front pages of Harlem tabloids when it came to interracial relationships.) It was an episode that had taken place right in the NAACP headquarters itself.

Walter White, executive secretary of the NAACP since 1931, was by all accounts a brilliant and brave man and a skilled genius in his direction of the NAACP. Many still greatly admired him because he had chosen to be a Negro: his complexion was so light, his eyes so blue, he could have passed as white. In the 1940s, *The New York Times* had estimated upwards of twelve thousand Negroes were "passing" as white every year. As they glided along the sidewalks in Anytown, U.S.A., their friends and neighbors were unaware they had Negro blood. Not Walter White. He was proud of the Negro blood in him. He had gone undercover and investigated southern lynchings; he had traveled the country giving thousands of speeches assailing the forces of racism and bigotry. And through the years, he had maintained close ties to whichever administration was in the White House. Walter White knew how to gin up publicity for a good cause, and reporters were eager to track him down. Then, in 1948, came a different kind of publicity.

That year, White divorced his first wife. The following year, he remarried. Poppy Cannon, his new bride, was a freelance writer and Vassar graduate. She was also a white woman. The uproar—Walter White, head of the NAACP, marrying a white woman—was swift. He received stinging letters, from blacks as well as whites. His two sisters, Madeline and Helen, excoriated him, telling him he had let the Negro race down. Emergency NAACP meetings were called to handle the fallout. White and his bride fled America, taking their honeymoon in Europe. There were threats that White would be fired by the NAACP. Thurgood Marshall supported White. The former first lady Eleanor Roosevelt, an NAACP board member, threatened to quit the organization if White were let go. Finally, it all calmed down. Those Negroes who had assailed White were made to feel ashamed. But it all had still alarmed Cissy Suyat. While Walter White did stay on at the NAACP, his powers were gradually decreased. It was as if the lion of the NAACP had been subtly forced to retreat into the shade. She couldn't stop wondering what Negro women in Harlem would think of her, believing they would turn against her, would accuse her of stealing one of Harlem's princes. Marshall reminded her that it all had worked out, that White and his wife, Poppy, were living their life. Then, suddenly, on March 21, 1955, Walter White died of a heart attack. More than a few wondered if domestic strife had hastened White's demise.

But Cissy Suyat soon realized she was no match for the debater in Thurgood Marshall. She finally said yes to his marriage proposal.

Marshall was wise enough to tell NAACP officials of his plans to marry Suyat, given the Walter White fallout and the need to gird for negative reaction.

The NAACP gave its blessing. Only after the marriage—which took place on December 17, 1955, in New York City, well-wishers pouring from the church into the cold to greet Marshall and his new bride—did they call a press conference to tell the world about it. Officials took pains to point out that Suyat had been a longtime member of the NAACP, that she believed strongly in civil rights—all of which left an impression that they would tolerate no criticism of Thurgood Marshall and his Filipino bride. There was no worrisome fallout, and it was a rare example of an interracial marriage in 1950s America of a well-known Negro drawing scant publicity. Suyat's family, however, was another matter. They were clearly disappointed in her choice of husband. "Her family was not particularly fond of blacks. Cissy was very independent—she didn't give a damn," recalled Monroe Dowling, a longtime friend of Marshall's.

Thurgood Marshall was quite eager to start a family. His first wife had had several miscarriages. Thurgood junior was born in August 1956, and another son, John, was born in July 1958. The boys, in those very early years, simply did not see a lot of their father. Cissy explained to them their father's all-important work out on the road. But children never stop asking questions. "Who's that man?" Thurgood junior had asked his mother one day upon looking at a picture of his father.

THAT MAN KEPT MOVING. He was seen in federal courthouses, at the U.S. Supreme Court arguing cases. His battles dawned all through the first half of the 1950s. The *Brown* desegregation ruling cemented his fame. He was quick to compliment those he knew believed in civil rights. In 1957 in Clinton, Tennessee, a Negro minister had been beaten up by members of the White Citizens' Council for escorting Negro children to the public school. The newspaper columnist Walter Winchell wrote a letter to the U.S. attorney general, Herbert Brownell, expressing his outrage for the attack upon the minister.

"Just read your recent column reprinted in Pittsburgh Courier on White Citizens Council, Klan and others," Thurgood Marshall wrote to Winchell. "Thanks a million for a marvelous column during a very trying period."

White America might not have seen the 1960s coming, but protesting Negroes certainly did. A short while after President John F. Kennedy took the oath of office at his inauguration in 1961, he was ensconced inside the White House. He was chatting with his brother Ted and Stephen Smith, his brother-in-law. They were peering from a window, watching a parade of cadets from the Coast Guard Academy as they marched by. The new president stared long and hard into the procession. A feeling came over him, and it was a feeling he did not like. There was not a single Negro among the coast guard cadets marching by the White House. Kennedy quickly summoned Richard Goodwin, one of his speechwriters. "Call the commandant and tell him I don't ever want to see that happen again," Kennedy said of the all-white parade procession.

When President John F. Kennedy came into office, the entire American federal judiciary was nearly all white. Kennedy intended to appoint a Negro to a federal court judgeship. And not just any Negro lawyer would do. The individual had to be dynamic, successful, beyond reproach. And Thurgood Marshall had the kinds of courtroom victories—*Shelley v. Kramer, Sweatt v. Painter, Brown v. Board of Education, Missouri ex rel. Gaines v. Canada*—that had changed American jurisprudence. "I think he had an extra sense that these individual cases were creating dramatic changes in their fields," says Berl Bernhard, an attorney who first met Marshall in the late 1950s. "He had a peculiar and abnormal instinct about which substantive cases could come together. Like ocean waves." He goes on: "You'd have to think about jobs and education and the right to vote. Thurgood was always on the hunt for what areas reinforced each other so they would come together for qualitative impact. It was a skill. I'd say he had really woven together this tapestry."

President Kennedy finally took Thurgood Marshall off the road, where he had labored for decades battling injustice, and brought him into the federal judiciary.

DAY TWO

FRIDAY, JULY 14, 1967

3

Battling with a Legendary
Country Lawyer

The Arkansas senator John McClellan—bruised by the 1957
Little Rock desegregation battle, which cast a harsh light on his state—
privately told constituents he would do all he could to stop
Marshall from ascending to the high court.

B Y BRINGING UP THE ISSUE of crime on the first day of hearings—
and insinuating Thurgood Marshall could be vulnerable on the
issue because of the *Miranda* ruling—southern Democrats believed
they had the kind of momentum that they craved and needed to derail
the nomination. Both Chairman Eastland and McClellan had been
informing colleagues that police department chiefs around the country
had been telling them how much they loathed the *Miranda* decision.

Southern Democrats now intended to go into another area they thought could severely hurt Marshall's confirmation chances: the U.S. Constitution. How well, exactly, did Marshall know the Constitution? How did he interpret that sacred document which had united the states upon ratification in 1788? This is what Senator Eastland wanted to find out, because he believed Marshall had subverted the Constitution, had joined with other "liberal" forces, twisting it around for political purposes. Eastland knew exactly whom he wanted to question Marshall on the breadth, scope, and meaning of the U.S. Constitution: the North Carolina senator Sam Ervin. Many believed Ervin the most brilliant figure in the U.S. Senate when it came to understanding and interpreting the U.S. Constitution.

The Constitution, of course, was the document that Thurgood Marshall had given so much of his life to—upholding it, interpreting it anew so that courts would grant his plaintiffs, Negroes, their rights. It was, in his mind, the grandest and most epic framework for individual rights and liberties. But the document, he fervently believed, also offered room for stretching, for amending—a process that he felt the original framers had intended for future generations to exercise and evoke. The document indeed spoke eloquently of liberty, justice, tranquillity, posterity, and general welfare. And yet Negroes had been, year in and year out, across decades, disenfranchised, maimed, and tortured in the shadow of that great document.

Proof in its elasticity could be seen in the nation's darkest hours. Before and during the agonies of the Civil War, many came to believe that slavery would never end. But in 1865, the Thirteenth Amendment to the Constitution outlawed slavery. In 1870, the Fifteenth Amendment to the Constitution granted black men the right to vote. Those amendments also unleashed bloodshed; thousands of lives were lost, and southern states threatened, time and time again, to secede.

Those flames in the mid-nineteenth century had now twisted and exploded into flames of the 1960s. It added a minute-by-minute tension to the hearings taking place inside room 2228.

When he was a boy, Sam Ervin and his father journeyed to Washington for a visit. They wound up at the Supreme Court. The elder Ervin was taken with language and considered himself something of an orator. He seemed to relish hearing the sound of his own voice. "The Supreme Court will abide by the Constitution though the heavens fall," the elder Ervin told his son during their visit to the court.

Senator Sam Ervin made it quite clear, at the outset of the second day's hearings, that he planned to focus solely on Thurgood Marshall's interpretation of the Constitution. Ervin, a large man with a jowly face, said he believed it was the dream of every citizen that those who sit on the Supreme Court interpret the Constitution "as written" in a literal manner. "I think that every Senator," Ervin told Marshall, "who has an official duty to perform in connection with the nomination of a Supreme Court justice has the right—indeed, that it is his duty, to determine to his own satisfaction whether or not the confirmation of a particular nominee will make it more certain that the American people will realize that dream, or whether or not the confirmation of that particular nominee will tend to make that dream vanish."

What was undeniably vanishing across the South, across Sam Ervin's North Carolina, was a way of life, what they called, with a great deal of nostalgia, the Lost Cause. And in the fevered smoke of that Lost Cause—"Negro Only" signs tumbling down, schools integrated, blacks rising up, the Constitution reexamined—sat the very man, Thurgood Marshall, whom Sam Ervin had prepared so long and studiously to derail. As a matter of fact, Ervin went to the Senate in 1954, the very year in which the Supreme Court issued its *Brown v. Board of Education* decision, a ruling that Ervin likened to the tyranny of Reconstruction after the Civil War, in which blacks received political rights. Because he owed his victory to his staunch campaigning against *Brown*, many in North Carolina expected Ervin to go into the U.S. Senate and settle scores.

SAM ERVIN was born in 1896 in the small mountain town of Morganton, North Carolina. His grandfather, a Confederate soldier, had battled the dreaded Yankees at Dingle's Mill. Ervin's father, also named Sam, was a lawyer. Young Sam went to the University of North Carolina, where he grew fond of poetry. He was precocious, so much so that when he entered Harvard Law School, he began taking third-year classes his very first year—and passing them. He went off to fight in World War I, before returning to North Carolina, marrying, and starting a law practice. He found himself appointed to a seat on the North Carolina Supreme Court in 1948, a job that he seemed to genuinely like.

Six years later, in 1954, North Carolina senator Clyde R. Hoey died in office. There was scrambling for his seat. Many felt that Irving Carlyle, a well-respected lawyer from Winston-Salem, might get the interim appointment. Carlyle had his own opinions about the *Brown* desegregation decision. "As good citizens," he told a North Carolina audience, "we have no other course except to obey the law as laid down by the Court." As they sat listening, audience members began swiveling their necks. Throats were cleared. This moderate declaration was not what they anticipated hearing. Not at all what they wanted to hear; such words were considered heresy, and Carlyle, just that quickly, had ruined his chances of being appointed. The governor intended to name someone who would attack this damnable *Brown* ruling. He found his man in Sam Ervin. "I love the South," Ervin said in response to the *Brown* decision. "Many persons whose blood runs in my veins died for a cause they believed to be right. I honestly believe that if usurpation by the court continues, the Constitution of the United States will be destroyed." This was the Sam Ervin North Carolinians so adored.

There were three figures in the South who rose high in the eyes of many of their fellow southerners for authoring the much-publicized Southern Manifesto: Senator John Stennis of Mississippi, Senator Richard Russell of Georgia, and Senator Sam Ervin of North Carolina.

The first big clash resulting from the *Brown* ruling took place in Little Rock, Arkansas, in the fall of 1957, when nine Negro children attempted to integrate Central High School. On their first day, they were met by a white mob. They were spat upon, pelted with rocks, and made to fear for their lives. The scenes were abhorrent and vile. Newsmen trying to cover the event were pummeled and bloodied. Governor Orval Faubus of Arkansas bewildered the Eisenhower administration by vowing to protect the students, then pulling a vanishing act. Eisenhower left his vacation home at Newport, Rhode Island, and, once back at the White House, made an announcement to the nation. "Under the leadership of demagogic extremists," Eisenhower said, "disorderly mobs have deliberately prevented the carrying out of proper orders from a Federal court. Local authorities have not eliminated that violent opposition." Eisenhower also said, "Mob rule cannot be allowed to override the decisions of the courts." (Thurgood Marshall swept into Little Rock to give solace and legal advice to the Negro parents and students.)

Federal troops, armed, would remain in Little Rock the entire school year.

In Ervin's mind, federal troops sent to Little Rock to protect Negro children represented "a tragic day for constitutional government in America."

IT IS NOT that Sam Ervin didn't have Negro acquaintances. He did, but they were his family's domestic help—maid, servant, cooks. Those were the Negroes whom Ervin knew. As a country lawyer, he had loved chuckling with them on his porch. He listened to their stories about scrapes with the law, about marital discord in their own relationships, and he'd retell these stories to wild laughter among his white friends. These stories would be interspersed with his oft-told tales of moonshine and whiskey runners in the backwoods of North Carolina. When Negroes visiting the Capitol from North Carolina during the 1960s wished to see Ervin, his staff would be so obliging. And as the senator began asking perfunctory questions—wondering what town in North Carolina they hailed from, wondering if he knew their folks—they would pipe up and warn him that segregation had to go, that it could not withstand the political winds. That's when an aide would interrupt, the meeting would come to a close, Senator Sam Ervin would offer his country grin, and they'd be ushered out the door, with such courtesy.

In early February 1960, four Negro freshmen from North Carolina Agricultural and Technical College in Greensboro (most referred to the school as North Carolina A&T) walked into an F. W. Woolworth store in downtown Greensboro. They took seats at the counter and asked to be served. "I'm sorry but we don't serve colored here," a waitress informed them. It soon triggered other sit-ins. Store executives were bewildered. The Negro students—sometimes joined by whites—were not going to go away. It spread to other cities—Nashville, Tallahassee, Jackson, Mississippi. Warning signs were posted by the white business owners: "We Reserve the Right to Service the Public as We See Fit." "Temporarily Closed." "Closed in the Interest of Public Safety." The students kept coming back. They were punched, doused with ammonia, cursed. Mayor William G. Enloe of Raleigh was furious. He called it "regrettable that some of our young Negro students would risk endangering these relations by seeking to change a long standing custom in a manner that is all but destined to fail." When asked about the sit-ins, Sam Ervin thought the solution simple: the students were trespassing on private property, and private property was protected by laws inherent in the Constitution—and these students should be arrested!

In the landmark U.S. Supreme Court case *Plessy v. Ferguson* of 1896, which upheld the "equal but separate" doctrine, Sam Ervin had a compatriot in Justice Henry B. Brown, who wrote the court's majority opinion. "If one race be inferior to the other socially, the Constitution of the United States cannot put them upon the same plane," Brown declared.

Some in North Carolina believed Sam Ervin very wrong on the integration issue and the shifting social and political landscape. One of them was Terry Sanford, a moderate governor elected in 1960. "The time had come for the liberation of the black man," Sanford said.

Those who were sometimes invited into Sam Ervin's library were astonished. Little wonder he possessed a brilliant mind—University of North Carolina, flying through Harvard Law School—because in his personal library were more than thirty-five thousand books, most of them about the law. He emboldened and filled his mind with constant knowledge. His beloved wife, Margaret, could not stop him from buying books. He'd go on trips and come back with more books. He'd order them out of magazines. He'd amble into bookstores and emerge with a stack under the crook of his beefy arms. But in none of those thousands and thousands of books did Sam Ervin—considered one of his nation's great experts on constitutional law—ever find anything pointing toward equality for the black man. It just wasn't there. He wrote notes about particularly resonant passages he had come across in some of his precious books. And in none of those passages, in his mind, was there anything that could convince him that the black man could—or should—walk side by side with the white man.

Someone had once said of Sam Ervin that when it came to race, he was "a great man whose mind is in chains."

ON THE SECOND DAY OF Thurgood Marshall's confirmation hearings, Sam Ervin ambled into the hearing room laden with books. He had scribbled notes to himself in the margins of some of them, as well as on pieces of notepaper. In those books, he had underlined important passages from major law decisions that had been issued from the highest court in the land—the Supreme Court—in the name of the Constitution. These were decisions that he thought sacrosanct.

Senator Sam Ervin came to room 2228 on Friday, July 14, intent on rattling chains.

Shortly into his questioning, he produced a twenty-two-page report that grew out of a 1958 California conference in which three dozen state supreme court justices issued a resolution saying that one of the "greatest" judicial virtues was "the virtue of judicial self-restraint."

The Ervin-produced resolution—written one year after the Little Rock school melee—seemed an attack on the *Brown* ruling and others of its kind. Ervin told Marshall that the state justices felt that many U.S. Supreme Court decisions had "represented unwarranted encroachments by the Supreme Court upon the powers reserved to the States by the Constitution itself." Ervin then bore in, asking Marshall, because more than half of the state justices in the nation had signed the resolution, didn't it mean that these justices felt the Supreme Court should "confine itself to its allotted constitutional sphere, that of interpreting the Constitution rightly"?

Marshall only said that the resolution "speaks for itself."

Ervin then summoned the name of Daniel Webster, the renowned New England politician. "Good intentions," Webster, now being quoted by Ervin, once said, "will always be pleaded for every assumption of authority. It is hardly too strong to say that the Constitution was made to guard the people against the dangers of good intentions. There are men in all ages who mean to govern well, but they mean to govern. They promise to be good masters, but they mean to be masters." Ervin wanted Marshall to respond to Webster's words. Marshall offered a poised reply, one that infused Webster's sentiment with modern reality: "I would not disagree with that as a statement, but it is based on the fact that the Constitution was to protect the people from what might happen temporarily in any governmental agency." (Ervin certainly felt no need to mention that during a heated debate about slavery in the U.S. Senate, Webster's reputation had been sullied when he attacked abolitionists and suggested strengthening the Fugitive Slave Law. "Mr. Webster has deliberately taken out his name from all the files of honour," an angry Ralph Waldo Emerson said.)

The country lawyer facing Thurgood Marshall seemed to be feeling more confident by the minute.

ERVIN: Does it not necessarily follow that the role of the Supreme Court as interpreter of the Constitution is simply to ascertain and give effect to the intention of its framers and the people who adopted it?

MARSHALL: Well, it is such a broad framework that I would say yes, but it is a very broad statement.

The answer did not appease Ervin.

ERVIN: I wish to repeat my question: Is it not the role of the Supreme Court simply to ascertain and give effect to the intent of the framers of the Constitution and the people who ratified the Constitution?

MARSHALL: Yes, Senator, with the understanding that the Constitution was meant to be a living document.

Eastland, the chairman, cut Ervin off and demanded from Marshall more clarity on the term "living document."

MARSHALL: Well, back in the early decisions of the 1880s or so, it was said specifically that the Constitution was a living document to be interpreted and applied as of the time that a particular factual situation came up, that it was broad terms, written with a broad stroke, and was not intended to meet each individual problem as it came up, but to be the broad . . .

Eastland cut him off again. The chairman knew he would have his time in the coming days—just as he had planned it—but he could not abide by the "living document" phrasing.

EASTLAND: Do you think that was the opinion of the founders of this country?

MARSHALL: I am certain of it, because the Constitution could not have foreseen what they obviously knew, that there would be changes in government.

Ervin was clearly dismayed with the answers he was getting. Something in all those thousands upon thousands of law books he had read told him Thurgood Marshall was not interpreting the same Constitution he was interpreting.

ERVIN: But has it not been established that in the construction of the language of the Constitution, as indeed in all other instances where construction of the language of a document becomes necessary, the justices of the Supreme Court must place themselves as nearly as possible in the position of the man who framed that instrument?

MARSHALL: I see nothing wrong with that statement.

ERVIN: Where the words of the Constitution are plain, there is no room for any construction whatever, is there? Where the meaning is obvious?

MARSHALL: Yes, Senator, I agree, and I also agree that there are differences on that. I have read opinions which said that—it was not speaking of the Constitution, it was speaking of an act of Congress if I remember correctly, and said that the interpretation discredited what would otherwise be plain meaning. I can conceive of that being a possibility, but I could not really foresee it.

In time, Ervin abandoned the Constitution questions and switched to the *Miranda* ruling and its potent issue of crime. He brought up an amendment clause.

ERVIN: I would like to invite your attention to this provision of the Fifth Amendment. No person "shall be compelled in any criminal case to be a witness against himself." Those words are fairly plain, are they not?

Marshall agreed.

ERVIN: Those words apply only to compelled or forced testimony, do they not?

Again, Marshall agreed.

ERVIN: For this reason, they cannot rightly be applied to any voluntary confessions made under any circumstances, because voluntary confessions are voluntarily made, are they not?

This time, however, Marshall did not agree. In his travels as an NAACP lawyer, he had simply come upon too many jailed Negro inmates with swollen eyes and bloodied lips; he had heard from too many fathers and mothers about their sons who had been beaten into confessions by law enforcement; he had gotten too many convictions overturned on technicalities, and those technicalities turned on a violation of an inmate's constitutional rights.

MARSHALL: Well, Senator, the word "voluntary" gets me in trouble. The real problem is whether a statement is or is not voluntary.

Aides in the Johnson White House had realized Marshall would have to address the *Miranda* issue, but they did not like the brush with which the southern Democrats were painting Marshall: soft on accused criminals; a civil rights lawyer who had bent the U.S. Constitution in directions it was not meant to be bent. Every flash of fire erupting on an American street that signaled racial clashes—and saw the arrests of large numbers of Negro youths—set the White House on edge.

Ervin stuck to his line of questioning.

ERVIN: Can you tell me how anyone who is willing to attribute to simple words in the English language their obvious meaning is able to say that the words of the fifth amendment, "no person shall be compelled in any criminal case to be a witness against himself," can apply to anything except compelled testimony?

MARSHALL: Yes, I think it can be interpreted differently.

The wily country lawyer imagined he had set a solid trap.

ERVIN: I wish you would give me the interpretation you think those words are susceptible of receiving. Is there some application they can have to testimony which is not compelled or forced testimony?

They went back and forth for several minutes. Those in their seats sat riveted.

ERVIN: "Compelled." Does not the word "compelled" imply coercion or compulsion?

MARSHALL: It implies coercion or compulsion, the degree not to be determined.

ERVIN: And not voluntary action?

MARSHALL: Voluntary can follow compulsion.

ERVIN: It can also precede it, can it not?

MARSHALL: Yes, sir. I tried a case in Oklahoma where the man "voluntarily" confessed after he was beaten up for 6 days. He "voluntarily" confessed.

This is the kind of word battle the Marshall partisans thought the nominee could win. Words printed on a page were now up against the real world in which Thurgood Marshall had lived and operated. Blood extracted viciously challenged any and all laws. But Ervin did not plan to retreat.

ERVIN: I would say any judge who would hold a confession induced by a beating is voluntary is not capable of discharging the duties of a judge.

Marshall—tutored by the White House to hold his emotions in check, especially in the face of relentless questioning—all but quietly snickered. There had been myriad cases throughout his career in which judges had accepted confessions from accused men who had been beaten—or had later whispered to Marshall personally of their beatings.

MARSHALL: I would not comment on that, sir.

Ervin went on to express grave frustration with Marshall, adding that the answers he demanded of Marshall were "relevant to this inquiry."

> MARSHALL: All I am trying to say, Senator, is I do not think you want me to be in the position of giving you a statement on the fifth amendment, and then, if I am confirmed and sit on the Court, when a fifth amendment case comes up, I will have to disqualify myself.

The answer agitated Ervin.

> ERVIN: If you have no opinions on what the Constitution means at this time, you ought not to be confirmed. Anybody that has been at the bar as long as you have . . . certainly ought to have some very firm opinions about the meaning of the Constitution.

Ervin—his large hands resting near his law books, the light reflecting off his bifocals—had warned his staff he aimed to bore in on Marshall with the contentious *Miranda* ruling.

> ERVIN: How can the words, "no person shall be compelled in any criminal case to be a witness against himself," apply to anything except testimony given in a court?

Marshall remained steadfast: he again stated he could not discuss *Miranda*. Ervin was flabbergasted.

> ERVIN: I would respectfully suggest that I am talking about 15 words which have been in the Constitution since June 15, 1790. Am I to take it that you are unwilling to tell me what you think those words, which have been in the Constitution since 1790, mean?

Senator Phil Hart felt a need to interject and asked Ervin for permission to do so, which Ervin granted.

HART: It would be interesting to know from the record how many cases have been litigated since 1790 over those very 15 words. It would be an enormously long hearing.

If Hart's interjection was seen as a reprieve, it lasted just briefly. Ervin would not back away. But before Ervin spoke again, Senator Eastland rose and headed for the door. He turned briefly and said he was canceling any afternoon hearing, saying that certain committee members would be absent. Members of the audience began shaking their heads, suddenly a bit confused. The heavy door slowly closed behind Eastland. There was nervous whispering among White House aides.

ERVIN: I think this is a very simple question. Did not the majority—that is, the five—who joined in the *Miranda* case on June 13, 1966, attempt to add to the provision of the fifth amendment something that never appeared in the fifth amendment?

Marshall replied that he was not going to criticize the Supreme Court—and thus the *Miranda* decision.

ERVIN: I am not asking you to criticize the Supreme Court . . . It is not criticism to express an opinion as to what is true or not. My question is simply, does not the *Miranda* case add some requirements to the fifth amendment which are not in the fifth amendment?

Marshall would not budge, and offered anew that he could not comment. But the country lawyer sensed a quick opening.

ERVIN: I believe you did admit that you agreed with me that these requirements prescribed a rule of conduct for the arresting or the detaining officer, did you not?

Heads now quickly swiveled inside room 2228.

MARSHALL: No, sir. I agreed that the words you read were in the opinion, Senator . . . That is all I meant to say, that they were in the opinion.

ERVIN: But the words I read are not in the Constitution, are they?
MARSHALL: No, sir.
ERVIN: And prior to that time, no decision of the Supreme Court even intimated that they were implicit in the Constitution, did they?

Marshall sensed another attempt at setting a trap and declined to comment.

Ervin shuffled some papers in front of him and produced the most recent issue of a magazine called *Case and Comment*, which was published by a group of lawyers in Rochester, New York. Ervin began quoting statistics cited in the magazine about a fear of crime among the American populace.

ERVIN: One third of a representative sample of all Americans say that it is unsafe to walk alone at night in their neighborhoods. Slightly more than one third say they keep firearms in the house for protection against criminals. 28 percent say they keep watchdogs for the same reason.

The recitation led Ervin to what he wanted to ask Marshall.

ERVIN: Do you not think that these facts point out this truth, that this is no time for judges to be inventing new rules to handicap law enforcement officers in the enforcement of criminal laws?

Marshall agreed.

ERVIN: Well, do you not think the Supreme Court invented new rules in the *Miranda* case?
MARSHALL: No, sir.

Ervin soon adopted another bit of phrasing.

ERVIN: Do you believe that outlawing of voluntary confessions as admissible evidence would have any effect upon the enforcement of criminal laws?

It was the type of question Thurgood Marshall seemed to be waiting for.

MARSHALL: My answer to that, Senator, would be the first case I remember was back in the 1930s that outlawed involuntary confessions, the case of *Brown v. Mississippi*.

Ervin told Marshall his response was "not quite a relevant answer to my question."

ERVIN: Do you believe that outlawing voluntary confessions would have no impact upon the ability of prosecutors to bring self-confessed criminals to justice?
MARSHALL: That is an arguable point.

Ervin went on to tell the kind of story he was accustomed to telling in North Carolina—a story laced with country humor that he thought would prove a compelling point. It was about two judges "who had been imbibing alcoholic beverages a little too much" and who jointly decided to only drink on days when it was raining. But a drought came, and the judges became thirsty. "They held a conference and decided that no matter how dry it was in Washington, their jurisdiction was very broad and that it was bound to be raining somewhere within their jurisdiction. Consequently, they concluded that they would not violate their agreement if they took a drink."

Ervin's point—and humor—seemed aimed at conveying to Marshall that the jurisdiction of the Supreme Court was vast and that he should not keep trying to escape answering questions about what might, or might not, come before the court.

ERVIN: Did not the Supreme Court in every case prior to these recent decisions . . . hold that the words of the Constitution that no person shall be compelled in any criminal case to be a witness against himself, did not apply to voluntary confessions for three reasons: First, the amendment applied to compelled testimony only; secondly, it applied only to testimony which an accused is required or permitted to give as a witness; and third, it applied only to such testimony when given in a judicial proceeding?

MARSHALL: No, sir, I do not agree.

Ervin wanted proof from Marshall of "some case that did not hold that."

Marshall yanked the hearing room's attention back to Mississippi and the 1930s and the *Brown v. Mississippi* ruling.

> MARSHALL: *Brown versus Mississippi* said a confession involuntarily obtained outside the courtroom could not be used, and Chief Justice Hughes said the rack and torture chamber shall not be used for due process.

Here is what happened on a tenant farm in Mississippi on March 30, 1934—thirty-three years before the Thurgood Marshall hearings began in room 2228. A white planter, Raymond Stuart, was murdered. Three Negroes, Arthur Ellington, Henry Shields, and Ed Brown, were quickly arrested. The accused confessed. So the prosecutor imagined the trial a mere formality. Prosecution witnesses testified that the men had killed Stuart, but they also said they knew the men had been brutally beaten by law enforcement—"the rack and torture chamber." One of the men was also strung up to a tree in a mock hanging. Still, the judge saw nothing amiss about their confessions. The trial lasted one day, and they were convicted. Their sentence: to be hanged by the neck until dead. Their appeal went, first, to the Mississippi Supreme Court. It upheld the hanging sentence. Then it went to the U.S. Supreme Court. In a unanimous decision written by Chief Justice Hughes, the court ruled that the constitutional rights of the men—the due process clause—had been violated because their confessions had been coerced from beatings. The high court remanded the case back to the lower courts. The defendants then pleaded guilty to manslaughter, and all received sentences ranging from six months to seven years in prison. The prosecutor in the case had been a young and rising Mississippi attorney whom many in Mississippi—though not Negroes—thought highly of. His name was John Stennis, and now, in 1967, he was in the U.S. Senate. And he, like all other U.S. senators, would be called upon to vote on any Supreme Court nominee.

. . .

AS THE SECOND DAY'S HEARINGS on the nomination came to a close, allies and well-wishers who were present complimented Senator Sam Ervin on his performance. Other senators joined in. This was what an Old Bull could still do: he could put a nominee in the crosshairs of the Constitution and the law. Ervin scooped up his papers as his staff members gathered around to carry off the books he had brought to the hearings with him.

There now began a rising worry among White House aides. They all agreed that Marshall had performed ably. It was the withering drumbeat provided by McClellan and now Ervin—all about crime and criminality—that they could not ignore. Americans were worried about crime. And the flames of the riots did not seem to be going away. They also had to consider that more big guns on the Judiciary Committee—Chairman Eastland and South Carolina's senator Strom Thurmond, among them—were looming in the days ahead.

Government officials and essayists had been predicting "a long hot summer," and now that very summer—beyond room 2228—was upon America. "This spring certain Negro activists have been using the threat of a 'long hot summer' as a device for stepping up the militancy of their followers by showing that only violence could win concessions from 'the white power structure,'" the editors of *Life* magazine wrote in an editorial. "Reciprocally, white extremists prey upon the fear of a 'long hot summer' to beef up their demands for more aggressive police tactics against demonstrators and to exhort white civilians to gird for trouble."

President Johnson was worried about the war in Vietnam. Senator Abraham Ribicoff warned the administration that its focus on the war was "overlooking the burning turmoil . . . [in] the cities of America." The administration disagreed with Ribicoff. Secretary of Labor Willard Wirtz fired off a round of statistics that, he said, claimed otherwise: $3.1 billion was being spent on educating and training poor urban youths, which was a tenfold increase over what had been spent in 1963; medical and health-related programs were up to $34.9 billion, an increase from $19.8 billion four years earlier.

Lyndon Johnson hated losing. He could already see inside room 2228 that the southern Democrats were trying to derail Thurgood Marshall. "Southern senators," the next morning's *Washington Post* stated, "made clear again yesterday that they are finding it hard to swallow the nomination of Thurgood Marshall for the Supreme Court."

If the senators would not take Marshall, then Lyndon Johnson would shove another accomplished Negro nominee right down their throats. He was hell-bent on integrating the U.S. Supreme Court. It wasn't that Lyndon Johnson was giving up on Thurgood Marshall. He was simply considering the reality of politics.

Johnson devised a fallback plan. He told his staff to get in touch with William Coleman, another gifted Negro attorney who had made his own mark in the annals of American law.

4

A "Philadelphia Negro"
Suddenly on Standby

When LBJ began worrying about the fate of his nominee Marshall, he secretly
held meetings with the Republican lawyer William Coleman [left] to gauge
his interest in the seat. Coleman seemed less of a threat to southerners than
Marshall. Attorney and civil rights leader Wiley Branton is pictured at right.

H ARRY MCPHERSON, one of Lyndon Johnson's closest aides and his
most gifted speechwriter, was already worried about the Marshall
nomination. He was trying to assuage feelings among all those senators who had been caught off guard by the abrupt announcement of the
nomination—especially those southern senators. But they didn't care
to have their feelings and egos massaged; they cared to put enough
doubt into the administration that either Marshall would step aside or

Johnson would ask him to step aside. It was torturous for the administration to even imagine such a scenario. McPherson well knew Johnson's admiration of Marshall. And McPherson certainly knew what black America thought of Marshall—"he was exemplar and father figure."

When President Johnson and Thurgood Marshall were seen together in Washington, they seemed to lift each other up; many sensed that here were two men committed to attacking and changing the racial dynamic in America from inside the government. In June 1966, Marshall had appeared at the White House to participate in a civil rights conference, and when President Johnson showed up in a "surprise" visit (that's what his aides would later say), gliding right up to Marshall, thunderous applause erupted, and there was an immediate standing ovation. And the Negroes in attendance seemed to take in the scene a little longer than everyone else because they wouldn't stop clapping until Marshall himself calmed them.

But a whole year had passed between that giddy moment in June 1966 at the White House and now—July 1967, when the Marshall hearings began. Soldiers were dying in Vietnam, and Molotov cocktails were whistling through the air of American cities. Steely-eyed senators were grilling Marshall, and Harry McPherson knew he had to respect these senators—and the power they wielded—even if he didn't care for some of their politics. "He could become agitated about the Communist menace," McPherson said of the Judiciary Chairman, James Eastland, "egged on by a mole-like staff man who, like the Romanian heavy in a Grade C thriller, served him up dossiers and intricate organizational charts." He also said of Eastland, "One heard about Byzantine games involving cotton subsidies, judgeships, anti-communism." McPherson took note of John McClellan, aware of the fact that he had once been a district attorney and, aside from his role on the Judiciary Committee, that he also chaired the Permanent Subcommittee on Investigations, "where he was at once judge and DA; as he could pick his targets, he chose crooked unions, the Mafia, Negro poverty-program managers who had conned the government—a highly selective and almost indefensible group with few friends in the Southern Establishment."

McPherson knew quite well what a rarefied world the Senate happened to be: "They had been DA's and county judges and state legislators and attorneys general and congressmen and sometimes governors. They had served in the European theater or as admirals' aides in the Pacific, and they had been awarded the Legion of Merit."

McPherson did not like the tone of McClellan or Ervin in the early rounds of the Marshall hearings. They had lost some battles indeed, but their war went on. The sharks were in the water, and they were moving with determination and clearly sniffing for blood. President Johnson and the White House thought there might be some goodwill coming from the civil rights leader Martin Luther King Jr. over the Marshall nomination and that he might finally dim his criticism of the administration's Vietnam policy. But they thought wrong. King considered the matter of war something that, as a man of the cloth, he could not shy away from. There was also a belief festering in minority communities that too many young men caught in the criminal justice system were being shipped off to war, sometimes with ultimatums—jail for their criminal act, freedom instead if they joined the military—issued by white judges, all the while as the politically well connected received deferments. It was a risky tightrope for King, who seemed to genuinely ache at the sight of so much hunger and so many lost opportunities while visiting the poor, because Johnson was waging a massive anti-poverty program. King's civil rights allies knew as much. Whitney Young, president of the National Urban League, warned King that his condemnation of Johnson's Vietnam policies would only jeopardize civil rights programs. "Whitney, what you're saying may get you a foundation grant, but it won't get you into the kingdom of truth," King told him.

Appearing on a stage in Los Angeles shortly before the Marshall nomination was announced, King held nothing back regarding his views on Vietnam. "When I see our country today intervening in what is basically a civil war," he said, "destroying hundreds of thousands of Vietnam children with napalm, leaving broken bodies in countless fields and sending home half-men, mutilated mentally and physically . . . and all this in the name of pursuing the goal of peace, I tremble for our world." The Johnson White House could only tremble with rage. "By the time of the Thurgood Marshall nomination," Nick Katzenbach, Johnson's attorney general, would recall years later, "I think Johnson was getting pissed off at Martin Luther King because of his views on Vietnam. I think Johnson was happy to support another black hero" in Thurgood Marshall. Katzenbach himself wondered if King had fully appreciated the contributions to racial justice made by Marshall: "Thurgood created the necessary legal conditions for King to take advantage politically. It is clear that the *Brown* court decision meant more than school desegregation."

In Thurgood Marshall, President Johnson had an ally in his belief that Martin Luther King Jr. was undermining the overall ambitions of the Johnson presidency. Marshall had long been wary of some of King's tactics, particularly his manner of organizing marches and ending up—sometimes with children—behind bars. Marshall had visited many southern jails and prisons, and he had stared into the faces of many southern sheriffs. He did not think the South a place to gamble on being arrested, especially when it came to women and children. "I used to have a lot of fights with Martin about his theory about disobeying the law," Marshall would recall. "I didn't believe in that . . . He kept talking about Thoreau, and I told him, I said, 'If I understand it, Thoreau wrote his book in jail.'"

No one knew how long the Marshall hearings would last. What the Johnson White House did know was that Senator Eastland, presiding over the hearings, was running a tight operation. There would be no surprise witnesses. When Senator Hart had said he wanted to continue the hearings on the second day into the afternoon following the lunch break, he was told that many senators in Washington would be going out of town because they wanted to get away for the weekend. So the gavel had been banged, leaving the Marshall allies on the committee clearly frustrated.

Harry McPherson had a lot to worry about as he began summing up the Marshall hearings after the first two days. He imagined what votes he might have in the Senate and what votes he might not have. He knew that presidents, so often, counted more votes in their favor than they actually had because of their belief in their own powers of persuasion. But when McPherson started his vote count, he was not at all sure of the outcome. The administration was hoping that the Republican senator Everett Dirksen, Judiciary Committee member, was working behind the scenes to rally moderate Republicans to support Marshall.

But that was hope, and hope was a tricky measuring stick to lean on given that Marshall had so many southern enemies.

Roger Wilkins—nephew of the NAACP's executive director, Roy Wilkins—worked as a lawyer in the Johnson White House. He also had known Marshall since he was a little kid in Harlem. And when he was in law school at the University of Michigan, Roger Wilkins had managed to get himself a summer job (his uncle helped) with Marshall at the NAACP Legal Defense Fund. Now, these years later, Wilkins was working in the Johnson White House, and he was witnessing his hero take a drubbing from the southern senators who had thus far questioned him. "McClellan was a motherfucker," Wilkins would say years later, still dripping with anger over the early part of the hearings. He also had an opinion about Senator Eastland: "a miserable bastard." Wilkins felt that Senator Phil Hart—"a wonderful man; I loved him"—and Senator Dirksen would be keys to the nominee's fate.

President Lyndon Johnson and Harry McPherson decided they needed a backup plan, that it would simply be prudent to have one in case of a Marshall defeat. It all led McPherson to get in touch with William Coleman. Johnson might well be forced to consider another nominee, but he was not going to deviate from the racial background of that nominee. The president's shrewd mind began churning feverishly. William Coleman was a Republican with a far less liberal background. That fact would certainly impress Republicans and make him more palatable to the southern Democrats. "The attraction of Coleman," the White House aide Joseph Califano would recall, "was he was a Republican."

When William Coleman picked up the telephone in his Philadelphia home and Harry McPherson identified himself, McPherson had to quickly insist to Coleman that the call remain confidential. Then Harry McPherson asked William Coleman to come to the White House on the approaching Sunday. Coleman thought it odd that he'd be asked to come to the White House on a Sunday and could not imagine what it would be for. But he could hardly say no to the White House, and besides, he wanted to see an exhibit of Dutch landscapes at the National Gallery; he figured he'd get to scoot over there during the quick jaunt to Washington. On the way down, however, he couldn't stop thinking about this secretive foray. He got to thinking perhaps the president wanted to name him to some kind of commission. In 1964, LBJ had named Coleman an assistant counsel with the Warren Commission, formed to investigate the assassination of President Kennedy. Presidents were always looking to name prominent attorneys to commissions. Coleman relaxed in his seat as the train rumbled toward the nation's capital.

WHEN WILLIAM COLEMAN—a short, compact man who wore thick wire-rimmed glasses—reached Washington and the White House, he was ushered in as quietly as possible, lest news reporters hear about it. Every time he stepped inside the White House—he had been there a few times—Coleman found himself in awe of the majesty of the place.

After small talk—asking about his family and the trip—McPherson cut to the chase with his visitor: concerns had arisen about the viability of the Marshall nomination, he told Coleman. Coleman could tell from the look on McPherson's face that the concerns were serious. "Our legislative people," McPherson finally revealed to Coleman, "are not sure they can muster the votes for confirmation." Coleman had been around long enough to realize that battles often took place behind the scenes for nominees. And he had known that the southern Democrats had given Marshall a hard time in the early going of the hearings. So he was immediately prepared to offer any help he could to the administration. He was a huge admirer of Thurgood Marshall's, believing him one of the greatest lawyers America had produced. He had worked with Marshall in the past. But William Coleman hadn't been called to Washington so the administration could ask him to help with the Marshall situation. Harry McPherson said that President Johnson had something else in mind: he wanted to offer William Coleman the appointment if the Marshall nomination fell apart. Coleman was not only stunned; he was speechless.

WILLIAM THADDEUS COLEMAN was born July 7, 1920, in Philadelphia. (He had been given his middle name in honor of Thaddeus Stevens, the fiery abolitionist.) Coleman's father, William Senior, became director of a Boys Club, earning enough to allow his wife, Laura, to quit teaching and devote herself full-time to raising their three children. The family's affection for the Republican Party could be traced not only to Abraham Lincoln but also to President Taft, who had given Coleman's grandfather an appointment as a postal worker. President Woodrow Wilson, a Democrat, had snatched government jobs from blacks—Coleman's grandfather was spared—and segregated the Washington workforce. Blacks never forgave Wilson.

Young William Coleman had quite an enviable upbringing for a Negro child in 1920s America. "Mother introduced us to the literature produced by colored Americans—Langston Hughes, Countee Cullen, James Weldon Johnson—along with the German classics of Goethe, Kant, and Schiller that she so loved." W. E. B. DuBois sometimes dined at the Coleman dinner table. Little William studied Latin and earned good grades. In elementary school, a teacher told him he should aim to become a chauffeur. He turned smart-alecky on her: "I said, 'Someday you may be working for me.'" The retort only got him sent to the principal's office.

He was a good swimmer by the time he reached Germantown High School. During the summers, he taught swimming, so he knew he'd make the varsity swim team. But the swim coach told him there had never been a Negro on the swim team, and there would not be one now. His parents raised a fuss. Because the school didn't want to appear to be condoning racism, it simply disbanded the swim team.

At the University of Pennsylvania, Coleman—one of only a dozen Negro students and viewed by some professors as flat-out brilliant—wondered to himself: law or medicine? He imagined he'd be successful in either profession. He chose pre-law, excelled in course work, and graduated with honors. He entered Harvard Law School in the fall of 1941. A Philadelphia Negro—to use W. E. B. DuBois's phrase—for all the world to see. Or not see.

DuBois was so fascinated by Negroes in Philadelphia that he had set about conducting a research project about their lives, habits, hopes, and dreams. He went door-to-door. He looked a sight: in suit and tie with his Vandyke beard and notebooks and pencils. He asked a ton of questions to those who didn't slam the door in his face. In 1899, the University of Pennsylvania published *The Philadelphia Negro*, the culmination of his groundbreaking study. It was a maverick piece of scholarship. Scholars had, in fact, never seen anything quite like it. Here was a collection of data—and personal reminiscences—about Negro life, about how difficult it was for Negroes to survive in practically all aspects of American life in a big city. It told of how hard it was for Negroes to gain an economic foothold, how they merely longed to make life better for their children, how they merely wanted to be respected enough to walk side by side with the white man.

Coleman just loved Harvard Law, where he was appointed to the *Law Review*. "My professors presided over their classes like Greek Gods," he recalled. Professor Paul Freund took notice of his smarts, just as Coleman took notice of Freund's sense of drama. The professor, in Coleman's mind, "entered into the lecture room like Laurence Olivier stepping onto the stage in *Henry V.*" Freund and a few other members of the law faculty would sometimes be visited by Charles Houston and William Hastie, the two Harvard Law graduates who had begun molding lawyers-to-be at Howard University. On occasion, they'd show up with a former pupil of theirs. It was the first time William Coleman laid eyes on Thurgood Marshall. He quickly sensed in Marshall something unique and special: Marshall was not in any way intimidated by the Harvard law professors. Coleman and his classmates—not easily awed—were in awe of Thurgood Marshall.

Coleman's law studies were interrupted by World War II. Down in Mississippi, he got in trouble with some other soldiers for trying to integrate an officers' club. They needed legal help. He phoned Thurgood Marshall, who suggested a nearby attorney. (Somewhere, someone always seemed to be reaching out to Thurgood Marshall.) By the end of 1945, Coleman found himself back at Harvard. The next year he graduated at the very top of his Harvard Law School class. It made national news, especially in the Negro press.

The *Law Review* members of Coleman's class knew they could look forward to job offers aplenty, in either tony law firms or coveted clerkships. Coleman received no such offers at the outset. He knew why. He insisted on being patient. He eventually accepted a clerkship in 1947 with the federal judge Herbert F. Goodrich, who had once been dean at the University of Pennsylvania Law School, a connection that obviously helped.

Negro attorneys across America were quite proud when they established the National Bar Association (NBA) in 1925. The American Bar Association remained segregated until 1943. The Howard Law dean, Charlie Houston, was seen waltzing around one of the NBA meetings with his law students Thurgood Marshall and Oliver Hill in tow. He was all but showing them off. William Coleman would eventually—because of his "personal commitment to enter the mainstream"—join the overwhelmingly white and recently desegregated American Bar Association.

In 1948, while sitting in his law office in Philadelphia, Coleman received a surprise phone call asking him if he would like to clerk for the U.S. Supreme Court justice Felix Frankfurter. Young, bright lawyers could only dream of such a call, and his "heart leaped to the skies," Coleman would remember of the moment. William Coleman became the very first Negro to ever clerk for a U.S. Supreme Court justice.

Frankfurter was considered a giant in American jurisprudence, and once on the justice's staff Coleman cherished every second. The hours were long, but the learning intoxicating. Coleman was invited to dinners with Mr. and Mrs. Frankfurter. On Sunday afternoons, he took walks through Georgetown. In the nation's capital, he avoided the establishments that wouldn't serve Negroes. Frankfurter grew fond of Coleman. "What I can say of you with great confidence," Frankfurter wrote to Coleman at the end of his clerkship, "is what was Justice Holmes's ultimate praise of a man: 'I bet on him.' I bet on you, whatever choice you may make and whatever the Fates may have in store for you."

Even with a Supreme Court clerkship, it was not easy for William Coleman to find a job in an East Coast law firm. Time and time again, he was turned away. Finally, he was offered a job in New York City at Paul, Weiss, Wharton & Garrison, at 61 Broadway. He believed he was the first person of color to be hired as an associate in a major American corporate law firm with a Wall Street address. His focus was tax and entertainment law.

Thurgood Marshall had a gift for recruiting other attorneys. And now, in 1950, with Coleman in New York City, Marshall brought Coleman into the NAACP Legal Defense Fund as a consultant to work on the *Brown* desegregation case. "I would like to invite you to a meeting early next month of about twenty-five lawyers to talk strategy," Marshall had confided to Coleman over the telephone. "Some of us believe this is the time to bring lawsuits attacking racial segregation head-on in the public schools in the South." Coleman was more than happy to join the fray. There was something else—aside from his keen legal mind—about Coleman that Marshall cherished: William Coleman could talk about the inner workings of the Supreme Court, specifically about the mind of Frankfurter, as the NAACP was embarking on perhaps the most pivotal case of the century. "We'd ask for integration forthwith," Coleman would remember of the planning sessions with Marshall, "not at some vague future date, because that was the only way to grant equality—now. We never brought a case after that where we'd concede equality without integration, but it was done within the traditional framework so that at the very least we could fall back on the equal-facilities argument. The point was that if we didn't win on constitutional grounds by getting *Plessy* reversed, we'd at least get the remedy we sought: integrated schools forthwith."

Both American political parties had wounds when it came to the Negro. The Democrats were crowded with Dixiecrats. The Republicans were seen as favoring big business over social and domestic programs. Coleman's Republicanism meant nothing to Marshall; Coleman's astute legal mind meant everything. Coleman—the corporate insider—found it thrilling to be working alongside Marshall and the forces Marshall had gathered. The mission gave him deep pride and a profound appreciation for the lawyer who had recruited him. "We respected him not only for his charisma and sagacity," Coleman would say of Marshall, "but also because of his courage."

Now, all these years later—across some of the most tumultuous years in America's racial history—William Coleman found himself seated on a cushy couch in the White House discussing Thurgood Marshall. He found himself listening to Harry McPherson say how worried he was about the hearings thus far and listening to McPherson tell him that President Johnson had asked him to "discreetly" inquire as to Coleman's interest if the Marshall effort should fail—"if we can't get Marshall confirmed," is how McPherson put it. LBJ wanted to bet on this Philadelphia negro. Coleman was suddenly "stunned"; he "stammered" and didn't know what to say. Thurgood Marshall was his dear friend. He wanted Marshall on the high court; now he was hearing that it might not happen. Coleman had to gather himself, his wits. "Well, you know, Harry, the Supreme Court, well, the Supreme Court, that's an entirely different job." He couldn't quite get a coherent response out. But McPherson needed an answer; President Johnson needed an answer—now. Would William Coleman be on standby? Would Coleman allow LBJ to send his name to the Senate Judiciary Committee should Marshall fail to be confirmed? Coleman gave a noncommittal answer: He confided he was just so torn. He said he was sure the White House would find a way to muster the votes. But the White House knew this was a dangerous and unpredictable time. These were not the answers Harry McPherson wanted to hear.

So William Coleman, the Philadelphia Negro, went back home. But there was, rather quickly, another meeting, this time face-to-face with President Johnson, who stared hard right into the eyes of William Coleman and told him his country might need him. And he told him he couldn't turn the president down. He thanked him again for the job he had done with the Warren Commission. He flattered Coleman by telling him how proud he had been to name him to that commission, what a great service he had done for America. The president talked about the North and the South, about black and white, about the politicians who hated him and who would always hate him because he was one of them—until he wasn't, until he roughhoused them and got the 1964 Civil Rights Act passed and the 1965 Voting Rights Act passed. But he told William Coleman he didn't care about their hate. All he cared about right now was getting a black man onto the U.S. Supreme Court. And the only way that could happen might well be with a Republican nominee. Coleman took deep breaths. He wanted to give a serious answer to the president of the United States. Finally, he talked about his family, about tuition costs and bills and his mortgage. "I said the pay was lousy" for Supreme Court justices. And even as he said it, he couldn't stop himself from wondering how many Republican votes he could get because he was a Republican. Against the hard vision of power, men can't help but dream.

William Coleman did offer President Johnson assistance. He said he would go visit some of the southern senators to lobby them on Marshall's behalf. Johnson told him he needed any help he could get. "The southerners knew I had argued cases before the Supreme Court where there had been no discussion of race," says Coleman.

One of the first senators Coleman went to visit was Hugh Scott of

Pennsylvania, a Republican member of the Judiciary Committee. In Philadelphia, Scott's family had known the Coleman family for years. Pennsylvania was certainly not the South, but Scott was Virginia-born. His grandfather had been a Confederate soldier. Harry McPherson knew that Senator Scott possessed certain gifts. He prowled the aisles of Washington politics cultivating relationships with Democrats and Republicans alike. McPherson thought of Scott as "a cultivated moderate with the political instincts of a jaguar."

On orders from the White House, the jaguar went about stalking other senators on Thurgood Marshall's behalf.

5

Thurgood Marshall
and His Southern Hero

The South Carolina justice J. Waties Waring sided with Marshall
and the NAACP at the state level on the case that would come to be
known as *Brown v. Board of Education*—and was ostracized.

Not every white southerner wanted Thurgood Marshall's Supreme Court nomination to be badly bruised—or derailed. One who followed the hearings—and with fervent hope on Marshall's behalf—was J. Waties Waring. The relationship between Waring and Marshall was rooted in Waring's home state of South Carolina—before the state turned on Waring and his wife and ran both of them out of town with epithets ringing in their ears.

The *J* in his name stood for Julius. He was a native of Charleston, born a decade and a half after the demise of slavery. His father and uncles were men whom he adored. He also would remember them as "fine, decent slaveholders." They were Confederate war veterans, heroes in a child's mind. "Most of the Negroes I knew were ex-slaves," Waring would recall, "and you loved them and were good to them. We didn't give them any rights, but they never asked for any rights, and I didn't question it." The North had pretty much ruined Charleston during the Civil War. Young Waring was witness to old men soaked in nostalgia for the Lost Cause.

Charleston had a wharf, and it was populated by Negroes scuffling on the waterfront in low-end jobs. DuBose Heyward, five years younger than Waring and also a white Charleston native, would become infatuated with the plight of the Negro. Heyward's first decent-paying job was working near the wharf. All about him were Negro workers: "Negroes in long lines trucking cotton on the wharves; dim figures in a deserted warehouse squatting over a crap game; spirituals bringing me up short to listen against the wall of a dilapidated church that I had to pass on the way to work." Heyward became a writer, and in 1925 his novel *Porgy* was published. The couple at the novel's center were named Porgy and Bess, two struggling Charleston Negroes. The *Chicago Daily News* called the novel the best fiction title of the season. In time, the world would hear a lot more about Porgy and Bess—Broadway, opera, film—from George Gershwin.

As he was coming of age, Waring couldn't help but see it as the natural order of things when Negroes cleaned up after him. He got admitted to a private school. Afterward, it was off to the College of Charleston. The law very much intrigued him, and he knew he wanted to study it. Waring became one of those men of the early twentieth century who "read the law" as opposed to going to a traditional law school. Those whom he studied under gave him high marks.

In time, there were judicial clerkships in which J. Waties Waring distinguished himself. President Woodrow Wilson appointed him assistant U.S. attorney for the Eastern District of South Carolina. Waring would become city attorney for Charleston. He brought the city back from the brink of bankruptcy, and his legion of admirers grew. He married, and his wife, Annie, had the right pedigree: a belle from a prosperous local family. To Negroes on the streets of Charleston whom he passed every day, J. Waties Waring was just another member of the city's white power structure. Most had no reason at all to come in close contact with him.

When Waring successfully managed a campaign for the U.S. senator Ellison D. "Cotton Ed" Smith—a renowned racist—the senator never forgot him and eventually recommended Waring for a judgeship. In 1941, President Roosevelt appointed the sixty-one-year-old Waring to become a federal judge. It was expected that the newly appointed judge would appreciate his place in Charleston society and simply join that long list of other southern judges who upheld segregation and all the customs that went along with it.

No one saw the radicalism of J. Waties Waring coming, but come it did.

Once Waring reached the courthouse, he began expressing different views from what Charlestonians expected of him. He allowed Negroes to sit anywhere they wanted to in the courtroom, ending a segregation policy. He appointed a Negro to be his bailiff, and the Negro press certainly pounced on that story. His wife warned him about the gossip, that he was making people angry. He didn't seem to care.

It was a cruel custom, but white farmers in South Carolina who wanted to punish field hands sometimes locked them in sheds for several days. When such a case landed in Waring's courtroom—of a Negro who had been held against his will—Waring ruled the farmer had violated the Negro's constitutional rights. He sent the farmer to jail. That really caused a ruckus among other white farmers. They cursed him in their fields and spat on his name. The judge, however, was just getting started.

In 1945, Waring ruled in favor of Negro schoolteachers who had sued over unequal pay. He could sense the winds of protest. "The whole thing worried me a great deal, and I knew the thing was coming to a showdown someday and was probably coming in my state," he said of the movement for equality.

That same year, Waring further alienated himself from Charleston society: He divorced his wife and married Elizabeth Avery Hoffman. She was a native of Detroit—a Yankee—and that fact only unleashed more scorn on Waring. Elizabeth Waring—quickly getting a full blast of Charleston society—told her husband she was proud to be his wife. And she also told him that America was far more bigoted than even he realized and that South Carolina, from what she was seeing, was among the most inhospitable places on earth for the Negro. Elizabeth Waring enthralled her husband. In the evenings, after supper, they sipped mint juleps and listened to soft music.

Elizabeth Waring's declaration about the South and the Negro was proven by an event that happened on the night of February 12, 1946.

Isaac Woodard was among a group of soldiers who had just been honorably discharged from Camp Gordon, in Georgia. Woodard, by all accounts, had bravely fought in the South Pacific. The soldiers were now heading home, traveling by bus through South Carolina. Woodard, a Negro, got into an argument with the white bus driver about making a restroom stop. When the bus reached Batesburg, the bus driver—alarmed at being challenged by a Negro—summoned the local sheriff. Words were exchanged, and Woodard was arrested for disorderly conduct. Woodard protested as he was being taken to the jail. The sheriff made a stop, in an alley, pulled out his blackjack, and gouged it into Woodard's eye. And only then did they proceed to the jail with Woodard twisting and howling in pain. The next morning, Woodard was found guilty of disorderly conduct and fined. The city suggested he proceed on his way, upon which he eventually landed in a medical hospital. The gouging from the sheriff left him permanently blind in one eye.

The story of a soldier abused so viciously reached the press. And it also reached the White House. "When a mayor and a City Marshal can take a negro Sergeant off a bus in South Carolina," President Truman wrote to a friend, "beat him up and put out one of his eyes, and nothing is done about it by State Authorities, something is radically wrong with the system."

Charges were filed against the sheriff who struck Woodard. The trial lasted twenty-eight minutes. It took place in the courtroom of J. Waties Waring. The all-white jury acquitted the sheriff of all charges and cackled loudly afterward. Judge Waring was outraged at the verdict. "I was shocked by the hypocrisy of my government," he would say later, but only in private.

When George Elmore, a taxi driver in Columbia, South Carolina, decided to sue the state over its all-white primary in 1947, it was Thurgood Marshall who came to his aid. Marshall traveled to Columbia to argue the case, which came before Judge J. Waties Waring. Waring was staring at the very lawyer, Thurgood Marshall, who had won the precedent over white primary rule in 1944 in the Texas case *Smith v. Allwright*. Waring cited Marshall's earlier case in making his ruling in favor of South Carolina's Negroes. "It is time for South Carolina to rejoin the Union," Waring said. "It is time to fall in step with the other states and to adopt the American way of conducting elections . . . Racial distinctions cannot exist in the machinery that selects the officers and lawmakers of the United States." A year later, more than thirty-five thousand Negroes voted in the South Carolina primary.

Someone burned a Klan cross on the front lawn of the judge's home. Waring received nasty and threatening phone calls. Some now said the *J* in his name might as well stand for Judas. He was told he was no longer welcome in the enviable social clubs he had once belonged to. Politicians running for office vowed they'd lead an impeachment drive against him. "Why," one white resident of the state said, "he'd never shown any interest in the Negroes before. Then he writes this decision, full of insults to the South. He says it is time for South Carolina 'to rejoin the union,' and so forth. It wasn't only the decision that made people angry. It was the way he did it. Something come [*sic*] over him."

Calls for his impeachment would not subside. They were heard in the halls of the U.S. Congress. Congressmen Mendel Rivers of South Carolina and John Rankin of Mississippi—both often cited in the Negro press for uttering virulent racist remarks—took to the floor of the House to discuss Waring.

> RANKIN [addressing Rivers]: I think you are slow about one thing in South Carolina. I am convinced, and have been convinced for some time, that Judge Waring is crazy. They ought to put him in a mental institution, confine him in a mental institution and get some sane judge appointed in his place.
>
> RIVERS: He has certainly lost his sense of direction, and I do not think that situation may be long in forthcoming.

Rivers would predict bedlam should Waring remain on the bench. "Unless he is removed, there will be bloodshed," he warned. "He is now in the process of extracting a pound of flesh from the white people of South Carolina because, through his own actions, he has been ostracized from their society."

Rankin and Rivers would be joined in their tirade by the South Carolina senator Olin Johnston. "We ought to have impeachment proceedings," Johnston urged, "to see exactly what the facts are." But Congress had too much on its agenda to bend to the desires of Rivers, Rankin, or Johnston.

What also galled the Warings was the fact that some members of the judge's own family seemed embarrassed that he was related to them, and even distanced themselves from him. Thomas Waring was a newspaperman and the judge's nephew. He got himself a free-lance job for *Harper's* magazine and penned a long article titled "The Southern Case Against Desegregation." The article tried hard to gar-ner sympathy for whites and their opposition to integration. *Harper's*, being a national publication, had wide readership. Those outside the South might have found the younger Waring's words difficult to take. "Negro parents as a whole—for reasons that white people may sym-pathetically deplore but which nevertheless exist—are not so careful on the average as their white neighbors in looking after the health and cleanliness of their children," he wrote. "The incidence of vene-real disease for instance is much greater among Negroes than among whites. Statistics to document this statement are difficult to come by, though the statement itself would be generally accepted in the South." The essay exhibited little nuance and hewed passionately to its overall mind-set as it went along. "For many years," Waring explained, "crime in the South has been more prevalent among Negroes than among white people. Though the Northern press no longer identifies crimi-nals by race, white Southerners have reasons to believe that much of the outbreak of crime and juvenile delinquency in Northern cities is due to the influx of Negro population. They believe the North now is getting a taste of the same race troubles that the South fears would grow out of mixed schooling, on a much bigger scale. They want no 'Blackboard Jungles' in the South." (The motion picture *Blackboard Jungle*, directed by Richard Brooks, opened in 1955 and was a gritty evocation of an inner-city high school in New York City. It starred, among others in a racially mixed cast, Glenn Ford, Richard Kiley, Vic Morrow, Anne Francis, Paul Mazursky, and Sidney Poitier. It was the first motion picture that used rock music, blaring Bill Haley's "Rock Around the Clock" as the movie begins. It did not fare well in southern box office receipts.) *Harper's* magazine, perhaps expecting strong reaction criticizing the piece, felt a need to add an editor's note to the Waring essay: "The point of view expressed in this article is far removed from that of the Editors."

In Charleston, Judge Waring's wife, Elizabeth, remained unbowed. She gave a blistering speech to the Negro YWCA in the city, castigating the entire South. Friends stopped returning her phone calls. The couple would be cold-shouldered on sidewalks. "We'd get in our car and drive through the night, miles and miles, just thinking and talking," the judge would say.

They invited Negro couples to dine with them in their home. Mrs. Waring was seen in front of the house hugging her Negro guests good-bye. Judge Waring himself was given security. Across the South, he became referred to as "the guy who let the nigger vote." Bricks came crashing through their front windows in the dark of night. "My opponents are the most unhappy people you can find," he said. "They're all torn apart inside. They try to make you believe that things that are not all right are fine, and they sweat as they search for the words to do it with. I don't have to engage in those mental acrobatics. I'm almost seventy, and I've got a cause to live for and a job to do."

Sometimes on out-of-town trips, Negro Pullman porters would stop the judge and tell him how much his court rulings and courage had meant to them. They would tell him nothing was more important to them than getting a good education for their children. It would bring tears to his eyes.

It was May 28, 1951, when Waring heard the first salvo in what would become known as the *Brown* desegregation case, with Thurgood Marshall standing in front of him yet again. "This was no ordinary test case," Marjorie McKenzie wrote in the Pittsburgh *Courier.* "It was a bare-bones challenge to the legality of segregation under the state's police power."

The case had the earmarks of being destined for the U.S. Supreme Court. A federal judge in the South—unconnected to the case and not wanting to reveal his name for obvious reasons—would opine, "It's going to be hard for the Supreme Court to side-step the issue. And it's going to be equally hard for them to face it, with the present-day political situation what it is. The case sort of puts them on the spot, and Thurgood has maneuvered that very cleverly."

Elizabeth Waring kept a diary during the historic *Brown* arguments, which were heard by her husband along with two other federal judges, John Parker and George Timmerman. Her diary is blunt, personal, and sometimes imbued with a stream-of-consciousness sensibility. She writes, "The technical witnesses for the Plaintiff were marvelous. Proving without a shadow of a doubt the harm done to both White and Negro children by Segregation itself irrespective of the dreadful physical condition of the Negro schools as compared to the White. Thurgood Marshall had thrilled the courtroom with his cross examination of the White School Board head—Crow—when in a surprise move Figg admitted the schools were not equal but threw himself upon the mercy of the Court to give them time with Governor Byrnes new Tax bill to improve the Negro schools."

In another part of her diary, she writes of the end of the arguments and her feelings about Judges Parker and Timmerman:

> Judge Timmerman just a dummy throughout. Timmerman the only HAPPY WARRIOR of the three Judges because completely sold on and the tool of White Supremacy. Parker knows better and was miserable rationalizing with his conscience and his eyes on the Supreme Court with the Republicans in power now with the alignment with the Dixiecrats who control Congress and the Senate . . . The die was cast for of course the two judges decision finishes the Case in this court but no doubt to be appealed to the Supreme Court. Parker tried to get my Judge [Waties] to make it unanimous by saying smoothly "You know we try in our court to all agree" etc. Waties told him firmly he was going to write a strong DISSENTING OPINION. Parker was furious.

With the appearance of Thurgood Marshall, John Parker was meeting the NAACP once again: it had led the protests years earlier in exposing Parker's racially charged comments about Negroes and the right to vote in North Carolina when he campaigned for political office.

Waring's dissent was, of course, the dissent heard throughout the South and around America. The epochal decision of *Brown* would follow in the spring of 1954.

Few were surprised at the southern politicians who derided the *Brown* ruling. "The abolishment of segregation in our schools," said the Virginia representative William Tuck, "will not enhance but, on the contrary, will lower the standards of public education, will tend to mar the cordial and understanding race relations which have existed for so long, and will in other respects be detrimental." Foreign nations considered the decision significant enough to offer comment. *The Daily Herald* of London said the decision points to "a sign that America is going the right way about a problem it does not always recognize for what it is—a colonial problem within its own borders." Also in London, the *Daily Mirror* said, "The ruling will rank in significance with Lincoln's Emancipation Proclamation." The Paris newspaper *Le Monde* published a front-page editorial, in which it opined that the ruling "marks the victory of justice over race prejudice, a victory for democracy."

In 1952, Judge Waring retired from the federal bench. The battle had worn him down. Soon he and his wife, Elizabeth, were communicating with friends in New York City—among them Kenneth Clark, the psychologist who had been an expert witness in the *Brown* case, and Thurgood Marshall. Clark, Marshall, and others encouraged the Warings to move to New York City, and they did. They packed their possessions. Some of their Negro friends were overcome with emotion upon their leaving.

They took an apartment in Manhattan on East Seventy-Seventh Street. Judge Waring felt they had been exiled. "Waties and Elizabeth invited my wife and me to their home in New York," Clark would remember, "and it was through a series of visits and talks that I was able to confirm all of my earlier speculations concerning the nature of this man."

The aging, retired justice and his wife enjoyed city life. The years began to roll by. There were formal affairs in which both Thurgood Marshall and J. Waties Waring were honored. The former judge joined human rights organizations. He became a director of the National Committee Against Discrimination in Housing. He became a trustee of the National Urban League. The American Civil Liberties Union invited him to join its board. Martin Luther King Jr. enjoyed yakking on the phone with both Warings. King couldn't stop thanking Waring for the bravery of his judicial decisions. "Negroes have thanked me for giving them the right to vote," Waring once said, "and that is sweetly flattering, but my colleagues in the law know that I gave them nothing. The right to vote belonged to them as much as to me, and I was just fortunate enough to be a judge, deciding the question according to law."

News of Thurgood Marshall's ascendancy to the federal bench delighted the staffers at the NAACP Legal Defense Fund, as well as all of Marshall's friends, the Warings among them. And when Thurgood Marshall was appointed solicitor general, the Warings were even happier. But their joy at his Supreme Court nomination quickly turned to worry and concern. They were from the South; they knew the Senate Judiciary Committee was ruled by southerners. The same men who had tried to thwart J. Waties Waring would certainly now try to thwart Thurgood Marshall. Elizabeth Waring remembered well the vicious verbal attacks on Marshall following the *Brown* court arguments before the three-judge panel. White socialites in Charleston—with husbands in powerful positions—had spread rumors that Marshall had been seen in town gambling and drinking huge amounts of liquor during the *Brown* arguments. (It sounded as if the gossipmongers had lifted Marshall from the pages of *Porgy and Bess*.) The rumors angered Elizabeth, and she was quick to express her displeasure to those spreading the gossip.

Thurgood Marshall had long kept a copy of Waring's historic dissent in the *Brown* desegregation case with him wherever he went. "I forgot to tell you that we mimeographed your Opinion on the Clarendon County case at the Convention and distributed it to every delegate," Marshall wrote to Waring. "The comments we have received on your opinion are unanimous. All of the laymen are thrilled and all of the lawyers are greatly encouraged."

In later years, a few southern friends, finding themselves in New York City, would be invited to the Waring home. The transplanted couple, getting on in age and slowed by ailments, did not get out much. But in the summer of 1967, all they could ponder was the fate of Thurgood Marshall's Supreme Court nomination. They asked their southern friends about Ernest Hollings and Strom Thurmond, arch segregationists and U.S. senators who represented South Carolina; Hollings had replaced Olin Johnston, who died in office. Both were segregationists. Perhaps they were softening? Perhaps their attitudes about race were changing with the civil rights movement in high momentum? Hardly, the Warings were told. Instead, both Hollings and Thurmond were telling people around South Carolina that they were going to do everything they could to stop Thurgood Marshall from reaching the highest court in the land. (Hollings may have been a more cosmopolitan figure than Thurmond, but he still left no doubt about where he stood on the issue of race.)

J. Waties Waring began telling people he hoped he would be alive to see the outcome of the hearings. His health was failing, and he was rooting for his friend.

6

The Chairman Goes AWOL,
and the Hunt Is On for Anti-Marshall Votes

The Mississippi senator James Eastland, chairman of the Senate Judiciary
Committee, which held the Marshall hearings. No one in the hearing room
that summer knew about the hidden Eastland family history.

H E WAS A SENATE BARON—a man with an office that had baronial-
like splendor: the thick carpet, the lovely drapes, the long table in
an adjacent room for his conferences, and that private bar in his office.
Some felt his power in the U.S. Senate was practically unmatched. It
was a dream job, of course, and attainable only by seniority, which
was possible only by getting elected and elected again. The state of
Mississippi—the entire South even—time and time again lauded
Senator James Oliver Eastland. Kiwanis Clubs and chambers of commerce and various political clubs gave him awards and citations. He

got so many speaking invitations from Tennessee and Georgia and Alabama and, of course, his own state that he could hardly accept them all. His office was festooned with plaques and commemorations. It was felt that the Confederacy, in the office of Senator James Eastland, was still very much alive. Mississippians loved him because he was doing exactly what they had sent him to the U.S. Senate to do: to maintain those cotton prices; to keep the Negro down. It was important to them that the walls of segregation remain high and sturdy.

And now, in the summer of 1967, they expected James Eastland to keep Thurgood Marshall from taking a seat on the U.S. Supreme Court. Eastland assured them he would do everything in his power to do so, and because he was chairman, he certainly had power. He had waited until the last minute to tell the White House when the hearings would even begin, all in hopes of limiting its preparation time. That gave him and his fellow southern senators a rise—LBJ and his aides over in the White House stewing!—and the Eastland camp chortled about the worry they had caused them.

Eastland knew that the White House—and Marshall himself—were worried about conservatives in both political parties, Democratic and Republican, who could not abide Marshall's legal views. That reality made Eastland feel damn good. But those numbers might not add up enough to derail the Marshall nomination. Eastland insisted that the West Virginia senator Robert Byrd ask the FBI to look into any links between Marshall and the Communist Party. (As a young man, Byrd had joined the Ku Klux Klan in his home state, later claiming it a mistake of youthfulness.) Byrd was only too happy to do what the chairman had asked of him. When trying to harm a Washington figure, conservatives found the Communist link a dependable ploy, and it still carried enough of a taint, if proven, to stop any appointee or federal job seeker. "Walter, I was amazed when I got to Washington to see the Communists in high places in the Government," Eastland wrote to a fellow cotton planter back in Mississippi shortly after arriving in the nation's capital. To the dismay of both Byrd and Eastland, the FBI could find no links between Marshall and the Communist Party.

On the third day of the hearings, Senator Eastland simply did not show up, surprising everyone. He sent word that the gavel was to be passed to Senator McClellan. Eastland was down in Mississippi. He was going to rally other southern senators, and he even hoped that some of their constituents would write to their own senators and express opposition to Marshall if they had not already done so. He was going to work the telephones. He was going to continue to plot strategy to besmirch Thurgood Marshall in hopes he could scuttle the nomination.

When Marshall realized Eastland's absence, it only heightened his worry. What could Eastland be up to? Marshall had confided to friends his constant and rising worry. He'd mentally try to decipher the position of each southern Democrat, recalling lawsuits he had filed in their respective states. He knew he had racked up victories all across the South, and he was proud of those victories. And he finally concluded there would be no forgiveness on the part of the southern Democrats because of the legal footprints he had left behind—from Virginia to Mississippi to Louisiana. His wife, Cissy, tried to comfort him; others told him that LBJ was no fool, that his White House—even if it was busy with a contentious war and a youth rebellion—had heady people on its staff. Jack Greenberg, Marshall's successor at the Legal Defense Fund, had only one word for the ongoing confirmation hearings: "bruising." Greenberg thought what was evident in the hearings was that "racism [had] once more reared its ugly head."

Those blacks walking into Senate room 2228 during those first two days cast long and wary glances at James Eastland. It was Eastland—and other segregationist senators—who had set their parents on their great migration journeys out of the Deep South. It was Eastland who had once stood on the floor of the U.S. Senate and thundered that "the Negro race is an inferior race." It was Eastland who had once said that Mississippians would "protect and maintain white supremacy throughout eternity." Sunday after Sunday, in the pulpits of Negro churches in the urban North, robed preachers assailed James Eastland. They waved articles about him and his incendiary language. The Harlem congressman Adam Clayton Powell Jr. was urging southern Negroes to leave the South and come up north. The Protestant Episcopal Diocese of New York charged that Eastland was guilty of "subversion just as real and, because it comes from a U.S. Senator, far more dangerous than any perpetrated by the Communist Party." It was James Eastland who had been attacking Thurgood Marshall and the NAACP for decades now. "If it came to fighting," Eastland had once said, "I'd fight for Mississippi against the United States, even if it meant going out into the street and shooting Negroes."

It is doubtful that anyone striding into room 2228 on July 18, 1967, knew much about the family legacy of Senator James Eastland—and the lynching of a black man that lay upon that legacy.

JAMES OLIVER EASTLAND was born November 28, 1904, in Sunflower County, Mississippi. His parents, Alma and Woods Eastland, operated a large plantation. Negro sharecroppers bent themselves beneath the hot sun working the fields beginning at sunrise. The Eastlands would have only one child, James, and upon his birth the chatter about the black man his father had lynched was very much in the air and the press. The episode was still being talked about far beyond the ississippi.

rs Woods and James Eastland—whom the future sena-
named after—owned and operated the huge family cot-
, two thousand acres and growing yearly, in Doddsville.
horses across the property and lorded over their Negro
, who lived in cabins that dotted the plantation's land-
Eastland was occasionally pulled into the domestic tra-
sharecroppers. One of them, Albert Carr, complained to James that another Negro plantation worker, Luther Holbert, had taken his girlfriend, Mary, from him. Angry words were exchanged between Carr and Holbert. Carr imagined Eastland would react swiftly because he had recently fired Holbert, and here he was now freeloading on Eastland property. Mary had indeed begun an affair with Holbert. Carr begged Eastland to do something, intimating that trouble could erupt.

On the morning of February 4, 1904, Carr informed Eastland that Holbert remained on Eastland land. Eastland simply could not sit by and swallow Holbert's belligerence. When a Negro was ordered off a plantation, he'd best scoot and not tarry about it. Eastland hopped on his horse and rode to confront Holbert; Carr was galloping alongside him. Holbert heard the hooves of the horses as the two riders neared. He grabbed his Winchester rifle while his lover, Mary, hovered in fear.

As soon as Holbert opened the door, the firing started. Mary screamed; the horses buckled. When the firing finally stopped, Carr and James Eastland were dead. The scene was horrific and bloody. Holbert had no intentions of waiting around to mount a self-defense claim, and he bolted into the woods with Mary.

A murdered Negro by the hands of another Negro might not arouse too much attention in early twentieth-century Mississippi. But a murdered white man at the hands of a Negro—and now a Negro on the loose—was a completely different matter.

Plantation workers had raced to the cabin after hearing gunshots in the distance. Woods Eastland arrived a short time later. When Woods stared down at the body of James, his slain brother, he did what any white man—given the customs of the landscape—would do: he vowed vengeance and vowed it with every ounce of strength he possessed.

A mob was quickly formed, consisting of "many prominent citizens of Sunflower County," and they brought with them the best hunting dogs in the county. The killings and manhunt were splashed across the front pages of newspapers throughout Mississippi and Tennessee. The Greenville *Daily Democrat* offered a description of the fleeing Holbert: "Holbert is a ginger-cake colored negro, has sideburns, light mustache, 5 feet 10 inches high, weight 170 pounds. Speaks well and has a good education." Woods Eastland was proclaiming, to whites as well as Negroes, that if he caught Holbert, Mary, or both, there'd surely be a lynching. Three days passed with no sightings of either. The couple were making their way through dense forests, trudging along swampy pathways. There were bears about and fearsome mechanical traps that had been set for those creatures. They had to be careful. The Eastland-led posse was moving swiftly. Two Negroes—who were neither Holbert nor his companion, Mary—saw the posse coming in their direction. The commotion frightened them. Not having done anything but feeling defenseless nevertheless, they decided to run in the opposite direction. It was not a wise move. They were gunned down, dying on the spot, and the posse, despite realizing its grave error, kept moving. In another gruesome mishap, a gun belonging to a posse member accidentally went off, sending an idling Negro woman to her knees, killing her also. Rains slashed, but the horses galloped onward, and when they were too tired, fresh mounts were provided by local law enforcement. Reports of reward money went out over the news wires. The hunting party kept growing, at one point reaching upwards of three hundred, some of the men traveling by train, peering from windows and into the spaces between railcars. The only hope for the fleeing couple was to get beyond the state of Mississippi.

A teenage boy believed he had spotted the two near Sheppardtown, Mississippi, about thirty miles from the scene of the killings. Holbert did not see the boy. The boy raced into town and told two locals— V. H. Lavender and E. L. O'Neal—that he had spotted the two wanted in connection with the killings. The men raced to the spot that the boy had described and found Holbert and Mary asleep. There was a brief gunfight; Holbert suffered two wounds to his leg, neither life-threatening. After their capture, both were turned over to authorities.

Woods Eastland and his mob quickly made their way to the sheriff's office. They browbeat the weak sheriff until he turned the suspects over to them. Press accounts were now referring to the couple as Luther and Mary Holbert. It was a Saturday morning when they were taken by Woods Eastland, and he immediately announced both would be lynched the next day—a Sunday—and on the grounds of a local Negro church. Eastland believed that black churches and their members had aided the couple during their escape. Killing them on the grounds of a Negro church was meant to serve both as a grievous insult to black pride and a future warning to all who would challenge white authority.

Eastland wasted no time in sending word out about the lynching. More than a thousand showed up in Doddsville on the fateful day. Luther and Mary were dragged to a tree and tied up. Then the ordeal began. Someone sliced their fingers off first, then their ears. Their howls were awful; blood squirted everywhere. A reporter for the *Vicksburg Evening Post* was on the scene: "The most excruciating form of punishment consisted in the use of a large corkscrew in the hands of some of the mob. This instrument was bored into the flesh of the man and woman, in the arms, legs, and body, and then pulled out, the spirals tearing out big pieces of raw, quivering flesh every time it was withdrawn." Then one at a time—so Luther could first watch Mary, even though both were barely alive—they were taken to a pyre and tossed in. A few people covered their eyes; some cackled. "It was a scene such as a man wants to witness only once in a lifetime," one of those gathered to watch would later say.

News quickly spread about the heinous act. "These barbarous scenes are more disgraceful and degrading to the people who inflict the punishment than to those who receive it," Booker T. Washington said, in an analogy that might have been difficult for the Negroes of Mississippi to understand.

The Memphis *News*, a white publication, weighed in: "The only plea that could be entered in palliation of this savagery is that it was necessary to strike terror in the negroes who might be tempted to murder other white men, but it is doubtful whether such horrible torture has as much effect in this respect as a legal execution."

There was enough uproar over the lynchings—most of it from those who lived outside Mississippi—that Woods Eastland was eventually brought to trial, indicted for the murders of Luther Holbert and Mary. Negroes were grateful that Eastland would stand trial but also suspicious, harboring grave doubts that a white man would go to prison for killing two Negroes.

The trial began in September 1904. U.S. Senator Anselm J. McLaurin, a prominent Mississippi lawyer and Confederate Civil War veteran, was Eastland's attorney. Ten of the twelve jurors selected were, like Eastland, farmers. At trial, McLaurin argued that the case against Eastland should be dismissed because it could not be proven that Eastland actually struck the match that started the fire in which the two burned to death. The judge agreed and quickly dismissed the case amid whoops and hollering. "A white man," the *Greenwood Commonwealth* had predicted before the trial, "will never be convicted for lynching a negro in Mississippi."

When Alma Eastland gave birth to her only son just weeks after the trial and named him James, she imagined and hoped it might bring some measure of solace to her husband after the death of his brother.

When little Jim Eastland was growing up, his mother, a member of the United Daughters of the Confederacy, would tell him about the Reconstructionists and how they ruined her beloved South. She would tell him about her grandfather Richmond Austin, who rode with the fierce Confederate general Nathan Bedford Forrest during the Civil War. (Forrest would become the very first imperial wizard of the Ku Klux Klan.) She would tell him, time and time again, about her distrust of Yankees—and Negroes. Beneath the roof of the Eastland household, it was the fierce dislike of the Negro that seemed to bind the family.

Following high school, young Eastland began a peripatetic college career. He attended the University of Mississippi, then Vanderbilt, and finally it was on to the University of Alabama for his senior year. Eventually goaded by his father to enter politics, James Eastland served in the statehouse from 1928 to 1932. Then he quit politics to devote time to the family's cotton plantation. He "read" the law and, in 1932, married Libby Coleman. In time, they would have three daughters and a son. They would move into a lovely white house in Doddsville. There was the usual makeup of household help for a family of such means: a Negro maid, cook, and laundrywoman. The Depression might have ravaged the nation, but the Eastland family seemed immune from the pain. "It was a fun place to be white and to be of a certain class," their daughter Anne would remember.

As time passed, a good many Negroes in and around Doddsville remembered the farcical trial of Woods Eastland. They could not forget what happened. The act had been so wicked—it needed no embellishment—that it left most Negroes across the rural landscape fearing the Eastland name.

JAMES EASTLAND first reached the U.S. Senate when Pat Harrison died in office and Governor Paul Johnson appointed him the replacement. It was just an interim appointment, lasting eighty-eight days. During those nearly three months in office, Eastland made speeches, plenty of them, and for the most part they were about the threat of Communism, Negroes whom he claimed were influenced by northern agitators, and the government's threat about limiting cotton prices. The two most frightening groups in the South were Communists and Negroes: the former invisible, the latter powerless but everywhere—in cotton field, on chain gang, in brick factory—and with outsiders, men like Thurgood Marshall, constantly fighting for their rights. Eastland confided to a hometown friend he thought the Communists were heading straight for the Mississippi delta: "I know that they desire to break up all farms over forty acres and to inaugurate a system of subsistent farming in the South, and especially in our section."

Eastland would come to launch a full campaign for the Harrison seat. In his campaign speeches, he returned to what he knew how to do best: attacking Negro activism, Communism, and the federal government. One day, he stood on the courthouse steps in Forest, Mississippi, and let loose, recalling his earlier interim stay in Washington. "I found," he said, attacking the Senate, "they were running a big house with plush carpets on the floor, and a marble swimming pool, and that they had electric baths, and a big yellow Negro in there to rub those old boys up so they could look pretty and pass a beauty contest." The crowd was roaring; they were slapping their knees. He went on: "Then upstairs there was a free barbershop, with some Negroes in there to doctor them up." They'd start screaming his name, howling with delight. His posters proclaimed him "Champion of the Farmer and the South." He crushed his opponent. He was sworn in on January 3, 1943. And he set his sights squarely on stopping the American Negro in his quest for equality.

It was World War II that catapulted the profile of Senator James Eastland as never before.

Military training camps would prove to be where many whites first spent time with Negroes on somewhat equal footing on a daily basis. Negro entertainment stars—Sammy Davis Jr., Joe Louis, Sugar Ray Robinson among them—all joined the war effort, either on the home front or abroad. Lena Horne sang for the troops while insisting to military brass that Negro and white soldiers sit side by side. But many, particularly in the South, did not like the intermingling of the races in the war effort. Eastland took to the Senate floor during a filibuster about the Fair Employment Practices Commission. He used his time to assail the Negro soldier, namely the all-Negro Ninety-Second Division serving in Italy. "The Negro soldier was an utter and dismal failure in combat," Eastland said. "When I make that statement, it is not from prejudice. I am not prejudiced against the Negro." It mattered little to Eastland that Generals George S. Patton and Dwight Eisenhower both refuted his charges. Patton said he found the Negro "to be a damn good soldier of which the nation could be proud." Newspapers weighed in on the Eastland charges. "Senator Eastland," offered *The*

Philadelphia Independent, which had a large Negro readership, "is trying to paint a mental picture of laziness and indifference as symbolic of Negroes in the minds of the American people so that he and others like him will be able to blind the masses of citizens to the justice of our fight for equity in these United States." The Louisville *Courier-Journal* opined that "there is no more cowardly device than that of attacking, under Congressional immunity, the courage and the Americanism of an entire race."

Days after attacking the mettle of the Negro soldier, Eastland made another charge, this one involving a gruesome incident on foreign soil. In April 1945, French troops took control of Stuttgart, Germany, following a long, hard battle. A great many of the French soldiers were of Tunisian and Moroccan heritage. Following the military victory, women were assaulted and raped. German authorities put the number of rape victims at fifteen hundred. In Eastland's retelling on the Senate floor of that awful saga, the rapists suddenly became "Senegalese"—dark-skinned brethren to the American Negro. A narrative so painful needed no exaggeration, but Eastland offered plenty. He said the number of rape victims was closer to five thousand; he also claimed the rapes went on for nearly a week in an underground subway. Stuttgart had no subway. Lieutenant General Augustin Léon Guillaume, who oversaw French troops in the city—and certainly had to be ashamed of his men's conduct beyond their defeat of the Nazis—told an American reporter who tracked him down that Eastland's Senegalese charge was "irresponsible and fantastic."

War begat politics, and the Mississippi senator remained on a roll. When the southern Democrats rode into Birmingham, Alabama, in a fevered sweat for their 1948 Dixiecrat convention, Eastland escorted Fielding Wright—the vice presidential pick alongside the presidential nominee Strom Thurmond—on his journey. The Dixiecrats went down to an ignominious defeat but were convinced they had launched a formidable movement. "You gave freely of your time and talents and I wish you to know that I am deeply grateful to you for the magnificent contribution you made to this great cause," Thurmond would write to Eastland just before Christmas 1948.

· · ·

AS IF IT WERE some sort of talisman attached to his political career, death would continue to play a large role in the rise of James Eastland.

On February 28, 1956, the Senate Judiciary chairman, Harley Kilgore, suffered a stroke and died. In the Senate, the rules of seniority dominated. The senator next in line to succeed Kilgore: James Eastland. The prospect sent shudders through blacks and liberal whites. "Maybe there is no easy substitute for seniority. There is no easy substitute for wisdom, either," *The New York Times* wrote in an editorial about the inevitable elevation of Eastland. "There is no substitute for faith in the American system of democracy. If something has to give way, it had better be seniority."

As subcommittee chairman who considered civil rights legislation, Eastland gloated that he had blocked all such bills. "I had special pockets put in my pants, and for three years I carried those bills around in my pockets."

The game of seniority was fixed and unalterable. Clarence Mitchell, a longtime friend of Thurgood Marshall's—he also hailed from Marshall's Baltimore—was the NAACP lobbyist in Washington during Eastland's rise. "A mad dog is loose in the streets of justice," he said of the Eastland ascendancy.

Eastland relished his newfound role as chairman. He had a very good time blocking civil rights bills for years.

It is little wonder that the mixture of Dixiecrat—southern Democrat—and conservative politicians continued to stymie the aspirations of so many blacks. "The Negro voter by and large appears convinced that it is the Democrats who prevent any legislative help in his race's striving for a better share in American democracy," opined *The Atlantic Monthly*. "The Negro voter, and the white voter, too, who feels strongly on the subject, sees only Mississippi Senator Eastland blocking the door of his powerful Judiciary Committee and backed by Southern Democrats determined to filibuster any civil rights legislation."

The Georgia politician Herman Talmadge was another heralded voice championing segregation. Talmadge wrote a book, *You and Segregation*, that was a tirade against integration and the *Brown* desegregation ruling. Serious publications ignored the book. Eastland happily endorsed it: "Herman Talmadge ably exposes and denounces the tissue of lies that surrounds the controversy over segregation. He reveals in simple terms the present threats to our republican form of constitutional government. He charts a course of action by which the people and the states can legally resist unlawful court decrees, maintain constitutional government, and preserve individual liberties."

By the mid-1950s, James Eastland had amassed an amazing amount of power in Washington. He was judiciary chairman and also presided over the Senate Internal Security Subcommittee—the committee charged with hunting Communists. When he went out on the road, crowds lined up to hear his talk. "People are starting to realize that we're not mistreating the Negro in the South," Eastland said in 1956 to a lily-white Tennessee audience. "And they're realizing we can make more progress with separate [educational] institutions." That very year, Eastland announced he was taking his children out of the Sidwell Friends School in Bethesda, Maryland, a Washington suburb. The school had admitted a Negro student, which he could not abide.

Clarence Pierce first met Eastland in the late 1950s and would later join his staff. Pierce hailed from Vaiden, Mississippi, a small cotton town. His family and the Eastlands had known each other for years. "He thought we were not ready for total integration," Pierce would recall decades later of Eastland's racial thinking. "Some children came from homes where their parents had no education. And you had to wonder if those children were even ready." Pierce had heard the stories about Eastland's father having lynched a black man. "He did not want to talk about that," Pierce says of Eastland. "The family lost control of that situation, and the Klan got involved."

Eastland spent half of his year on his Doddsville plantation. He employed about a hundred Negro families there. The sharecroppers lived on the premises. "They seldom ever left," Pierce says of those families. Eastland liked to brag that the Negroes who worked for him wouldn't dare seek to cause him any trouble.

When Nell Eastland, the senator's twenty-two-year-old daughter, was crowned Miss Confederacy 1956, Eastland and his wife simply could not stop beaming. The ceremony took place inside a lavish ballroom in Washington as Negro servants glided about smoothly and silently. A marine planted a kiss on Nell Eastland's cheeks as the flashbulbs popped.

To visit the Senate office of James Eastland was like stepping into a shrine to all things Dixie: there were photographs—actually, they were steel engravings—of General Robert E. Lee, John C. Calhoun, and the KKK wizard Nathan Bedford Forrest. Eastland revered all of them. He smoked imported Cuban cigars and sometimes handed them out as very special gifts. (One of his admirers shipped him boxes of the smokes.) As he was smoking those cigars, he sometimes began to tell stories of his beloved Mississippi and his ancestors who fought so proudly for the Confederacy. Confederate knickknacks were strewn about the office.

As was customary at the opening of Senate sessions, Eastland had to face a vote in 1957 to retain his chairmanship. In the clubby world of Senate decorum, it was considered all but unthinkable to challenge an incumbent's chairmanship. Only one man, Senator Paul Douglas of Illinois, a liberal lion, dared vote against Eastland. "Most Congressmen realize the high standards of Eastland's work," *The Monroe News-Star* of Louisiana said on its editorial page.

Roger Greene, an Associated Press correspondent, knew the muscle of Eastland's power. "Due north of Eastland, they say, lies the 20th Century," he wrote.

In 1960, there were about one million Negroes in the state of Mississippi; fewer than sixty thousand were registered to vote. To counter Negro activism, a group known as the White Citizens' Council was born in the state. Clarence Mitchell, the NAACP lobbyist, proclaimed the council to represent "the rebirth of the Ku Klux Klan under another name." Eastland vehemently disagreed. "The Councils prevent violence," he said. "We have no riff-raff, and I know of no hot-heads who would desire to commit violence."

At the University of Mississippi, commonly and proudly referred to as Ole Miss, a Negro had never set foot in a classroom as a student. But in 1961, the Fifth Circuit of the U.S. Court of Appeals ordered the school to admit James Meredith, who was born in Kosciusko, Mississippi. Meredith was a military veteran. He possessed a near-messianic determination to achieve any goal once he set his mind to it. "My mission was to destroy white supremacy and all connected with it," he would say of his desire to enroll at Ole Miss. (The voting rights activist Medgar Evers had put Meredith in touch with Thurgood Marshall, who provided legal guidance for Meredith.)

Meredith needed the power of the Kennedy administration to ensure his enrollment. The ensuing melee on the campus was brutal. Thousands of students hurled epithets at Meredith when he arrived. In *The New York Times*, the headline proclaimed, "U.S. Is Prepared to Send Troops as Mississippi Governor Defies Courts and Bars Negro Student." The in-state *Jackson Daily News* headline propped up the local passions: "Thousands Said Ready to Fight for Mississippi." On September 30, Meredith, with federal troops escorting him, finally moved into Baxter Hall on campus. Rioting erupted that very night. There were marauding students and goons from as far away as Texas. Someone ran up on Paul Guihard, a French journalist, and shot him in the back of the head, killing him. Before it was over—before James Meredith had cracked Ole Miss open before the world—two dozen federal marshals would be hit with bullets (all survived) and dozens arrested.

Many across the country were appalled by the violence. Letters poured into the state and onto the Ole Miss campus. One arrived in the mailbox of Sidna Brower, the editor of the Ole Miss student newspaper. She had written an editorial simply urging an end to the violence. One of the letters that reached her came from Danville, Virginia: "Dear Miss Brower: . . . Despite all their red herring speeches, the real purposes of the NAACP is the ultimate destruction of the white race, and our civilization that has required more than a thousand years to develop . . . Negroes are famous (or rather infamous) for their Saturday night brawls and razor fights, but are worthless as combat troops in the defense of our country. Their chief concern in Europe was, and is, white women, if you will pardon my expression. Yours sincerely, Ezra L. Austin." There were letters and telegrams of a different mind-set as well. The great chanteuse Josephine Baker telegrammed from Paris: GOD IS GOOD JUST AND SURE . . . WE ARE ALL HAPPY FOR THE RIGHT OF MAN.

Not long after voting rights activist Medgar Evers had been assassinated on the night of June 12, 1963, in the driveway of his Jackson, Mississippi, home, a very gifted writer, a white Mississippian by the name of Eudora Welty, sent a short story to *The New Yorker*. Welty lived right there in Jackson, on Pinehurst Street. She had recently turned fifty-four. The story, which *The New Yorker* quickly published, was titled "Where Is the Voice Coming From." It was about the in-cold-blood murder of Evers. It was told in the first-person voice of the assassin; it was fiction but seemed written from the hard ground of truth:

> I'd already brought up my rifle, I'd already taken my sights. And I'd already got him, because it was too late then for him or me to turn by one hair. Something darker than him, like the wings of a bird, spread on his back and pulled him down. He climbed up once, like a man under bad claws, and like just blood could weigh a ton he walked with it on his back to better light. Didn't get no further than his door. And fell to stay.

In 1994, Byron De La Beckwith, the man who murdered Evers, was finally brought to trial in Mississippi. He was convicted of first-degree murder and died in prison seven years later. Years after publication of her story, Eudora Welty was asked how she could capture, with such sharpness back in 1963, the voice of Beckwith before he had even been identified. "We all knew who did it," she said, "because we all knew Beckwiths. It wasn't necessary to know that man, Beckwith."

Byron De La Beckwith had been a proud member of Mississippi's White Citizens' Council.

THERE WAS A TANGLED RELATIONSHIP between the Kennedy administration and Senator James Eastland. Its roots lay in the dynamics of the Kennedy campaign, which had to traverse the landscape of race, politics, and the South.

The campaign pitted the Massachusetts senator John F. Kennedy against Vice President Richard Nixon. Nixon relied on the still-tingling and romantic imagery of Republicans as the party of Abraham Lincoln. Kennedy had a riskier tightrope: he wanted to wrest as many Negroes as he could away from the Republican Party but could not be seen as overly aggressive regarding civil rights. "More profile than courage," the Senate majority leader and now vice presidential candidate, Lyndon Johnson, had once quipped about Kennedy in a mockery of Kennedy's book *Profiles in Courage.* It helped candidate

Kennedy ingratiate himself to Negro voters when he phoned Coretta Scott King, Martin Luther King Jr.'s wife, to tell her he was thinking of her and her husband, who had been arrested on an old traffic charge in Georgia and was being held in the notorious Reidsville state prison. Such a courtesy was very warmly received and appreciated. "Please ask them not to worry about me," King urged his wife in one of his first letters written during his confinement. "I will adjust to whatever comes in terms of pain."

Shortly before he announced his candidacy, Kennedy had summoned the renowned civil rights attorney Thurgood Marshall for a private lunch. He struck Marshall as charming, but Marshall was worried about the laissez-faire attitude concerning civil rights. "I didn't pull any punches with him," Marshall would say, adding, "It was a lunch and we spent about two hours together. But he got the story. He knew what it was. But I don't think [Kennedy] realized the urgency of it."

What seemed to really ignite newfound Negro interest in candidate Kennedy—besides the phone call to Coretta Scott King—was the Harlem congressman Adam Clayton Powell Jr. The Kennedy camp had brought Powell into the fold as a paid "urban affairs consultant." (Powell was a cagey and sometimes unpredictable politician: He bolted the Democrats in 1956—drawing heated anger from fellow Democrats—and supported the Republican Eisenhower's reelection. Powell maligned Democrats—displaying a nerve his fellow Democrats lacked—for the Dixiecrat wing of their party.) Kennedy's Catholicism was being assailed, and Powell, as a minister himself, was called on to counteract the Kennedy attacks. Powell possessed a quick wit. He caused a ruckus among some members of his Harlem church in 1944 when he divorced his first wife, Isabel, and took up with the jazz chanteuse Hazel Scott. "I thought you were a man of the cloth," someone snapped at Powell. "I am," Powell shot back. "Silk."

Powell set off on a jaunt around the country for the Kennedy camp, coast-to-coast. He appeared before congregations extolling Kennedy's virtues. He said the attacks on Kennedy's religion were coming from southerners and Republicans, and he referred to them as "bigots in the pulpit." But the potent Powell touch was truly felt when he displayed a blown-up replica of a mortgage deed, which he carried from rally to rally. The deed belonged to Richard Nixon, and it showed that

Nixon had sold his home with words in the deed that the property not be sold to a Negro or a Jew. This was in direct violation of *Shelley v. Kraemer*, the 1948 landmark Supreme Court ruling—argued by Thurgood Marshall—that lawfully forbade states to enforce restrictive covenants.

In October, Kennedy came to the Harlem of Thurgood Marshall and Adam Clayton Powell Jr. There was a campaign speech outdoors, on 125th Street. Thousands were in attendance, lining the streets, peering from windows and restaurants and shoe-shine stands. The old Democratic guard was represented by Eleanor Roosevelt. In his speech, Kennedy talked about an America he felt was in decline, but one that still held a reverence in the hearts of foreigners. He said children abroad had been named after American heroes like Thomas Jefferson and George Washington. "There may be a couple called Adam Powell," he said.

"Careful, Jack," Powell—who had a reputation as a playboy—quickly piped in. The laughter was loud.

Kennedy's down-to-the-wire victory was only by 118,000 votes.

Thurgood Marshall had been forced to remain publicly aloof from 1960 presidential politics because of his nonpartisan role with the NAACP Legal Defense Fund. Politicians in that campaign were certainly more than a little aware of Marshall's continued prowess. On March 29, 1960, in Baton Rouge, Louisiana, a group of sixteen Negro students calmly walked into Sitman's Drugstore, sat down in the "whites only" section, and refused to leave. They were arrested for disturbing the peace. The students sued. The case went all the way to the U.S. Supreme Court, where it was argued by Marshall. In a unanimous decision—and yet another notch in Marshall's winning legal belt—he won the case, *Garner v. Louisiana*, which became the first sit-in case heard by the justices.

But shortly after Kennedy was sworn in, the president wanted to feel Marshall out on the direction of civil rights in the country. He sent his brother Bobby to talk with him. Soon into that meeting, Marshall became impatient with Kennedy's nonstop directives and ideas about civil rights. "He spent all his time telling us what we should do," Marshall would recall. Marshall listened and stewed, not wanting to interrupt, until he could not hold himself back any longer. "I told him that so far as I was concerned we had been in the civil rights

business since 1909, and he'd been in the President business a year."
(In mentioning 1909, Marshall was referring to the year the NAACP
was founded. At that time, more than 85 percent of Negroes lived in
southern communities.)

President Kennedy adopted a consistent habit of giving important
personal assignments to his brother Bobby, appointed his attorney
general. Bobby might be told to contact someone the president was
interested in hiring and to feel him or her out. If there was one man
in Washington the president felt he could trust to keep confidences, it
was his brother. So he told Bobby to get in touch with Thurgood Marshall. The president wondered if Marshall was interested in a possible
judicial appointment.

Even though Marshall was now wary of Bobby Kennedy, he thought
it impolitic to refuse to meet with him. Shortly after Marshall arrived,
Bobby Kennedy made his pitch: the president wanted to know if he
was interested in possibly being appointed a federal judge in New York
City. At the age of fifty-three, Thurgood Marshall knew well what he
wanted in life and what he didn't want. He said he wasn't interested.

"Well, why?" Kennedy demanded, suddenly alarmed that anyone
would turn down an overture from the president.

"My boiling point is too low for the trial court," Marshall told him.
"I'd blow my stack and then get reversed. But I could go on the court
of appeals."

Kennedy immediately rebuffed him, even as Marshall told him he
knew there was an appeals court opening. "You don't seem to understand," Bobby Kennedy sharply said, "it's this or nothing."

Marshall, a fiercely prideful man, was quickly reminded of why he
disliked Bobby Kennedy—the arrogance and condescension. He knew
the Kennedys came from money, were pedigreed. "Well, I do understand," he told young Bobby. "The trouble is that you are different
from me. You don't know what it means, but all I've had in my life is
nothing. It's not new to me, so goodbye." And Thurgood Marshall
turned and walked out on the president's brother. "Bobby," Marshall
would later say, "was like his father. He was a cold, calculating character. 'What's in it for me?' I mean, not like his brother. He had no warm
feelings. None at all. With that big old dog of his, walking around,
cocking his leg up on your leg."

Louis Martin, the well-connected Negro political operative and

Democratic National Committee member—sitting right there in the Oval Office on the day of the Marshall Supreme Court announcement—finally prevailed upon the Kennedy White House to nominate Marshall to the U.S. Court of Appeals for the Second Circuit. It was the judgeship he wanted.

Marshall knew there would be an intense background search, delving into his personal life and legal reputation. Some of it would be conducted by the FBI. Marshall resided in a Harlem apartment building, and his neighbors were a bit bemused at the types of questions FBI agents asked them about Marshall. One day, Marshall ran into the building janitor, who told him he had been visited and questioned. Marshall was curious as to what kinds of questions he had been asked. "Well . . . about how many people visited you, and how many liquor bottles came out, and all like that." The nominee could only chuckle.

There were more eyebrow-raising episodes regarding the background search. One day, Marshall and his fellow NAACP Legal Defense Fund attorney, Jack Greenberg, were walking down a New York City street, having just finished lunch. A policeman appeared out of nowhere and accused Marshall of following a white woman walking several feet in front of him. Marshall and Greenberg both were bewildered, wondering if it were some kind of a joke. The policeman was not joking and demanded Marshall's identification. He then scribbled something down on a scrap of paper before walking away. Marshall was shaken by the scene: a bizarre report about his following white women would surely play into the hands of those senators who wanted to torpedo his appeals court nomination. "Of course," Greenberg would recall, "Thurgood hadn't been following anybody, other than all those people who happened to be on the sidewalk in front of him as he returned to the office. But he was worried, if word of the episode got out it might affect his prospects for the judgeship." Marshall wondered if he should approach the New York City Police Department, as he strongly felt someone was trying to set him up. He finally decided against it. "I have wondered how history might have changed if an eager reporter with an interest in politics had come across Thurgood's name in the policeman's report," Greenberg would muse later.

It was considered a common courtesy for judicial nominees to meet with the powerful senators who would be conducting hearings.

Bobby Kennedy escorted the appeals court nominee Marshall around the Senate during his meet and greets. Marshall now saw a different Bobby Kennedy striding along the Senate hallways, the toothy grin all wide, the handshake pumping away. "You'd think he was the nicest guy in the world," Marshall would remember. "Taking all the credit for it." In and out of offices they went. They came upon the office door of the Mississippi senator James Eastland, chairman of the powerful Judiciary Committee. "Oh," Kennedy said to Marshall, "we have to stop here. We have to pay our respects."

Marshall stopped and told Kennedy he wasn't going in there to meet with Eastland. Kennedy was dumbfounded; this was Eastland, the chairman. "Well, you ought to," Kennedy testily warned him. Again, Marshall refused.

John F. Kennedy's alliance with southern Democrats also had exposure back at the 1956 Democratic National Convention. There was a battle between Democratic senators vying for vice president. Kennedy and Estes Kefauver were in the mix. But the southern senators loathed Kefauver of Tennessee. He was one of three southern senators—along with his fellow Tennessean Albert Gore and Lyndon Johnson of Texas—who did not sign the Southern Manifesto, a screed railing against the Thurgood Marshall–led *Brown* desegregation ruling. The authors of the Southern Manifesto proclaimed *Brown* "a clear abuse of judicial power." Kefauver believed in integration and was proud of the position he staked. So instead of supporting Kefauver, southern senators threw their votes behind Kennedy, which he accepted during his party's roll call. "I'm going to sing 'Dixie' for the rest of my life," Kennedy said at the time.

When Kennedy finally reached the White House a little more than four years later, the powerful southern segregationist senators sat back and all but made him sing "Dixie" as they sent judicial nominees to him that he rubber-stamped. There were complaints about the judges, and he addressed them at a press conference. "I think that the men that have been appointed to judgeships in the South, sharing perhaps as they do the general outlook of the South, have done a remarkable job in fulfilling their oath of office."

Some disagreed with President Kennedy's assessment. Among them was Roy Wilkins of the NAACP, who bitterly complained about Kennedy's early judicial appointee, William Harold Cox. "For 986,000 Mississippi Negroes, Judge Cox will be another strand in their barbed-wire fence, another cross over their weary shoulders," Wilkins told President Kennedy.

It did not take very long for Wilkins's fears to be realized. As soon as his first voting rights case came before him as a federal judge, Cox could not contain himself. "A bunch of niggers . . . acting like a bunch of chimpanzees," is how he referred to the Negro plaintiffs.

Cox had not worried a bit about his chances at confirmation. He had an insurance policy that was quite potent. His college roommate had been Senator James Eastland, the Senate Judiciary Committee chairman.

AS TO MARSHALL's federal appeals judgeship, the nomination languished. Three months turned to five, which turned to seven. Eastland would simply not release the nomination for a vote. "Look, do you understand this problem?" President Kennedy explained to Marshall in a phone call. Marshall assured the president he understood the gravity of the situation.

Marshall was soon sitting as an interim appointment. But that wouldn't do for the long run, because after a year sitting on an interim basis, his pay would cease. Marshall told Kennedy he had been hearing rumblings that a group of Negro masons throughout the South—they felt indebted to him for his past legal work—would help him financially. But that, of course, was a dubious plan complicated by all manner of ethical issues.

If the segregationist federal judge William Cox possessed an ace up his sleeve in his college roommate James Eastland, then Marshall, languishing on an interim basis, also had an ace: Henry Luce, the powerful founder and publisher of *Time* magazine. Both Luce and his wife, Ambassador Clare Boothe Luce, had been admirers of those brave men and women who were changing the course of American history in the South. Henry Luce's *Time* had put Marshall on its cover in that 1955 issue; two years later, it put Martin Luther King Jr. on the cover highlighting the Montgomery bus boycott. Marshall told Luce—"my good friend Henry Luce"—about the holdup on his nomination. Luce's *Time* magazine reached millions. The magazine could enlarge reputations—or diminish them. And it was common knowledge that Henry Luce feared no one. Luce got in touch with the southern Democrats blocking the Marshall appointment. He demanded to know what, if anything, they had on Marshall that would make them stifle his nomination. "Luce just said he didn't think it was fair," Marshall would recall. "And if they had something on me, bring it out." Luce warned the southern Democrats that if Marshall's nomination were not released, he would put something glowing about Marshall in the magazine every week, the supposition being that such stories would reflect harshly back on the southern Democrats themselves.

It took nearly a year, but Thurgood Marshall was finally confirmed for his appeals court seat.

The southern senators on James Eastland's judiciary committee—along with Eastland himself—had been beaten. And they did not take kindly to being beaten.

AS THE 1960S ROLLED INTO VIEW across Mississippi, the college kids came and kept coming, staging nonviolent protests. They came into Eastland's Sunflower County, where they defiantly made contact with Eastland's plantation workers, men and women making about $3 a day. "If you were on the plantation you couldn't take any part," recalled Earline Tillman, a worker on Eastland's land, referring to the protests. "If you took part you'd have to move."

Three of the civil rights workers who had come to Mississippi by the middle of June 1964 were Andrew Goodman, James Chaney, and Michael Schwerner. Twenty black churches had been burned by the Klan that summer. The way to fight the inequality, Goodman and his fellow workers believed, was to register Negroes to vote—which, of course, could be a risky endeavor. Schwerner was especially brave: Jewish and from New York, he had been the first white person to have a full-time civil rights job in Mississippi and beyond the somewhat safe confines of Jackson, the capital. "You have been slaves too long," Schwerner told a group of blacks standing amid the ashes of the burned-to-the-ground Mount Zion church one day in Neshoba County.

On the afternoon of June 21, Goodman, Schwerner, and Chaney were on Highway 16 in Neshoba County. Chaney, the Negro, was behind the wheel of the blue station wagon. By the time they neared Philadelphia, Mississippi, they found themselves with a flat tire. Deputy Cecil Price pulled up. Price told them they had been speeding. He also told them he wanted to question them about church arsons. The civil rights workers knew this was ominous and began to worry. Other deputies arrived on the scene alongside Price. The three were arrested and taken to the Neshoba County jail. Later that night, they were released. And like puffs of smoke, they vanished. Just days earlier, during training on the campus of Western College in Oxford, Ohio, the civil rights workers had been told to avoid being out at night in rural areas. And to always check in with the Jackson office if a problem arose. No one in Jackson received a call from the three workers.

The news of the missing workers sent shivers through their colleagues. The White House was quickly informed, as well as the national media. Mississippi had no full-time FBI agents working in the state, and President Johnson ordered the FBI director, J. Edgar Hoover, to launch a manhunt for the three. In time, the FBI would link the Neshoba County sheriffs Lawrence Rainey and Cecil Price to the disappearances. By the end of the second week, it was widely suspected the three had been murdered. "There's just nothing, no violence, no friction of any kind," Senator Eastland told President Johnson regarding the missing young men. Many knew otherwise. Cadets were dispatched to search the woods and swamps in and around the county where they were last seen. Soon they were dragging the Pearl River. Locals lined the bridge above the river. "Hey," a local man shouted to the naval cadets, "why don't you hold a welfare check out over the water. That'll get that nigger to the surface." An editorial appeared in *The Meridian Star* after Hoover visited Jackson to announce the opening of an FBI office in the state. "The student volunteers, the beatniks, the wild-eyed left wing nuts, the unshaven and unwashed . . . go on meddling and muddling. The poison pen sweepings of the gutters of journalism go on printing their lying trash."

A sign at the time was seen proudly displayed in the back window of a car rolling down a rural Mississippi road: "You Are in Occupied Mississippi. Proceed with Caution."

The search for the missing three civil rights workers went up to and beyond thirty days. It was FBI reward money that drew out an informant, who told the agency that the three were buried in an earthen dam at the old Jolly farm off Highway 21. It took a Caterpillar bulldozer hours to dig deep into the earth. The three were found after forty-four days. The autopsy would reveal Schwerner and Goodman had been shot once; Chaney, the Negro, three times.

Nearly two dozen men would be charged with the killings. A Mississippi state court, however, dropped all charges. Then the federal government brought charges against eighteen of those originally charged. Mississippi authorities did not sit by, and they felt that the federal government had no right to bring such charges. The case went to the U.S. Supreme Court, where it was argued in the fall of 1965. The case to be argued on the federal government's behalf fell to the solicitor general, who based his argument on a Reconstruction-era law that attacked any conspiracies used to deny blacks their rights under "color of law." The solicitor general standing in court on behalf of the United States was Thurgood Marshall. The justices issued a unanimous decision in favor of the federal government.

A REVOLUTION had swept across the South, and Eastland resented it. On his trips to Mississippi, he had begun urging radio and TV stations—as well as newspaper editorial boards, who needed no such encouragement—to attack the NAACP, Thurgood Marshall, and all followers of Martin Luther King Jr. "We lost the Voting Rights Bill yesterday," he confided to a constituent in the late spring of 1965. "In fact, there were only 19 votes against it. The whole country seems to be swept with a kind of hysteria on this civil rights matter."

In the mid-1950s, Senator Eastland had begun issuing announcements about Supreme Court decisions. They were either "pro-Communist" or "anti-Communist" decisions. "Jim Eastland," the *New York Post* would write in a widely discussed 1956 editorial, "is a dreary figure fighting the holy war of the Southern white supremacists. He disgraces the USA as long as he is permitted to sit in judgment on the loyalty of other Americans. He is beyond the pale of honorable debate." It concluded, "Those who let him use 'anti-communism' to cover his tracks are political racketeers playing an old and dirty game."

James Eastland was convinced, in the summer of 1967, that the

Supreme Court nominee Thurgood Marshall had been on the side of Communism for decades. He had to convince fellow senators of such a belief—and of the torment, he proclaimed, that all those Marshall-led court decisions had caused his beloved South. Even many children in Mississippi had been made aware of the exploits of Thurgood Marshall. "I remember when I was six years old hearing people raise hell about Thurgood Marshall," says David Lambert, who grew up in a small Mississippi town and would later join Senator Eastland's staff. "I didn't know what 'a Thurgood Marshall' was."

James Eastland, absent from the third day of Marshall's confirmation hearings in Washington, was doing more down in Mississippi than just puffing on one of his cigars and gazing out over the Negroes working his plantation. He was plotting anew over the Marshall nomination. (He would never forgive Marshall's snubbing of him—the chairman!—when the nominee refused to visit him in his office, where he might have been treated to a shot of bourbon and seen all of Eastland's Confederate memorabilia.) Just as he used to keep those civil rights bills deep in his pockets, Eastland now began to decipher how many senators would join him—how many he had in his pocket—in opposing Marshall. He knew there were stalwart members of the Senate—men he had been in the fight with against integration for decades—whom he could certainly count on. He could depend on John Sparkman and Lister Hill of Alabama. Robert Byrd of West Virginia would stand with him. Ernest Hollings of South Carolina and Russell Long of Louisiana would not let him down. Strom Thurmond would be all too happy to join him, as would Allen Ellender of Louisiana and Spessard Holland of Florida. He had other senators he imagined he could count on, among them Richard Russell of Georgia and George Smathers of Florida. There was also John Stennis, his fellow Mississippian, and Paul Fannin of Arizona, who was just as rabidly conservative as his friend Barry Goldwater, who ran for the presidency in 1964.

With the hearings still ongoing, dozens of votes had yet to be pinned down regarding Marshall. The reality made the White House nervous. The country was a racial tinderbox. And the president could hardly take his eye off the quagmire of Vietnam.

As chairman of the Judiciary Committee, James Eastland set the order of the hearings. In many ways, he set their tone and bent the hearings to his will. He set opposition strategy against Thurgood Marshall. Eastland figured, given the nation's social upheaval, that no issue in American society was more potent than crime, punishment, and patriotism. His big stalwarts in those areas on the Judiciary Committee were unquestionably Senators Sam Ervin and John McClellan. Even though they had completed their questioning—or so they had stated—Eastland decided he needed them again. He wanted them to intensify their attack on Marshall over those contentious issues of crime and urban mayhem—which had become code words for the anger brewing in black America. Ervin and McClellan were far superior lawyers to Eastland himself. They possessed more depth about the law, and Eastland knew it. They had been savvy, hard-nosed prosecutors. The nation had seen and admired both Ervin and McClellan and realized they knew how to trip witnesses up, how to catch criminals off guard, how to expose weaknesses. And they knew well the element of surprise.

The chairman left Mississippi to return to Washington with a new-found strategy. He was going to unleash McClellan and Ervin once again on the nominee Thurgood Marshall. And if the so-called Young Turks on the committee—Kennedy, Hart, Tydings, all of whom the White House was depending on to help Marshall—didn't like it, well, that was just tough luck.

7

"The Jew"

In 1916, President Woodrow Wilson nominated the Boston attorney
Louis Brandeis to the U.S. Supreme Court. The nomination unleashed
a wave of anti-Semitism and a bottleneck in the U.S. Senate.
(Brandeis is shown at right with former president and
U.S. Supreme Court Chief Justice William Howard Taft, c. 1929.)

THURGOOD MARSHALL was not the first Supreme Court nominee
who ignited bold headlines, editorials, personal invective, and sensa-
tional commentary because of the roots of his ethnicity. That distinction belonged to Louis D. Brandeis.

In 1916—following the death of Justice Joseph Lamar just after
New Year's Day—President Woodrow Wilson nominated Brandeis, a
renowned Boston attorney, to replace the justice. Considering that by
1916 only sixty-six men had sat on the U.S. Supreme Court since its
beginning, the nation knew what a laborious and significant amount

of concentration a high court appointment demanded from the White House.

But someone of Jewish heritage? From President Wilson? Few expected it.

Wilson was born in the Deep South, and despite his Princeton background his sentiments continued to lie with the South. American Negroes were appalled that Wilson segregated the nation's capital and the federal government workforce—separate bathrooms and facilities—upon taking office. At a White House screening, he showed the film *The Birth of a Nation*, based on the novel about Klansmen attacking blacks who they charged had defiled white women. Wilson heaped praise upon the film. Black leaders, such as W. E. B. DuBois and William Trotter, turned against Wilson and criticized the film for its racist overtones. Trotter went so far as to raise his voice at the president during a White House event, a breach of protocol that got him hastily removed from the premises.

Wilson's aides had toyed with the Washington press corps up to the moment of the Brandeis announcement, allowing a variety of names to be floated without comment. On January 28, Wilson sent a brief message to the Senate, telling it he was nominating Louis Dembitz Brandeis. Just a few reporters were in the press gallery that day, and they immediately dashed away to spread news of the announcement. It wasn't only that Louis D. Brandeis was a surprise choice—a wonderfully kept secret, although he and Wilson were acquaintances—it was also because Louis D. Brandeis was Jewish. In a nation quick to turn race or religion into a tinderbox issue when it came to all manner of politics, this was, on Wilson's part, a daring and explosive nomination.

Hardly anyone could argue with Brandeis's reputation or legal acumen. A Harvard Law graduate—and a co-founder of the *Harvard Law Review*—he quickly impressed those whom he worked under. "I consider Brandeis the most ingenious and most original lawyer I ever met," said the Massachusetts chief justice Horace Gray, who had offered Brandeis a clerkship. Brandeis founded a corporate law practice in Boston that became highly respected. His rise took place during the Industrial Revolution, and Brandeis mastered the intricacies of corporate America. But he also became a reformer, fighting for women's rights and the rights of the aggrieved. In 1908, the State of Oregon submitted a brief to the U.S. Supreme Court hoping to limit the hours women worked, especially in laundries and similar industries. Brandeis argued and won the case. His brief, full of emotion and concerns about the welfare of women, was a landmark victory for women's rights. It became known as the Brandeis Brief.

So, if they couldn't argue about Brandeis's legal skills—which were practically unmatched—his opponents, in trying to derail his nomination, aimed to argue about his so-called radicalism, which quickly unleashed currents of anti-Semitism. And the nation had recently seen what unchecked anti-Semitism could do.

In 1915, a year before the Brandeis nomination, a Jew had been snatched from a jail cell in Milledgeville, Georgia, taken to Marietta, and hanged from an oak tree—an echo of the kind of violence usually meted out to Negroes.

On April 27, 1913, a night watchman at the National Pencil Company in Atlanta discovered the lifeless body of thirteen-year-old Mary Phagan. The cause of death was strangulation. Suspects were questioned. Two Negroes—Newt Lee and Jim Conley—came under quick suspicion, a fact both realized could lead to their own swift deaths. Conley—who had a criminal background and a slippery manner with the truth—would come to finger Leo Frank, the plant manager. Frank was Jewish and a transplant from New York. He said Conley's claim was outrageous. All the while, Frank casually admitted that he indeed believed he was the last one to have seen Mary Phagan alive. Frank was charged with the murder.

PHAGAN'S FUNERAL attracted more than ten thousand mourners. Little seemed as precious as white womanhood in the South, and the crime drew national attention.

Leo Frank hired a defense team. And he calmly told anyone who would listen that the authorities simply had the wrong man.

Tom Watson, one of the yellow journalists of the era, wrote nonstop about the Phagan murder, and his stories, dripping with anti-Semitism, quickly gained a wide readership. He described Frank as a "typical young libertine Jew" who had a "ravenous appetite for the forbidden fruit—a lustful eagerness enhanced by the racial novelty of a girl of the uncircumcised." Frank had his day in court. "Hang the Jew, or we'll hang you!" were some of the shouts he heard while seated. The judge wisely suggested Frank and his attorney not be present when the verdict was reached. He was found guilty by a kangaroo court—and sentenced to death. (Conley got sentenced to a year imprisonment, convicted of being an accomplice.)

There were appeals on Frank's behalf. He quite clearly had an unfair trial, with its howling mobs ever present at the courthouse. On April 19, 1915, the U.S. Supreme Court shockingly upheld the death sentence. Justice Oliver Wendell Holmes—wounded three times in the Civil War—wrote a dissent. "I understand that I am to assume that the allegations of fact in the motion to set aside are true," Holmes wrote. "On these facts I very seriously doubt if the petitioner (Frank) has had due process of law—not on the ground of his absence when the verdict was rendered so much as because of the trial taking place in the presence of a hostile demonstration and seemingly dangerous crowd, thought by the presiding Judge to be ready for violence unless a verdict of guilty was rendered." Frank's partisans only had one move left: to appeal to Georgia's governor, John M. Slaton, for a commutation. Others hoped for a complete pardon. Slaton knew the weight of his decision. An attorney, he decided to study every aspect of the case himself. He told his aides to give him solitude as he went over the entirety of the case and trial.

While Slaton was considering the request for a pardon, there was a mass meeting in Marietta, Phagan's hometown, which close to a thousand attended, voicing their shock that a pardon would even be considered. They had the fierceness of a mob. "Let him hang!" came the cries. Fred Morris stepped to the front. Everyone knew Morris. He was a local and respected lawyer. But he had also been a University of Georgia football legend. "Mary Phagan was a poor factory girl," Morris bellowed. "What show would she have against Jew money? When they found they couldn't fool the people of Georgia, they got people from Massachusetts, New York and California to try and raise trouble. Well, we throw the advice of these outsiders back in their teeth. To hell with what they think."

Governor Slaton found numerous holes in Conley's accusations. After poring over crates of documents, Slaton could not convince himself of Frank's guilt beyond a reasonable doubt. "I would rather be the widow of a brave and honorable man," Slaton's wife told him, "than the wife of a coward." Governor Slaton was no coward. "I can endure misconstruction, abuse and condemnation," he said, "but I cannot stand the constant companionship of an accusing conscience, which would remind me in every thought that I, as governor of Georgia, failed to do what I thought to be right."

Slaton commuted Frank's death sentence to life imprisonment. Goons wasted little time in storming the governor's mansion in protest. Slaton had to declare martial law to ensure his own safety. He was hanged in effigy. "Had Georgia sent Frank to the gallows," *The New York Times* declared in an editorial, "the good name of the State would have been blackened and its people would have been under reproach. Governor Slaton has saved Georgia from herself." (Negroes throughout the state of Georgia—and even beyond—expressed sympathy for Frank, while behind closed doors they could only bemoan their own tales of justice gone wickedly awry.)

Frank was sent to a prison farm to begin his sentence. It was there, on the night of August 16, 1915, that seven carloads of armed men, proclaiming themselves the Knights of Mary Phagan, stormed the prison. They pulled their weapons on the warden and his guards and snatched Frank away. They rode hard toward Marietta, Phagan's hometown, with the terrified Leo Frank now in death's grip. Terror was mingled with the pain in his neck: a crazed inmate had recently stabbed him with a butcher knife. He owed his life—in the seconds following the stabbing—to the quick reaction of inmates and the prison doctor. The cars with the kidnappers wheezed along country roads until they reached the edge of Marietta. Frank, blindfolded, was dragged from the car. Everyone in town knew Newt Morris; he was a judge. He was also part of the mob. A noose was slipped over Frank's head. Then someone viciously kicked the table out from under him. Blood sprayed from his knife wound as his body swung, draining all life from him.

The lynching produced outrage from northern cities. "Georgia is reaping what she sowed," cried the *Pittsburgh Dispatch*. "For years she had tolerated mob violence against one race . . . The mob that is allowed to set its belief above the law in one case, will not hesitate to arrogate to itself the same power in another." The *Chicago Daily Tri-*

bune opined that "the South is half educated. It is a region of illiteracy, blatant self-righteousness, cruelty and violence. Until it is improved by the infusion of new blood and better ideas it will remain a reproach and a danger to the American republic."

Just months after the Frank killing, with the case still in the air, "the Jew"—as Brandeis's antagonists were calling him—was nominated to the U.S. Supreme Court.

"President Wilson sent a bomb to the United States Senate yesterday," the AP quickly wrote of the Brandeis nomination. "The bomb exploded. With the reading of the nomination Senators started for the cloakrooms. To them it was the biggest sensation of the session." A New York *Sun* headline—"He's First Jew Ever Picked for Bench"—foretold of struggles to come. The *Detroit Free Press* quickly staked its position: "Of all the Americans who have passed before the public view in the last ten years Louis D. Brandeis is in temperament and in training perhaps the least fit for the calm, cold, dispassionate work of the Supreme Court of the United States . . . It is the solemn duty of the Senate to reject this nomination." The former president William Howard Taft thought he might get the nomination that went to Brandeis. He expressed his anger and animus toward Brandeis in a letter to a friend. "He is a muckraker, an emotionalist for his own purposes, a socialist, prompted by jealousy, a hypocrite, a man who has certain high ideals in his imagination, but who is utterly unscrupulous in method in reaching them, a man of infinite cunning, of great tenacity of purpose, and, in my judgment, of much power for evil." Taft's heft seemed to power his language, and he went on: "The intelligent Jews of this country are as much opposed to Brandeis' nomination as I am, but there are politics in the Jewish community, which with their clannishness embarrass leading and liberal and clear-sighted Jews."

Many senators—unable to assail Brandeis's intellect—were careful about publicly expressing their opposition to his heritage lest they seem anti-Semitic. However, it did not stop them from expressing such feelings in personal correspondence, often marked "confidential." "A man ought to be appointed without any reference to his race or religion, and solely on his fitness," said the highly respected senator Henry Cabot Lodge. "If it were not that Brandeis is a Jew, and a German Jew, he would never have been appointed and he would not have a baker's dozen of votes in the Senate. This seems to be in the highest degree un-American and wrong."

When judiciary subcommittee hearings got under way, witnesses for and against Brandeis made their way to their seats. Those against the nominee thought he had been too harsh on big business, and those for the nominee praised his social reform skills and progressive mind-set. A clique of Massachusetts power brokers—bankers, insurance company owners, the president of Harvard University, all numbering upwards of fifty prominent citizens—sent a letter to Senator Lodge opposing the Brandeis nomination. The Harvard law professor Felix Frankfurter felt otherwise: "Mr. Brandeis' mind is at once luminous and creative, and a passion for justice is his dominating motive."

Many of Brandeis's foes were upset that having once worked for corporate interests, he now attacked corporate interests in favor of the common man and woman. But constantly hovering—like curlicues of smoke—was the nominee's ethnicity. There was not a single person of Jewish heritage in the U.S. Senate when Louis Brandeis was nominated to the high court. "I have kept myself fully informed," the labor leader Samuel Gompers told a reporter about Brandeis, "as to the character of the testimony against his confirmation, and it discloses the fact that it is prompted by either greed or prejudice, and has no real foundation in fact."

After forty days, the Brandeis hearings finally came to a close. But just as quickly, and bizarrely, they were reopened by the force of an effort fueled by Austen George Fox. Fox, a Wall Street attorney and Harvard Law graduate, had alliances in the Senate. Such was his reputation that when he said he needed more time to offer additional testimony, it was granted to him. Fox, along with Taft, secured a statement from six former presidents—as well as the reigning president—of the American Bar Association, all condemning the Brandeis nomination. This was not something that could be overlooked, and senators took notice. "The undersigned," the statement began, "feel under the painful duty to say to you in their opinion, taking into view the reputation, character and professional career of Mr. Louis D. Brandeis, he is not a fit person to be a member of the Supreme Court of the United States."

The attack was answered by those who supported Brandeis. "There is probably no man on the present Supreme Bench who has more than a small fraction of Brandeis' acquaintance with the living and thinking of the 85 percent of the American people who earn their way in humble station," the *Record*, a newspaper in Stockton, California, proclaimed.

At long last, a majority report was issued on the nomination, written by the West Virginia senator William E. Chilton. Chilton concluded Brandeis had been a victim of reckless charges. "I am not willing to endorse a campaign of slander," he said. Senator Thomas Walsh of Montana felt otherwise: "The real crime of which this man [Brandeis] is guilty is that he has exposed the iniquities of men in high places in our financial system. He has not stood in awe of the majesty of wealth."

Some in the Senate remembered well that President Grover Cleveland had been rebuffed with two court nominees. When senators could ultimately not make up their minds, the Brandeis nomination became stalled in committee. And while it was stalled in committee, a campaign was afoot alleging that Brandeis did not believe in the written Constitution. Brandeis, silent throughout the hearings—it was not yet the custom for nominees to appear before the committee—felt an obligation to answer such a charge. "It was sufficiently trying throughout two months of the hearings to have lies and misrepresentations spread in regard to me without the opportunity of being heard by the Committee and the public," he said, "but to have these lies circulated privately after the hearings are closed seems to me not in accord with American conception of fair play."

There were senators now wavering about Brandeis, and the Wilson White House realized it. "The prospects for the confirmation of the Brandeis nomination darkened still more today," *The Wall Street Journal* said on May 4, 1916, following another voting delay.

The worry of Democrats on the committee deepened. They decided to implore President Wilson to write a letter to the committee, explaining his decision to nominate Brandeis. Realizing the urgency of the request, Wilson did so. "In every matter in which I have made test of his judgment and point of view," Wilson wrote, "I have received from him counsel singularly enlightening, singularly clear-sighted and judicial, and, above all, full of moral stimulation. He is a friend of all just men and a lover of the right; and he knows more than how to talk about the right—he knows how to set it forward in the face of his enemies." Rabbi Stephen Wise believed the time had come for a more aggressive backing of Brandeis. "All we need do is to help the American people to see that a crime is being committed against them," he wrote to a friend about the smears against Brandeis.

Wilson and the White House had no choice but to become more engaged than ever in the fate of the nomination. The egos of certain senators had to be stroked, and were. Wilson lobbied friends who had known some of the wavering senators since their childhoods, hoping they could offer words of persuasion.

On May 24, the committee finally met to vote on the nomination. If the committee deadlocked, the nomination would be thrown to the full house, where it might well die from a filibuster. The vote came in, 10–8 for Brandeis. Because Democrats controlled the Senate, it all but meant Louis D. Brandeis was going onto the Supreme Court. In a surprising editorial, *The New York Times* expressed disappointment over the inevitable confirmation of Brandeis. "To place upon the Supreme Bench judges who hold a different view of the function of the court, to supplant conservatism by radicalism, would be to undo the work of John Marshall and strip the Constitution of its defenses," the newspaper wrote. "It would introduce endless confusion where order has reigned, it would tend to give force and effect to any whim or passion of the hour, to crown with success any transitory agitation engaged in by a part of the people, overriding the matured judgment of all the people as expressed in their fundamental law."

The Senate vote to confirm Brandeis was 47–22.

When Brandeis reached the doorway of his summer home without yet hearing the conclusion of the vote, his wife—who had been informed—greeted him as she had never done before. "Good evening, Mr. Justice Brandeis."

The first Jew on the Supreme Court would become one of the great justices of the high court, a titanic figure who served for twenty-three years and whose rulings on the right to privacy and freedom of speech would become landmarks.

The high court justice was eternally proud of his religious faith, a birthright that had guided him and enlarged both his mind and his heart.

Louis D. Brandeis died in 1941.

Forty-five years later, on March 11, 1986, Leo Frank—kidnapped and hanged in 1915 for the murder of Mary Phagan—received a post-humous pardon from the State of Georgia. The pardon, however, did not completely exonerate Frank from the murder in a case that remains shrouded in mystery. It found, instead, that the State of Georgia had denied Leo Frank his constitutional rights by allowing him to be snatched from a so-called secure prison and murdered by anti-Semitic vigilantes.

{ 8 }

The Long Memory
of Evangeline Moore

In 1951, Klansmen placed dynamite beneath the Florida home
of Harry and Harriette Moore. Harry died immediately, his wife days later.
Thurgood Marshall had once slept in their home while on yet another
NAACP legal crusade.

WHEN THE ANNOUNCEMENT CAME that Thurgood Marshall was
being nominated for the U.S. Supreme Court, Evangeline Moore
was suddenly filled with enormous joy. She was a government worker
in 1967, living in the Washington, D.C., region. The hearings were
not televised—as they would come to be in later years—and so when
they started, all she could do was bend an ear when some bit of news
about the proceedings was on the radio. She'd also scan the newspapers. She had no idea if Marshall would be confirmed.

Evangeline Moore originally met the nominee when she was a young girl. Long before violence had altered her family's life forever, she knew quite well the distaste southern senators had for Thurgood Marshall.

FOR THE FIRST twenty-one years of her life, Moore lived in the world that Thurgood Marshall traveled, braved, and survived. It was the 1930s and 1940s world of the Deep South, where men plotted criminal acts in the sunshine, where men slapped one another on their backsides and talked about doing harm to the Moore family, who lived in a clapboard house off the old Dixie Highway in Mims, Florida.

Evangeline Moore—still alive in 2011—is sitting in her Maryland living room. She's eighty-one years old now. She is decades removed from it all, though it never seems to go away. She can't forget that world and those times. Just as she can't forget what those moments felt like when she stepped into her Florida home that January day in 1952, when she moved about slowly, as if she sensed evil were still lurking. In her parents' bedroom, she noticed large indentations in the ceiling when she looked up. The bodies had smacked hard up against the wall, such was the force of the dynamite.

Harry and Harriette Moore met in 1926 at a card party in Cocoa, Florida. The game of the moment was bid whist, and it felt better if some home fries and shrimp were on the table or just being pulled off the stove top. He was of medium build with close-cut hair; she was stout with kind eyes and favored bangs, which drooped over her right eye. Southern days were not always terror filled when it came to the Negro populace: there were picnics with heaps of food, and on fragrant nights folk gathered in modest homes on weekends in Mims and sipped brew, shared laughter, and flicked playing cards back and forth across a table. Crickets sang in the night air. Harry and Harriette soon married and turned into a family of four. Annie was their first-born, then, two years later, Evangeline arrived. She was named after the Henry Wadsworth Longfellow poem. Her father, Harry, loved poetry. The Moores taught in the Negro elementary schools in nearby Titusville. But discrimination gnawed at Harry Moore. In 1934, he founded and became the first president of the Brevard County branch of the NAACP, and that began his communication and letter writing with Thurgood Marshall. Harry Moore had plans: he wanted better wages for the Negroes working in the orange groves; he wanted to start a voter registration drive. He wanted teachers to be given equitable pay. It was dangerous work, and he knew it. "Our kitchen table was my daddy's office," remembers Evangeline Moore.

Thurgood Marshall encouraged Moore to get out and about, and he did, signing up NAACP converts around Florida. Some were too nervous to join up, shaking their heads no out of fear, gently closing the door on him. But he crusaded on, drawing admiration from both Walter White and Thurgood Marshall. "I can remember the first time I saw Thurgood Marshall," Evangeline Moore recalls. "He came down and spent the night at our house in Mims. Daddy picked him up from the train station." Harriette, her mother, prepared supper that evening. Marshall was curious about the girls' schoolwork, asking them questions about history and math. But following supper, the grown-ups had to talk about serious issues, and the girls were shooed off to bed. When Evangeline rose the next morning, her father and Marshall had already left, off to spread the gospel about the NAACP.

Harry Moore did not talk much to his family about his work that took him to all regions of the state. Sometimes he was gone for several days and nights. He'd wade into orange groves and talk to the workers. He'd corral Negro preachers in their homes. Harriette worried herself sick. But it was west Florida—the panhandle—that worried Harriette Moore the most when her husband was away on his investigations. "The panhandle was very dangerous," remembers their daughter.

And the Claude Neal case happened in the panhandle. "That was one of the first cases my daddy investigated," she says.

In the early 1930s, Florida had the highest rate of proportional lynchings of its black citizens of any state in the nation. The most dangerous part of Florida was in the panhandle, in Jackson County, where the town of Marianna sat and where Claude Neal was raised. In the 1930s, Jackson County seemed frozen in time. Many still jawboned about the Civil War skirmish that happened in Marianna in 1864 when Union troops—aided by the Eighty-Second and Eighty-Sixth Negro Regiments—defeated a local force. In 1931, a local newspaper editor, recalling the battle, wrote, "Most of our killed were butchered and beaten to death after they had surrendered by the infernal Negro troops who finding them in their power took advantage of it."

Three small farming towns sat inside Jackson County—Cottondale, Graceville, and Greenwood. Their economies operated on shipping: fruits, cotton, and peanuts. It was close to the Alabama border and relatively isolated. Negroes held no political power, and those who had jobs worked, for the most part, on the white-owned farms.

Claude Neal worked as a laborer and lived with his mother and aunt. He had a reputation of being brassy and talkative. Neal knew nineteen-year-old Lola Cannidy, who hailed from a poor white working-class family. The two had played together as children, and when he grew up, Neal worked awhile on the Cannidy homestead. On October 18, 1934, around noon, Lola—her parents were away visiting relatives—trooped off alone through nearby woods to a water pump. When Cannidy's parents returned home and Lola was missing, an all-out search ensued. Her battered and lifeless body—she had been bludgeoned with a hammer—was found early the next morning in the woods. Sheriff W. Flake Chambliss was quickly on the scene, and so was a local and vengeance-seeking mob. Rumors swirled of two suspects seen in the area, one black, one white, and when the white suspect's alibi was accepted, Claude Neal was accused and arrested. A piece of bloodied cloth was found near the scene, and it was quickly linked to Neal, a damning revelation, proof enough to the mob. Neal's mother admitted she had washed her son's bloodstained clothes the evening before. Within days, a coroner's report—announced publicly—named Neal the murderer. Sheriff Chambliss, as if anticipating the announcement, had spent the previous days with other deputies transporting Neal between jails on both sides of the Florida-Alabama state line for his own safety. For all of the investigation's hastiness, the circumstantial evidence against Neal was powerful. Five days after the murder, secreted inside a Brewton, Alabama, jail—three hundred miles away from the scene of the crime—Neal confessed to the murder and rape of Lola Cannidy.

THEY CALLED THEM "boom stick boys" because they carried makeshift bombs and sticks of dynamite. They were familiar with dynamite because they used it on the stumps of trees they had to blow out of the ground in the orange groves. But they also had other uses for dynamite. They bombed homes of civil rights agitators and voting rights activists. They were the men who plotted crimes in the sunshine. And now three carloads of them were on their way from Jackson County to the small town of Brewton to get Neal, having likely been tipped off by someone connected to Alabama law enforcement. When the men rushed the jail—with guns pointed and sticks of dynamite under the crooks of their arms—they demanded that the cell doors be unlocked so they could look over the Negro prisoners. There was commotion all about. Neal himself was in the back, in the so-called death cell, away from the others, but when he popped to the front of the cell to ask what was going on, he fatefully revealed himself. "One of the men was behind the ones that held guns on me and had an arm full of dynamite," a jailer would later recall. "He said that he would blow the place off the corner if they did not find what they were looking for." They got Neal out of the cell and whisked him away.

Back in Jackson County, Neal was kept hidden and guarded in the woods a few miles from the Cannidy home, near the Chattahoochee River. The plan was to have a public lynching for the benefit of the Cannidy family. Neal's captors announced their intentions in loud and gossipy pronouncements. There were headlines within hours: "Florida to Burn Negro at Stake: Sex Criminal Seized from Brewton Jail, Will Be Mutilated, Set Afire in Extra-legal Vengeance for Deed." That headline, from a nearby Alabama newspaper, caught the attention of the Associated Press, and it quickly got the story out on its wires. The news reached Walter White and Thurgood Marshall. The NAACP rushed off a telegram to Florida's governor, David Sholtz, pleading for intervention. The telegram went unanswered.

A crowd upwards of a thousand had gathered at the Cannidy home on the evening of October 27 for the spectacle. Moonshine was gulped; bonfires were lit. But as the night wore on, those in the woods holding Neal had second thoughts about bringing him before the crowd, fearing that bedlam would result and harm would be done to bystanders. So Neal's captors made a decision: they would lynch Neal themselves and then bring his body before the crowd. The torture began around ten that night. Neal's penis was sliced off. Then it was stuffed into his mouth. Knives sliced in circular motions around his body. A finger, then a toe, was cut off at intervals. Someone lifted an iron, red-hot, and poked and singed his body. His crying out was useless. The captors would hang Neal from a rope, then drop his body to the ground, still alive, only to repeat the maneuver again. When the men were sure that Neal was dead, they tied his body to the back of a car and drove it up to the Cannidy house, whereupon George Cannidy fired three shots into Neal's skull. Eventually, the revelry disbursed, and the men, women, and children ambled home through the darkness.

When Jackson County residents awoke the next morning, many saw Neal's naked body hanging from a tree near the Jackson County Courthouse. It was left to Sheriff Chambliss to cut the body down and bury it. But the whites of Jackson County were not finished. Many, after daybreak, began assaulting Negroes. The melee was terrifying for the town's Negro populace, and after hurried appeals, the governor finally dispatched a caravan of national guardsmen.

In the ensuing months, with outrage growing over the Neal lynching and the fact there had been no state or federal intervention to stop it—with Harry Moore slyly rolling around the panhandle, then sending news clippings and reports about the aftermath up north—there was a renewed effort in Washington to pass a federal antilynching bill. The Maryland senator Millard Tydings—father of Senator Joseph Tydings, Senate Judiciary Committee member during Thurgood Marshall's hearings—was courted to support the legislation but hid behind the argument of states' rights, claiming that local matters were best left in the hands of local officials. Tydings received a letter—wordy but pointed—from one of his state's constituents, Thurgood Marshall. "This bill does not deprive the states of a single right which they now have," Marshall wrote. "When the officers of the state either act on behalf of the mob or fail to use reasonable means to prevent them from acting, as was done in the lynching of Claude Neal in Florida; when daily newspapers told of the proposed outrage and invited all to attend; and when the lynching was over, the lawless element with the sanction of the officials of the state continued to spew their venomous wrath upon innocent, law-abiding tax-paying Negro citizens . . . how in the name of justice and decency can anyone talk of protecting the rights of such a state when it has forfeited all rights to be classed as a state because of open treason and rebellion?" Since 1900, there had been thirty-five hundred recorded lynchings in the United States; there had been only twelve convictions. President Roosevelt agreed with the need for an antilynching bill, but he retreated from southern opposition to it, and the bill gained no traction.

CLAUDE NEAL'S DEATH—no one was arrested for his abduction and killing—introduced Harry Moore to the more dangerous aspect of civil rights work. But it hardly deterred him. When his daughter Evangeline turned eleven, he began taking her on trips, rolling down rural roads in the 1937 Model T Chevy he owned. His wife, Harriette, would pack Vienna sausages and crackers. Evangeline loved the getaways, the sunshine splayed all about them. Her father had brought her along for a reason: she was wonderful at reciting his speeches before crowds. Harry Moore was painfully shy; Evangeline was fearless, at least when it came to appearing in front of audiences. She'd often recite a poem after delivering her father's speech. The speeches—one was titled "The Negro's Struggle for Complete Emancipation"—would often be about black uplift, about the goals of the NAACP, and they would also touch upon Harry Moore's latest lynching investigation. He let them know he knew someone important up north, in New York City, and that someone was Thurgood Marshall. Moore and his family would travel to churches and lodge halls; they'd pass out NAACP literature and plead for folk to join the organization. He'd tell audiences that the NAACP was proud of the work the brave people in Florida were doing. And they'd keep going, out on the road again and again. Many would often walk up to Harry and Harriette Moore afterward and compliment them on their daughter's composure and fine speech. While roaming about, however, Harry was careful with his wife and daughter. He handpicked the places he took them. He took them to places where he could turn right around and get them home before nightfall.

After Thurgood Marshall's 1944 Texas primary voting rights victory, Harry Moore and other Florida NAACP officials emerged from a meeting in the small community of Lake Wales—there had been much discussion of Marshall's victory and the momentum it was inspiring—where they formed the Progressive Voters' League. The aim of the organization, which was led by Moore, was to canvass Florida and encourage ministers and business leaders to assist blacks in registering to vote. It was a bold plan, and Moore knew there would be risks in implementing it. There were rumblings from whites.

Jesse James Payne lived just outside Madison, Florida. He was thirty years old and a Negro sharecropper, which is to say he was poor. In the summer of 1945, Payne asked his employer for a small cash advance. The employer—brother-in-law to the local sheriff—refused the request. Payne couldn't shake the employer's brusque refusal and told the employer he'd report him to the federal government because he had planted too much tobacco, exceeding the allotment. If it was an attempt at blackmail, it was foolish. The next day, Payne found himself accused of attempted rape, the victim being his employer's five-year-old daughter. Payne told family members—and any others who would listen—that the charge was outlandish, that he was being set up, and as he was telling them, he also fled, not trusting any investigation to clear him. A lynch mob pursued him. Gunmen found him and shot him three times. Miraculously, he survived and was rescued by a Florida patrolman, who thought it wise to deliver Payne directly to the Florida State Prison, in Raiford, for both medical care and safety. Payne continued to profess his innocence. Nevertheless, he was taken from Raiford and returned to the jail at Madison. The very night of his return, a lynch mob, realizing the sheriff was asleep in a nearby dwelling, pulled Payne from his cell. The next morning, Jesse James Payne was found on a roadside, dead, having been hanged. As soon as Harry Moore heard the news, he hopped in his 1937 Chevy. Payne's family was in hiding, but Moore found them. He obtained sworn affidavits regarding Payne's argument with his employer and the fact that the employer had pulled a gun on Payne—before any charge of rape had been lodged. Newspapers in St. Petersburg, Tampa, and Jacksonville argued for the firing of the sheriff. The governor refused to do so. A specially formed grand jury brought no indictments in the lynching. Harry Moore got in touch with both Roy Wilkins and Thurgood Marshall. Marshall asked for and received a private meeting with Justice Department officials, who promised an FBI investigation. The Justice Department ultimately concluded, however, it had "no jurisdiction" in the case.

Despite warnings in the succeeding months that promised harm if he continued his investigations, Harry Moore wouldn't retreat. He put together a booklet, titled *Pamphlet on Lynching*, and mailed copies around the country. It landed on the desks of congressmen, college professors, religious leaders, anyone who Moore thought might help his cause. He fired off yet another telegram to Thurgood Marshall, telling him he was "anxious for action" in pursuing local lawsuits to open the voter rolls. Sometimes Marshall just shook his head in wonder at the bravery of the men, women, and children of the civil rights movement.

Harry and Harriette Moore still managed to teach; Harry had actually been appointed a school principal over in Titusville. But at the end of the 1946 school year, officials wouldn't renew the Moores' contracts. Local Negroes felt—as did the Moores—it was because of their activism. A petition was circulated, which was useless. "My parents were fired," Evangeline Moore says all these years later.

In the summer of 1946, the two young daughters of Harry and Harriette Moore couldn't help but wonder, every day, how their parents would make do without their jobs. The family needed an income. Harriette eventually found work as an insurance agent with the Atlanta Life Insurance Company, a highly popular agency throughout the South because it catered to Negroes. Harry Moore became a full-time organizer for the NAACP. His contacts with Thurgood Marshall worked in his favor. Now Harry Moore could travel the state of Florida with one mission: to organize, full-time, potential voters and raise money for the NAACP. He had his eye on Gadsden County, which was located in the dangerous panhandle.

Harry Moore did get Negroes registered in Gadsden County, but it came with a price. One voter whom he had registered had dynamite tossed onto his porch; several others who had been threatened fled the county. Moore told Thurgood Marshall that Gadsden County "remind[s] one very much of Mississippi." But he kept at it, investigating, firing off more telegrams to the NAACP and Marshall, to the state's congressional delegation, even to President Truman himself. In time, he established several dozen local NAACP chapters. He was a tireless worker.

Moore worked on a case that erupted in tiny, rural Groveland, Florida, and that would eventually bring Marshall to Florida yet again. It would become known as the Groveland case.

Norma Padgett, seventeen years old, had been out to a dance hall with her husband, Willie, the evening of July 16, 1949. Their car got stuck on a rural road and wouldn't start back up. Two young Negro men, Walter Irvin and Samuel Shepherd, who were army vets, happened upon them and stopped to help. The car's battery was dead; it was not going to start. Willie, semiliterate, poor, but accustomed to bossing Negroes, had an edge in his voice as he commanded the two to push harder. Shepherd in particular didn't like his tone. Norma, worldly in a backwoods sort of way—she was known to party with Negroes—didn't want trouble and thought to share the couple's whiskey bottle with the two Samaritans. She passed it from Shepherd to her husband, Willie, who scoffed at her. "Do you think I'm going to drink behind a nigger?" Shepherd grabbed Willie Padgett around the neck and threw him violently to the ground. Perhaps it was cowardice, or maybe just the whiskey slowing his reflexes, but Willie Padgett did not fight back and simply stayed down. He had insulted two black men who had gotten a taste of freedom in Uncle Sam's army. Norma Padgett had never seen such a sight: a Negro accosting a white man with such impunity.

By the next day, Norma Padgett had concocted a story, saying that she had been raped by some Negro men and her husband left on the road near Groveland—left for dead. A rider took her out to look for her husband, Willie. Oddly enough, Willie was found, upright and unharmed. But the terrible tale Norma had unspooled was now cascading around the community.

Like always, men reached for guns and vowed vengeance. Once such a tale had escaped the bottle, there was no getting it back inside. In a short time, three Negroes were arrested: Charles Greenlee, Samuel Shepherd, and Walter Irvin. (Greenlee just happened to have been in the wrong place at the wrong time—a convenient enough Negro.) They were quickly beaten by deputies, extracting confessions as men howled and bled. It was a black man's worst nightmare. A fourth suspect, Ernest Thomas, was running, unsure of what he was supposed to have done but having the sense to flee when he heard what was taking place. He was cornered, unarmed, and shot dead by law enforcement on July 26 after being chased into the swamps by bloodhounds who had been charging ahead of upwards of a thousand men. "That is him," Norma Padgett said when taken to a funeral home to identify a man whose face was riddled with bullets—a man she had never in her life seen before.

It soon became clear to the Negroes in the community that a rape had never taken place. The suspects recanted their confessions, admitting they'd been beaten. That hardly mattered: Negro homes were destroyed in a spasm of violence by Klansmen, and Negro families told to flee. Thurgood Marshall weighed in: "The resources of the association will be thrown behind the defense of these boys, and at the same time, we will insist upon protection of other Negroes in the area."

When it came to a timeline—of where the suspects were when Norma Padgett was supposedly raped—their attorney proved that none of them could have raped her. But the Florida attorney general scoffed at that reasoning, claiming that Negro men consummated their sex act with blinding and even inhuman speed. "Mrs. Padgett," he told the jurors, "didn't have any idea how long the four negroes took to rape her. While sexual intercourse can be a prolonged affair in some settings, it is probable that these four negroes, goaded to a sexual frenzy by the prospect of having intercourse with a young white woman, took about as much time as a bull put to a cow in heat. Cover her, a few rapid thrusts, all over, and off again."

At trial, death sentences were meted out to all save Greenlee, who had been only sixteen years old when accused of the crimes. The all-white jury needed no medical evidence to support their beyond-a-reasonable-doubt guilty verdicts. The two defense lawyers were chased from town immediately following the trial. "Horror in the Sunny South," shouted the *New York Post* headline about the case.

The U.S. Supreme Court ordered a new trial, citing the tension surrounding the given confessions. "Won new trial for Walter Irvin in Supreme Court of the United States," Thurgood Marshall wired to Dellia Irvin about her son.

It was on April 9, 1951, that the Supreme Court overturned the convictions of Walter Irvin and Samuel Shepherd. Justice Robert Jackson wrote that the Groveland convictions didn't meet "any civilized conception of due process of law."

On November 6, 1951, while transporting the prisoners Shepherd and Irvin from prison back to the Lake County jail to await another hearing, Sheriff Willis McCall pulled off onto a little-traveled road. He slowed his car, telling the handcuffed prisoners something was wrong with it. He ordered them out. And when they got out of the car, their backs to McCall, he pulled his gun and shot both, killing Shepherd and—unbeknownst to him—leaving Irvin riddled with bullets but alive. McCall quickly concocted a story claiming he had been attacked. Thurgood Marshall received the news in his New York City home. He bolted for the Florida panhandle.

From a hospital bed, Irvin told the FBI and Thurgood Marshall what the sheriff had done. He told the agents that right after McCall shot them, he dashed to his car radio. "I heard him say 'I got rid of them, killed the sons of bitches' but I still did not say anything . . . I heard him say 'Pull around here right quick . . . these sons of bitches tried to jump on me and I have done a damn good job of it.' I wondered what he meant by that, because we hadn't done that . . . and then in about five or ten minutes Deputy Yates was there."

The local prosecutor refused to bring charges against the sheriff. Again, Irvin was sentenced to death. Greenlee would be paroled in 1962. Thurgood Marshall made a promise to Irvin's mother he would save her son from his death sentence. He delivered: in 1955, Governor LeRoy Collins commuted Irvin's death sentence. Irvin was finally released from prison in 1968 for a crime he never committed.

HARRY MOORE kept working beyond the horrors of the Groveland case. He tried to calm NAACP members who recoiled at a hike, in 1949, in yearly dues, from $1 to $2. "I just wish we could have increased the membership fee in 1944 or 1945, when everybody was making plenty of money," Moore confided to an NAACP official. "A extra dollar would not have been noticed much then."

But there was also joy in Moore's life. His wife, Harriette, who missed teaching, returned to the classroom, getting a job at an elementary school. The only disappointment was that the school was one hundred miles away. They moved closer to the school, returning to their Mims home on weekends and special family occasions. Harry didn't mind the move; Harriette loved teaching, and she had been so supportive of his work. The Moore girls were now away at college, at Bethune-Cookman, a mostly black college in Daytona Beach. Harry missed Evangeline giving speeches for him on the road, but he steeled his own nerves as he climbed up on stages in lodge halls and churches.

When Evangeline graduated from Bethune-Cookman in 1951, she began working in the registrar's office on campus. She was whiling time away—and earning a little money—until she could find something more promising. One of the campus deans asked her to take the federal civil service exam. "They had just started recruiting from black schools," she says of the federal government. "I wasn't thinking about leaving home at all." Her father also convinced her it would be a good idea. Evangeline took the exam in Daytona Beach and was soon boarding a train in nearby Titusville to take a job she had been offered in Washington with the stenography pool at the Department of Labor. Harry and Harriette saw their younger daughter off. Everyone was happy.

She arrived in Washington on a weekend, and Evangeline Moore went straight to the YWCA and checked in. She rose excitedly on her first day to report to work. Before reaching the Department of Labor, she stopped at a local drugstore that also served food. She wanted breakfast and sat down at a counter. She ordered coffee and a pastry. The waitress delivered her order to her in a bag, then told her she couldn't eat there. She had come face-to-face with segregation in Washington, and it appalled her. "Here I am in the nation's capital," she would remember decades later, "and I couldn't eat." But she enjoyed her job. Eventually, she moved out of the YWCA into a rooming house where students from Howard University boarded. She delighted in receiving mail from home but could not tell from her father's or mother's letters if anything was amiss in Florida. Evangeline's parents kept their letters to her airy and light.

But in 1951, the state of Florida remained a very dangerous place for Negroes. In the spring of that year, Melvin Womack endured a flogging and then was shot and killed. Womack's brother-in-law, a janitor, had been accused of walking into a girls' bathroom filled with white students; Womack was mistaken for his brother-in-law. It was later revealed that the brother-in-law, after suffering a brutal clubbing—and a gunshot that he, unlike Womack, survived—had been wrongfully accused himself.

In the early fall of that year, Negroes, under armed guard, integrated a Miami public housing project. Two of the empty units were blasted with dynamite. (There were also attacks on Jewish synagogues in the area.) Harry Moore kept a shotgun in his house and also packed a .32-caliber pistol. "I'll take a few of them with me if it comes to that," he confided to Harriette and others. Harry Moore considered nothing more important than the safety of his family.

But nothing would stop Moore from doing his work. That December, Walter White and Thurgood Marshall pointed to Moore's influence when they appeared in the state to address rallies on behalf of justice. The Groveland case remained on the minds of many at the time. "We seek no special favors," Moore wrote that month in a letter to Governor Fuller Warren, referring to the case, "but certainly we have a right to expect justice and equal protection of the laws even for the humblest Negro." Warren—who had admitted his own former Klan membership—didn't bother to answer Moore's letter.

With Christmas approaching, both Harry and Harriette looked forward to being back in Mims with their two daughters. There would be large meals and holiday presents. They planned to drive Evangeline around to visit relatives. They both were home on December 18. Harriette busied herself getting the house ready for the holidays. Harry—when not thinking of his NAACP duties—worked in a little orange grove he had been planting.

But up in Washington, Evangeline Moore was having a difficult time securing a reservation on the train in the days leading up to the holiday. The bookings had been so feverish, in fact, that she couldn't get a seat until December 26, the day after Christmas. When she told her family over the telephone that she would miss Christmas by a day, there was no less joy in their voices about her imminent arrival. "We'll hold the presents," her mother promised her.

On Christmas Day 1951, the Moores—Harry, Harriette, and their other daughter, Annie—drove over to the nearby home of Annie Simms, Harriette's mother, for Christmas dinner. Harry's mother, Rosa, was also visiting. At the door, they were met with delicious aromas. Annie Simms was dismayed Evangeline was not among the

arriving guests but delighted at news she was on her way. Those walking through Annie Simms's front door, however, did make a fuss over
another family member: Harriette's brother George was home on
leave from the army in Korea. More than a dozen people sat down at
Annie Simms's table for dinner. The talk seesawed from world affairs
to who might want second helpings of food, to Harry's work with
the NAACP, to Harry and Harriette Moore's twenty-fifth wedding
anniversary—also on Christmas Day—to the giddiness about seeing
Evangeline again.

The Moores arrived back home that evening and looked forward to
a little relaxation before bedtime. Harriette set some dessert plates out
and sliced into a fruitcake. They were a still-in-love couple, married
twenty-five years, and devoted to the fight for equality just as long. It
was around 10:00 p.m. when Harry and Harriette Moore finally went
to bed. The Christmas lights remained on and were twinkling.

Evangeline Moore spent her time on the Silver Meteor train en
route to Florida—in the segregated compartment—reading a novel.
She thought of her parents, her cousins, her grandmother, the faces
she'd surely recognize on the streets of Titusville, where she would get
off. She thought of how she had only been away for five months, yet
it seemed so much longer. When her eyes wouldn't let her continue
reading, she dozed off. She couldn't wait to get home. She arrived in
Titusville the next day, full of joy and excitement. When she stepped
off the train, she spotted family members: aunts, uncles, her sister,
Annie. Her eyes kept roving. She didn't see her parents. She thought
it was a little odd, but she didn't say anything. Maybe her parents were
home putting the finishing touches on the day-after-Christmas meal.
She hadn't expected to see her uncle George. She had always admired
his coolness, his steadiness. Everyone began walking toward the car,
and now—with no mention yet of her parents—she started to worry.

"I got in the backseat and said, 'Where's my mom and dad?'"

Her uncle George, behind the wheel, hadn't started the car up yet.
He turned around to face her.

"Your house was bombed last night," he told her. "Your dad's dead.
Your mother is in the hospital."

She didn't cry or let loose any anguished sounds from her throat.
She just told her uncle George she didn't believe a word he'd said. It

was Christmastime. How could anyone die—be blown up!—at Christmastime in their own home, their own bedroom? It made absolutely no sense. The car was silent. She finally said, "The only way I'll believe it is if I see him." They wondered if she had gone into shock already. Uncle George started the car. They were headed to Sanford Hospital, thirty miles away. It was the closest hospital to Mims that accepted Negroes.

They took her to her mother first. Harriette Moore was conscious, and she brightened a bit at the sight of her daughter. But she was in severe pain. There were wounds in her stomach. The doctor told her family members that if Harriette Moore could hang on for a week, she might make it. Evangeline was then taken to see her father's mangled body. Things seemed blurry to her, dizzying.

J. Edgar Hoover had been contacted; the FBI chief had agents immediately on their way from field offices in Jacksonville, Miami, and Orlando to start an investigation into the bombing. Thurgood Marshall was crestfallen. He had slept in the Moore home, several feet from their bedroom where the dynamite exploded.

For several days, Evangeline, as if webbed in a horrible dream, kept trooping back to the hospital and her mother's side, well aware of the doctor's warning. Her uncle George would not allow the two Moore girls to sleep in the same place on two consecutive nights: he feared whoever had planted the dynamite might intend to kill the entire family. "We were in a different location every night," remembers Evangeline Moore. "No one knew where we were at except Uncle George."

News flashed across both national and international wires about the Harry and Harriette Moore bombing, how dynamite had ripped through their house on one of the holiest days of the year. President Truman was notified; editorials in *The New York Times* and *Newsweek* condemned it. To the editors of the *Pittsburgh Courier*, the bombing represented "a point of no return in American race relations." Eleanor Roosevelt discussed the bombing at the United Nations. One of the first telegrams into the offices of Florida's governor, Fuller Warren, came from Moore's friend Thurgood Marshall. Marshall warned that "unless they can be secure from lawlessness no one in Florida is safe from destruction." Harry Moore was the first NAACP official in the nation to be murdered. Many connected Moore's murder to his ongoing investigation into the Groveland shootings as well as the many unsolved lynchings in the state.

When Thurgood Marshall arrived—he wanted to make sure the FBI was doing everything it could and also check in on the Moore family—the bureau quickly assigned a young agent, Wayne Swinney, to drive Marshall around. As Swinney would recall, the bureau was "worried that physical harm might come to Marshall since racial tension was very high after the bombing." Marshall met with agents and filled them in on the various projects he knew Moore had been working on over the years. The agents scribbled notes down furiously. Marshall fretted about the Moore family. But he was not on the ground very long, because the FBI insisted he finish his business and leave: it feared someone might try to kill him. It was Swinney's responsibility to get Marshall back to the airport, and he did. At the counter, though, an Eastern Air Lines agent said they were "booked solid," and Marshall couldn't leave that day. Swinney snapped, "I don't care how booked you are, you better find a seat for this guy so he can get out of here." The airline found a seat.

Harriette Moore wanted to attend her husband's funeral, but it was out of the question. Her most severe injuries were in her chest and abdomen, although her head had swelled to twice its normal size. She instructed her daughters to buy a simple coffin for Harry, reminding them that she and Harry were plain people. She died nine days after the bombing. "There isn't much left to fight back for," she had said just before her death. "My home is wrecked. My children are grown up. They don't need me." Upon her death, her daughters sank even deeper into grief.

The NAACP announced a $5,000 reward for any information leading to the conviction of those responsible for the murders.

AS HARRY AND HARRIETTE lay sleeping, the four men were on the move. They certainly would have already opened Christmas gifts with their families and filled their stomachs with Christmas food. Maybe they had already started getting liquored up before they hit the night air and had their rendezvous out there on the old Dixie Highway. They rolled along in two separate cars. All four—Ed Spivey, Joe Cox,

Earl Brooklyn, and Tillman Belvin—were Klansmen, and they considered it crazy luck that thick fog had rolled across the landscape: it offered extra cover for their mission. They cut the engine before they reached the Moore home. Not many people were out on the roads—it was Christmas night; there was the worrisome fog—but they still were careful not to make eye contact with anyone passing by. Still, one driver would recall seeing the men and thought they looked like "bank robbers dividing the loot." Brooklyn and Belvin stayed behind, while Spivey and Cox tiptoed their way up to the Moore house. They were carrying sticks of dynamite. They had made and studied a crude map of the interior of the Moore dwelling, devising it from memory following a break-in while the Moores had earlier been away. For weeks, they had been planning, guffawing over beers at drinking establishments over in Fort Pierce. They knew the exact location—northeast corner—of the master bedroom. The twinkling Christmas lights caught their attention but hardly stymied them. Cox and Spivey crept about closer, moving like feral cats. Spivey could see inside. It was quiet.

The house, as was customary with homes in Florida, sat eighteen inches up off the sandy terrain. Cox crawled underneath the master bedroom and roped the dynamite in place. Afterward, as quietly as possible, he and Spivey made their way back to their cars. Then the two cars rolled away.

At 10:20, the house exploded. Doors flew off hinges; windows shattered; the bed that Harry and Harriette were sleeping in rose up off the floor—like in a ghost story—and crashed back down. Their daughter Annie, miraculously unhurt, jumped up, feeling sheer terror: She rushed to her parents' bedroom. She saw blood; they were covered in rubble and debris; she heard moans; she screamed; there was a hole beneath where the bed should have been and the bed had dropped into the hole—as if they were buried alive. She screamed more; she ran to get help, bursting through the back door of the house. The explosion shook cars on the roadway; some thought there had been a gas plant explosion. George Simms, her uncle, who was sleeping in a house down the road, heard the explosion, and it rousted him. He was met by Annie's screams as soon as he went outside. He ran down the road and into the house and saw what Annie had seen: Harry and Harriette writhing in unimaginable pain. He knew he had to get them to a hospital, so he ran back and got his car. He was joined by a couple of other relatives, and they placed, as gingerly as possible, Harry and Harriette into a car. There was a hospital in nearby Titusville, but it didn't admit Negroes, so George pointed the car in the direction of Sanford, thirty miles away, where there was a hospital that would take them. Shortly into the drive, Harry gurgled up a good deal of blood, and it terrified his daughter.

By the next night—with a crowd of hundreds standing nearby and gawking—FBI agents were crawling around beneath the house looking for clues. A little Negro boy, without anyone's directing him to, also scooted underneath the house, banging a stick. He was trying to help: he told the agents he had to do it to force the rats to scurry lest they get in their way. The agents thanked him. "The house was in shambles, the bedroom was—it looked like a cyclone had hit it," an FBI agent who was on the scene would recall. One of the more bizarre structural revelations in the wake of the explosion was the chimney: it had blown up off the house, only to drop right back down into its original spot, like a piece of a puzzle lost then summoned back into place. Agents were constantly huddling, taking notes, scanning the crowd of those gathered for possible clues. Perhaps the culprit had circled back just to gawk at the destruction? Within two days, FBI agents—in a county with more than a few known Klansmen—had a suspect in mind: George Simms, Harry Moore's brother-in-law. Simms and his relatives were aghast. But he had to endure the questioning. The agents had zeroed in on Simms because he had military training with explosives. But Simms's alibi—he was asleep in a house across the road from the Moore home—checked out. The FBI chief, J. Edgar Hoover, wanted results and sent in more agents.

It was Richard Ashe, an FBI Klan undercover operative, who offered a crucial name: Earl Brooklyn. Brooklyn had a notorious reputation in the county for kidnapping Negroes and taking them into the woods for beatings. Ashe revealed that Brooklyn told him—unaware, of course, of Ashe's connections to law enforcement—four people were involved in the Moore bombing: Spivey, Cox, Belvin, and Brooklyn himself. Investigators began questioning all four men. They were fidgety; their alibis didn't check out on deeper probing. The agents followed other leads, stretching across four states, but they kept coming back to the same four names. Still, there were no arrests. But nationally, the spotlight on the horrific murders would not go away. In January and February 1952, massive rallies were held across the country. On January 27, in Pittsburgh, twenty-five hundred people appeared at a protest. Roy Wilkins of the NAACP addressed an emergency meeting in Jacksonville. Wilkins was normally a reserved man and did not have a reputation for being an electrifying speaker. On this day, he changed that perception: "Since Christmas Day they've found some tracks," he said of the FBI. "That's not progress. There are tracks all over Florida. If it had been a white couple that was killed, they would have had a hundred blacks in jail by sunrise—any hundred . . . they thought that because of what happened to Moore we would be afraid to meet here. But those people don't understand us. Bombs bring us together." Those in their seats were applauding wildly, rising to their feet, wiping away their tears. He went on: "We're going to turn the South upside down."

The agents kept searching and interviewing potential witnesses and suspects. They sent Teletypes almost daily to Hoover because he demanded it. But months passed and passed, the South remained upright, and there were no indictments. It proved difficult for the agents to get anyone to talk on the record, such was the level of fear in the county. The agents also were concerned about being ambushed and murdered themselves. Then some spooky things began to happen. On March 29, 1952, the day after he had endured intensive questioning by FBI agents, Joe Cox, a leading suspect, picked up a shotgun and committed suicide. In August 1952, Tillman Belvin died. On December 25, 1952, exactly one year after the bombing, Earl Brooklyn died. Both deaths were attributed to natural causes. Still, rumors flew: Had the men turned on one another?

In February 1953, a grand jury did take up a massive state bombing case—which included the Moore bombing—and in June brought back perjury indictments against seven Ku Klux Klansmen. But not a single indictment related to the Moore case. In 1955, federal officials gave up and turned their findings over to the State of Florida. But no one expected that to yield anything, and it did not. In August 1955, the U.S. attorney in Florida, James L. Guilmartin, said the Moore case "did not develop any evidence showing a violation of the victims' civil rights." Those who wanted justice for the Moores felt crushed.

And there were many. It was estimated that during his lifetime Harry Moore helped more than 100,000 black Floridians register to vote.

One FBI agent, despite the bureau's lack of success in the case, would come to see some reward in the probe because it "lit a fire in Washington that led to an investigation of the Ku Klux Klan all over the country."

But the case of Harry and Harriette Moore—lifelong sweethearts—did not end in 1955 with those FBI and Florida law enforcement decisions to abandon the case.

In 1978, an ailing Ed Spivey contacted the Brevard County sheriff and Brevard state attorney. Spivey told them he had some information related to the case. He said Joe Cox participated in the bombing and had told him about it. Spivey's intimate knowledge of the bombing persuaded Florida officials to reopen the case. Still, they were not able to bring indictments, and Spivey himself died two years later. (The state attorney who reopened the case in 1978 paid a price: he lost his subsequent bid for reelection; black voters lamented the defeat.)

Eleven years after Spivey's death, in 1991, a woman contacted state officials claiming her husband had been involved with the Moore bombing. Governor Lawton Chiles ordered an inquiry, but again officials came up with nothing.

In 2003, Florida had an attorney general by the name of Charlie Crist. A Republican, he was known as a friend to both environmentalists and supporters of civil rights. (Crist was later the first sitting Florida governor to ever speak before an NAACP convention.) An appeal was made to Crist to reopen the Moore investigation, many realizing the bombers—and probably their co-conspirators—were already dead. In 2004, Crist agreed to reopen the case, and he vowed to put muscle behind it.

The new probe was directed by the attorney general's Office of Civil Rights and aided by the Florida Department of Law Enforcement, which had done little over the years regarding the bombing except gain the enmity of those who suspected a cover-up. But as months stretched on, the new Moore inquiry was proving to be the most extensive investigation ever undertaken in Florida concerning a civil rights murder case. Investigators conducted a hundred interviews. They excavated the crime scene using state-of-the-art equipment. They pored anew over old records. The 335-page report, released by Crist on August 16, 2006, after a twenty-month investigation, was both devastating and heartbreaking for the Moore family descendants. Four men were identified as the culprits: Earl Brooklyn, Joe Cox, Tillman Belvin, and Ed Spivey, who did not identify himself as one of the killers when he spoke to investigators in 1978. The report cites a reign of terror that permeated the Mims and Titusville areas—as well as the panhandle—during the time that Harry Moore launched his civil rights investigations and sought to register blacks to vote. It was Cox, the report allows, who probably planted the dynamite. "It is very likely," the report stated, "that there are person(s) still alive that have information about the Moore investigation that neither have nor will they ever come forward for whatever the reason." The report concluded with a haunting coda: "So many people suffered at the hands of a few."

It is true, and unfortunate, that for years Harry Moore seemed to drift from history. The 1960s—in all of its painful and prideful marching and protests—came roaring into view. There were other heroes, other martyrs.

Evangeline Moore, as years passed, would rarely discuss the bombing. She migrated—as so many had done—up north. Her sister, Annie, two years older than Evangeline, died when she was forty-four years old. No one could convince Evangeline that her sister did not die from the heartbreak she endured after the deaths of their parents.

From 1951 on, Evangeline Moore has suffered from depression. The holiday seasons have proved nearly unbearable. The Crist report seemed to help. Then—as if the State of Florida were trying to atone for the tragedy that befell Harry and Harriette Moore—came tangible proof of her parents' legacy. In 1996, an $18 million courthouse—the Harry T. and Harriette V. Moore Justice Center—was dedicated in Viera, Florida. Brevard Community College named its multicultural center after Harry Moore. There now stands a museum and park at the site of the bombing. Sometimes the snowbirds cruising through the state will drive over to Mims—forty miles from Orlando—and get a pretty good introduction to the life and sacrifices of Harry and Harriette Moore.

· · ·

SO, AN ELDERLY LADY sits all alone in a house in her living room in Bowie, Maryland, nearly sixty-five years removed from a Florida bombing and her memory of Thurgood Marshall's walking in the front door of her family home. She is grieving still. Evangeline Moore has read and reread the Crist report, fully believing, as the report intimated, that there are still people alive who had a part in the bombing. She wants them brought to justice. (In 2007, President George W. Bush signed the Emmett Till Unsolved Civil Rights Crime Act into law. Its purpose was to help heal a nation's wounds that continued to fester because of civil rights murders. But so much time had passed that even many supporters—while appreciating the expressions of the act—considered it little more than symbolic. And yet, in 2010 the FBI opened an investigation into the murder of the lynching victim Claude Neal, one of Harry Moore's first investigations.)

Evangeline Moore still sees a psychiatrist. She has been married three times; none of the marriages lasted. She wonders how much of her life's disappointments and anguish can be traced back to December 25, 1951, a day evil men lurked beneath her family home in the shadow of the family Christmas tree.

A couple of years after the release of the Crist report, some cold case investigators started poking into the case yet again, and they gave Evangeline Moore a renewed feeling of optimism. But the case still went nowhere. She still writes letters to the Justice Department. She has good things to say about J. Edgar Hoover. It's a sentiment that cuts against the grain of Hoover's reputation held by civil rights advocates who point to the bureau's wiretapping of Martin Luther King Jr. But she feels Hoover truly tried to solve the case. She says the NAACP abandoned her father, even as he continued to do NAACP work. She can recite the last names of those cited for the bombing—Spivey, Cox, Brooklyn, Belvin—like some people can recite names of particular jazz albums, even if she fairly spits their names from her lips. It all disturbs her sleep. Those men might as well be under her house now, crawling.

Sometimes it is difficult to imagine what Evangeline Moore hopes for: the last of the identified men, Spivey, died in 1980. There have been buildings erected in her parents' name, a public television tribute to her father. "I am determined," she says, "that before I close my eyes for good, my dad have his proper recognition."

Perhaps it's only understandable if you are her, having heard the train conductor's voice lift you excitedly up out of your seat as you pulled in to the train station that December morning in 1951 with a full heart, with a redcap hustling to help you with your luggage, only to have it all replaced by the darkest kind of nightmare.

So, in the summer of 1967, it all came back—her father and mother, her sister, and Thurgood Marshall. The president had nominated her father's friend for the U.S. Supreme Court, and she could hardly believe it. She'd corner friends in her neighborhood and get to talking about it. She rattled on and on about the nomination to friends in the South. She saw his picture in her cherished Negro magazines that she subscribed to. She had heard about those first two days of hearings, about the senators' giving Marshall such a hard time. She had no idea if he would be confirmed. And that only made Evangeline Moore pray that much harder.

ONE OF THE FINAL political campaigns Harry Moore was involved with came in 1950, a year before his death. It was a Democratic primary campaign that pitted the incumbent U.S. senator Claude Pepper—who had been an early supporter of Roosevelt's New Deal while in the Senate—against George Smathers, a World War II vet and current congressman. Many told Smathers not to run against Pepper, reminding him that in the state's history no incumbent Florida senator had ever lost a reelection campaign. But Smathers had a multilayered strategy: he would assail Pepper as a liberal and link him to pro-Communist groups, court the businessmen who ran the orange groves in the state, and attack the rise of Negro voters—voters who had benefited from Thurgood Marshall's 1944 Texas primary voting rights case. Of all the southern states, Florida had the largest increase in the Negro voter rolls in the aftermath of the Texas primary case. During the Pepper-Smathers primary battle, *The Miami Times*, which catered to a black audience, opined that "not since the Reconstruction Period have Negroes representing a state-wide political organization been able to sit down and talk with high state officials as full-fledged voting citizens." Smathers himself ran a newspaper advertisement that featured pictures of Negroes registering to vote. "Doesn't this make your blood boil?" Smathers asked in the ad.

It took Smathers little time to attack any hint of racial moderation on Pepper's part. Pepper had once been photographed with the black activist Paul Robeson, and Smathers reminded white voters of it. As well, Pepper had supported, during wartime, President Truman's Fair Employment Practices Commission (FEPC), which was an attempt to outlaw discrimination in the defense industry. "This vicious legislation," Smathers said, "conceived in Communistic Russia in 1917, is sponsored by Senator Pepper in an attempt to regiment and control our way of life, and with whom we work, worship and associate." (Smathers was exaggerating Pepper's role in the FEPC, as the legislation—which died from southern filibustering—was hardly Pepper's brainchild. And Pepper distanced himself from the legislation the further along it went in committee.)

Pepper was hardly anyone's idea of a liberal when it came to race, telling audiences he believed in separation of the races. Something else made Pepper quite vulnerable: he had shown an affinity for Stalin and had been a supporter of the onetime vice presidential candidate Henry Wallace, a genuine liberal, an appellation that was anathema to most white Florida voters. Harry Moore encouraged his voters to cast their votes for Pepper, linking Smathers to wide support among Klansmen. Smathers further alienated Moore when he charged that union officials were helping to register Negroes. Smathers charged that "some Negroes had received $1.50 and $2.00 for registering, and in Miami we are told some were handed free movie passes." The heated campaign was covered by both national and state media. The *St. Petersburg Times* charged that Smathers had launched his campaign "with an appeal to ignorance, and prejudice and sly bigotry."

On election eve, both candidates felt good and predicted victory. Smathers stunned Pepper by winning by more than 67,000 votes. National publications were quick to weigh in. "The defeat of Claude Pepper in Florida," claimed *The New Republic*, "demonstrates the power of the smear. Senator Pepper was driven from the office he had held with honor and distinction for 14 years by an emotional appeal to the basest prejudices of the Florida voters." *The New York Times* said that Smathers "spent much of his considerable energies in attacking Senator Pepper for being too friendly to Negroes and to Communists." George Smathers won his general election and was soon headed to Washington.

In Washington, Smathers became known as a sociable sort. He liked parties and anyplace where the beautiful people congregated. He forged friendships with Senators John F. Kennedy and Lyndon B. Johnson. And his affiliation with Negroes went only as far as their serving him drinks and platters of food. George Smathers voted against all civil rights bills that came before him. He considered it a prized moment when he was invited to join the Senate Judiciary Committee. By the 1960s, Smathers had been in Washington long enough to be considered a personal friend of President Kennedy's. (He attended Kennedy's wedding.) He also hosted President Johnson on his boat in Florida—seagulls overhead, the wine flowing, the boat bobbing.

In Florida in 1963, plans were unveiled—partially overseen by Smathers himself—and a committee named to commemorate the four hundredth anniversary of St. Augustine, known as the nation's oldest city. Not a single Negro was on the committee, which struck the Negro populace as insensitive inasmuch as St. Augustine had once been a bustling slave market. The Southern Christian Leadership Conference announced plans to boycott the segregated city and bring attention to the fact Negroes were not allowed to eat in its restaurants or swim in its local swimming pools. By late spring of the following year, the boycott was in full motion, with local Negroes and college students being routinely arrested for picketing. The Ku Klux Klan, in full view of law enforcement, taunted and kicked the protesters. At the Monson Motor Lodge in town, Negroes jumped into the all-white swimming pool. The manager screamed and threatened to pour acid into the pool, which he did, emptying it. He followed that up with sending an alligator into the pool. Martin Luther King Jr. vowed to come to the city. So did Mary Peabody, a white patrician and mother of Governor Endicott Peabody of Massachusetts. She aimed to join the protesters. She soon arrived in the city with several quite prim and proper lady friends, among them Esther Burgess, a very light-skinned Negro whose ethnicity was nearly indecipherable. Peabody thought her presence just might go a long way in desegregating the city. She and her friends went straight to McCartney's, a local restaurant, sat down, and ordered. The waitress was kind, scribbled down their orders.

"How nice it is that you serve colored people here," she told the waitress.

"We don't," the waitress told her.

"Well," Mrs. Peabody answered, looking in the direction of her friend, "Mrs. Burgess is colored."

They were quickly evicted, although Burgess, the Negro, was arrested.

Peabody and company were aghast. It didn't take long before they too were arrested, landing inside the St. Johns County jail. Peabody was a sight to behold inside the jail—"every inch the Boston blueblood," as one story noted. She looked lovely in her pink suit.

One of those previously arrested for protesting at the jail was struck by the sight of Mrs. Peabody.

"You look just like Miss Eleanor Roosevelt."

"We are cousins," Mrs. Peabody answered.

An announcement was made that Dr. King was coming to St. Augustine. Before his arrival, the address of the cottage he was to stay in was publicized in the newspaper. Hooligans riddled the house with bullets; no one was hurt. When King reached St. Augustine—rowdy Klansmen were awaiting him—he proceeded to the Monson Motor Lodge. The owner rebuffed him and announced to the press on June 11 that his restaurant would remain segregated. King was quickly handcuffed and arrested. Movement followers feared he would be lynched inside the local jail. Senator Smathers didn't like the national publicity that came with King's arrest. He wrote King a letter, promising to pay his bail—if King would proceed to leave the state of Florida. King refused. He eventually paid his own bail.

Three years later, Thurgood Marshall was facing members of the Senate Judiciary Committee. And Johnson aides had to inform Marshall that even though Senator Smathers had personal friendships with both President Kennedy and President Johnson, they could not get him to come around on the nomination. Smathers was already so sure of his vote on the Marshall nomination that he felt no need to even show up for the hearings. Marshall began to feel the deck was stacked against him and complained bitterly to the White House.

DAY THREE

{ 9 }

Return of the Prosecutors

The Harvard Law School graduate and North Carolina senator Sam Ervin,
perhaps the foremost constitutional law expert in the country. Senators
Eastland and McClellan were confident Ervin could damage the Marshall
nomination enough to force a filibuster.

B Y THE TIME THE THIRD DAY of confirmation hearings began at
10:30 a.m., Thurgood Marshall had already been subjected to more
hours of questioning than any other nominee in history. It was an
unsettling omen, and White House aides did not like it.

It was in 1925 that a Supreme Court nominee first appeared before
the Judiciary Committee. Harlan Stone, nominated by President
Coolidge, had been summoned because of concerns about his role as
attorney general when he investigated the Montana senator Burton K.
Wheeler. Wheeler had demanded the U.S. attorney general, Harry
Daugherty—Stone's predecessor—be investigated for his depart-

ment's lack of aggressiveness in the Teapot Dome oil leasing scandal. Daugherty felt enough pressure to resign in 1924. It didn't stop there. The Justice Department then indicted Senator Wheeler for alleged shenanigans with his Montana law practice. Wheeler scoffed, claiming the Justice Department was seeking revenge against him for having driven out Daugherty. The Senate investigated Wheeler and fully exonerated him. It did not sit well with Stone, now the U.S. attorney general, that the matter had been left to the Senate to investigate one of its own. Stone continued the investigation of Wheeler, despite many encouraging him to drop it. When Stone received his high court nomination, senators demanded he appear before them, a most unusual order but one President Coolidge reluctantly agreed to in an attempt to salvage the nomination. Stone drew plaudits for his five-hour ordeal and was easily confirmed. Wheeler himself was eventually cleared of all charges.

For many years, it took a set of unique circumstances, tinged with controversy, to get a nominee to appear before the Senate Judiciary Committee. In 1939, Felix Frankfurter was obliged to appear because of scandalous charges aligning him with Communist sympathizers. "My attitude and outlook on relevant matters have been fully expressed over a period of years and are easily accessible," he told the committee. "I should think it not only bad taste but inconsistent with the duties of the office for which I have been nominated for me to attempt to supplement my past record by present declarations. That is all I have to say." Then he left.

Not until 1955—thirty years after Harlan Stone's surprise appearance—did the Judiciary Committee officially begin making it a requirement for nominees to appear before it.

In 1957, William Brennan's questioning was completed in a brisk three hours.

Thurgood Marshall was not so lucky.

The nominee had been privately grumbling about the hearings because he did not know when they might end. The lack of a time frame was part of the Eastland strategy in hopes of rattling the nominee. And even if they were to end on any given day, Marshall knew he had to suffer the possibility of being called back for more questioning and testimony.

Marshall might have thought he was finished with Senators Ervin and McClellan as the third day of hearings got under way, but he would quickly find out he was not. McClellan began by informing the committee and those gathered that Eastland had turned the gavel over to him for the day. The absent Eastland had directed both McClellan and Ervin—the two former prosecutors—to bear down harder on Marshall. They relished the opportunity.

"So," McClellan said, beginning the hearings and glancing at Ervin, "go right ahead."

Ervin—once again laden with law books and thick briefing papers—began peppering Marshall with questions about another significant criminal case, *Escobedo v. Illinois.* The case grew out of the suspect Danny Escobedo, who, while under arrest, had been prevented from seeing his lawyer. He also had not been informed of his right to remain silent. Escobedo thus made a confession. On June 22, 1964, the Supreme Court tossed the confession aside, ruling that Escobedo's constitutional rights had been violated. The decision, like the subsequent *Miranda* ruling, angered conservatives.

ERVIN: Did not the Court hold in the *Escobedo* case for the first time that the right of counsel arose not at the time of the commencement of the criminal prosecution, but arose whenever an officer having him in custody began to suspect in his mind that the person in his custody might have some connection with the crime he was investigating?

MARSHALL: I think he went a little further, Senator. It was not that he thought so, but that his investigation up to that time centered in on a particular person as a suspect.

ERVIN: Is that not, in effect, that when the officer began to suspect that the man in his custody had a part in the commission of the crime he is investigating, then his right to counsel arose?

The Marshall response was potent.

MARSHALL: Bear in mind that in the *Escobedo* case, the lawyer was standing outside trying to get in.

Ervin was forced to concede Marshall's logic, even as it apparently pained him to do so.

> ERVIN: The *Escobedo* case was a hard case. Hard cases are the quick-sands of law. The Court ought to have held, in my opinion, in the circumstances there that it was an involuntary confession and excluded it on that basis. Instead of doing so, it undertook to change the meaning of the Constitution. Instead of saying that his right to counsel arose when the criminal prosecution was begun, the Court held it arose when the officer having the accused in custody began to suspect that he was the guilty party. I do not know how you can invade the contents of the officer's mind and determine when a suspicion arises in it.
>
> MARSHALL: I think it is not just a suspicion, it is that the man is a suspect. It is a little more.

Fearing that Marshall was pulling him into quicksand of a different sort—where Ervin's logic was disappearing by the second—the senator changed course.

Ervin flowed right into the issue of voting rights, citing *South Carolina v. Katzenbach*, a 1966 case in which South Carolina legislators challenged the legality of the 1965 Voting Rights Act. The high court decision not only upheld the constitutionality of the bill in its ruling; it granted Congress the right to punish those states with egregious patterns of voting discrimination. This was the only way, the court ruled, the country could eradicate "the blight of racial discrimination in voting." In essence, the court ruled that federal oversight over these named southern states could and must continue.

> ERVIN: Do not those two provisions of the Constitution make it plain that the State has the power to prescribe qualifications for voting for State and Federal offices, subject only to the limitation that they cannot deny or abridge the right to vote by reason of race or sex?

Marshall knew Ervin was referring to the 1965 Voting Rights Act and told him that the discussion had already taken place in the halls of Congress—and was decided.

ERVIN: It was.

MARSHALL: And Congress decided it was within their province to pass that bill.

Neither senator nor nominee was prepared to budge.

ERVIN: Now, how can you reconcile that holding with the declaration in *Ex parte Milligan* that the Constitution of the United States is a law for rulers as well as the people and that no doctrine involving more pernicious consequences was ever invented by the wit of man than that any of its provisions be suspended during any of the great exigencies of government?

The question could be translated thus: Ervin believed that southern states had been bullied into accepting the 1965 Voting Rights Act. He claimed justice officials in Washington did not trust southern election administrators to protect the voting rights of blacks, no matter what they promised.

MARSHALL: Well, I rely upon the opinion of the Supreme Court. That argument was made to the Supreme Court and the Supreme Court rejected it.

Ervin continued this line of questioning for several more minutes, those in their seats riveted by the parrying between him and Marshall.

ERVIN: If as the Supreme Court holds in *South Carolina v. Katzenbach* such an act as that constitutes or affords due process of law, then Congress has the power to provide that in all civil cases the only court that could have jurisdiction would be a Federal court sitting in the island of Guam, would it not?

A look of confusion suddenly appeared on the face of Senator Tydings as Ervin summoned up the *Escobedo* case again. Tydings and Birch Bayh were among the so-called Young Turks—along with Senator Kennedy—who abhorred the Old Bulls Ervin, Eastland,

McClellan, and Thurmond, but there was nothing they could do about them. They had seniority; they had genuine power. But Tydings couldn't take it any longer. He broke in before Ervin could say another word.

> TYDINGS: I do not understand your question, Senator. I am mixed up. You were in the Voting Rights Act, and you jumped to *Escobedo.*

Ervin was taken aback by the intrusion.

> ERVIN: I beg your pardon. I am asking about the Voting Rights Act. I have not gone back to *Escobedo.*

Ervin, having swatted the Tydings comment away, redirected his gaze at Marshall and continued. He was aggressive in painting a picture of southern officials' being maligned by virtue of geography.

> ERVIN: Do you think it is a handicap and an obstacle to State elections officials in Southern States to have to journey anywhere up to 1,000 miles and bring witnesses that distance in order to establish their innocence of a congressional condemnation rather than a judicial condemnation?
> MARSHALL: The main problem is there is no problem of cost. The States can afford it. No. 2, with air travel today—

Ervin cut Marshall off.

> ERVIN: As a matter of fact, that bill as originally framed did not even provide that they could obtain a subpoena that would run more than 100 miles from the District of Columbia. I raised the point and Congress amended the bill so that the court in its discretion could authorize a subpoena to run further than that. Do you not think the State election officials in North Carolina or Mississippi are denied the right to due process of law when they do not have a right to compulsory process to bring the witnesses here?

MARSHALL: I do not know whether you are right or wrong on that.

ERVIN: You do not? Well, you have no opinion whether that is right or wrong?

The audience sat eyeing two learned men who were battling over words, philosophies, legal recall—and a lifetime court appointment. Marshall provided Ervin with an answer.

MARSHALL: As an abstract proposition, I say I do not have an opinion, Senator. It is an abstract proposition.

The answer did not sit well with Ervin.

ERVIN: It is a very concrete proposition in the case of North Carolina. We have the election officers of 40 of our counties condemned by [an] act of Congress and denied the right to exercise the constitutional powers of the State of North Carolina in those 40 counties. Under the Voting Rights Act, they have to come to the District of Columbia and bring witnesses all the way to the District of Columbia to prove their innocence . . . And under this act, they do not even have the right of compulsory process to obtain the attendance of their witnesses. They cannot even enjoy such right unless the court here grants it to them as a matter of grace.

MARSHALL: My answer, Senator, would be that if that were presented to me as a Justice of the Supreme Court, I would consider it on both sides and make up my mind as to whether it was constitutional or not.

ERVIN: Well, I am not a Justice of the Supreme Court and never will be, but if I were a Justice of the Supreme Court, I would say that was too shabby a course of procedure to constitute due process of law.

Tydings felt compelled to interject.

TYDINGS: Is the Senator asking him how he would rule if the case came before him?

ERVIN: No, all I am asking him is on the decisions of the Supreme
    Court that have been handed down.
TYDINGS: Those are the past. I do not think it would be fair to
    ask him a hypothetical fact question about a case in the future.

For the moment, Ervin relented.

IT WAS NOT LOST on Senator Tydings that the best-known Supreme
Court justice from Maryland—home state of Marshall and Tydings—
was Roger B. Taney. Taney hailed from a family of well-to-do tobacco
farmers. He would come to marry Anne Key. Her brother Francis
Scott Key wrote "The Star-Spangled Banner." Taney was respected as
a Maryland legislator, rising to be elected state attorney general. That
led to appointment as attorney general of the United States. President
Andrew Jackson eventually appointed Taney chief justice of the U.S.
Supreme Court. It was Chief Justice Taney who wrote the 1857 *Dred
Scott* decision, a devastating blow that all but reminded Negroes they
had no place in the land of the free. Dred Scott, born in Virginia, was
a slave who had once been freed by his master. Crisscrossing in and out
of slave state and free state, Scott felt sure of his eternal freedom. The
established law in Missouri had been "once free, always free." But the
Missouri Supreme Court upended that tenet and ruled, in 1852, that
Scott be returned to slavery. Scott's lawyers sued, and the case landed
in the lap of the U.S. Supreme Court. Chief Justice Taney wrote the
court's majority opinion. The court ruled that Negroes were not citizens and thus had no right to sue for their freedom. Anger ensued in
the aftermath of the decision, yet another flame on the path to the
cannon fire that landed at Fort Sumter.

A SHORT WHILE LATER, Ervin returned to the narrow 1966 *Miranda*
ruling by the Supreme Court. Thurmond and McClellan nodded
approvingly. It was a planned tactical move on Ervin's part, given Marshall's earlier refusal to revisit *Miranda* because areas of the case would
likely be discussed before the high court in the future.

    Again, Marshall said he would not discuss *Miranda*. The wily Ervin
nevertheless announced he would like to proceed by talking about

the *Miranda* decision himself, thus giving the audience—fresh from headlines about black inner-city unrest and criminality on American streets—a soliloquy about crime, punishment, and its constitutional antecedents. Sam Ervin had a syrupy voice. And even in these years far removed from his youth, he still spoke with a kind of literary confidence. Some thought the voice spellbinding.

> ERVIN: The *Miranda* decision is based upon these words of the fifth amendment: no person shall be compelled in any criminal case to be a witness against himself. Those words became effective as part of the Constitution of the United States on the 15th day of June 1790. They were uniformly interpreted . . . from the 15th day of June 1790 until 13th day of June 1966 to have no possible application to voluntary confessions. The decisions held that this was true because the words clearly apply to compelled testimony only which a person testifying as a witness against himself gives in a judicial tribunal in a criminal case or a case of the nature of a criminal case.

Marshall listened as heads swiveled from him to Ervin and back again.

> ERVIN: I further assert for whatever it is worth that the judges who joined in the majority opinion made a voluntary confession in the opinion that they were adding to the Constitution requirements which were not there, when they called these requirements "the principles announced today" and "the systems or warnings we delineate today." I construe that to be a voluntary confession on the part of the majority of the Court that it was creating new requirements which were not a part of the Constitution prior to the 13th day of June 1966, notwithstanding that the constitutional provision involved had been in the Constitution since June 15, 1790.

Ervin was so confident in his attack on the high court he imagined Marshall would not let it go unchallenged. But Marshall once again declined to offer a response.

Ervin would not be deterred.

ERVIN: I would like to ask you this question: . . . As a result of your experience in practicing law, what percentage of persons who commit murders, rapes, robberies, burglaries, and other serious offenses do not already know that they have a right to remain silent and do not already know that whatever they say derogatory to themselves will be used against them in court and do not already know that they have the right of counsel at the time they are interrogated?

MARSHALL: I would say, Senator, that the percentage would give me great difficulty, but that the violent crimes, for the most part, are spur-of-the-moment crimes and the person per-petrating the crime does not consider *Miranda* or anybody else. That runs from that scope to the calculating, so-called white-collar crimes. They are not worried about *Miranda*, because they have a lawyer. So I say the figures would get me in great difficulty.

As those gathered could clearly see—and against Marshall's own protestations—Ervin had drawn him out on *Miranda*. Marshall's self-confidence, and knowledge of constitutional law, would not allow him to now retreat.

So they continued.

ERVIN: Do you not know that when the question of ratification of the Constitution was under consideration in this country, Elbridge Gerry of Massachusetts, a great lawyer, and George Mason of Virginia, another great lawyer, pointed out that there is really no actual limitation in the Constitution upon the pow-ers of the court, and stated in substance that under the guise of interpreting the Constitution, the Justice of the Supreme Court would exercise the power to change its meaning?

MARSHALL: I think you are correct. My history is not as good as yours.

There was light chuckling.

ERVIN: Did not Gerry and Mason state at that time that when judges did change the meaning of the Constitution while pro-

fessing to interpret it the errors they committed in so doing
were without remedy for all practical intents and purposes?
MARSHALL: I do not agree on that. Congress is still here.

As more minutes ticked off the clock, Ervin could sense—as he
acknowledged—that others wanted to question Marshall. But he asked
their indulgence, as he had just one more question. "Do you recall the
Stovall case?" he asked Marshall.

And Thurgood Marshall said he did. It was among the cases the
White House had hoped would not come up during the hearings. All
eyes in the hearing room were on Marshall.

His given name really was Theodore Roosevelt Stovall. He was
working a job at a store in Brooklyn, New York, during the summer of
1961. He lamented his low wages and decided he needed more money.
He knew well-to-do families lived out on Long Island—big lawns,
chandeliered dining rooms—because he lived out there with his sister,
but in a poorer section, Hempstead, and he resented those who had so
much more than he did. On the night of August 23, Stovall ventured
out to well-heeled Garden City on Long Island. He aimed to break
into one of those lovely homes and make off with whatever loot he
could get his hands on. He came upon the home of Paul Behrendt,
and his wife, Frances, both physicians. Once inside, he began rum-
maging around. The two doctors were asleep upstairs. They heard
something. Paul rose and crept downstairs. As he stepped into the
kitchen, he came upon Stovall. A vicious fight ensued. Stovall plunged
a knife into Behrendt, killing him. The jarring noise swiftly brought
his wife, Frances, downstairs, and she came upon the horror-filled
scene, screaming, staring at the wild-eyed intruder, blood everywhere.
Stovall easily overpowered Frances Behrendt, stabbing her a total of
eleven times against the din of her screams. Then he fled. Frances
Behrendt struggled to the telephone and dialed the police. When the
police arrived, they came upon a ghastly scene. Mrs. Behrendt was
rushed to the hospital, sirens wailing. While canvassing the house,
police discovered important evidence. The intruder had left behind
a key to a locker, which, by the next morning, the police had traced
to a Brooklyn store. The investigation led to the locker of Theodore
Roosevelt Stovall. The police then went to a nearby bar and found a
man who knew Stovall and who mentioned Stovall might well be at

his sister's home, out in Hempstead. And that is where police arrested Stovall—and obtained clothing that had bloodstains on it which matched the blood type of Frances Behrendt.

On August 25, Stovall was arraigned and charged with first-degree murder. He could not afford a lawyer and was told one would be assigned to him. Frances Behrendt lay in the hospital with serious injuries. Police officials decided to take Stovall to the nearby hospital and see if Behrendt could identify him. Without hesitation, Frances Behrendt identified Stovall as the man who killed her husband and had left her for dead. Stovall was eventually convicted and sentenced to die in the electric chair at Sing Sing prison.

Then came the appeal, which would be heard in the earlier rounds by a panel of New York appellate judges, including Thurgood Marshall. The appeal centered on the contention that Stovall's Fifth, Sixth, and Fourteenth Amendment rights had been violated by having him taken to Mrs. Behrendt's hospital room to be identified without counsel present. (Stovall was handcuffed to a policeman as Mrs. Behrendt looked him up and down.)

Because Marshall had felt that Stovall's constitutional rights had indeed been violated, he voted in favor of the appeal when the case came before his three-judge panel. Ervin intended, once again, to portray Marshall as soft on crime.

ERVIN: Then before Stovall had gotten a lawyer of his own choice, or before one had been appointed for him, the police officers, not knowing whether Mrs. Behrendt would live or die, took Stovall from the jail to the nearby hospital in which she was a patient.

MARSHALL: No, sir, they took him directly from the arraignment, the original arraignment, and instead of returning to the prison, which the law of New York required, that very same day took him immediately to the hospital.

Ervin took the hearing room through the meandering process of where the Stovall appeal was heard, six times before it eventually reached the U.S. Supreme Court. But when the case reached the panel of appellate judges in New York, where Judge Henry Friendly sat along with Judge Leonard Moore and Judge Thurgood Marshall, Friendly wrote an opinion saying that Stovall's constitutional rights had been violated. Marshall had concurred with that opinion.

> ERVIN: . . . This [Friendly's] opinion held that the provision of the sixth amendment provision giving a person the right to counsel in all criminal prosecutions rendered made it unconstitutional for Mrs. Behrendt, the victim of the crime and a witness of the crime, to look at Stovall while he was in custody unless an attorney representing Stovall was present.
>
> MARSHALL: I do not think the opinion says that, Senator. I think the opinion says that once the man was arraigned, the criminal process had started, and once the criminal process had started, he was entitled to have a lawyer before anything further was done. The man was arraigned, he was warned of his right to a lawyer, and that arraignment was postponed or continued, whatever the word was. We said at that moment, he was entitled to a lawyer, at the time of arraignment.

Ervin went on, slow, courtly, and determined, assailing the Friendly ruling.

> ERVIN: You joined Judge Friendly in making this decision, did you not?
>
> MARSHALL: In every word he wrote I joined it; in every word he wrote. My question would be, "How would that have injured anything if they had appointed a lawyer and took him and she identified him?" What harm could that have done to the enforcement of criminal process?

Marshall—his voice dripping with sarcasm—had turned the tables and tossed a question at Ervin.

> ERVIN: I will tell you one thing. She could have died without having an opportunity of identifying him. That would have prevented his being tried for her murder.
>
> MARSHALL: Well, she did not.

The other senators who wanted to interrupt chose not to, allowing the two combatants to keep at it.

> ERVIN: In the ultimate analysis, the decision was because the lawyer was not present. Did he [Friendly] not hold that that was unconstitutional for Mrs. Behrendt to look at Stovall with a view to determining whether he was or was not the person she saw commit the crime because he was not accompanied by counsel?
>
> MARSHALL: It was, because he was taken from the arraignment officer and, instead of being taken back to jail, was carried over to the hospital for that purpose. It was what they did to him, not what she did.

Ervin, moments later, began angling to strike a blow he hoped many would not forget.

> ERVIN: And you joined Judge Friendly's opinion, which held that the accused must be freed unless the case was retried without the use of the testimony of the only person on earth who could identify the man from personal observation?
>
> MARSHALL: You mean we said she could not testify?
>
> ERVIN: Yes.
>
> MARSHALL: No, we did not say that.
>
> ERVIN: Then why did your opinion say that a writ of habeas corpus could issue to free Stovall unless the State, within a reasonable time, afforded him a new trial?

Marshall sensed the trap.

> MARSHALL: That is a normal procedure in any habeas corpus case. We did not want to turn that man loose.

Ervin charged Marshall—and Friendly—with creating a new slant on the law.

> ERVIN: Judge Friendly and you, in effect, wrote into the sixth amendment something that nobody had even suspected was there before.

The accusation clearly irritated Marshall.

MARSHALL: We did not write anything into the Sixth Amendment. We applied the law of the land, which was at that time that when a man reached the stage of arraignment, he was entitled to a lawyer. He had reached that stage, he did not have a lawyer. So any identification question or what have you after that should be withheld until he gets a lawyer. That was our position, as I remember it.

The unbowed senator pressed on.

ERVIN: Since the prosecution did not offer any evidence except courtroom identification, why did Judge Friendly and you not hold that her own attorney opened the door to this evidence which you all decided for the first time in history, so far as I know, was unconstitutional?

MARSHALL: I repeat, Senator, the right of a lawyer at arraignment was not established in *Stovall*. It was established long before *Stovall*.

It went unmentioned during the hearing—but was apparent from the police reports and news accounts out of Garden City, Long Island—that Theodore Roosevelt Stovall was a black man. When taken to Mrs. Behrendt's hospital room, he was handcuffed to a policeman and was the only black person in the room. Thurgood Marshall, in a lifetime of travels, had been well aware of the fate of black men being wrongfully identified. While true that the Stovall appeal turned on a constitutional aspect of the law—not his race—Marshall was cognizant, in 1965 during the appeal, of the unmentioned racial dynamic at play. In Marshall's mind, the law needed to be adhered to fully and constitutionally, lest another defendant fall through an unfilled crack. (Stovall, in a sense, won the spirit of his appeal, but it was a Pyrrhic victory: while the appeal judges ruled that Stovall's constitutional rights might well have been violated, they concluded it was not enough of a violation to overturn his conviction and sentence.)

It had been a long session thus far, and Sam Ervin felt a need to explain himself before his fellow committee members, the nominee, and those sitting in the seats.

> ERVIN: The reason I am conducting this examination is because I have a solemn responsibility as a Member of the Senate in passing on and determining whether or not I shall vote for the confirmation of the nominee to the Supreme Court. My personal opinion is, and I say it with reluctance, but I say it because I believe it to be true, that the road to destruction of constitutional government in the United States is being paved by the good intentions of the judicial activists, who, all too often, constitute a majority of the Supreme Court.

Ervin continued, before drawing to a close.

> ERVIN: As Chief Justice Stone said, the members of the Supreme Court have the power under the Constitution to restrain the President and the Congress in their actions, but there is really no power on earth to restrain the members of the Supreme Court in their action except their own self-restraint.

By now Michigan's senator Phil Hart was fuming.

> HART: Mr. Chairman, could I inquire of the Senator from North Carolina if this concludes his interrogation of the witness, subject only to the development of other aspects?

The word "interrogation" seemed to echo inside the hearing room. Ervin said he was indeed finished.

Now Senator McClellan—the other prosecutor—raised his voice in the direction of Marshall.

> MCCLELLAN: Something that gives me a little concern—this does not pertain to you directly any more than to other members of the Court. We regard Supreme Court decisions interpreting the Constitution as being the law of the land, do we not?

Marshall answered yes.

MCCLELLAN: And we hold, too, that all citizens should be amenable to the law of the land?

Again, Marshall said yes.

MCCLELLAN: Now, do you feel that that applies to everybody
except Supreme Court Justices?
MARSHALL: I think that the Supreme Court Justices must be more
responsive to their oath than any other judge because of that.

McClellan didn't see Marshall's logic.

MCCLELLAN: Then how can they consistently overrule a former
decision holding an act constitutional or an act unconstitutional
and then say they have been amenable to the law of the land?

Marshall said he felt it was necessary for the Supreme Court to "slow
down" and take a long look at important cases up for reconsideration.
McClellan quickly followed that with a question about reversing
earlier decisions with constitutional ramifications. Marshall said he
felt the justices were free to do so.

MCCLELLAN: If you feel they are free, would you have any hesitancy in overruling the *Miranda* decision when it came up for
consideration if you became convinced that that decision was
wrong?
MARSHALL: If I became convinced that the *Miranda* decision was
wrong, I would, of course, vote my conscience, which would
say yes.

McClellan—the prosecutor—seemed to sense he had Marshall
right where he wanted him.

MCCLELLAN: Then the previous court decision does not bind you,
although it is the law of the land?

Marshall remained unbowed in his sentiments.

MARSHALL: It binds the Supreme Court as well as it binds every-body else in the land.

MCCLELLAN: That is an inconsistency, is it not? . . . I have to obey it because the Supreme Court says so, but tomorrow, when you reconsider that decision, in your capacity you do not have to conform to it; you can overrule it and you can change the law of the land. Is that not so?

MARSHALL: I think that is the job of the Supreme Court.

For several seconds, both men kept cutting off each other. Then:

MCCLELLAN: I think that changing the law of the land in the fash-ion it is doing it is bringing chaos and confusion to our system of justice. One judge—I think it is Judge Lombard –

"Chief Judge Lombard," Marshall quickly corrected McClellan, before he went on.

MCCLELLAN: Yes, Chief Judge Lombard testified before . . . the Subcommittee on Criminal Laws and Procedures that today when he is trying a criminal case, he feels like he is in a topsy-turvy world because he does not know what the law is and what the Supreme Court is going to say it may be, and he is absolutely in a state of confusion . . . It is a tragic situation. The instability, the unreliability on what the Court said yes-terday as being the law of today.

MARSHALL: I can say this, Senator: . . . I hope you do not interpret me to say it is the duty of the Court to reverse decisions. It is the duty of the Court to keep stability of the law.

MCCLELLAN: To what?

Marshall repeated what he had just said.

MCCLELLAN: How do you keep it [stability] when one year you hold one thing in the Court and next year hold something else? Is there any stability in that?

MARSHALL: It happens often in the exact same Court.

McClellan told Marshall that was not the definition of stability. Marshall quickly disagreed.

> MCCLELLAN: Then your interpretation and definition of the word "stability" is that one day it is one thing and another day it is something else.
> MARSHALL: You would not need the Supreme Court any more?
> MCCLELLAN: Unless it reversed itself?
> MARSHALL: Sir?

Senator Ervin was greatly admiring this back-and-forth, feeling confident in his colleague's cross-examination.

> MCCLELLAN: Except that it reverses itself you would not need it?
> MARSHALL: No, sir; I think the Constitution as a living document needs somebody to interpret it.
> MCCLELLAN: But once you interpret it, it becomes the law of the land, when the Supreme Court interprets it. You admitted that.

Senator Ervin was nodding; Senator Hart glaring.

> MARSHALL: Yes, sir.
> MCCLELLAN: Now you say you can change the interpretation at will and give it another interpretation.
> MARSHALL: Yes, sir.

Ervin suddenly had his opening to reenter the debate.

> ERVIN: I am always intrigued by this statement that the Constitution is a living document and, therefore, must change. That statement does not mean that the Constitution is dead and we are ruled by the personal notions of the temporary occupants of the Supreme Court.
> MARSHALL: I do not agree with your constantly referring to the Judges' personal views.

Tempers were noticeably edgy—to the audience's delight—as Hart now reentered the debate.

> HART: Just this comment, that also involved here is a realization that the assignment of the Court is not the pursuit of certainty but of justice, and sometimes justice requires overruling of previous decisions.

McClellan, listening, taking it in, had a question for Hart.

> MCCLELLAN: Can you make any justice out of turning a criminal loose because some policeman failed to give him a lawyer?

So it came back to the murderer.

> HART: If he is found to be a criminal by reason of ignoring the constitutional safeguards, yes; just as we say we do not like the rack because—
> MCCLELLAN: Why not punish the officer who violated the Constitution instead of turning the criminal loose?
> HART: I am for both.

Moments later, McClellan asked Senator Hart if he had any more questions. Hart said he did not. Hart had already thought these hearings had gone on too long. In his mind, they had become an "interrogation," and he wished them to end. But Chairman Eastland had not been present, so these hearings would not be concluded today. They would go on. McClellan confirmed that reality when he said they would resume the following morning at 10:30. Marshall looked bewildered, already allowing his mind to race—wondering if he had said too much, if he had not said enough. Wondering how he had fared against Senator Ervin.

It had been a day when so much history, and so many events, had been summoned: ghosts and murderers had been brought into the courtroom from long-ago legal cases. But one thing Thurgood Marshall was content about was his reiteration of his decades-long belief that the Constitution was a living document. That it was not something that stayed pressed between sheets of glass; that it involved people, and the spanning of time; that it involved words such as "liberty" and "justice" that had to be expanded to include Negroes, the black populace. In Thurgood Marshall's mind, the world was spinning—had spun—away from the likes of Senators Ervin and McClellan because of the amendments to the Constitution and rulings by the Supreme Court. He knew the law, and deep in his mind, Thurgood Marshall felt the logic of the law would not abandon him.

Marshall, having risen from his seat, made his way past the standing-room-only crowd and all those who had been at the hearings now milling about the Senate hallways.

Senator Phil Hart, however, couldn't shake the day. The White House expected him to gauge these hearings, to watch over them. But of course in the hearing room, he was limited; Eastland and McClellan held seniority, and they had yet to make time for friendly witnesses. Hart had to make sure the nominee made it out of the committee.

Many in the U.S. Senate thought Phil Hart was one of the best men in that body.

HART WAS BORN in Bryn Mawr, Pennsylvania, in 1912, into a well-heeled family. There were Negro servants and summer vacations. "He had culture," a high school classmate said of Hart. The family had a social conscience, and when Hart turned seventeen, his father presented him with an NAACP membership as a gift. His father took him to the Democratic National Convention in New York City in 1924. The young Hart saw the internecine battle played out between southern Democrats—with their anti-Negro sentiments—and eastern Democrats. He entered Georgetown University in 1930, where he became, like Thurgood Marshall, a college debater, and graduated from the University of Michigan Law School in 1937. He fought in World War II, even sharing a meal on Christmas Eve 1944 in Luxembourg with the war correspondent Ernest Hemingway.

During the war, Hart—tall, angular, handsome in a beatnik kind of way—had returned to Michigan. He reacquainted himself with Janey Briggs, sister of one of his college classmates. He asked her to marry him. She laughed, until she realized he was serious. The wedding took place in 1943. Janey's father, Walter O. Briggs Sr., was an auto magnate who owned the Detroit Tigers baseball team. They would never have money worries. After the war, Hart and his wife settled in Detroit and began raising a family. In 1947, while vacationing on Bois Blanc Island in Michigan, their three-year-old son, Flip, ambled off a pier alone and drowned. Thereafter, many would comment on how serious a man Phil Hart seemed to be, and they wondered if he truly got joy from life. There would be other children. There would be laughter. But it was forever tempered.

Hart was pulled into Michigan politics by the gravitational force of the liberal governor Mennen "Soapy" Williams and was elected lieutenant governor. He befriended blacks; he interrupted people who uttered racial slurs in public. In 1957, he started contemplating a run for the U.S. Senate because he didn't like the slow pace of school integration on the heels of the *Brown* desegregation ruling. He campaigned on "the failure of leadership that produced Little Rock, and the silence in the White House over integration." He seemed fearless. He went after Eisenhower for his "hideous failure" in enforcing the *Brown* ruling.

Hart won his election. And as soon as he reached Washington in 1959, he began speaking out on behalf of civil rights. The Kennedy administration was not doing enough, he believed; southern Democrats were stifling progress the country desperately needed to make in terms of equality, he told gatherings. He got a prized appointment to the Senate Judiciary Committee, then ran up against the powerful segregationist Eastland. "We have to face the facts of life about that committee," he once said. There were those who told Phil Hart he should go along to get along, that there were rules and political party expectations he should respect. He wouldn't listen. "Lifelong Democrats," opined a Michigan newspaper about Hart's progressive approach to politics, "might be hesitant about a senator who presses with such emphasis in a civil rights movement promising to threaten their own way of life." Hart became one of President Johnson's key strategists for the epochal 1965 Voting Rights Act. He soon began driving through the South just to look at the face of black progress for himself. He'd find some recently elected officeholders who were black, walk right in, and introduce himself. He'd identify himself, and they were stunned that a big-time U.S. senator had come south to meet and talk with them. This was the beautiful part about politics to Phil Hart: it could make a difference. Between a country road and a little shack set off from that country road and the souls who lived in that little shack, he could see the U.S. Constitution in all its glory at work. Just look what the Voting Rights Act had done! They'd be staring at him from the windows of the offices he'd just left, and he'd wave and smile and climb back into his car.

Phil Hart wanted so badly for things to turn out beautifully for Thurgood Marshall.

But the urban riots kept coming. And those protesting were saying more bills were needed, more help was needed after centuries of second-class citizenship. The southern Democrats—Phil Hart's own party—were intransigent and even bellicose. They pointed to the mayhem on the streets—just as Judiciary Committee members were doing with Thurgood Marshall in their sights. Hart assailed them: "And I do say, too, that those who obstruct and hinder civil rights legislation are contributing to the very disorder and violence in our lives that they so loudly decry."

Hart certainly knew the black populace in his native Detroit quite well. He knew that they were emotional about Thurgood Marshall's reaching the Supreme Court. Many of those blacks were autoworkers and held jobs in the Hart family business by virtue of his marriage to Janey Briggs. Union leaders in Michigan's urban areas were fond of Hart as well. So when he left room 2228 on the third day of Marshall's confirmation hearings, he knew that many in Michigan were following him—and the Judiciary Committee—and he would remind them to do what people had always done in history: get out stationery and write to their senators; and he would tell them to tell their relatives down south to write to those senators, because now blacks were going to the polls like never before. And they would keep going.

Hart had to explain to reporters that there would be no vote on the Marshall nomination today—just as there had been no vote at the end of the first day or the end of the second day. He suggested to Marshall he get some rest and prepare for the next day's hearings.

Senator Tydings, in the hearing room that third day, knew all along that his colleagues who supported Marshall would have to fight. "We would have to fight for Thurgood just like we fought for the voting rights bill," he would recall.

The White House itself was under no illusion going forward, especially now that it realized the hearings were purposefully being prolonged. "They thought Johnson was a traitor," recalls the White House aide Joseph Califano about southern Democrats on the Judiciary Committee. "They despised Johnson."

The southern Democrats on the Judiciary Committee were hardly the only problem the White House faced when it came to the Marshall hearings. Other woes were hovering—an errant congressman, a war that devoured the president's attention, and those whirring Molotov cocktails being tossed by beret-wearing blacks throughout urban America. They were all hard and ominous shadows being thrown against the progress of the Marshall nomination.

10

Painful Interruptions for a
President and His Nominee

Congressman Adam Clayton Powell Jr. (center)—whose rise in the American
mind-set mirrored Thurgood Marshall's—in 1942 leading aides into the
U.S. Capitol to protest discrimination. He bedeviled the White House
with his antics at the time of the Marshall hearings.

I N THE SUMMER OF 1967, President Lyndon Johnson had a great
deal on his mind. His signature legislative accomplishments were
often met, within the same week even, with another round of seis-
mic woes. The streets were afire as urban rioting—and college protests against the Vietnam War—were erupting on both coasts as well
as in the Midwest. Writers, singers, and poets kept weighing in on
the demonstrations, using melodic and lyrical phrasing to assail the
years of antigovernment disenchantment that seemed to be cresting.

None of it stopped the national guardsmen and tanks from arriving at urban zones and zigzagging through public housing projects, angering blacks even more. The war in Vietnam, Johnson kept telling the nation, was winnable, despite the gloomy and dire dispatches showing up on the front pages of the nation's metropolitan dailies and inside all those weekly magazines. As if that were not enough, a rapscallion figure—and a quite gifted politician—by the name of Adam Clayton Powell Jr. showed up to ride all of this protest as Thurgood Marshall was engaged in his contentious confirmation battle.

Congressman Powell had been in trouble—and literally on the run—with fellow House members about ethics violations, which involved overseas trips and comely women. Powell, like Marshall, was black, and many—especially southern whites—looped the two men together as proof of black empowerment gone astray. The White House was not amused. "I hope you will vote no on the seating of a Negro to the Supreme Court," began the letter to Senator McClellan from John Buch of Buffalo. It went on: "The endorsement of Adam Clayton Powell by the Harlem voters . . . I did not hear one major Negro denounce Adam Clayton Powell, the scoundrel." Another missive found its way to McClellan from Ella Brown of Sioux City, Iowa: "The United States isn't ready for a negro on the Supreme Court. They just don't think in terms other than black and white. Even Senator [Edward] Brooke, when asked on TV if he thought the unseating of Adam Clayton Powell was discrimination, said he thought it was. He knew better."

Powell had been a staunch ally of Johnson's vaunted War on Poverty, sending millions of federal dollars into distressed areas throughout the nation. As chairman of the Education and Labor Committee, he wielded enormous power. But some of Powell's current torment was, like Marshall's, rooted in a decades-long battle with the American South. (He began calling the War on Poverty the War on Powell.)

POWELL WAS BORN IN 1908, making him the same age as Thurgood Marshall. His parents were middle-class. His father, Adam Clayton Powell Sr., had become a popular minister of the Abyssinian Baptist Church. Everyone in Harlem seemed to know the elder Powell and his wife, Mattie. Adam junior—handsome and so light of complexion he looked white to the unsuspecting—was sent to Colgate University. There were only a few Negroes at the school then. He let none of them know of his ethnicity, casually strolling around campus in the white world, a phenomenon that would come to be known as "passing." When discovered that he was actually a Negro, he profusely apologized to the few Negroes on campus—and to his father, who scolded him and warned him of the shame he had brought on himself. It seemed to have been his Waterloo.

Young Powell also became a minister, progressive and determined, leading Harlem boycotts of stores that forbade Negroes to try on clothes and use the restrooms. He led protests against bus lines that would not hire Negro drivers. The activism got him elected to city council in New York, which launched a mesmerizing run for Congress in 1944. Standing atop flatbed trucks in a white suit against the darkening Harlem sky, he gave speech after speech, assailing discrimination and timid politicians. Victory was historic when he became the first Negro congressman elected from the East Coast. "The people have purged this community of carpetbaggers, compromisers, and Uncle Toms," he said following victory.

He hardly minded controversy: Powell left his first wife, Isabel, on the eve of his election, going to Washington with plans to marry Hazel Scott, the glamorous jazz pianist.

Negroes were proud of his election, and liberal whites eagerly looked forward to his arrival in Washington. Before his swearing in, he stepped into a House elevator in Washington with Hattie Dodson, his secretary. He was unrecognized by the two other men in the elevator. "We're just waiting for that nigger to come down here from New York," one of the men said.

Southerners might not have been able to lay claim to the White House, but they stayed in Congress and the Senate long enough to accrue seniority. Everywhere Powell turned, there seemed to be a southerner leading a committee. Some of those southerners were quite nasty men. The Mississippi congressman John Rankin had taken to the House floor and called the newspaper columnist Walter Winchell "a little kike." Powell responded swiftly. "Last week democracy was shamed by the uncalled for and unfounded condemnation of one of

America's great minorities. I am not a member of that great minority, but I will always oppose anyone who tries to besmirch any group because of race, creed, or color." Powell then called for Rankin's impeachment—a hollow pronouncement as it would never happen, but the southerners never forgave him. In due time, southern chairmen kept Powell from rising on any committees. When his wife, Hazel Scott, was stopped from appearing at Constitution Hall by the Daughters of the American Revolution (DAR) because of her race, Powell suggested the DAR member and first lady, Bess Truman, quit the organization in protest. She refused. Powell then called Truman "the last lady of the land." Harry Truman, outraged, would not allow Powell to set foot inside the White House while he remained in office.

Powell became a spokesman, a national politician by dint of fearlessness and his matinee idol looks. Democratic Party leaders could not control him and quickly realized it. "Walk out," he suggested to southern blacks about the South. "Leave your doors and windows, if you have any, wide open." Many southern politicians had plantations; they needed black labor; their animus toward Powell only grew.

Powell drubbed his election opponents but still could not rise in Washington on the committees that he sat on. On weekends, he could be seen in Harlem at the jumpy nightspots, Small's Paradise or the Red Rooster, where he might run into any array of Negro celebrities—Lena Horne, Joe Louis, Sugar Ray Robinson, Thurgood Marshall. There would be good food, drinks, jazz, a reciting of the most recent stories that had appeared in Negro publications about any one of them: Sammy Davis Jr. on Broadway; that *Brown* school decision; Lena up for another Hollywood role. The famous gravitated toward the smooth and handsome congressman, as he did to them.

But the southern Democrats were completely another matter. Powell relentlessly attacked them and their segregationist policies. The Eisenhower administration went after segregation on military bases, and those "Colored Only" and "White Only" signs were removed. Powell was impressed. He began meeting with Eisenhower staff members, rubbing a thin cigarillo along his lips, passing along his ideas about the country and politics. "You'd sit with him and you'd think he was a sage of wisdom about the race problem," Eisenhower's aide Sherman Adams would recall. "He was about the smoothest guy I ever saw." Powell had praised the Marshall-led *Brown* desegregation ruling—"democracy's shining hour"—and was gratified when Eisenhower told the nation to support the ruling. When Powell wrote an article in *Reader's Digest* praising Eisenhower, White House aides began wondering—dreaming!—if they could get Powell to support Ike in the 1956 election. It was considered suicidal for a Democrat to bolt his party and support another party's candidate. It would be a coup and, Republicans knew, a slap at Democrats. Powell, cagey—and tired of members of his own party who would do nothing to challenge southern Democrats—announced a startling position: he was going to support Ike! Democrats, as expected, were aghast and vowed revenge. Tammany Hall, the muscular New York political machine, went on a recruiting mission to find someone to challenge Powell in his next election. They came after Franklin D. Roosevelt Jr. He said no. Then they came after Thurgood Marshall. He was beloved, held a national reputation. But Marshall also declined, telling the Tammany emissaries that he and Powell were "fighting for the same thing."

If Marshall was the steady drumbeat to Powell's jazzy horn, Marshall nevertheless knew that Powell possessed unique gifts. "The greatest showman in the business," Marshall said of Powell. He would add,

> He could raise any amount of money, and his influence with his people was just unbelievable. I don't know how many of us were sitting down one night. There must have been six or eight of us. And we decided that, at that time, in his heyday, if you had a mass meeting in Harlem with Ralph Bunche, Walter White, Roy Wilkins, Thurgood Marshall, [A. Philip] Randolph, you name them—and at the same time, had one with Adam Powell—he'd have everybody, and you'd have nobody . . . he was the most effective committee chairman in Congress. And you'll never see that in writing any place, but it's true.

TWO YEARS LATER the unpredictable Powell had switched back to the Democratic fold. He returned to attacking Eisenhower. For those not watching, Powell had been accumulating seniority himself. If a Democrat should win the 1960 presidential campaign, his committee chairmanship ticket would be punched. Powell supported the Missouri senator Stuart Symington during the 1960 Democratic primaries. But he told his followers, in a sermon, that the southern senator Lyndon Johnson should not be unfairly judged. "Any Negro who automatically dismisses Lyndon Johnson because of the accident of birth automatically qualifies himself as an immature captive Negro, and a captive of his own prejudices." Powell went on: "Mark you, Lyndon Johnson brought the 1957 bill [the 1957 Civil Rights Bill] to a vote despite the fact that the outstanding Presidential candidate, Senator John F. Kennedy of Massachusetts, voted to send that bill back to Mississippi Senator Eastland's committee to be killed." The Powell sermon seemed to morph into an endorsement. "Let us not forget that when the Southerners issued their manifesto, it was Lyndon Johnson who led the vast majority of the members from Texas away from the Southern Manifesto and refused to sign it, thus proving where he stood. That was a long time before there was any thought in his mind of the Presidency." That last line was laughably naive, and Adam Clayton Powell was not a naive man.

Upon the inauguration of President Kennedy and Vice President Lyndon Johnson, Adam Clayton Powell Jr. became chairman of the committee on education and labor, overseeing a large staff. It was a profound turnabout for a congressman who had been in the committee wilderness. Now he lorded over vast interests! He announced a furious amount of legislation, lining up behind Kennedy's New Frontier agenda to attack poverty and discrimination. Southerners blocked much of that agenda, then, upon Kennedy's death, President Johnson and Powell teamed to steamroll it through Congress. Now it was the War on Poverty, and bills were passed attacking the hunger, discrimination, and wide-scale inequality that had haunted and scarred the nation for decades. Nearly $7 billion worth of domestic legislation had come across Powell's desk—then another $7 billion more. More than sixty major bills passed through his twin committees. Now he was a baron—just like all those southerners—and he gloried in the role. There were celebrations, drinks poured. He was given all those oversized plaques, and they adorned his big suite of offices. The president bragged about Powell's legislative prowess. Johnson sat in his Oval Office one day swooning about all of the success. Powell was there along with other Johnson aides. As a souvenir, Johnson tossed Powell a jeweled cigarette lighter. "Now, Adam," Johnson said, "don't go losing this in no whorehouse." Others cackled, but not Powell. "Mr. President," he said, "Adam Clayton Powell doesn't have to buy pussy."

That all of Powell's success happened while he was being investigated by Congress only pointed to his endurance.

In the early 1960s, Powell began an investigation of the New York Police Department for corruption. One of his targets was Esther James, a grandmotherly Harlem woman with a criminal background—she had been shot on one occasion; on another, she stabbed a man—who Powell charged was running numbers for the mob. James sued Powell for libel and in 1963 won a judgment for $245,000. Powell laughed. A judge, however, would not dismiss the amount, and it would not go away. Penalties kept accruing. An attorney for Powell finally suggested he pay the judgment. "The hell with the bitch," Powell said. A warrant was issued for Powell's arrest. The police informed him if he visited New York any day of the week—save Sundays—he'd be arrested. Now it was hard to laugh.

In 1966, a robed Powell addressed the graduates of Howard University. He coined a phrase that day—"black power"—and it would spread like wildfire around many college campuses, especially in urban areas. In a time of riots and unrest, the phrase was loaded. Politicians were appalled. They did not, however, feel a need to examine the entirety of Powell's speech that day. "There are those who scream, 'Burn, baby, burn,' while pretending to be clothed in the majestic mantle of 'black power,'" he had said. "Black power is a constructive approach to the new life of freedom for black people in the Great Society. Violence must play no part in its fulfillment . . . Instead of 'Burn, baby, burn,' we should be shouting, 'Learn, baby, learn' and 'Earn, baby, earn.' Instead of lighting up the sky with Molotov cocktails, we should be brightening the skies with the stars of millions of registered voters in 1968."

A short while later, Powell—his direction now clouded and unfocused—called a "black power" conference in his baronial offices on Capitol Hill. Black students and college radicals arrived, their huge Afros bobbing and colorful African garb drawing stares. Powell looked around, drew some sustenance by quoting *Hamlet*, smiled, and let the meeting begin. The alliance he was forming with black student radicals only further alienated him from members of Congress. Northern and southern congressmen warned Powell to corral his black-power-oriented activities. "The deep southerners hated his guts," recalled the Ohio congressman Wayne Hays. "They couldn't stand him." Efforts were begun to curtail and even strip him of many of his powers.

Powell easily won reelection in 1966. Democrats still controlled the House, 248–187, but Republicans had picked up forty-seven seats in the election. And now House members—particularly southern Democrats, egged on by Republicans—were threatening to deny Powell his seat at the 1967 swearing in. They were citing not only the Esther James libel case but also Powell having taken a junket on taxpayers' money with two attractive secretaries—one black, one white—to European capitals. On the day of the vote, when House members were to be sworn in, Powell, in a 364–64 vote, was stripped of his chairmanship. Weeks later, he was denied his seat altogether. Not since 1807 had Congress denied an elected member his seat and right to take office. To deny that right was tantamount to denying the citizens of that particular community the effectiveness of their vote. New York's senators, Robert F. Kennedy and Jacob Javits—both of whom later introduced Thurgood Marshall at the start of his judiciary hearings—were alarmed that Powell was stripped of his seat. They said it was unconstitutional.

Governor Nelson Rockefeller was forced to call a special election. It was held April 11, 1967. Again, the voters of Harlem elected Powell; his winning margin was seven to one. By the summer of 1967, the two most talked-about Negroes in Washington were Adam Clayton Powell, Jr. and Thurgood Marshall. Powell hovered about the Marshall confirmation hearings like a side act showing just next door. The White House prayed that the rising anti-Powell fever would not unduly harm its nominee.

Racial fireworks seemed to be everywhere for the White House. The 1964 Civil Rights Act, the Voting Rights Act, and the Marshall nomination, says Califano, the LBJ aide, were equivalent to "a declaration of war against Eastland and McClellan." Additionally, President Johnson further angered many southern politicians serving in Washington when, in 1967, he appointed Walter Washington, a

Negro, D.C.'s city commissioner, a position tantamount to the city's mayor. The nation's capital was a federal city, and thus its mostly black populace did not have the political powers of statehood. They had no member of Congress or the U.S. Senate. For years, southern senators were named chairman of the U.S. Senate Committee on the District of Columbia. They were white men who, for the most part, had grown up on plantations and were accused of treating the citizenry of D.C. with grave indifference—as if the city were another plantation. The Mississippi senator Theodore Bilbo had presided over the Senate committee for the district and constantly espoused segregationist policies while using vile language to do so. The South Carolina congressman John McMillan—who was chairing the House district committee in 1967—was angered that Johnson named a black man to preside over the city. When Mayor-Commissioner Walter Washington sent in his first budget, McMillan plotted a reply: he had watermelons delivered to Washington's office. That particular fruit—prevalent on southern plantations—had long taken on a stereotypical slant when it came to blacks.

In Prattville, Alabama, Stokely Carmichael had been tossed in jail, charged with inciting a riot. Police claimed he had been yelling "black power" at them. The Student Nonviolent Coordinating Committee chairman, H. Rap Brown, hearing of Carmichael's arrest, quickly sought to cast blame. "We feel that this is a part of America's Gestapo tactics to destroy SNCC and to commit genocide against black people. We are calling for full retaliation from the black community across America. We blame Lyndon Johnson."

When whites were polled in the midst of the riots, nearly 50 percent attributed the dangerous unrest to agitators "with Communist backing." Yet more than two-thirds of the black populace who had been polled pointed to police brutality.

And there was Vietnam.

White House aides who wanted to update the president on the Marshall hearings—and the cat-and-mouse movements of Adam Clayton Powell Jr.—had to contend with his mind focused almost obsessively on Vietnam.

The antiwar protesters were marching outside the White House. The placards provided plenty of rich photo opportunities: "Jesus

Christ Didn't Carry No Draft Card." Johnson felt the war would wind
down because of attrition. "Once the Communists know, as we know,
that a violent solution is impossible," he said, "then a peaceful solution
is inevitable." The comment landed between the crosshairs of double-
speak and wishful thinking. In his 1964 State of the Union address,
Johnson announced that America must be "better prepared than ever
before to defend the cause of freedom, whether it is threatened by
outright aggression or by the infiltration practiced by those in Hanoi
and Havana, who ship arms and men across international borders to
foment insurrection." Lee Lockwood, a *Life* magazine photographer,
entered North Vietnam by way of Havana and scored an interview
with Premier Pham Van Dong. "President Johnson says he is prepared
to go more than halfway in the interest of peace," Dong said. "What
is 'halfway'? He comes from the other side of the Pacific to wage war
against us. We are already here!"

North Vietnam's leaders were being compared to Hitler. Communism would seep upon American shores if Pham Van Dong were
not crushed, American military leaders began to fear. Eisenhower
had passed the rattling war saber to President Kennedy, who had
sent upwards of 16,000 American soldiers and advisers into the thick
green jungles before his assassination. Johnson's huge 1964 election
victory had fueled his hubris. Now the men around him directing
the war—Robert McNamara, McGeorge Bundy, General Maxwell
Taylor—were bragged about as being geniuses. They were mostly
Harvard and Yale men, now given great powers, rushing the nation
upfield and into war with wild arrogance. The Gulf of Tonkin Resolution had given Johnson immediate and unchecked war powers. By
1965, he was committing American ground forces—500,000 and
counting—headlong into Vietnam. "I don't see that we can ever hope
to get out of there once we are committed," he said in private. "It's just
the biggest damn mess." He kept going, kept sending troops, the ghost
of Kennedy—war hero, beloved—haunting his psyche. He kept rushing into the quagmire.

In the American inner cities and ghettos, the war took on psychological interpretations that left uneasy feelings. Judges had begun giving many convicted black males options: jail or the army, which meant
Vietnam. As measured against their percentage of the population,

more blacks than whites were being sent to fight the war—and dying. Between 1965 and 1967, black deaths in Vietnam were 20 percent higher than those of whites. Black leadership across the country—having praised Johnson for his civil rights and domestic programs—began to condemn him for the war. Two months before Johnson's nomination of Thurgood Marshall, Martin Luther King Jr. appeared at the Riverside Church in Manhattan and proclaimed that the Great Society was being lost because of the Vietnam War. There was applause.

When Adam Clayton Powell Jr. reappeared on the scene—he had been sunning down in Bimini on his boat, *Adam's Fancy*, in the summer weeks of 1967—he announced plans for a speaking tour. He would rail against the Vietnam War and against cutbacks in social programs. He referred to himself as "the old man of the black revolution." While true that only senators would vote on the Marshall nomination, House members were watching, reading the winds, knowing that voters wrote letters to Congress and to the Senate. If certain House members who opposed Marshall saw a need to share their sentiments with the White House, they certainly would.

The White House was left to bemoan that the names Adam Clayton Powell Jr. and Thurgood Marshall had become linked while Marshall was being grilled about urban riots and the rights of criminals. It did not calm the White House either to be constantly reminded that Abe Fortas, President Johnson's first high court nominee, had, two years earlier, sailed through his hearings in less than a day.

BECAUSE HIS WORK in the federal government had pretty much taken him off the lecture circuit, many of the people attending the hearings, black or white, had never before seen Thurgood Marshall, or his wife, Cissy, up close. As a federal appeals court judge, then solicitor general, Marshall had been all but invisible to a newer generation. But some of those who were crowding into the hearing room were from this new generation; they were coming of age and being influenced by a black-is-beautiful mantra. No black man had ever had such a public coming-out in America, where his life's work had been laid out and examined, as Marshall was now going through. Additionally, it was rare to see a public figure in an interracial marriage.

Cissy Marshall—elegantly attired every day of the hearings, wearing her thin white summer gloves—endured the stares alongside her husband with grace. For years and years, there had been these stares, these moments of awkwardness—should she simply explain she loved her husband? That she was better than America's racial nightmare and interracial hang-ups that others harbored? The NAACP had steeled her for years against these slights and the meanness of others. She had patiently explained to her two sons their racial heritage, that it was mixed and that they should be proud. She had managed to ignore the unkind whispers in grocery stores that sailed in her direction through the years. Some things, however, she simply could not forget: her father had fretted about just how dark the skin of her firstborn child would be.

Cissy Marshall smiled as she walked through the hallways outside the hearing room. Occasionally, someone from Hawaii would stop and introduce himself. Filipinos—who shared her heritage—were as rare in the halls of the Senate as Negroes were.

An interracial marriage like Thurgood and Cissy Marshall's was so rare in the public sphere of America that it still startled. On the other side of the country, in Hollywood, Stanley Kramer and William Rose knew as much.

Rose was a screenwriter. He was born in Missouri but had come to spend a great deal of his life in Europe. He received Oscar nominations for his screenplays, *Genevieve* and *The Ladykillers*. In 1966, Rose was in Beverly Hills, visiting the director Kramer. Kramer was well respected, having received acclaim for directing *The Defiant Ones* in 1958—a groundbreaking interracial story starring Sidney Poitier and Tony Curtis and set against the backdrop of a prison escape—and *Judgment at Nuremberg* in 1961. In the conservative mind-set of Hollywood, Kramer was considered progressive. During his visit with Kramer, Rose mentioned yet another idea for a film. It would be about a young white woman who falls in love in 1960s America with a Negro. She then must bring him home to meet her parents. Kramer's eyes lit up. He knew it sounded shocking, but America was engulfed in talk about race. It was unavoidable, even if Hollywood was choosing to look the other way. Actors wanted to work with Stanley Kramer. He had no trouble assembling a cast: the screen legends Spencer

Tracy and Katharine Hepburn would play the parents. Sidney Poitier would play the Negro. Katharine Houghton—Hepburn's niece in real life—would play the daughter. It would be called *Guess Who's Coming to Dinner*. The answer: a Negro! The movie was filming just as the Johnson administration was preparing for the Marshall nomination. The Poitier character was drawn as the Super Negro, a scientist and all-around do-gooder, someone good enough for his white bride-to-be.

Cissy Marshall's husband might have been super, but he had his flaws: he drank and smoked and slipped into speakeasies and sometimes could turn into a roué around women. She loved him all the same; her husband lived in the real world, and she knew it.

By the time of the Marshall hearings, *Guess Who's Coming to Dinner* had finished filming—though was not yet released—and studio executives in Los Angeles were nervous, wondering about its fate. The made-up story that sprang from the mind of William Rose would go on to Oscar glory.

Negroes actually gave Thurgood Marshall a wide berth. He and his Filipino wife deserved to be left alone. Besides, in the minds of Negroes, Thurgood could do no wrong. He had saved black men from the electric chair, and he had done it time and time again. Negroes had gone to see that movie back in 1962, *To Kill a Mockingbird*, about a white lawyer, Atticus Finch, who defends a Negro accused of rape. He gets the Negro acquitted, but, alas, the town mob murders the Negro. That was movie stuff. Negroes, however, would tell you that Thurgood Marshall lived in a realistic and gritty world. And he had gone into dangerous southern towns at night. And lived to tell about it. Negroes would tell you Thurgood Marshall was Atticus Finch before Atticus Finch.

Beyond the stares and looks of curiosity she received around room 2228, Cissy Marshall had a simple desire at the conclusion of every day. She wished to get her husband home and serve him dinner.

11

Dear Mr. President

White House staffers were awed by the warmth black audiences showed LBJ.

PRESIDENT LYNDON JOHNSON might have been bewildered and
disillusioned about the Vietnam War, but he held no such feelings
about the torment of black pain and how that pain was deepening a
schism between black and white America. That was a situation he
understood quite clearly. Plenty of people, he realized, "worked hard
every day to save up for a week's vacation or a new store and they
look around and think they see their tax dollars going to a bunch of
ungrateful rioters." He expected goodwill expressions about the nomination of Thurgood Marshall, but the hearings were still going on, the
battle for that nomination still taking place, and the public hosannas

were, for the most part, held in check. Why, hadn't Senator McClellan tried to link Marshall's feelings about the *Miranda* ruling and other criminal cases to showing sympathy for criminals—which by extension pointed directly to the rioters out on the streets right now?

In regard to the Supreme Court, what seemed to grab Negro attention in the late spring of 1967 was the court's ruling in *Walker v. Birmingham*. The suit flowed from the beginning of the protest marches and boycotts in Birmingham, Alabama, led by Martin Luther King Jr. The town fathers had long presided over what was referred to as the most segregated city in America. Their sheriff, a bigoted figure by the name of Eugene Connor, who liked to be called "Bull," glared menacingly into TV cameras as he directed his men to spray both adult and child alike with powerful fire hoses. Houses had been dynamited in Birmingham; marchers and boycotters sent off to the local jails. But King would not yield. He was jailed, right along with the protesting children, for violating the city's injunction. His lawyers got him out. But Alabama wanted him tossed back in jail. City attorneys took the case to court, and it wended its way to the Supreme Court. The high court ruled, 5–4, on the side of Alabama authorities. It sent tremors through the civil rights movement. "Now even the Supreme Court is against us," is how Martin Luther King Jr. felt.

Turmoil was everywhere. Johnson had actually leaned on Marshall before he nominated him to the high court, dispatching him in early 1966 to confer with various civil rights leaders. Marshall met with both Roy Wilkins of the NAACP and Whitney Young of the National Urban League in Wilkins's office. They were all old friends, and their bonhomie was genuine as they slapped backs and exchanged warm handshakes upon seeing one another. They'd all been through various incarnations of the civil rights wars. But there were, as always, grave matters at hand. The trio discussed the national scope and dimension of black unrest throughout the country and how, despite much legislation, misery and agony—and anger—were still prevalent.

Marshall reported back to President Johnson the results of his meeting. There was a litany of woes to share: increased black voter registration in the Deep South was taking place, but there were still challenges and outright threats; foundation money for civil rights aid was drying up; the NAACP itself "was broke." Still, Marshall—proudly aware that he and Johnson were conjoined—sought to encourage the president. "I will not give up because we cannot give up," he told LBJ. It was at such moments that President Johnson's admiration of Thurgood Marshall seemed to soar even more. LBJ realized that many of Marshall's high court victories had all but laid the foundation for both the 1964 Civil Rights Act and the 1965 Voting Rights Act. "The real hero of this struggle," Johnson had told the nation, "is the American Negro." Johnson's measures expanded Marshall's earlier court victories and put the muscle of the White House and federal government behind them. So Johnson abhorred what the southern Democrats were doing to his Supreme Court nominee. And he lamented that to fortify his own confidence in the outcome, he had courted William Coleman in case Marshall's nomination failed. But he knew this was high-stakes politics and he had to try to stay ahead of his opposition.

Johnson skulked about the White House. Quietly, he claimed he'd kill as many Vietcong as he had to in order to win the war and keep America safe from Communism. And he fumed that Adam Clayton Powell Jr. had gotten himself into such a mess—and the timing could not have been worse. As for the poor, did they even love him anymore? After passage of that monumental civil rights bill? Did they care about all the money and the food programs he had poured into the desperate inner cities of America? He felt that "the woman I really loved—the Great Society"—was now slipping away to "that bitch of a war."

And the bitch kept haunting his sleep.

Those chants outside the White House only got louder: "Hey, hey, LBJ, how many kids did you kill today?" He was trying to save the damn world, and they just didn't know it. He knew they were secretly pining for their so-called golden boy, Jack Kennedy, but Jack was gone. He was not coming back. He was that eternal flame over at Arlington National Cemetery. So it was up to him, Lyndon Baines Johnson, to fight and win this war.

And to get this black man onto the United States Supreme Court.

When the president smiled during these dark days, it sometimes made his aides practically jump with joy themselves. When they had a hand in making him smile, well, there was nothing better. And sometimes the letters that poured into the White House made him smile. So they'd bring him letters, especially the wonderful letters that had arrived about Thurgood Marshall and his nomination. The letters—"My Dear Mr. President"—came from all over the nation, from black and white, rich and poor. From the Reverend J. H. Screven of Newark, New Jersey: "You have in the Supreme Court every nationality but one, and that is Negro. I think it would be fitting and a good example, since all nationalities are serving and giving supreme sacrifice in Vietnam, if you would have a Negro gentleman who is qualified; not because he is a Negro, but because he is qualified and capable for the job, and he should be given the privilege to share as other nationalities have . . . Mr. Thurgood Marshall is the gentleman I have reference to." From William Jones of Brooklyn, New York: "I believe in these very emotional times it would be a wise decision to name Thurgood Marshall to the Supreme Court . . . especially now that the appalling Adam Clayton Powell case is upon us; it is necessary for some act of good faith to be shown. I believe Negroes will react gladly if the white man rewards a Negro who has been intelligent and qualifies."

Harry Lurge, explaining that he was a senior citizen and had lost most of his eyesight, wrote in from Van Nuys, California: "Recalling the conditions in the early part of this century when the Jews were segregated and harassed as much as the Colored people have been today . . . I remember the change that came about when President Woodrow Wilson nominated Louis Brandeis to the Supreme Court. Being Jewish myself . . . I take the liberty to suggest the name of Thurgood Marshall to the Supreme Court, whom I am sure will do well for the good of our country." From a bed at a veterans hospital in Canandaigua, New York, John H. Siebert got himself to a typewriter and praised Marshall: "Such an appointment would indicate clearly that your administration is dedicated to raising the status of Negroes in this country and to securing for them the rights that our laws indicate are theirs but which have been denied to them for so long." A group of Virginia NAACP members—who had witnessed the state's closing its school doors rather than abiding by the 1954 *Brown* school desegregation ruling—expressed their profound joy about Marshall's nomination: "By this action . . . you have earned the admiration and gratitude of the majority of colored Virginians." Robert E. Jones of the Unitarian Universalist Association believed the nomination "will be long remembered as a milestone in the history of race relations in the United States." Clement D. Fowler of New York City felt compelled to couch his missive in political voting dynamics: "A white man, I applaud most earnestly your appointment of Thurgood Marshall to the Supreme Court . . . Now if you could show equal courage in working out a détente in Vietnam . . . I would be even more proud—and glad to vote for you in 1968." Ben Ramey, an attorney down in Houston, wrote, "The appointment of Thurgood Marshall . . . is the best news I have heard on the radio for a long time. When I was learning to practice law here in Houston and running errands for Thurgood and Bill Durham, we used to speculate on when the day would come." Mary Jane Wing wrote to the president from Atlanta: "Having just heard of your appointment of the Hon. Thurgood Marshall to the Supreme Court . . . I say again: Bless you!" She added a postscript: "A WASP—and a middle-aged, deep down South female one, just to keep the record clear." A telegram arrived from David Grant of St. Louis. "History will be unable adequately to assess your understanding of the impelling needs of our claimed democracy," he wrote in quite a mouthful to LBJ. "Your nomination of Mr. Marshall as a one-ninth, last resort guardian of our liberties demonstrates the depth of your conscience . . . No matter the repercussions, God Bless you."

Congressmen of course had plenty to keep themselves busy dealing with the Powell situation. But Marshall also was never far from their minds. "It will naturally be unpopular in some quarters," Congressman Thomas Foley wrote and warned the president, "but it is thoroughly justified by . . . Marshall's personal and legal qualifications with total disregard for his race." Foley cited the hope for equal opportunity in America and, in conclusion, wrote, "If history fails to record you as the greatest contributor to that cause since Abraham Lincoln, you have been misjudged." The letter from C. M. Keever, mayor of Tuskegee, Alabama, had to hearten President Johnson inasmuch as it went right at the crux of the southern problem. "His legal prowess and knowledge," Keever wrote of Marshall, "are matters of record and performance, if Southerners are honest with themselves in weighing his qualifications."

A handwritten letter arrived from Harlem. It must have touched members of the White House staff because it also made its way to the president's attention. In the letter, one sensed an elderly lady, perhaps sitting alone with pen and paper by a window's light in one of those Harlem tenements in which Marshall himself had at one time lived. "I have written you once before when you passed the Civil Rights bill and now you have done it again in promoting Mr. Marshall," Ida Wright wrote to the president. "I think you made a good choice. Want you to know I think you are wonderful. Did more than any other president . . . You are a friend to my people." And doubtless one of the more meaningful letters that landed on LBJ's desk came from Horace Busby, his longtime Texas friend who had once served as Johnson's speechwriter and had been in Washington with him since the 1940s. Busby knew Johnson as few in Washington did—what drove the man, what was inside his heart, his fears and ambitions—and his ongoing psychological warfare with his fellow southern Democrats. Busby also knew that the longer the Marshall confirmation hearings went on without a resolution, the more determined Johnson would become to emerge victorious. "He was a creature of war," Busby would recall of Johnson. "His whole life had been shaped in the buildup to World War II."

And the hearings had become nothing less than war.

"Apart from the history-book significance," Busby told Johnson about the Marshall nomination, "the man, in my opinion, merits the appointment as a man and lawyer—and that is the most significant aspect of all." Busby had first met Marshall in the mid-1940s when Marshall was bouncing in and out of Texas working on the all-white voting primary cases and trying to integrate the University of Texas, as well as the assorted other urgent cases that pulled him into the state. "Twenty years ago," Busby's letter continued, "when he came to Austin to argue the first University of Texas integration case for the NAACP, Marshall won over everybody covering the case or connected with it. We all sat around then talking about how unfortunate it was that a lawyer of such distinguished ability had, because of race, so little opportunity for recognition."

Of course not all the letters were full of sweetness and light. Plenty of letters and telegrams flowing into the White House had a far different tone and slant. After opening her letter with an anti-Marshall salvo, Irene Johnson of Pittsburgh candidly shared her sentiments: "I don't have a fence around my house nor do I live on a ranch out in God's Country. Myself and most of the rest of the people in this Country have to walk down the same street with them (without Secret Service Men protecting them), shop in the same stores, sit in the same shows, and now they have invaded my Church." She was, of course, referring to black people. John Miller wrote from Santa Ana, California, "Your recommendation of one Thurgood Marshall to the U.S. Supreme Court is completely insane." J. R. Christians wrote from Grand Rapids, Michigan, "You appointed Mr. Marshall. Why not Stokely Carmichael." Gerald Johnson's note arrived from Little Rock, Arkansas. "Today's liberal Supreme Court appointment," he allowed, "is appalling. You will need a lot of luck in 1968." And from Winchester, Massachusetts, came Carl Dane's sixteen words: "You Despicable Bum How Do You Have The Guts To Do It Coming Out Of Texas."

SO LBJ SWEATED as he read the letters about Thurgood Marshall. And he implored his aides—and Phil Hart, and all the senators whom he trusted through the years and whom he had helped in the past with special favors and appointments—to help him get his nominee onto the Supreme Court. Few presidents worked the phones as he did. He kept the White House operators hopping at all hours of the day and night, then he'd bark for a butler to bring him some stomach medicine, and after he had taken his medicine, he'd get back on the phone offering a torrent of praise about his Supreme Court nominee. And when aides told him maybe he'd better get some sleep, he told them, time and time again, that nights were for other men who wanted to sleep, but not him, not LBJ.

The White House—and Washington—was poised for day four of the Thurgood Marshall confirmation hearings. The White House took note that Chairman Eastland was back in town.

DAY FOUR

12

A Rebel's Last Roar

South Carolina's senator Strom Thurmond, a onetime presidential candidate
on the all-white Dixiecrat party ticket—and quite proud of his fitness routine—
showed no hesitancy in expressing his dislike of Marshall and his judicial
philosophy during the hearings.

CISSY MARSHALL had seen her husband go through a variety of trib-
ulations in the past. Even before they were married, she had been
aware of the everyday challenges he faced heading the NAACP Legal
Defense Fund. It gnawed at him deeply when he couldn't save someone
from an outrageously long prison sentence—or the electric chair—and
his heavy sighing could sound almost like rumbling. She had watched
him endure the assaults on his legal legacy during the long wait for
his federal court of appeals seat. But this battle of wills and stagecraft
with the southern senators who opposed her husband's Supreme Court

nomination was different because the stakes were so high. If the nomination failed, would they move back to Harlem? Thurgood Marshall sometimes salved his wounds with drink—in his most melancholy moments, he would say a stain of alcoholism ran through the family genes—and now his wife wondered if he would turn to drinking too much if all went asunder.

Thurgood Marshall couldn't keep himself from turning over numbers in his brain, imagining yet again which senators would vote for him and which ones would vote against him. Rather than ease his worry, the tactic only seemed to exacerbate it. He bemoaned the gag order he was under from the White House. He would have loved to have cornered some of the Capitol Hill reporters and spilled his guts about what he had seen in the South, and about how constitutional rights of Negroes had been trampled upon, and about how he thought the hearings were revenge for the legal success he had in the South. But he could not. When the White House would tell him it was working behind the scenes, it meant little to Marshall, because the Kennedy camp was supposedly working behind the scenes on his federal appeals court nomination, and it took Henry Luce's intervention to get that nomination moving after months and months had passed.

As a debater—first in college, then in courtrooms all around the country—Thurgood Marshall relished a good fight. He had a keen sense of competitiveness. He *wanted* to be on the U.S. Supreme Court. That was Olympus for lawyers. He had argued so many times before the court that he practically felt at home there. He could look around room 2228—standing room only, Negroes and whites intently listening—and know how much it especially meant to Negroes that he ascend to the highest court in the land. "It was the equivalent of Jackie Robinson in baseball," says Jack Weinstein about Marshall's nomination.

Weinstein had worked with Marshall on the *Brown* desegregation case and later became a judge. In the summer of 1967, he too found it complicated trying to read the tea leaves about what was going to happen inside room 2228. He felt deeply the worry and concern the Marshall family was enduring.

·   ·   ·

A RESTLESSNESS was now becoming palpable among some Marshall partisans on the committee. Eastland, the chairman, was back presiding, his one-day absence causing Marshall to worry about what he might have been up to. (For one thing, he had been plotting anew with Strom Thurmond.) Eastland's thick right hand reached for the gavel. When he banged it, the room grew quiet, and the proceedings once again got under way. It was Thurmond's turn.

STROM THURMOND came of age in South Carolina knowing no other way of life except Jim Crow, one race subjugated to the other. After the Civil War, Reconstruction lifted blacks in South Carolina into the political world in ways previously unimaginable. They headed local offices, became business owners, were even elected to the U.S. Congress. But following the end of Reconstruction, blacks were attacked and massacred; federal troops often had to be dispatched into the southern states to keep them safe.

In 1897, J. William "Will" Thurmond—Strom Thurmond's father—counted himself a fervent ally of "Pitchfork" Ben Tillman's. Tillman, a virulent racist who was blind in one eye, was a South Carolina governor, then a U.S. senator. Will Thurmond took any slights against Tillman very seriously. One morning, walking to his office, Thurmond was called a "low, dirty scoundrel" by an anti-Tillman agitator. Thurmond pulled out a pistol and shot the man dead. Onlookers, aghast, scattered in shock. A man had clearly been murdered, right in front of them. Thurmond did go to trial for the shooting, but his quick acquittal on the murder charge was linked to the muscle of the Tillman machine.

Will's son Strom attended Clemson Agricultural College, and was soon in the broil of politics—state senator, judge, then governor. When Thurmond was governor, twenty-one convicts were escorted to the electric chair. All were Negro. "I didn't know what color they were," he unconvincingly proclaimed. As governor, he couldn't abide President Truman's integration of the military, which is why he offered himself up as the Dixiecrat presidential candidate to run against Truman. "I want to tell you, ladies and gentlemen," he thundered as he accepted the Dixiecrat presidential nomination from a stage in Birmingham, Alabama, "that there's not enough troops in the Army to force the

Southern people to break down segregation and admit the Negro race into our theaters, into our swimming pools, into our homes, and into our churches." While President Truman squeaked out victory, Thurmond, on the ballot in sixteen states, won four of those states, acquiring more than a million votes.

In 1954—the year of Thurgood and the *Brown* decision—Thurmond throatily attacked the court ruling and launched a write-in candidacy for the U.S. Senate. He pulled off a surprising win, landing in Washington against the glow of one of Marshall's enduring court victories. Ten years later, in 1964, Thurmond—who had abandoned the Democratic Party for Barry Goldwater's Republican Party—took the floor of the U.S. Senate, joined by other southern senators, to stage a weeks-long filibuster against the 1964 Civil Rights Act. It was quite a sight to see Thurmond, an angular man, his brow sweating, his arms waving wildly, howling on the Senate floor for so long. In 1957, Thurmond's filibuster lasted more than twenty-four hours against Eisenhower's Civil Rights Bill but failed to stop the bill.

Lyndon Johnson did not want a filibuster of his Supreme Court nominee. The mere thought of the possibility made him furious.

Before the hearings got under way again, some attendees cornered Phil Hart and Joseph Tydings, wanting to know just when the hearings might conclude. The senators told them they had no idea.

SENATOR EASTLAND began the proceedings by producing a copy of a May 15, 1966, edition of the *American Bar News*, a popular periodical known by all lawyers.

> EASTLAND: Now, the *American Bar News*—you know what the *American Bar News* is?

Every lawyer knew about the *American Bar News*. Marshall had been cautioned anew between the hearings about not letting any of the questions—nonsensical or otherwise—get him riled up, and he calmly answered yes.

> EASTLAND: You are quoted in this article as having said that your concern was not with those "who resist any change in

the status quo with fury," but those "whose criticism of recent Supreme Court doctrine stems from a more intellectual level."

Marshall agreed the quotation was accurate.

EASTLAND: Well, then, doesn't that reflect that—isn't the meaning of that that the U.S. Supreme Court is an instrument and should be an instrument of social change?

MARSHALL: I don't think I was talking about the Supreme Court. I was talking about the people in general and especially the bar.

Eastland shifted to Marshall's interpretation of the Constitution, the ongoing war over words encouraged by both McClellan and Ervin, asking Marshall to again express himself on the matter.

MARSHALL: Well, I would make my every effort to read the Constitution of the United States, to read it all, and to apply it to the facts as I get them with emphasis on applying the law to the facts without regard to any personal predilections one way or the other.

EASTLAND: And do you agree that you can't have any—that the Constitution of the United States meant in the 19th century just what it means in the 20th century?

Marshall knew the question demanded a deft answer.

MARSHALL: The words mean the same; yes, sir.

EASTLAND: In deciding cases will you make a selection between constitutional principle based on your own sense of right and wrong?

Heads were already turning back and forth between Marshall and Eastland; those in the hard pew-like seats were all wide-eyed.

MARSHALL: Well, my own sense of right and wrong is the Constitution itself.

Hart, Kennedy, and Tydings liked that answer. But Marshall already knew Eastland was closing in on a point he wished to make.

EASTLAND: Will you decide cases on the basis of asking yourself the question, "Is this a fair proposition?"

MARSHALL: I would hope that my own ideas of fairness are based entirely on the Constitution, and I would not under any circumstances find—where the Constitution says this and my "personal feelings" say that, I would go with the Constitution. I am obliged to.

Eastland was inching closer to his ultimate question.

EASTLAND: Now, you have been in a lot of institutions in the Southern States.

Eastland knew this fact quite well. Most in the hearing room knew it.

EASTLAND: Are you prejudiced against white people in the South?

It was the penultimate question, and the gazes of the southern Democrats bore into Marshall. Merely by asking the question—loaded with racial history and naked curiosity about Marshall's relations with whites—Eastland had asked the question he felt millions of white southerners beyond room 2228 would want answered. This was the Civil War and Reconstruction and the great escape by Negroes from the South and the civil rights movement all rolled into one searing question. Marshall's pending answer—whatever it happened to be—would provide grist for the next day's newspapers, particularly across the American South.

MARSHALL: Not at all. I was brought up by what I would say way up South in Baltimore, Maryland. And I worked for white people all my life until I got in college. And from there most of my practice, of course, was in the South, and I don't know, with the possible exception of one person that I was against in the South, that I have any feeling about them.

It was a response untroubled by the reality of all the dangerous situations Thurgood Marshall had found himself in while traveling the South for so many years. Men had wanted him jailed. Men had threatened to kill him. It was but a tactical and political answer so that the proceedings would keep moving. Eastland's question, however, was the perfect opening for Strom Thurmond, who had been so quiet, who had waited for his moment.

Eastland turned toward Thurmond.

"Senator Thurmond?" he said.

NO ONE IN THE HEARING ROOM was quite like Strom Thurmond. He was sixty-four years old and, as the presidential candidate for the breakaway whites-only Dixiecrat party, had elevated himself much higher than Senators McClellan and Ervin had ever been. They had an almost iconic reverence of him. And now, in 1967, Strom Thurmond had to endure the 1960s having steamrolled his life and his beloved South. He wasn't, however, so quick now to brag about his onetime presidential campaign. In hindsight, it looked like an army of bigots disobeying and trying to undermine the U.S. Constitution. Their crusade seemed almost vulgar to 1967 eyes. The black college kids touring Capitol Hill would sometimes peek into his Senate office to see if he was there, just to see what he looked like. He had wisps of red hair, which he was losing, and his long face was speckled with spots. They didn't believe him for a minute when he started talking about states' rights and how he was trying to stop the encroachment of federal power. They thought it pure racist code. Waltzing through the hallways, some onlookers simply found it hard not to think of Thurmond as some kind of southern relic, still around from the Civil War itself. His voice retained a proud and hard rebel twang. He was more than ready for Thurgood Marshall.

THURMOND: Do you know who drafted the 13th amendment to the U.S. Constitution?

The Young Turks—Kennedy, Tydings, Hart—could not believe it. Such a question was eerily reminiscent of the questions southern voting registrars had been asking blacks for decades: How many marbles in this jar? How many judges are in the state of Mississippi? How many dots on the state map of Georgia? They were, of course, turned away when they couldn't provide the answers. Marshall answered no, then again answered no to a follow-up question of similar composition. Thurmond was unyielding, now swaying backward to the nineteenth century amid confused glances from audience members.

> THURMOND: Turning to the provision of the 13th amendment forbidding involuntary servitude, are you familiar with any pre-1860 cases which interpreted this language?
> MARSHALL: Well, Senator, I might say, frankly, I don't know of any case I had that involved the 13th amendment. My research on it would be very limited, on the 13th amendment.

Thurmond—reading from his notes—hardly allowed for a moment's breathing room as he quickly followed one question with another.

> THURMOND: Does the provision against involuntary servitude, in your view, abolish all compulsory labor for the benefit of a private person, and if not, what limitations would you read into this language, and on what legal basis would you establish such limitation?

Marshall again allowed that he hadn't been presented with a need to research the Thirteenth Amendment, but if he were required to do so, he would. Thurmond, undeterred, seemed empowered by what he believed to be the righteousness of his own questioning.

> THURMOND: Do you agree with an article by Prof. Alfred Avins in the Cornell Law Quarterly of 1964 that the provision against involuntary servitude in the 13th amendment prevents either Federal or State legislation which requires any person to render personal services to any other private person, whether the refusal to render such services is motivated by racial or religious discrimination or for any other reason, and if you do not agree with this view, why do you think that the provi-

sion against involuntary servitude does not forbid legislation requiring personal services?

The looks on the faces of many of the audience members registered near-total incomprehension.

Marshall told Thurmond he had no idea what he was talking about inasmuch as he had not read the article. Thurmond—who wore hearing aids—asked again.

THURMOND: What kind of legislation would, in your estimation, be forbidden by the provision against involuntary servitude?
MARSHALL: I don't know.

Moments later, Thurmond's next question left little doubt he was back into the bruising Civil War–era debates.

THURMOND: What is the significance, if there is any in your view, in the interpretation of the 13th amendment, that it was first rejected by the House of Representatives, which did not have a two-thirds Republican majority, and finally proposed only because of a switch of votes of a group of Union Democrats?

"Union Democrats" was a phrase not heard in official Washington in a mighty long time. Perhaps not since the Civil War.

Marshall allowed that he could not verify Thurmond's facts, and so he had no opinion.

THURMOND: Do you believe that the Civil Rights Act of 1866 was constitutional before the ratification of the 14th amendment?
MARSHALL: I researched that when the school cases were up, and I consider it unimportant because the amendment was adopted and they were reenacted.

Thurmond was relentless; Eastland seemed to be enjoying the back-and-forth.

THURMOND: Under what legal theories was the constitutionality of the Civil Rights Act of 1866 supported by its proponents?

Marshall was charmingly blunt in his answer.

MARSHALL: I think it was based on the 13th amendment, if I remember correctly. I could be wrong. That I don't remember. My last real digging on that was more than 10 years ago.

More and more, Thurmond's questions—their obtuseness began to elicit a rolling of the eyes from some committee members—seemed quite typical of the kinds of questions high school students might be asked on an academic game show.

THURMOND: What theories were then current in the Republican Party which gave support to the position that the Civil Rights Act of 1866 could be constitutionally passed by Congress to enforce the privileges and immunities clause of article IV section 2 of the original Constitution?

Marshall simply confessed he didn't remember.

It went on and on, the last rebel roar now being heard from Senator Strom Thurmond of South Carolina.

THURMOND: What constitutional difficulties did Representative John Bingham of Ohio see, or what difficulties do you see, in congressional enforcement of the privileges and immunities clause of article IV, section 2, through the necessary and proper clauses of article 1, section 8?

Senator Edward Kennedy could take it no more. He cut in.

KENNEDY: Could we just have some further clarification so all of us can benefit? . . . I was just wondering if the Senator . . . if we could have some further clarification of the question, because I really am confused as to what actually you are driving at, and I would like to hear the answer of the person that is called upon to answer.

Thurmond was stunned at the interruption and told Kennedy he had already repeated the question twice. There was impatience in his voice. Kennedy then asked Thurmond if he could perhaps pose the question a different way.

THURMOND: I don't think I can make it any plainer, if you know the answer.

Kennedy asked Thurmond how the question pertained to Marshall. Thurmond sensed he was being disrespected by Kennedy.

THURMOND: Well, I could tell you that article IV, section 2, did not set forth the powers vested in the United States. That's the answer.
KENNEDY: That's the answer. I see.

Those in their seats suddenly burst into laughter—as if Kennedy had found a way to ridicule Thurmond—which prompted Eastland to pick up his gavel and demand order. The snickers continued for a bit.

Thurmond, shuffling papers, his head rising and lowering from Marshall to his sheaf of papers, simply continued. This was his moment. The seats were all filled.

THURMOND: What did the term "civil rights" mean in 1866, and what rights were included thereby?
MARSHALL: The rights included in the phrase "civil rights" in 1866 meant the rights that were considered civil rights at that time. The delineation of them is not clear as of this day.

It was an acknowledgment, by Marshall, of all the turmoil going on beyond the windows of room 2228 at that very moment.

Thurmond wouldn't relent. There were plenty of reasons why. Marshall had once set foot in South Carolina and come away with that Waring judicial dissent, which had brought more media into South Carolina, which had catapulted Waring into hero status—outside the South, that is. And that had given impetus to what would become known as the *Brown* decision—which is why Strom Thurmond landed in the Senate in the first place. Which is why Thurmond had prepared so hard and been waiting for this very morning to tangle with Thur-good Marshall.

> THURMOND: What provisions of the Slave Codes in existence in the South before 1860 was Congress desirous of abolishing by the civil rights bill of 1866?
>
> MARSHALL: Well, as I remember, the so-called Black Codes ranged from a newly freed Negro not being able to own prop-erty or vote to a statute in my home state of Maryland which prevented these Negroes from flying kites.

The Marshall retort—heavy with naked injustice heaped upon blacks—seemed to rattle Thurmond a bit, so he quickly switched direction.

> THURMOND: Now, on the 14th amendment, what committee re-ported out the 14th amendment and who were its members?

It was followed by several more similarly arcane questions, to which Marshall's responses were "I don't know, sir," "I don't know, sir," "I don't know," "I don't know."

> THURMOND: In the equal protection clause, what is the reason for limiting equal protection to persons within the jurisdiction of the State?
>
> MARSHALL: I don't know any reason for that. It applies to every-body in the United States.

Thurmond couldn't stop himself. This was one-on-one, him and Thurgood Marshall.

> THURMOND: In 1862, the laws of Ohio barred Negroes from vot-ing, intermarrying with white persons, or attending school with white children. On April 11, 1862, [Representative John A.] Bingham was asked what rights Negroes held under Ohio law, and in particular, whether they could vote or engage in miscegenation ... Keeping in mind that Bingham was an

experienced Ohio lawyer and legislator who had been at the bar for 20 years, and was talking about the statutes of his home state, do you find this remark relevant in interpreting the equal protection clause as it applies to the right to vote, enter desegregated schools, or engage in miscegenation?

MARSHALL: I certainly agree that it's relevant, but certainly not controlling. All of this was litigated in the *Brown* case. Both sides, everybody, researched it. The Supreme Court found that there was nothing clearly derived from those debates.

There had long been stories—and photographs—of Strom Thurmond's physical stamina. He was an exercise fiend before exercise became a craze. In high school and college, he was a long-distance runner. When he first arrived in the Senate, he showed off photographs in national magazines of his standing on his head for long periods of time, which, to him, proved his stamina. And now, on behalf of his beloved South, he would prove to everyone the potency of his strength, his sheer will. He would put his beloved South on his shoulders and embarrass Thurgood Marshall.

THURMOND: Do you think that the Supreme Court must adhere to the original understanding of the Constitution as set forth by its framers, or may it ignore the intent of the framers and hold that a provision of the Constitution means whatever the Court chooses to have it mean at the moment?

MARSHALL: I don't agree with that statement at all, because I know of no instance where the Supreme Court has done what you said.

Moments later, Thurmond rolled back into the pages of the Constitution.

THURMOND: I want to advert to the theory you propounded last week that the Constitution is a living document which does not have to be interpreted historically, but may be construed in accordance with the needs of the hour . . . If your theory is followed, if Congress is not bound by the historical meaning of the clause, may Congress give the President authority to take reprisals on rioters, for example, by shooting them on sight?

MARSHALL: Certainly not.

Thurmond just as quickly flitted into yet another arena. He opened the door onto *Loving v. Virginia*, a case that delved into the emotional and historic tapestry of sex, race, love, and the American South.

On a summer night in June 1958, Virginia police broke into the home, and bedroom, of the married couple Richard and Mildred Loving, rousing them from sleep. He was white; she was black. They were arrested for being in violation of Virginia's 1924 Racial Integrity Act. At the time, Virginia was one of sixteen states that had laws prohibiting interracial marriage. The Lovings were sentenced to a year in prison, but the judge stated he would not enforce the sentence if they left the state. They moved to Washington. Missing family and friends back in Virginia, they sued, and the case reached the U.S. Supreme Court on April 10, 1967, and was decided June 12, 1967—a mere four weeks before the Marshall confirmation hearings began. The high court, in a unanimous and historic decision, ruled that the constitutional rights of the Lovings had been violated, and it overturned the nation's racial integrity laws. (Prior to 1967 under Virginia law, because of his interracial marriage, Thurgood Marshall and his wife, Cecilia, would have been subject themselves to arrest.)

> THURMOND: Do you know of any specific evidence relating to antimiscegenation laws which was presented to the Supreme Court in *Loving v. Virginia* which contradicted the historical evidence of the Commonwealth of Virginia that the 14th amendment was not intended to affect antimiscegenation laws, and if you do not know of such evidence, how do you justify the Court saying that the historical evidence was not conclusive?
>
> MARSHALL: I am only familiar with the opinion. I did not read the record in that case.

Thurmond doubted Marshall's answer, reminding him that the case had just recently been decided.

MARSHALL: It was one of 150 this term, 150-odd, and I can't read all of them.

And with that—an image of a white and black couple beneath bedroom sheets in violation of American law now lingering in the hearing room—Strom Thurmond, one of the last lions of the Dixiecrat South, brought his questioning of Thurgood Marshall to a close. He felt mighty good about himself. He accepted approving nods from McClellan, Ervin, and Eastland. In their collective minds, they thought Thurmond had proven that Marshall was fallible on his knowledge of the law and the Constitution. They thought that Thurmond had proven that there were grave concerns the Senate at large would have to consider before deciding if Marshall was fit for a seat on the highest court in the land.

THE AMERICAN SOUTH was a place of innumerable secrets. It would be revealed, in a detailed investigative *Washington Post* story in 1992 by Marilyn Thompson, that Strom Thurmond had carried on an illicit sexual relationship in his native South Carolina with Essie Butler, a black woman who worked for Thurmond's family. Thurmond was twenty-two and Butler sixteen when the relationship began. And from that relationship, a daughter, Essie Mae, was born in 1925. The child would be sent away by her mother to Pennsylvania, where she grew up. The story of Strom Thurmond's black daughter was explosive and drew condemnation from Thurmond family members when it was published. They categorically condemned it. Essie Mae—later Essie Mae Washington-Williams—also denied the story for years. But in 2003, six months after Thurmond's death, Washington-Williams revealed to a packed ballroom in South Carolina that she was indeed the daughter of Strom Thurmond. She said she finally decided to talk for the sake of history and that her children and grandchildren persuaded her to unburden herself. She died in 2013. "Ever since I was a child," James Clyburn, a black South Carolina congressman, would recall about Strom Thurmond, "I often heard that he had black children—under the definition that this country gives to what makes one black. The thing that was news is that it was told to white South

Carolinians in a public context." But in 1967, Strom Thurmond's sexual past with black women was just a secret rolling around the Negro grapevine in South Carolina, far removed from room 2228. And white America had no reason at all to pay attention to the mysteries of the Negro grapevine.

Chairman Eastland followed Thurmond's questioning, and he too had a particular angle he now aimed to pursue.

Eastland proceeded to ask Marshall about a book, *A Documentary History of the Negro People in the United States*, by Herbert Aptheker, that Marshall had once cited in a speech. Aptheker—who preferred the term Marxist historian—had, like W. E. B. DuBois and Paul Robeson, aligned himself with Communist sympathies in the 1940s and 1950s. The movement had found a foothold in some corners of Harlem and elsewhere, only to collapse against the treachery of spies, traitors, and Senator Joseph McCarthy, who ruined innocent victims in the naming of names. America, in 1967, was in a nasty war trying to stave off the spread of Communism in Asia. The word "Communism," whenever uttered, still carried dangerous underpinnings.

> EASTLAND: Well, now, of course, I don't want to leave the impression that you have ever been a Communist or anything like that, but did you know that at the time you cited this work the author of that book, Herbert Aptheker, had been for many years an avowed Communist and was the leading Communist theoretician in the United States?

Hart, Kennedy, and Tydings once again grew angry. One could see it on their faces. They clearly saw what Eastland had done: he had, however subtly, linked Marshall with a Communist.

Marshall quickly answered that he did not know of Aptheker's background.

Minutes later, Senator Hart asked Eastland if the hearings were now concluding for the day.

> EASTLAND: No, sir. We have got opposition.

Some committee members were suddenly surprised, as not all knew about the Marshall witness now waiting to testify against him. To dim whatever might be said in opposition to Marshall, Senators Hart and Kennedy voiced their approval of Marshall for the record. Hart proclaimed Marshall's "record of success" as solicitor general to be "magnificent." Senator Kennedy allowed that he looked forward to casting a favorable vote for Marshall in committee as well as on the Senate floor. Senator Ervin, though, wound up a soliloquy in which he unmistakably expressed doubts about the nominee: "I think that in passing upon the qualifications of an appointee to the Supreme Court, it is not only important for a Senator to determine whether the nominee has sufficient knowledge of the law or sufficient legal experience, but also to determine whether he is able and willing to exercise that judicial self-restraint which is implicit in the judicial process when that process is properly understood and applied by this, I mean whether or not he will base his decisions upon what the Constitution says rather than upon what he thinks the Constitution ought to have said."

Eastland then asked the witness opposed to Marshall to identify himself. His name was Michael D. Jaffe, and he was of counsel to a company known as Liberty Lobby, an organization he said represented 170,000 subscribers.

JAFFE: Liberty Lobby is strongly opposed to the confirmation of Mr. Marshall's nomination to the highest court in our Nation. Our opposition is based both on his lack of qualifications, and on the unfortunate attitude toward the law of the land which has marked his public career. Decisions handed down by the Supreme Court over the past 15 or so years revolutionizing virtually every area of American life have created a genuine crisis of public confidence in the impartiality and objectivity of the judicial branch of our government.

He went on and on, assailing Marshall for statements or speeches he had made in either churches or courtrooms over the past two decades. (It was never mentioned in the hearing room, however, that Jaffe's Liberty Lobby—formed in the shadow of McCarthyism—had been accused of anti-Semitism and a fascination with the teachings of Adolf Hitler. And that two of the group's biggest supporters were Senator Strom Thurmond and the Mississippi Supreme Court justice Tom Brady, an avowed segregationist and Eastland ally.)

JAFFE: Now, Mr. Marshall's associations with groups of questionable loyalty is clearly relevant to his fitness to serve as a Justice of the Supreme Court, and we believe that the committee should give these matters serious consideration. This unfortunate penchant for associations with organizations of a subversive nature runs throughout the nominee's career.

In concluding, Jaffe said he felt the "American people have a right to know the record and the legal philosophy of a man appointed to a position with the awesome powers and responsibilities of a Justice of the U.S. Supreme Court, and we commend this committee for attempting to bring these matters into the open."

Chairman Eastland—figuring Jaffe's testimony quite a resounding note to end on—announced an adjournment and hammered his gavel. Marshall remained silent, but Senator Hart did not. He took objection to Jaffe's testimony and wished to have introduced a statement by Alfred H. Kelly, a Wayne State University historian who had befriended Marshall during preparations revolving around the *Brown* court case. "It may be worth observing here," Kelly's statement said, "that I have also heard Marshall express personally his powerful conviction that communism and Marxism are fatal pitfalls for the American Negro which must be avoided like the plague . . . On more than one occasion Marshall in my presence bespoke his intense conviction that the destiny of the American Negro is to be fulfilled in terms of the American constitutional system."

But Kelly's statement was entered as an exhibit, and those in the hearing room would not hear it spoken. They would be left with Jaffe's testimony, which had been uttered loudly—though not so clearly, as Eastland had to caution him several times to slow his rapid-delivery speech down.

The patience of Marshall supporters on the committee—as well as that of the White House—had by now evaporated. They were clearly stunned that these hearings were still taking place at all. Senator Kennedy, exasperation dripping from his voice, asked Eastland when he planned to bring these hearings to an end. "I cannot answer that question," Eastland said.

Thurgood Marshall, his wife by his side, silently ambled out of the hearing room.

Strom Thurmond shook the hands of admirers. His aides circled him as if he were still the gallant southern hero.

Little could anyone foresee that an event was about to take place five hundred miles away that would rattle these hearings even further and send shivers of profound worry through the Marshall camp—not to mention the White House.

13

Flames

The deadly Detroit race riots—ignited by allegations of police brutality—
erupted during the Marshall hearings. They caused heightened worry
for both the White House and its Supreme Court nominee.

N O MARSHALL HEARINGS WERE SCHEDULED for Thursday, July 20, or Friday, July 21. It was up to the chairman's discretion as to when the hearings would resume. The strange postponement worried Thurgood Marshall and bewildered the White House. Marshall had cultivated contacts all over the nation in his legal career and especially in Washington. He called on some of those contacts during this interim to see what they knew, if anything, about the behind-the-scenes maneuverings of the Judiciary Committee. He could not find out anything that calmed his worries about the fate of his nomination.

Then, on Sunday, July 23, the nation was forced to shift its attention to Detroit.

In the long march toward black freedom in American history, riots, as destructive as they are, have always managed to snap those in power to attention. There were race riots in the early part of the twentieth century, and it is acknowledged that the so-called Red Summer riots of 1919 shifted the perception of the nation when it came to blacks and their demands for equality. That same summer, there were also race riots in Chicago; Knoxville, Tennessee; Omaha; Elaine, Arkansas; Charleston, South Carolina; Longview, Texas; and, among others, Washington, D.C. "Before the very gates of the White House," a *New-York Tribune* correspondent would write, "Negroes were dragged from streetcars and beaten up while crowds of soldiers, sailors and marines dashed down Pennsylvania Avenue, the principal thoroughfare in the downtown section, in pursuit of the fleeing Negroes. In one instance a restaurant, crowded with men and women diners, was invaded by a crowd of uniformed soldiers and sailors in search of Negro waiters." Willie Marshall—Thurgood Marshall's father—was traveling through Washington at the time and found himself caught in the uprising. His light skin might have saved his life, confusing would-be tormentors on both sides of the racial chasm as they spotted him blurring by them. The elder Marshall would tell his eleven-year-old-son, Thurgood, of the horrific riot. "He had a hell of a time," Thurgood would later recall. "The Negroes would run one place, the white folks were running the other. So, he was running back and forth. Wherever he went, he was wrong . . . I know that was a tough riot." An industrialized nation, two generations removed from slavery, could not remain quiet when one race was legally bound to second-class citizenship by law. "Your prophecies of serious race conflicts begin to come true," the newspaper columnist H. L. Mencken would write, in 1919, to the celebrated black writer James Weldon Johnson. Many years later, there would come another declaration. "Violence," the college dropout and radical black spokesman H. Rap Brown would say in the summer of 1967, "is as American as cherry pie."

Detroit had endured its own headline-making race riot in 1943. The wartime riot erupted between blacks and whites over the issue of jobs. There were thirty-four deaths, twenty-five blacks among them. At the time, the NAACP lawyer Thurgood Marshall had investigated police response to the riot. In Marshall's report, he concluded that whites had been repelled by police with "persuasion," while Negroes had received "the ultimate in force."

Now, against the backdrop of Thurgood Marshall's confirmation hearings, Detroit was about to explode again. And again, it would all revolve around the American trip wire of race.

In the early morning hours of July 23, 1967, two Negro undercover vice squad officers with the Detroit police went to a speakeasy on Twelfth Street. The speakeasy establishments were dotted around the city and frequented by blacks, an outgrowth of being denied admission to bars and restaurants in downtown Detroit during the 1950s. The establishments were illegal, generally opened around 2:00 a.m., and played host to a variety of characters—pimps, gamblers, prostitutes, the unemployed, the barely employed, the thankfully employed, soldiers just home from Vietnam. The speakeasies—sometimes oddly referred to as "blind pigs"—agitated higher-ups in the police department. They were intent on shutting them down, a determination put into action, operators of the speakeasies would say, when police were not getting their payoffs. The Negro undercover officers lolled around outside the Twelfth Street speakeasy for a bit, and at 3:45 a.m., confident of their plan of action, they called for backup. The celebration going on inside was in honor of two soldiers just home from Vietnam. Soon after the police call went out, other officers arrived. A sledgehammer was used to bust the door open. Amid the wafting rhythm and blues music and the toppling bottles of booze, men and women tried to scatter. They could not get out the front door of the dark establishment, because it was now blocked. Bodies were slammed up against walls. Screams flew from the women, grunts of protest from the men. Everyone inside the speakeasy was arrested. One eyewitness would say he saw police "dragging people down the stairs." Women, already in skimpy dress because of summery weather, had clothing that came undone because of rough handling by police. A woman poked her head out of a police wagon. "Brutality," she yelled.

A crowd gathered and grew as the police wagons drove away, the air scented with anger and unpredictability. For years, blacks in the city had complained about oppression at the hands of the overwhelmingly white police force.

William Scott III's father was a part owner of the just-raided speakeasy. Scott remained on the scene while his father was handcuffed and taken away. "Are we going to let these peckerwood motherfuckers come down here any time they want and mess us around?" he asked the on-edge crowd. They answered with thundering voices that they most certainly were not.

Because it was a Sunday morning, there were no summer school activities, and knots of youths came out on the street; they were joined by some adults, those with pent-up anger, but it was mostly the young who could no longer keep their rage in check. And they kept coming. By 8:00 a.m., upwards of nine thousand were on the streets. Some complained loudly they were tired of being taken to jail without reason; others protested they had acquaintances who had been arrested at the speakeasy; still others protested about raw racism. It was a misbegotten mélange without a common voice or leadership. It did not take long at all for the looting to begin. The police—they were not at full capacity because of the weekend—arrived and were shocked by the large number of youths now scattering about in all directions.

The first flames went up before 9:00 a.m., a case of arson, and then the fires started spreading. Adults—blacks and a few brave whites—tried to stem the rampaging but quickly found themselves cowering and forced to take cover. John Conyers, one of the few blacks in Congress—elected from Detroit in 1964—happened to have been home for the weekend. He raced to the scene of the rioting with an aide. He hopped atop a car and pleaded for peace. The marauding youths scowled at him. He was yelled down. "You try to talk to those people and they'll knock you into the middle of next week," he said, beads of sweat covering his face. Conyers would soon come to find out his own district office had been ransacked. He later mused that the only person who could possibly have communicated effectively with the rioters was Malcolm X, who, when he himself had participated in criminal activities in the city, carried the hipster name Detroit Red.

Four hours turned to six, which turned to eight, and only then—with flames everywhere, looters running amok, and the police on orders not to shoot unless their lives were in imminent danger—did Governor George Romney conclude he needed federal intervention.

City officials came to inspect the damage and were aghast at what they saw. Mayor Jerry Cavanagh, widely respected, had said just weeks before the riot that you "didn't need to throw a brick to communicate with City Hall." Now the bricks were flying everywhere. Youths were clutching them like cans of soup. Cavanagh, try as he might, had failed to digest the deep and underlying tensions in his city over jobs and housing—as well as the constant drumbeat of complaints about his belligerent police force. "The Negroes in Detroit feel they are part of an occupied country," the NAACP had declared two years earlier.

The reports of sniper fire that began crackling over police radios were particularly harrowing. The mayor took no time in realizing Washington had to help. "It looks like Berlin in 1945," he said.

The FBI director, J. Edgar Hoover, got an assessment report of the Detroit crisis from his agents in the city. He reported to President Johnson, telling him the scene was grim, offering dark premonitions that other cities might erupt as well. "They have lost all control in Detroit," Hoover told the president. Johnson was hesitant to send federal troops. He told aides he was being blamed for soldiers being killed in Vietnam, and now he would surely be blamed for Negroes—women and children!—shot down by federal troops on the streets of Detroit. But the consensus from the White House emerged that troops had to get to Detroit. Johnson dispatched the Michigan National Guard, Second Battalion of the 182nd Artillery.

The Detroit police felt ashamed that national guardsmen had to come help, as if they could not be depended on to do their job. They grew even angrier at the rioters, and some of them vowed revenge. "Those black son-of-a-bitches. I'm going to get me a couple of them before this is over," a Detroit police officer said within earshot of a reporter.

The Michigan National Guard rolled into the city heavily armed. Like the Detroit Police Department, it was an overwhelmingly white organization. Many of the guardsmen had avoided the draft, came from the suburbs or small Michigan towns, and were ill-equipped to handle an urban riot. They fanned out with rifles and bayonets at the ready, ducking fire and bricks and hearing the shrieks of innocent victims all around them. "I'm gonna shoot anything that moves and that is black," one guardsman vowed. As expected, libraries and recreation centers were closed the following day, Monday, then Tuesday as well. The Detroit General Hospital put its disaster plan into full effect. It hadn't done so since World War II.

President Johnson went on national TV on the evening of July 24 to talk about the flames in Detroit. He said looters would be arrested; he said pent-up anger was no cause for destruction and violence; he said the Republican governor George Romney had been unable to bring order to the city, so he was sending in federal troops. Republicans saw it as a dig at Romney and began privately blaming the president's War on Poverty and other social measures enacted to attack discrimination for the mayhem. "There were dark days before," Martin Luther King Jr. said of Detroit's riot, "but this is the darkest."

Grim news started surfacing in the besieged city: a four-year-old girl had been killed in her apartment from the spray of fire from a .50-caliber machine gun tank. A black man was cornered, then told by police to run. He was later found dead, a gunshot in the back. It was—as had been reported after the 1943 riot by Thurgood Marshall—the ultimate in force now being exercised. The deaths were mounting. Aging women in house slippers were rousted from their homes by gunfire—fired by police onto rooftops—and lined up, police insisting they must be shielding looters. Some fainted in the heat and stress.

On the night of July 25, around midnight, a contingent of police, state troopers, and guardsmen was protecting an insurance company near Woodward Avenue. They reported sniper fire from a block away and rushed toward the scene, which was the site of the Algiers Motel and an adjacent motel annex. The motel was on its last legs, suffering from urban blight and lost revenue. It now operated as a transient motel. But the police, upon arriving, were quickly directed to the annex out back, a place that also housed guests. There they found a group of twelve people inside, ten black males and two young white women who had worked as go-go girls in Chicago. They were just in the city to have a good time. It would later be revealed none of them had anything to do with the riot, but someone among them had fired a starter's pistol at the sky, which brought the men with heavy artillery to them in the first place. One at a time, several of the young men were dragged into separate rooms in an effort to get information about the "sniper." They were berated about having sex with white women, just as the white women were berated for consorting with "niggers." The young men pleaded for mercy, saying they knew nothing at all about a sniper and so could not point a finger at anyone among them. They were punched and pistol-whipped. Then, to deepen their fear of mortal danger, a gun was fired into the floor near each man's head. The guardsmen had witnessed enough of this type of terrorizing and decided to depart, leaving the Detroit police inside. And by the time the police left, Fred Temple, Carl Cooper, and Auburey Pollard Jr., three of the young black men, lay dead. Each had taken shotgun blasts to the chest and stomach areas. The other members of the group fled, escaping with their lives, shaking with fear, eager to tell anyone who would listen about what they had witnessed. In time, three white officers, David Senak, Robert Paille, and Ronald August, were arrested and charged with murder.

Auburey Pollard Sr., a military veteran, tried talking about his teenage son Auburey Junior. "I went in the service when I was sixteen years old—lied about my age—and I was only a baby," the father said. "That's the only way I learnt life, that's where I learnt my life. I wouldn't be hard like I am now if I hadn't have been. I learnt the hard way. But the poor little thing, he never knew what hardness was, he had to crawl through a bucket of blood. The poor little fellow, he didn't even know what life was really all about. Auburey was a beautiful kid, but he was just a baby, that's all. Just a baby."

Auburey's brother Chaney was rushed home from Vietnam, where he had been fighting for his country. At the funeral home, he broke down. "Momma," he said, looking at his mother, then at his brother in the casket, "they don't kill them in Vietnam like that!"

The trials of the police officers were moved out of the city to Lansing. The accused officers claimed the three who died at the Algiers Motel had been snipers and they were defending themselves. Those were lies, exposed in a prizewinning piece of journalism by reporters at the *Detroit Free Press* weeks after the riot. The accused white officers were acquitted. To much of the outside world, the verdict reeked of courtroom trials in the South in the 1940s and 1950s, when whites were exonerated for the cold-blooded killing of blacks. Thurgood Marshall himself followed the news closely of the Detroit riots. He was not surprised at the bloodshed. It all reminded him of an article he had written in the August 1943 edition of *The Crisis* magazine following his investigation into the Detroit riots that took place in June 1943. "The certainty of Negroes," Marshall had written, "that they will not be protected by police, but instead will be attacked by them, is a contributing factor to racial tensions leading to overt acts. The first item on the agenda of any group seeking to prevent rioting would seem to be a critical study of the police department of the community, its record in handling Negroes, something of the background of its personnel, and the plans of its chief officers for meeting possible racial disorders."

Forty-three deaths were recorded in the 1967 weeklong rioting. Among them were two firemen and a policeman. More than three thousand had been arrested. President Johnson would refer to it as one of the toughest weeks of his presidency. "It could be," Hugh Sidey would write in *Life* magazine, "that the thing missing in Johnson's city effort is some sense of communication between ghetto and White House . . . L.B.J. has an impressive box score of dollars and legislation, but he still has not struck that spark of sympathy in the cities."

In Washington, legislators were working the phones, watching the news reports from Detroit on television, and analyzing Johnson's nationwide speech.

A day after the riot had erupted, Senator James Eastland sent word through aides that the Marshall hearings would resume Monday morning, July 24. He was not going to let this moment pass. There was chaos on the streets. In Eastland's mind, this is exactly what he and Senator McClellan had been talking about, the *Miranda* ruling and all that came with it, liberties for the accused. Marshall had shown too much concern for criminal misfits—and some of those misfits were loose on the streets of Detroit right now! The White House realized there was nothing it could do about the sudden announcement of resumption of the hearings, even at the outset of a brewing national crisis. The Michigan senator Phil Hart wanted to get to Detroit, but he couldn't: he had just been told the Marshall hearings were resuming Monday morning. As Sunday night, July 23, wore on, Eastland, who sat on an internal subcommittee, came up with a plan he was sure would yield dividends. He would have Senator McClellan—the crime buster who had made his name conducting Senate investigation hearings—preside over the hearings when they resumed.

As Thurgood Marshall made his way to the Senate hearing room on Monday morning, the news was everywhere in Washington: Detroit was burning and engulfed in a racial nightmare.

DAY FIVE

MONDAY, JULY 24, 1967

14

The Constitution

Marshall's wife, Cissy, beside him at the hearings. Marshall's reputation
was so indomitable in the Negro community that their interracial marriage—
her ancestry is Filipino—drew little comment.

THE MOOD INSIDE room 2228 was worrisome. A major American
city was under siege. Senator Hart, who had been communicating
with Michigan officials most of the morning, looked exhausted. But he
knew the White House was counting on him to help guide Marshall as
the hearings moved forward. Chairman Eastland and the other southern Democrats—desperate to stop Thurgood Marshall from reaching
the Supreme Court—figured it a potent time to bring up issues of
crime and security, which they imagined would greatly weaken Marshall given his reputation as an attorney who had fought to give the
accused equal rights. Video footage of Detroit's ongoing rioting had
been playing on TVs in Senate and House offices all morning long.

In their efforts to stem crime nationwide, police departments had expressed to McClellan and Eastland that the use of wiretapping, and the need to negate the rights of criminals, was essential to the nation's security. (Eastland skipped the Monday hearings to glean what he could from FBI and intelligence sources about Detroit, confident that the master interrogator John McClellan would continue to expose Marshall's perceived weaknesses.)

Senator McClellan wasted no time as the hearings resumed; he started by asking Marshall about an issue that revolved around the plotting of criminal acts—wiretapping.

> MCCLELLAN: I am very concerned . . . about a condition that prevails in our country today, not only with respect to crime generally, but with respect to the tools that are made available to, or withheld from, law enforcement officers to use in their efforts against crime. And wiretapping or electronic surveillance has become a matter of national concern . . . I wanted to ascertain your views because apparently you have given a public statement which was quoted in the press. I refer . . . to the Washington *Evening Star* of Thursday, December 1, 1966, headlined "Marshall Tells Investigators Bugging Is Out," and subtitled, "Solicitor General Cites Recent Ruling by the Supreme Court."

(In *Berger v. New York,* decided just prior to the start of the Marshall hearings, the high court overturned another case and sided with a Brandeis position that the Constitution protects privacy.)

Marshall explained to McClellan that electronic surveillance simply would not stand up in court. He also told McClellan he had been referring to federal cases inasmuch as he had been talking to federal investigators.

> MCCLELLAN: I don't care whether it is Federal or State. We can talk about Federal as far as I am concerned.

It had grown testy just that quickly.

> MARSHALL: Under the rules the Federal investigators are not allowed to trespass except on security matters.

McClellan told Marshall—his voice quick and snappy now—he was talking about "a statute," upon which Marshall told McClellan he was bound by the recent *Berger* decision, "in which the decision left open to the legislature, the Congress and the State legislature the authority to set up regulations by which eavesdropping could be done by State order."

> MCCLELLAN: Are you saying that you do not subscribe to the doctrine or the belief that it is unconstitutional to provide by statute for such surveillance?

Marshall confessed he had "not made up my mind on that one way or the other."

McClellan grew exasperated. Beyond room 2228, Detroit was burning. Fears were spreading that the city might collapse entirely. Those fears had raced to the forefront of McClellan's determination to block Marshall's nomination.

> MCCLELLAN: I know we get criticized for trying to find out the philosophy of a nominee for the Supreme Court of the United States. But they are possessed of and they are exercising a power that is lethal in my judgment to the security of this Nation. And if we can't get some idea of the nominee's views with respect to the Constitution of the United States, then how am I to exercise my judgment and meet my responsibility in passing upon the suitableness of that nominee? . . . If we can't find out some of the philosophy with respect to the Constitution, what will be constitutional and what will not be, in a matter as grave as the crime crisis in this country, I am in a quandary . . . I perform my function—if there is a clash of philosophies, one of which is dangerous to the country in my viewpoint, and the other makes the country safe, and I have got to choose between them, and I can't find out the philosophy of the nominee, how am I going to function?

Senator Hart—his state and his city were afire—broke in, saying to McClellan that his was "a question that calls for an opinion, and a very tough one, on a constitutional question which the nominee may be confronted with if he is confirmed. I think there is a lot of difference between philosophy and how much more than a court order is connected with a thing like that."

McClellan accused Hart of simply trying to "rationalize" Marshall's answer.

> MCCLELLAN: But I know there is a crisis in this country, a crime crisis. And I know that the philosophy of the Supreme Court one way or the other on these vital issues is going to be of untold consequences, and has already been, in my judgment, of serious consequences to the crime situation . . . You talk about democracy and liberty and all these things; I think they are in jeopardy in this country. Look at the riots everywhere . . . No wonder the fellow out in the street, thinks that, if the Supreme Court has no regard for precedent in law, and can change it when he wants to, why can't I do as I please? We have an intolerable situation in this country, and I would like to find some way to check it . . . You may lecture me if you want to. I have told you what I think.

It was raw theater and those in their seats sat in rapt attention. Marshall quickly told McClellan he was not trying to lecture him. McClellan then turned to the issue of trespassing, citing a 1966 article from the Washington *Evening Star*.

> MCCLELLAN: You are quoted in the first paragraph of this article as follows: "Solicitor General Thurgood Marshall warns U.S. prosecutors that all eavesdropping is illegal, no matter how it is done."

McClellan demanded to know if the quotation was accurate.

> MARSHALL: The statement, Senator, was qualified by, if there is an unlawful trespass.

McClellan, staunchly believing that wiretapping was a useful tool against crime, remained undeterred, homing in on the issue of trespassing and intimating that Marshall's interpretation of the Constitution merely provided a boon to criminals.

> MCCLELLAN: I cannot support the nomination of anybody, I don't care who he is, from a brother up and down, who I think will not sustain the right of the sovereign to protect itself against internal danger, especially with the Constitution authorizing a reasonable search and seizure.

Marshall responded that the government had the ability and talents to meet whatever situations might arise in the country and that the country could meet them "in a constitutional fashion."

> MCCLELLAN: We haven't been meeting the crime situation very successfully.
>
> MARSHALL: I agree.

Senator Ervin entered the debate, offering a long discourse about search and seizure and the powers of the president.

> ERVIN: For some reason too strange for me to fathom, people who are very much inclined to condemn unwarranted exercise of constitutional power by the President or by the Congress seem to regard the exercise of such power by the Supreme Court as something rather sacrosanct.

He went on to talk about safeguards and judicial self-restraint, Marshall simply staring. (Every now and then during the hearings, Marshall could be seen turning his head backward and conferring with a White House official seated directly behind him. Marshall had been under strict orders not to veer into controversial territory or to become noticeably harsh while answering questions. White House officials had reminded him that while America was certainly following these hearings, the American South—its Dixiecrat politicians and rising Republicans especially—was following with a particularly close ear in hopes of hurting LBJ's reelection chances should Marshall's comments be deemed anti-South. Marshall privately chafed at the directive but knew the significance of his nomination and followed the playbook.)

> ERVIN: I love the Constitution, I am absolutely convinced that the faithful observance of the principles of the Constitution by the President, by the Congress, and by the Supreme Court is essential to the preservation of constitutional government in America. Apart from the Constitution, our country and all the human beings in it are without any security against anarchy on the one hand and tyranny on the other.

Senator Thurmond eyed and listened to all of this with grave interest. With a nod from Senator McClellan, he posed a question, asking Marshall what he thought about a Supreme Court justice who doesn't follow the Constitution and the possibility of his impeachment. The question swirled about like dark matter.

> MARSHALL: I have no position on that, because I can't conceive of a situation you are talking about. If you mean that a Supreme Court Justice, or indeed the Supreme Court itself, interprets the Constitution differently from the way Congress wants it interpreted, that Congress has a right to impeach, I don't believe that.

Thurmond had gotten himself entangled in murky water and Marshall knew it. Nevertheless, Thurmond was confident of his thesis.

> THURMOND: I was afraid you would take that position.

Senator Ervin, sensing the quizzical looks on some faces regarding Thurmond's comments, sought to come to the aid of his fellow senator, albeit while having them listen to a little bit of homespun native history.

> ERVIN: We had a great law teacher in North Carolina: Dean Mordecai of Trinity College, now Duke University. He said that the law makes strange requirements of different people; that it

requires the layman to know every jot and tittle of the law; and that it requires the lawyer to know a reasonable amount of the law, but that it does not require the judge to know a damned thing. I have to differ with my friend from South Carolina about the power of impeachment. I don't think the House can impeach a member of the Supreme Court because of his ignorance of the law or because of his lack of fidelity to the meaning of the Constitution when he undertakes its interpretation. The Constitution authorizes the House to impeach public officials for high crimes and misdemeanors. I don't believe a Supreme Court Judge's ignorance of the Constitution or his lack of ability to interpret the Constitution correctly is a high crime or a misdemeanor regardless of its serious consequence to the nation.

Marshall listened, a stony look on his face. Senator Thurmond had a final comment.

THURMOND: I think when a Supreme Court Judge blatantly violates the Constitution, it is in a different category than just an ordinary case of interpretation. And I want to make that distinction.

Once again, Thurmond's thinking seems to have lost followers. Senator McClellan began glancing around. There was silence. "Very well," he said.

Then McClellan shared with the committee and the audience that a gentleman had unexpectedly shown up—was in the audience—by the name of George Williams, from Baltimore, and wanted to testify. McClellan said Williams had told aides to the committee he wished to appear before the committee, in a chair and seated before a microphone, to make a statement. McClellan related that Williams had no prepared statement to share beforehand with committee aides, which had made them a bit nervous. McClellan did not say if the unknown Williams had come to praise Marshall (highly likely because he had come from Marshall's hometown of Baltimore) or to criticize him. Nevertheless, McClellan explained that Williams would not be offering testimony because he needed to run such a request by Chairman Eastland, who was absent.

McClellan realized everyone was curious as to when Eastland would return—and the future fate of the hearings. "I have no instructions from the chairman about closing the hearing, or adjourning it," McClellan offered, then called for a recess.

The riots in Detroit had hovered over the day's hearings, and senators wanted to get to their offices to check on the situation. Their aides had been close by, waiting with updates.

AS DAYS BEGAN TO PASS with no word from Eastland, Marshall demanded information from the White House about what Eastland might be up to, but it could offer no detailed insights. Marshall supporters on the committee were eagerly looking forward to resumption of the hearings, which would present them with their opportunity to praise him in as fulsome a manner as possible.

The riots in Detroit, of course, would rage for several more days, days in which Eastland called no confirmation hearings for Thurgood Marshall. Some Democrats thought it was political, allowing the scenes of mayhem to settle permanently into the nation's consciousness with hopes that it might boomerang and have an adverse effect on Marshall's chances. Voters fired off more pro and con letters about Marshall to their senators. Editorials about the Detroit riots appeared in newspapers, expressing sadness and dismay.

Back in their offices, southern Democrats ordered aides to look into any reactions Marshall had voiced in the past following major outbursts of rioting. They came up with nothing incriminating.

From his Senate office, Eastland finally announced that he would call no more hearings, that the Thurgood Marshall hearings were over! Marshall allies—especially the committee members who did not get a chance to speak up on his behalf—were both stunned and outraged. This was not the manner in which they wanted the hearings to end. But there was not a thing they could do. Eastland was the chairman. Those who backed Marshall huddled and concluded that they would have to begin working, right away, on their majority report, a compilation of their feelings and sentiments about Marshall's fitness to serve on the high court. Those who opposed Marshall would also write up a report.

A period of silence began to set in.

In the nation's history, a Supreme Court nominee had never appeared in person before a committee as long as Thurgood Marshall. His nomination had been announced when there was fire on the streets in Tampa, and now his hearings had concluded with fire on the streets in Detroit. It was hardly biblical, but the elfin writer James Baldwin—who had been roaming in and out of the Deep South and launching caustic barbs toward White House policy for years—had said something about the fire next time. Prominent names and lines from speeches flew from history books that had been carried into the hearing room. Race, sex, and crime—the triptych of the American story when it came to black and white—seeped into the hearings.

As fires rose in the distance—and a nation remained on edge—a Supreme Court seat was at stake. America would be asked to wait for the outcome. There was, as well, a kind of coda to the end of the hearings, as awkwardly as it came. Senator Everett Dirksen managed to have a letter, from Carl Shipley, chairman of the Washington, D.C., Republican Committee, inserted into the final day of hearings. "At a time when race relations in the United States seem to be regressing," Shipley wrote, "to a point where we may join the historical pattern of perpetual racial hostility similar to that that exists between Greeks and Turks in Cypress, or French and English in Canada, or Arabs and Jews in the Middle East, or French and Algerians in North Africa, it is important to the Nation to have a qualified member of the Negro community sitting on the Supreme Court."

The introduction of the letter, orchestrated by the powerful Republican senator Dirksen, meant to show Marshall's support across party lines.

NONE OF THOSE who had been sitting—or standing shoulder to shoulder—watching the Marshall hearings could have imagined how large a role the wide state of LBJ's Texas had played in the career of Thurgood Marshall. Or, for that matter, in the battles for Negro freedom waged in blood, honor, and sacrifice through the years.

15

Thurgood Marshall's Stand
in LBJ's Texas

The Brownsville riot of 1906, involving Negro soldiers and local citizens, was
one of many Texas stories Lyndon Johnson heard about when growing up and
that gave him uncommon sensitivity concerning the American Negro.

W HY WAS LBJ WILLING to risk so much for Thurgood Marshall? A
good part of the answer lay in LBJ's own Texas, where Marshall
had gone years earlier and altered the political landscape—a move that
began to change the outlook for Democratic politicians like Johnson.

When Johnson was growing into manhood in Texas, it didn't take
long for him to hear stories about Negroes and their struggle to gain
the vote and social freedoms. Against the backdrop of those stories
were other stories—about Negro riots and about what happened with
those Negro soldiers at Brownsville who were dishonorably discharged
by President Theodore Roosevelt because of a shooting incident within
the city's limits.

Lyndon Johnson saw the faces of those Negroes in his native Texas. And while they could vote in federal elections, they could not vote in the party primaries, diminishing their constitutional right. This is what Lyndon Johnson shared with fellow senators when he picked up the telephone to encourage them to vote for his Supreme Court nominee. He would tell them how wrong it had been to deny the Negro the right to vote, and how Thurgood Marshall had fought to gain them that right in his very own state of Texas, and how that had made the whole of America a bit more free when he won that big Texas primary case down there. And he would tell them that the Negro was not going to backslide; he would implore them to look out onto the streets of America; he would beseech them to look at the fires burning and the looting; he would tell them, time and time again, that Thurgood Marshall was the right man at the right time to go onto the Supreme Court.

When Thurgood Marshall first ventured into Texas in 1940—having written to his then wife, Buster, about "the really beautiful country down here"—he did not anticipate he'd find a Negro population in the city of Houston that would harness resources to fight the kinds of cases he wished to fight. But he would, indeed, find a Negro who resided in Houston and who—like many other Negroes across the state—had a powerful desire to vote in the Texas Democratic primary. But the State of Texas denied Lonnie Smith, a Houstonian, the right to vote in the primary because he was a Negro, just as it had denied others of his race before him. Marshall would take Smith's case all the way to the U.S. Supreme Court. That case would crack open a dimension of the Constitution and ultimately enable thousands—millions in fact—of other Negroes to walk into voting booths and mark the ballot of their choice. And that case would come to greatly improve the future fortunes of the Texan Lyndon Johnson as he launched a bid for the U.S. Senate and, in time, harbored larger dreams. With his arrival in Texas in 1940, Thurgood Marshall unknowingly was playing a kind of visionary role for the man who would, twenty-seven years later, nominate him for a seat on the U.S. Supreme Court. But like so many other places where Thurgood Marshall ventured—Texas would prove to be no different—there had been heated clashes that preceded his arrival, and those clashes had often been followed by the spilling of blood.

In 1828, the government of Mexico did away with slavery. That did not, however, stop the practice of slave smuggling, which continued in the territory and along its borders. It was a tricky dilemma for America when it began voicing interest in the 1840s in annexing part of the country to create another southern state. Many in the northern states of America were opposed to slavery, and if annexation happened, it meant America would be ushering a slaveholding state into the "land of liberty." Abolitionists howled and took to church lecterns and outdoor stages. It took some years—and the aftermath of bloody battles with the Mexicans—but the pro-slavery forces had their way as Texas was finally annexed into the Union in 1845 as a slaveholding state. (The city of Houston had been named after Sam Houston, who received great admiration for leading soldiers in the Battle of San Jacinto as Texas gained its independence.)

In Texas, southern planters and capitalists made themselves at home. As expected, with the election of President Lincoln in 1860, Texas cut its umbilical cord with the Union and joined the Confederacy. The move had to further frighten Negroes who had been forced into Texas with their owners, as they surely must have realized their only chance of freedom now lay with war. And war, of course, surely came.

Texas had long been a nightmare—as if there were any other word—for its slaves. In Houston, slaves were auctioned, right along with horses and mules, over at the Tattersalls and Auction Yard. Free Negroes did reside in Houston, but local officials resented their presence: there was a fear that free Negroes were plotting in darkened corners and corresponding with abolitionists. In the summer of 1860, in Dallas—which was a mere village then—a fire broke out in the business district and practically annihilated it. Business owners were befuddled by the fire's origins. A newspaper editor with an itchy pen wrote that the fire was the result of "a general revolt of the slaves, aided by the white men of the North in our midst." The same editor charged that Negroes were planning to gallop throughout the town poisoning wells with strychnine. Hundreds of Negroes across the state were rounded up as the false and wild charges spread. Slaves were beaten into making false confessions. Then they were hanged. Northern whites visiting the state who crossed paths with the marauders were also lynched. "Schoolboys," reported one newspaper account, "have become so excited by the sport in hanging Abolitionists that the schools are completely deserted. They . . . will go 15 or 100 miles on horseback to participate in a single execution of the sentence of Judge Lynch's court."

When freedom finally came for the Negro upon slavery's demise, those in Houston settled into what would become known as the Third, Fourth, and Fifth Wards of the city, forming their own enclaves. They held few illusions about their second-class status in the city. In early 1903, Negroes were forced to boycott the city's railcars because they no longer wanted to ride in the back of them. That same year, a Houston ordinance expressed sentiments about the Negro and the vote, stating that in a white primary only whites could vote.

It was the Negro soldier, at the turn of the century, who provided the Negroes of Texas with pride, determination, and, as it were, sometimes sorrow.

On August 13, 1906, a scuffle erupted inside a bar in Brownsville, Texas. A white bartender lay murdered and a white police officer injured. Just outside Brownsville sat Fort Brown, which housed soldiers of the all-Negro Twenty-Fifth Regiment. Some of them had fought at San Juan Hill in Cuba—"the last great mounted maneuvers in American military history," it was called—alongside the Rough Rider Teddy Roosevelt himself. But the soldiers, who arrived a month earlier, did not take easily to the racial limits put on them in Brownsville, and there had been mild skirmishes. There had also been "reports" of Negro soldiers acting aggressively in their conversations directed toward white women. Following the shootings of the bartender and the policeman, townspeople quickly cried that it was the Negro soldiers who shot the two men. They couldn't name any names, of course, because they didn't dare traffic with Negro soldiers themselves, but they knew it was them, would swear to it; they had seen a Negro here, a Negro there, fleeing. Their word and feverish emotions were plenty for the mayor, and within two days he was wiring President Theodore Roosevelt: "After firing about 200 shots, the soldiers retired to their quarters. We find that threats have been made by them that they will repeat this outrage. We do not believe their officers can restrain them." He went on: "Our condition, Mr. President, is this: our women and children are terrorized and our men are practically under constant alarm and watchfulness . . . We look to you for relief; we ask you to have the troops at once removed from Fort Brown and replaced by white soldiers." Roosevelt ordered an investigation by the War Department. The Negro soldiers categorically disputed the allegations. Evidence somewhat supported the claims of innocence made by the soldiers. Charles W. Penrose, the white commander of the battalion, had blown the whistle for roll call on the night of the melee—and not a single soldier missed it. Brigadier General William S. McCaskey commanded the army's Southwestern Division and had a bead on racial tensions in Brownsville. In a telegram, he expressed doubts to the War Department: CITIZENS OF BROWNSVILLE ENTERTAIN RACE HATRED TO AN EXTREME DEGREE . . . PROVOCATION GIVEN THE SOLDIERS NOT TAKEN INTO ACCOUNT.

Roosevelt was unmoved. Within days, he ordered the Negro regiment out of Fort Brown. This news was met with grave disappointment from Negroes around the country, who began, for the first time, doubting the sincerity of the Republican Party—the party of Lincoln—when it came to their quest for justice. The Negro soldiers continued their denials, even with the revelation that army shell casings had been found near the scene of the shooting, possibly pointing but not definitively pointing to a soldier who went on a solo mission to cause mayhem. Nevertheless, every Negro soldier was ordered to Fort Reno, in Oklahoma. Army investigators were adamant they had been involved: surely the townspeople hadn't seen dark-skinned and tanned ghosts! Still, as for positively identifying a single Negro soldier, an army official told Roosevelt that none could be made. Nevertheless, Major Augustus P. Blocksom sent his report to President Roosevelt on August 29. "That the raiders were soldiers of the Twenty-fifth Infantry cannot be doubted," he said. Blocksom—as if by way of further explanation—also reported that "the colored soldier is much more aggressive in his attitude on the social equality question than he used to be." Roosevelt announced he was going to dismiss the Negro soldiers from the military. An anguished Booker T. Washington pleaded with the president to not do it. "If you possibly can avoid doing so, I very much hope you will not take definite action regarding the Negro soldiers in the Brownsville affair," he wrote to Roosevelt, "until after your return from Panama." But as soon as Roosevelt returned stateside, he swung his big stick and dismissed the soldiers. There were ten million Negroes in America at the time, and it seemed as if his decision sank the emotions of all of them. In "almost . . . hours," according to Booker T. Washington, Roosevelt's popularity among Negroes plummeted. The New York *World* newspaper referred to the dismissals as "executive lynch law."

The Brownsville saga would mark the beginning of defection away from the Republican Party nationwide for Negroes.

One day, a short while after the Brownsville imbroglio, Roosevelt was strolling along the Potomac with his longtime friend Owen Wister. "When you turned those niggers out of the army at Brownsville," Wister asked him, "why didn't you order a court of enquiry for the commissioned officers?" The commissioned officers were white. Roosevelt had no satisfactory answer for Wister, save for his penchant for quick action and decisiveness. It would take decades, until 1972, before the soldiers of the Twenty-Fifth Infantry received justice. President Nixon, following an investigation conducted by the Defense Department, would be the president who finally pardoned the Negro soldiers. At the time, only one survivor, Dorrie Willis, was still alive. He received $25,000 and the restoring of his honor.

Eleven years after Roosevelt's ill-fated decision, what had been a leap of racially scarred imaginings in Brownsville took on a different degree of lethal reality in Houston.

On July 28, 1917, soldiers of the Third Battalion of the Twenty-Fourth Infantry rolled into Houston as part of a guard unit at Camp Logan to protect supply lines for the military. The city, a strong cotton port, boasted a population of 130,000 residents. The Twenty-Fourth Infantry was also an all-Negro unit with white officers. Houston officials were taken aback by the appearance of the Negro soldiers bearing arms but could do nothing about it. In previous postings, the soldiers had served in Manila, Cheyenne, Wyoming, and San Francisco and had not complained of any overt racial mishaps. But Houston was the Deep South. The public insults were immediate. When they rode streetcars, the soldiers felt compelled to yank the "Colored Only" signs down. "Look here," one soldier said to a local white citizen, "I want you to understand that we ain't no niggers." But many amongst the Negro citizenry looked upon the soldiers with a swelling pride. In a few short days, many in the community—women and especially children—came to look upon the soldiers as gallant figures. They'd watch them stride through town, wearing their crisp khakis, their shined shoes, their sharp hats. The soldiers were invited to social events, to dinners in private homes. And when they were in those private homes, they were astonished how consistently they heard—time and time again—about the incidents of police brutality that plagued Negroes in the city.

On an afternoon in late August, Rufus Daniels, a particularly brutish and muscular white policeman whom the city's Negroes had warned the soldiers about, pistol-whipped Private Alonzo Edwards as he sought to ask about paying a fine for a woman Daniels had arrested. When Charles Baltimore, another Negro soldier, rushed to inquire about Edwards, Daniels proceeded to beat him as well. Within hours, word raced back to the men of the Twenty-Fourth that Baltimore had died from his injuries. They became agitated; their whisperings were ominous. White officers told themselves the bubbling anger would soon dissipate. When Baltimore showed up at the base camp a day later—his face was badly bruised, but he was quite alive—it seemed to justify the feelings of the white officers. However, that night—August 23—upwards of 120 Negro soldiers, led by Sergeant Vida Henry, staged a mutiny and marched into Houston clutching their Springfield rifles. They were bent on revenge for their weeks of mistreatment and the savage beating endured by two members of their unit. They walked into town in formation in the dark and with utter control. And once they reached their destination, they began firing indiscriminately, ushering forth two hours of violence and horror. Bodies dropped, children among them; men leaped out of cars and fled, bullets whizzing all about them. Once the mayhem started, there was no stopping it. The soldiers raced around corners and across yards, sometimes stopping to kneel as they took aim, alternately killing or wounding another victim. Rufus Daniels, the police officer who had pistol-whipped the two Negro soldiers, came running toward the mutinous infantrymen firing his pearl-handled revolver. It was a brazen move, and he was quickly cut down. Negro civilians were spared, even as they froze with eyes full of panic watching the soldiers commit acts of murderous mayhem. Lance Corporal Henry Peacock, breathing heavily, glancing about the darkness, realizing white soldiers would surely be coming any minute, stumbled upon a Negro taxi driver. "Well," he told him, "if we die, we'll die like men." The firing proceeded, but it began to sink into some of the soldiers, weary from all the firing, that there would be no escaping this night. Eventually, some fled into the woods, as if to gather their thoughts; others finally loped off back to camp. One soldier, sensing futility, committed suicide in the woods. Fifteen whites lay dead, among them two white soldiers. Townsfolk were yelling into phones for help. National guardsmen were quickly dispatched by railroad. The train's engine roared noisily; the reinforcements arrived within five hours. With the infantrymen back on base, and military officials now alert to the mayhem, the scene was one of disbelief and bewilderment. The Negro soldiers were ordered to give up their rifles. One of their superiors told them the military now had two obligations: to keep them safe from the vengeance-seeking mob that was forming in town and to extract military justice for their crimes. Within two days after the shootings, the soldiers of the Twenty-Fourth Infantry were shipped out of Houston. Many of the Negro civilians left behind quickly followed them, fearing reprisals from townsfolk. News of the mayhem had spread nationwide. *The Houston Post* penned an editorial after the soldiers had departed: "The negro soldiers resent our separate coach laws, our customs which prohibit mixed schools, mixed service at places of public enterprise, but this measure of separation is absolute and will be maintained."

Sixty-three members of the Twenty-Fourth Infantry would eventually be charged in connection with the killings. The courts-martial, which began three months after the soldiers had left Houston, took place in San Antonio. The proceedings lasted three weeks. Five men were acquitted of the charges. Forty-one received life sentences. Thirteen others were less fortunate: their sentences were death by hanging. And in the predawn darkness of December 11, 1917, the men, secretly escorted by more than two hundred soldiers—the army feared a last-minute assault and effort to free them—were taken to a spot just east of San Antonio and on the edge of a training camp. The men could see the scaffold and gallows as they climbed from the trucks. Their coffins sat nearby but out of their sight. A Negro minister and two white chaplains were in attendance. The men refused to wear blindfolds and appeared preternaturally calm. They began singing, in unison, "I'm coming home, I'm coming home." It echoed like an old Negro spiritual. The nooses were placed around their necks. The morning light was still struggling to break through the trees. Birds were chirping. When they dropped—nine feet—a loud thud could be heard along with the creaking of the scaffold as their bodies twitched and swayed. Birds were scattering in all directions.

In the aftermath of the Houston tragedy, the Negroes in the city—and throughout the state—continued about their daily lives with a practiced instinct for survival, suffering all the indignities that came with second-class citizenship. The "Colored Only" signs were once again prominently displayed inside Houston's railway cars.

But there was no denying that through it all a political muscle had been awakened. In Houston, the Negro population had been making intermittent challenges to the law that forbade them to vote in the Democratic primary. But in 1923, another statute regarding primary voting was issued, which stated, "In no event shall a negro be eligible to participate in a Democratic party primary election held in the State of Texas, and should a negro vote in a Democratic primary election, such ballot should be void." Even if the state was large and vast, there were enough Negro doctors, nurses, funeral parlor directors, and teachers in Texas to form an impressive and noticeable middle class. Those middle-class men and women knew well the events of Browns-ville and Houston. They also knew that the State of Texas—never mind their college degrees—did not want them to vote and they would have to do something about it. Local branches of the NAACP were opened in El Paso, in Houston, in Dallas, in Corpus Christi, in any city where there were enough of them to sustain a branch of the civil rights organization.

Lawrence A. Nixon was a physician who resided in El Paso. He had earned his medical degree at Nashville's Meharry Medical College in 1906. He arrived in El Paso four years later. He easily stood out—a Negro physician with a growing clientele—among the other Negroes in the city. Nixon soon purchased a drugstore and also became a domi-nant voice in the local NAACP. His drugstore served as a meeting place to discuss political issues of the day; disenfranchisement was always a hot topic. Nixon believed his relations with whites in the city to be good. They shopped in his drugstore, could see that he had stature in the community. His stature gave him independence; he was not dependent on a paycheck from whites. Without fear of financial ruin, he could stand up for what he believed in. On July 26, 1924, he decided to attempt to vote, challenging the statute that forbade Negroes to do so. "The judges were friends of mine," Nixon would come to recall, "they inquired after my health, and when I presented my poll-tax receipt, one of them said, 'Dr. Nixon, you know we can't let you vote.'"

Nixon did not intend to sit idly by. His local NAACP assured him it would support a legal challenge. Fred Knollenberg, a local white attorney who was well respected among the city's Negro population, was hired. He firmly believed Texas, when it came to Negroes and the vote, was violating both the Fourteenth and the Fifteenth Amendments. The national headquarters of the NAACP in New York City deemed the case important as well and threw its financial support and legal assistance behind it. The case wended its way to the U.S. Supreme Court, where arguments began on January 4, 1927. (Knollenberg, however, would be replaced by two NAACP-affiliated attorneys: Louis Marshall—no relation to Thurgood—a crack constitutional lawyer who had worked on the Leo Frank case; and the ageless Moorfield Storey, also a constitutional lawyer and one who had, from 1867 to 1869—in the Civil War's aftermath—served as an aide to the abolitionist senator Charles Sumner.) Two months later, in a 9–0 decision written by Oliver Wendell Holmes, the court ruled that Texas had violated the equal protection clause of the Fourteenth Amendment. The court would write, "We find it unnecessary to consider the Fifteenth Amendment, because it seems to us hard to imagine a more direct infringement of the Fourteenth . . . That Amendment not only gave citizenship to persons of color, but it denied to any State the power to withhold from them the equal protection of the laws."

It sounded like victory, and to many Negroes in Texas and beyond it smelled like victory. But sharp-eyed legal analysts noticed what was missing from the decision: there was no mention of Fifteenth Amendment violations and redress, which would have included reinforcing the right to vote regardless of race. The decision only answered a citizenship question. It unwittingly gave Texas officials "an escape hatch" by putting voting decisions in the hands of local, so-called private committees. And Texas officials realized as much. "The Supreme Court has held the Texas Democratic primary law prohibiting negroes from voting unconstitutional, but they can't keep the various local executive committees from passing rules prohibiting the negro vote," Texas Democratic officials huffily countered. Private committees could determine who, in Texas, was qualified to vote. Dr. Nixon refused to give up.

Nixon recruited new attorneys, and these attorneys came from Houston, a city whose Negroes had endured riots and were not afraid of a fight. James Nabrit, Carter Wesley, and Jack Atkins had a Negro law firm in Houston. Nabrit and Wesley had studied law at Northwestern; Atkins attended Yale. They possessed sharp legal minds and plenty of confidence. Between them, they also owned a real estate venture, a newspaper, and an insurance company. Nixon believed in them, believed they could succeed in garnering him the right to vote. The attorneys, however, were defeated in the Texas courts, where the case would always be an uphill battle. Still, in 1932, Nathan Margold took Nixon's new case all the way to the Supreme Court again. Nixon was challenging tricky new rules adopted by Texas Democratic officials in the aftermath of his original court victory to keep Negroes from voting. The Supreme Court this time ruled—yet again—in Nixon's favor. *Nixon v. Herndon* was close, 5–4, but Benjamin Cardozo, writing for the court, ruled that Texas had adopted unconstitutional measures to keep the ballot slip out of the hands of the Negro.

Not surprisingly, Texas officials reacted swiftly: they convened in their legislature and repealed those parts of the measure that caused the five justices to rule in Nixon's favor. The dispute dovetailed around party machinery—the state Democratic convention bylaws as opposed to those of the state executive committee. Nixon's "victory" allowed room for the Texas Democratic Party to wrest power back from the executive committees simply by doing away with primary election statutes, whereby they themselves could exclude Negroes, and did so, as they now stated that "all white Democrats who are qualified under the Constitution and laws of Texas and none others are to be allowed to participate in the primary elections." The editor of *The Austin Statesman* admired the newly adopted footwork of the Texas Democratic Party: "This is a white man's government way down here in Texas. This is a white man's country . . . the Texas negro . . . is popular in his place—that of hewer of wood and drawer of water." In 1932, Dr. Nixon went to vote in the Texas primary. He was again denied. Both the National Bar Association and the NAACP made appeals to the Department of Justice to get involved. An agent in San Antonio with the Justice Department's Division of Investigation (later the FBI) was ordered to look into the matter of voting complaints by Negroes. After a cursory probe, the agent, Gus T. Jones, told his superiors that a deeper look wasn't necessary because "the denial of the negro the right to vote was not a matter of fact but a matter of law."

By 1934, Negroes all over the state were feeling the pangs of the Democratic Party's shiftiness. While in the small towns, a few Negroes might be allowed to vote, supplanting the primary rule, it was in the larger cities—Dallas, San Antonio, and Houston—where whites enforced the rule with strictness. The door that had appeared to be opening by virtue of Supreme Court rulings had now slammed shut again. Nixon's so-called victories were proving meaningless. The Texas maneuver—adopting other statutes or doing away with existing ones—was mimicked by other southern states as they boldly changed state constitutions and amendments to continue thwarting the Negro vote. And there was always a much cruder option: violence.

The Negroes of Houston had a couple of prominent watering holes, places where many would go to meet, plan, commiserate, slap one another on the back, but especially talk politics. The best-known places were the Third Ward Civic Club and the Harris County Negro Democratic Club. Richard Randolph Grovey was a well-known gadabout who belonged to both organizations. He was born out on the prairie, near Sweeny, Texas. He had been a rural school principal before moving to Houston in 1917—the very year of the infamous uprising by the Negro soldiers. Grovey opened a barbershop in Houston. He'd pause—scissors in the air, above an unfinished head—to expound on city government, President Franklin D. Roosevelt, wrongs done to the Negro. He had moxie, and plenty of it: He'd show up at rodeos, and standing just outside the gates, he'd start talking about equality and politics. Some spat tobacco juice at his feet; he didn't care and kept the monologue going. Many were surprised when he showed up back home, in one piece. He was happiest in the environs of his political club. Grovey wanted to bring the lower-class Negroes of Houston together with its middle class. "We didn't go out and organize the school teachers and the doctors and write down a program for the 'little' Negroes," he recalled. "We called the washerwoman, the maid, the ditch-digger, the businessman, the cook, the preacher, the hod carrier, the dentist, the bricklayer, the teacher, the longshoreman, and the gentleman of the press." It was a shrewd move and forced Negroes from varying backgrounds to rally behind a common cause—their liberty. As Grovey put it, "We plan to use reason, the public press, and the Courts to let the world see Texas Democracy as it really is. We will broadcast these tactics of the Democratic Party managers to perpetuate civic injustice, unfairness in the Courts, police brutality—all behind the shibboleth: social equality."

One of those men pulled into Grovey's orbit was Hobart Taylor. Taylor, a powerfully built man who was born in 1890 in Wharton, Texas, showed up in Houston in 1925. It wasn't unusual that he happened to be the grandson of a slave—many local Negroes shared that family identity—but it certainly was impressive that he owned land and had earned an advanced college degree in business. After his undergraduate studies, at Prairie View A&M, Taylor went to work for Standard Life Insurance Company in Atlanta; he cemented his business savvy there by becoming one of its first salesmen to be responsible for $1 million worth of business in a single year. When he arrived in Houston—his graduate degree earned at the University of Pennsylvania—he had letters of introduction from financiers and bankers back in his hometown. They vouched for his trustworthiness. It was uncommon for a Negro at the time, but in 1928 Taylor secured a $10,000 loan in Houston and used it to purchase a taxicab business. The H.T. Cab Company, with offices on Dowling Street, had upwards of two hundred employees, and as profits rolled in, Hobart Taylor would become a very well-off man. (It was important to him that whites ride in his taxicabs, and they did.) He was proud of telling people, in that world of segregation, that he never walked through anyone's back door. He never heard the evil whisperings of men who muttered about a lynch rope. His father had both protected him and befriended the whites who lived in the rural community where Hobart had grown up. The whites of Houston—especially the business class—came to respect Hobart Taylor. He knew how to curry favor as well as charm: he'd send gifts to judges and police officials at Christmastime or upon their publicized promotions. But Taylor lamented that no matter how nice he happened to be, or how well trained and courteous his taxi drivers were, or how much money he himself made, his people, Negroes, could still not vote in Texas. Those two Supreme Court rulings had indeed upheld their *right* to vote, but Texas officials were still grinning mischievously because of their successful efforts to thwart their voting. They aimed, however, to keep fighting. As Walter White of the NAACP put it, the Negroes of Texas aimed to "immediately . . . test this latest subterfuge."

Negroes had certainly needed money to support those earlier cases as they wound their way to the U.S. Supreme Court, and Hobart Taylor was one of those who had been quick to reach into his pockets and help supply some of that money. In 1932, he got himself voted an officer of the Harris County Negro Democratic Club, the platform from which Richard Grovey did a lot of his protesting. And now, as Hobart Taylor was seen out and about on Dowling Street, or over at the Third Ward Civic Club, he couldn't help but hear what remained on everyone's mind: the raw desire to vote.

The national office of the NAACP had begun telling Grovey and others in Texas that it was going to mount another challenge to the Texas white primary system. Grovey—who had been chafing at the fact the NAACP national office often relied on white attorneys because of the scarcity of Negro attorneys in so many towns and cities—didn't like this call for patience. And he sensed something suspicious: he believed it all amounted to condescension on the part of the national NAACP office toward Houston. He talked about his feelings, from barbershop to civic club, in homes of acquaintances on weekends, standing in the sunshine outside church, and he finally convinced himself he knew what was best when it came to legal challenges, and what was best was to strike now, and he implored Houston's own legal brain trust to back him. He asked men and women to open wallets, and they did—Hobart Taylor and his legion of taxi drivers among them—because he was going back to court. He wanted Carter Wesley and Jack Atkins—the local Negro attorneys who had played a part in the first two challenges, working alongside NAACP lawyers—to fight his case as well. Wesley was particularly eager to launch a new voting case on Grovey's behalf. Wesley, a Houston native, had moved to Oklahoma after law school and won more than 80 percent of the cases he had argued before the Oklahoma Supreme Court. Now that he was back home in Houston, he felt he knew the vibe of Houstonians better than any outsiders did—such as those national NAACP attorneys. Wesley took great pride in his legal education (Northwestern School of Law), and that pride gave him as well as his good friend Jack Atkins (Yale Law) a bit of cockiness. They were two Negroes who had been successful at white law schools. And wasn't Yale Law and Northwestern School of Law far superior to Howard Law, where a good many Negro lawyers had studied? A fund was set up—the Grovey Primary Fund—and the dollar bills began to roll in to support Grovey's planned legal challenge. By January 1935, $1,500 had been raised. Couples strolled into the Grovey Benefit Ball—it was a hot ticket—wearing beautiful clothes, nodding at one another, talking about changing not only Texas but the entire South. "Never before," Wesley crowed, "since Negroes were disfranchised by the Terrell Election Law has there been such widespread interest on the part of Negroes all over the state in a common point of view and common objective." Through some smart legal moves, Wesley and Atkins got their client's case before the U.S. Supreme Court, where it was argued on March 11, 1935.

One of the things the NAACP had warned Atkins and Wesley about was that in 1935 this was a conservative Supreme Court, a court that had already shown eagerness to bite into Roosevelt's progressive New Deal legislation. The national NAACP's reasoning was if this court was going to be challenged anew, it was best to use more formidable legal arguments, which it was still trying to formulate. There was also a gnawing fear among many Negroes that if the court was given a chance to strike down the past two Texas voting rights victories—never mind that they lacked genuine muscle—it could result in a profound setback. Atkins and Wesley put forth their position to the court, which was that the Texas primary, constitutionally speaking, amounted to a real election and nothing else. They argued that Texas party officials had commanded ballots be given to everyone—except Negroes. The justices listened intently. Three weeks later, April 1—April Fools' Day, 1935—the decision came down. It was unanimous. And it went against Grovey, harshly confirming the fears of the NAACP. The door that had been cracked open a little by virtue of those earlier decisions not only had started to close—Atkins and Wesley must have heard it creaking in the questions posed by the justices—but was now being slammed shut. Wesley and Atkins were dumbfounded. And because three of four Negroes in America lived in the South, the heartbreaking decision seemed to go against black America as a whole.

It was Justice Owen Roberts who issued the court's ruling. Roberts had been the justice the NAACP lauded after he was chosen by President Hoover to replace the failed nomination of John Parker. The civil rights organization now felt double-crossed by Roberts. The high court said it was simply following a Texas Supreme Court decision, *Bell v. Hill*, which declared that Texas had a right to give leeway to its private associations and that those bodies could make their own decisions about membership. The justices concluded the plaintiffs had confused "the privilege of membership in a party with the right to vote for one who is to hold public office." To Negroes in Texas—and beyond—it sounded like gobbledygook. *The Houston Informer* ran a lengthy headline: "In 1935 the Supreme Court of the United States in Grovey v. Townsend Makes Political Slavery in Texas and the South Constitutional Just as the Dred Scott Decision Made Slavery Constitutional 78 Years Ago." Walter White of the national NAACP was crestfallen. "It should not be difficult to imagine the gloom we all felt," he said of the decision. "Years of hard work and heavy expense appeared to have gone for naught." Democratic Party officials in Texas—and elsewhere throughout the South—were ecstatic about the decision. "So the Negro is endowed by law with the privilege of exercising the ballot, and deprived by political considerations of exercising it with anything but consummate futility," said the editors of the *Texas Weekly*.

If those concerned with freedom looked backward from the *Grovey* decision, they could see two other decisions that, coupled with *Grovey*, seemed to construct a triple and devastating blow against the Negro desire for full emancipation. The so-called *Slaughterhouse Cases*—argued before the Supreme Court in 1873—had emanated out of New Orleans during Reconstruction. The cases involved, at least on the surface, the butchering of animals but turned on protections provided by the Fourteenth Amendment. The court proceeded to gut some of the protective clauses regarding the Negro when it came to that amendment. The *Plessy v. Ferguson* decision drove the "separate but equal" coinage into American law. And now *Grovey*—the denial of the Negro right to vote in primaries. One historian, citing those three decisions, referred to the *Grovey* ruling as the "nail in the coffin" of black aspirations. Thurgood Marshall was not with the national NAACP office when the *Grovey* decision came down. But he would get his chance to express his views in a letter to Carter Wesley, one of Grovey's lawyers, in the years to come. "If you want to know what I think about it," Marshall wrote to Wesley, "I think *Grovey vs. Townsend* was not only one of the biggest mistakes made in the fight for Negroes' rights, but it set the fight against primary elections back at least fifteen years." The NAACP now needed someone to pull the nail out of the coffin.

Richard Grovey's lawyers had plenty of time to ponder what went wrong in their presentation before the court. President Roosevelt abhorred some of the decisions the court had been making, and two years after the *Grovey* ruling he launched his "court packing" maneuver, which boomeranged against him, causing much embarrassment. (Roosevelt never uttered a word about the *Grovey* setback for public consumption, careful not to upset his white southern supporters.) Walter White of the NAACP was determined to continue the fight for voting rights at the highest levels—which meant a hopeful return before the U.S. Supreme Court. White now sought "the ideal circumstances and litigant" to forge ahead in the legal battle. Texas, with its assortment of progressive organizations—the Texas Negro Chamber of Commerce, the Interdenominational Ministerial Alliance, the Texas Council of Negro Organizations among them, as well as groups of Negro farmers—still remained fertile ground, and White knew it. No other state could boast the muscle of its collective Negro civic groups. And in Houston, Hobart Taylor, with his vibrant taxi business, was still whistling up and down Dowling Street and willing to open his deep pockets for voting equality. But sensing that there was now bad blood regarding the national NAACP office and the NAACP in Texas, White decided to visit the state to mend relations. He met with leaders across the state: clergymen, editors of weekly Negro newspapers, and those whites who supported the NAACP cause in the state. Once relations were mended, White and other NAACP officials set about looking for a client on whose behalf they'd launch another voting challenge. The NAACP eventually found that ideal client, right in Houston. His name was Lonnie Smith. By now, Thurgood Marshall was the go-to NAACP lawyer, and Walter White knew right away he wanted him to wade into the tough battleground of Texas.

In 1940, Lonnie Smith was elected a Houston branch NAACP official. Smith, along with other newly elected NAACP officials, did not wish to replay the *Grovey* drama and decided to welcome the direction provided by national NAACP officials in renewing the white primary fight. Smith was born in 1901 in Yoakum, Texas. He attended Prairie View A&M before being admitted to Meharry Medical College in Nashville to study dentistry, from which he graduated in 1924. By 1929, he had moved to Houston, where he set up a dentistry practice and became involved with NAACP causes. He married, but had no children, and devoted much of his nonworking life to civil rights activities.

In May 1940 in Texas, there was a meeting of all statewide NAACP branches in Corpus Christi. Thurgood Marshall was in attendance and urged the members to unify in defeating the white primary. The Texans listened raptly to the New York lawyer. Marshall realized, however, that the Negroes of Texas were getting wary of these judicial setbacks. "We want you to know, this is the last go-round," he recalled being told by one of the local NAACP members. "We've contributed four times before, if you lose this one, forget about it." Soon enough, the Democratic Primary Defense Fund was established. Negroes who cleaned the homes of wealthy whites, who drove taxis, who worked in the oil fields, who hauled trash, who shoveled up horse manure on farms, all contributed to the fund. The dollars and coins came in from across the state. Marshall himself was surprised by the fund-raising success: "We raised all that money—and it was around two hundred thousand dollars altogether—for expenses." *The Houston Informer*, the Negro-oriented newspaper, was ecstatic, proclaiming that "at last Negroes will work together instead of separately in a lot of weak cases."

It was on July 27, 1940, that the challenge officially began anew as Lonnie Smith tried to vote in Houston. He was denied a ballot by the Houston election judge S. E. Allwright. Marshall would eventually meet with Smith in Houston and proceed to file a complaint on his behalf, which wound its way to the Court of Appeals for the Fifth Circuit, located in Fort Worth. Marshall lost there too.

"Well, I'm going to the Supreme Court," Marshall told Chief Judge Joseph C. Hutcheson.

"Of course," Hutcheson replied, as if he sensed the inevitability of it all.

It was a bold threat on Marshall's part. The court had ruled for the white Texas primary system nine years earlier in *Grovey v. Townsend.* Now Marshall was vowing to meet up with the justices on the very same issue again. Marshall's boast could easily have been seen as an act of bravado: At the time he told Hutcheson of his intention, Thurgood Marshall had never appeared before the justices of the U.S. Supreme Court on any case approaching this magnitude. And in reality, if he were to reach that hallowed courtroom to take on Texas, he'd be taking on all the states below the Mason-Dixon Line, because they had punishing white primary systems of their own. He'd be shouldering the hopes and prayers of Negroes who were eager for the right to vote everywhere. Marshall's hope was that he could find judges who would not "blind themselves as judges to what they know as men."

THE MAN WHO NOMINATED the first Negro to the U.S. Supreme Court was born in 1908 in the harsh Hill Country of Texas. The Johnson family lived in a small farmhouse near the Pedernales River in Blanco County. In 1913, Sam and Rebekah Johnson moved to Johnson City, which was still inside Hill Country, a vast and barren expanse of land that measured twenty-four thousand square miles. Despite the last name, the Johnsons had no link to the heritage of Johnson City, even though their son Lyndon was quick to brag that they did. Sam Johnson got himself elected to the state legislature and sometimes took his growing and gangly son with him to the state capitol in Austin. Lyndon liked the environment—the rush of ideas, the battles over legislation, the ego of politicians on display. But when his father, after six terms, was out of the legislature, the family's fortunes turned: money grew tight; sometimes food was scarce. After high school, young Lyndon—fretting over college tuition costs—lit out for the western territory and spent two years in California. He did an assortment of menial jobs; it was the America of can-you-spare-a-dime reality, and it was a harsh comedown for young Lyndon Johnson. "All his life," one of his biographers would note, "he had 'talked big'—had boasted, bragged, swaggered, strutted, tried to stand out, shoved himself into the forefront—so incessantly that he had revealed a *need* to talk big, a desperate thirst for attention and admiration."

Within two years, Lyndon Johnson had abandoned California and was back home. He quickly turned his attention to college. In 1927, Johnson enrolled at Southwest Texas State Teachers College at San Marcos. He had a gift of gab and was a campus gadfly. When he graduated, in 1931, he soon found himself in Houston—that landscape of dreamland (job opportunity) and heartbreak (the riots of 1917; the ongoing white primary battle) for Negroes. Johnson was hired as a schoolteacher in Houston. At his high school, he became a debate coach and distinguished himself. It is most certain that Johnson came in contact with more Negroes in Houston than he ever had anyplace else in Texas. "I never had any bigotry in me," he would remark later in life. "My daddy wouldn't let me. He was a strong anti-Klansman. He wouldn't join the Methodists. The Klan controlled the state when I was a boy. They threatened to kill him several times." Johnson left his teaching job in Houston after nearly two years and took a job as an administrative aide to the Texas congressman Richard Kleberg. It was what he really wanted to do: be around those who made legislation, who changed lives. He was energetic, cocky; in Kleberg's office, he quickly seemed as big as Texas itself—whirling about, suggesting ideas, dictating letters to constituents back in Texas.

In Washington, the young Johnson found himself surrounded by the aura of President Roosevelt's New Deal, the unprecedented whoosh of ideas and legislation unspooled to attack the ravages of the Depression. He got the attention of not only Kleberg but, in time, Sam Rayburn, the powerful Speaker of the House who also hailed from Texas. And when First Lady Eleanor Roosevelt persuaded President Roosevelt to do something about the youths of America—jobless, losing hope, dropping out of school—he created the National Youth Administration (NYA). It would be a nationwide jobs program aimed at putting the young to work. There would be directors in each state across the country. For Texas, Sam Rayburn had just the ideal candidate in mind:

Lyndon Johnson. The Roosevelt administration—though it took a little bullying on Rayburn's part—followed his suggestion, and soon Lyndon Johnson, all of twenty-six years of age, found himself back in his home state, directing a statewide program out of an office in Austin, with an impressive title. He also had a staff that he worked very hard. He relished the job. Young people were put to work on roads and bridges; there were programs to encourage going to college. It was a bureaucracy, but he had the flexibility to think on the fly. Because Johnson's domain was all of Texas, little wonder he quickly found himself back in Houston—face-to-face with Negroes, who needed more help, it seemed, than anybody. And he was not shy about helping them. "In the middle thirties we didn't know Lyndon Johnson from Adam," a Negro leader in Texas would remember of Johnson's presence there. "We began to get word up here that there was one NYA director who wasn't like the others. He was looking after Negroes and poor folks and most NYA people weren't doing that." Johnson roamed the Negro college campuses in the state, offering help. When things didn't move as fast as he wanted them to—he was constantly complaining about bureaucracy—he demanded his aides move the damn paperwork faster.

As Johnson himself would recall of his interactions with Negroes in the state, "What I did was go around and get people to donate money for the equipment in the white areas and then apply that saving to Prairie View [a Negro youth job site] and use it to build dorms which they so badly needed. I'd stop over there to see how they were doing, on my way to the Houston office. Stayed overnight, ate with them." In time, it seemed a great many of the Negroes across Texas—out in the fields, in the factories—were hearing about young Lyndon Johnson; Hobart Taylor of Houston, who had been helping to fund those challenges against the white primaries, certainly heard about him. (Taylor would become a financial contributor to Johnson's earliest political campaigns.) And yes, Lyndon Johnson could be heard—now and in the years to come—uttering the knifelike racial epithet so commonly twirled against Negroes in those days—"nigger"—but the issue of race would prove not to have darkened his heart but to have widened it, enlarged it, suffused it with a kind of light. It clearly set him apart. "Well, the day I announced for Congress which was soon after the funeral of the man who'd had the seat, by the next night the announcement had been in the Sunday papers," Johnson would recall. "Four cars drove up to the apartment where we lived on the second floor, and out tumbled ten to twelve Negroes. They said they'd come to let me know that they'd find every Negro in my district and make sure they voted for me."

Who knows, given the impediments put forth by white election officials across the state, how many Negroes actually got to cast ballots for the congressional candidate Lyndon Johnson in 1937? (While Negroes were forbidden to vote in the primaries, they could vote in federal elections in the state.) Certainly some took advantage of that vote. More important, Lyndon Johnson had set himself on a course that would enable him to understand, better than most, the second-class citizenship for millions of its citizens that haunted black America—and America itself. "Somehow," he would say years later, "you never forget what poverty and hatred can do when you see its scars on the hopeful face of a young child."

Before Thurgood Marshall bounded up the steps of the U.S. Supreme Court (his co-counsel was the former federal judge William Hastie) to argue the Smith voting rights case, he and other NAACP officials had studied, closely, the May 26, 1941, decision, *United States v. Classic* that had been issued by the high court. It was one of the first cases brought by the newly created civil rights section within the Justice Department. It grew out of complaints made by white—not black—voters in Louisiana who told the Justice Department that their ballots were not counted in the 1940 federal elections there. Government attorneys charged Louisiana officials with illegalities. Assistant Attorney General Herbert Wechsler, standing before the court on behalf of the government and the Louisiana plaintiffs, argued that "election officials who willfully alter or falsely count and certify ballots" in primary elections were operating under state law—and thus violating citizens' rights inasmuch as the South was a one-party state and the primary results were tantamount to an election. Wechsler argued that federal authorities could indeed take on discrimination that had been proven to have occurred within the state electoral process—violations of both the Fourteenth and the Fifteenth Amendments. If Wechsler's argument held, it would lay a bull's-eye on the two cases, *Newberry v. United States* and *Grovey v. Townsend*, that had disenfranchised black voters as well. The court did not mention *Grovey* per se, but in a 5–3 decision it overruled *Newberry*, stating that Congress had power to "regulate primaries when state law makes the primary an integral part of the procedure for choosing candidates for federal office." The court, in the NAACP's mind, appeared to clearly be stepping away from *Grovey*, intimating that it, like *Newberry*, was in violation of the Fifteenth Amendment. It was a ruling that made Thurgood Marshall happy. Houstonians were quick to take note of it. "Whereas the Democratic Party had had all the protection and Negroes have been forced to scurry and hunt like beavers for a hole to get through," the Houston *Informer and Texas Freeman* wrote, "now the Negroes seemingly are sitting on top of the world, and the Democratic Party will have to burrow and hunt and dig to find a way to get by the famous Classic case."

It seemed natural for Thurgood Marshall to approach both Attorney General Francis Biddle and Wechsler concerning the *Smith* case, and he did, asking if the government would join with the NAACP on behalf of Smith. The request made Solicitor General Charles Fahy nervous. "We have already assisted the Negroes by winning the Classic case which gives them their principal ammunition," Fahy confided to Biddle. "Should we go further in their behalf and make a gesture which cannot fail to offend many others, in Texas and the South generally, in a case in which we are not a party? I think not." Biddle took Fahy's advice, and the government refused Marshall's request for assistance. "We were a governmental department," Wechsler would reflect years later, "and we had to get along with the Senate Judiciary Committee, which was dominated by the Southerners—and this seemed an unnecessary fight. When I told Thurgood that the answer would be no, he took it very well. He said, 'I'm sorry, we'd like to have you with us, but we'll just have to go it alone.'"

Just as President Franklin D. Roosevelt had been good for the career of the young Lyndon Johnson by virtue of his government appointment, Roosevelt was also good for Thurgood Marshall's legal aims. From the time Marshall had first set foot in Houston, in 1940, until the time he had been scheduled to step into the courtroom of the Supreme Court to argue the *Smith* case, in 1944, a notable shift had taken place on the high court. Three new justices—Frank Murphy, Robert H. Jackson, and Wiley B. Rutledge—had all been nominated and confirmed to the court in that time span. All were Roosevelt appointees. The court had clearly become more liberal; it was Stone himself who had written the recent *Classic* decision for the court.

For those who wanted to inhibit the Negro right to vote, and those who wanted to guarantee it, the *Smith* case was tantamount to a grave game of chess played by constitutional lawyers on both sides. It wasn't terribly surprising when both the federal court—Marshall had ventured into Texas yet again—and the court of appeals sided with Texas at the outset of the *Smith* challenge. It was on June 7, 1943, when the U.S. Supreme Court granted a writ of certiorari, agreeing to hear the case. With his own government on the sidelines, Marshall knew he would have to, figuratively, go it alone. He had little doubt, as well, what was at stake. Negro attorneys throughout the nation offered their emotional support and well wishes. Marshall would refer to the *Smith* case as "the first real big one I had."

On the day of opening arguments of *Smith v. Allwright*, November 10, 1943, the Supreme Court was crowded: Negroes, having been alerted to the importance of the case by the Negro press, seemed to be everywhere—outside and inside the courtroom. When Mary McLeod Bethune sashayed into the courtroom, the whispering commenced and heads turned. Bethune was one of the most famous Negro women in America. In 1904, she had founded the Daytona Educational and Industrial Training School for Negro Girls; after a merger, it became known as Bethune-Cookman College. The Roosevelt administration named her, in 1939, director of Negro Affairs for the National Youth Administration; she administered the programs for those Negro youths Lyndon Johnson was helping in Houston and other places in Texas. It was difficult to predict how a court might rule, but it did not go unnoticed that this Supreme Court was one that featured new and decidedly liberal justices, who actually seemed eager for a voting rights case. William Hastie and W. J. Durham were the attorneys assisting Marshall. Marshall opened by telling the justices what he had been saying all along: that the Texas primary simply undermined Negro voting no matter how state officials argued otherwise. Hastie went on to attack the *Grovey* decision. The justices were quiet; as one attendee would remark of Marshall, Hastie, and Durham, they were "surprised and baffled when the Justices sat on the edge of their seats to listen but asked no questions." The Texas attorney general, Gerald Mann, as expected, argued that the earlier ruling supporting Texas did not violate any of the constitutional amendments being debated. The justices, at the conclusion of arguments, had to ponder a question: Does the Constitution embrace "private" discrimination? They were certainly aware of their recent decision, in *Classic*, that had decided that Congress does possess regulatory powers over federal elections. At the conclusion of deliberations, Chief Justice Stone went back and forth in his own mind about who would issue the court's ruling. He first chose Justice Frankfurter. That selection gave pause to Justice Robert Jackson, who shared his concerns about Frankfurter's ethnicity, saying that Frankfurter "in the first place, is a Jew. In the second place, he is from New England, the seat of the abolition movement." Stone sided with Jackson's sentiments and chose Justice Stanley Reed, a southerner—and a Democrat. Reed never graduated from law school, though he did study at the University of Virginia Law School for a year as well as at Columbia Law. As solicitor general, it fell to him to defend Roosevelt's New Deal programs before the Supreme Court when they came under attack. The justices issued their *Smith* decision on April 3, 1944.

If it had been a chess game, the Marshall-led defense checkmated those who would deny Negroes the vote. Justice Reed, in writing the court's sweeping and landmark 8–1 decision, ruled on behalf of a humble Houston dentist and Negroes everywhere, as he cited this court's very own *Classic* decision in overruling *Grovey*, allowing that citizens were protected from discrimination by the Fifteenth Amendment. "The United States," the court wrote, "is a constitutional democracy. Its organic law grants to all citizens a right to participate in the choice of elected officials without restriction by any state because of race. This grant to the people of the opportunity for choice is not to be nullified by a state through casting its electoral process in a form which permits a private organization to practice racial discrimination in the election."

It was a profound voting rights victory for the NAACP. As soon as word of the decision reached Thurgood Marshall in his New York City office, there was joy and celebration. The phones began ringing; reporters wanted quotes. Someone dashed to get spirits; drinks would be poured, and there would be toasts. Marshall remained a bourbon man. The Supreme Court justice Frank Murphy tried to reach Marshall by phone to offer congratulations, but couldn't get through. "I apologized profusely, and Murphy agreed that a guy had the right to get drunk at a time like that," Marshall would recall.

Houstonians heaped praise on Marshall. Lonnie Smith, the Houston dentist on whose behalf Marshall took the case, called it a "great achievement" and pointed out that well-meaning whites had helped as well. Jack Atkins, who had been one of Grovey's attorneys, referred to the long line of white primary battles in Texas as "one of baffled hopes, sickening disappointments and grim deathless courage" that had been marked by "the patience, and endurance, and character of the Negro race at its best."

Thurgood Marshall deserved a victory lap, and there were plenty of speaking invitations to get him out on the road. "There is no reason," he told an NAACP gathering in Chicago after the *Smith* victory, "why a hundred clear cases of this sort should not be placed before the United States Attorneys and the Attorney General every year until the election officials discover it is both wiser and safer to follow the United States laws than to violate them." In Chicago, he cited the example of the Houston dentist Lonnie Smith, allowing that "the NAACP can move no faster than the individuals who have been discriminated against . . . We must not be delayed by people who say, 'The time is not ripe,' nor should we proceed with caution for fear of destroying the status quo. People who deny us our civil rights should be brought to justice now."

Once the joy died down over the *Smith* decision, however, a deeper reality began to take root. Poll taxes and literacy tests could still thwart the Negro vote, along with harassment and outright physical brutality. Marshall himself had little doubt that "new contrivances to bar Negroes from voting in primary elections" would be unveiled. Politicians who resented the *Smith* ruling wasted little time in expressing their opinions. John Overton, the Louisiana senator, was appalled by the *Smith* decision. "We're not going to submit to Negro voting in our elections," he vowed. "We don't need white primaries, or poll taxes. We can keep them out on educational qualifications." And the Mississippi senator James Eastland—the future Marshall antagonist as chairman of the Senate Judiciary Committee—allowed that the ruling portrayed "an alarming tendency to destroy State sovereignty."

There was no denying that in those months during the fall of 1943—the beginning of the *Smith* case arguments before the high court—and early winter of 1944—the conclusion of them—a great many eyes fell upon Texas when it came to furthering the emancipation of the Negro. The white primary battles had lasted nearly two decades. Thurgood Marshall emerged from those Texas primary wars a legal star. During Marshall's earliest years roaming in and out of Texas, he met Aubrey Williams. That meeting would lead to Marshall's first hearing about Lyndon Johnson. Williams, a native southerner, was born poor in Alabama. His grandfather had owned slaves. Williams knew the way to escape poverty was getting an education; he eventually received a doctoral degree from a university in France. He wanted to be a social worker, to help the downtrodden, and during the New Deal he caught the attention of the Roosevelt administration. Williams was appointed director of the National Youth Administration. He forged a close alliance with the NYA director in Texas—Lyndon Johnson. Williams had also come to know Thurgood Marshall as Marshall was driving and flying around Texas on the white primary cases. Williams told Thurgood Marshall that Lyndon Johnson was someone Negroes could trust. Marshall found out that the NAACP leadership in Texas at the time was "enthusiastically" behind Johnson the political candidate. "The Negroes down there, they know each other pretty well," Marshall would recall. "They were a pretty hard bunch. We followed their judgement." At the time, Walter White, the NAACP executive secretary, did arrange a meeting with Johnson, and White went on to convey to Marshall that Lyndon Johnson was a white southerner whom the NAACP could trust.

In 1946, Thurgood Marshall received the Spingarn Medal—the most prestigious honor bestowed by the NAACP and given for having made a distinctive contribution to the betterment of Negro life. Paul Robeson, the great activist, had received the honor the year before Marshall.

As for Lyndon Johnson, the pain on the faces of Negroes that he had witnessed in Texas, his home state, had undeniably touched him. He now carried emotions and memories that would reverberate throughout his life.

In 1948, Congressman Lyndon Johnson ran for the U.S. Senate in the Texas primary against Coke Stevenson, onetime governor. Stevenson was not a friend of the Negro in Texas. He was a segregationist. There had been a widely publicized case in which a black man—accused of raping a white woman—had been dragged from his hospital bed in Texas and lynched. Negroes were outraged. Appeals were made to Governor Stevenson; letters were written to Attorney General Francis Biddle, pleading for help. Biddle made inquiries to Stevenson about the incident. "Certain members of the Negro race from time to time furnish the setting for mob violence by the outrageous crimes which they commit," Stevenson told Biddle.

When Lyndon Johnson ran for the Senate in that 1948 primary, Negroes were not going to throw their support to Stevenson. Johnson found friendly faces among Negroes, Negroes who now, because of Thurgood Marshall and the *Smith* decision, could vote without disruption in the state. "We put money in and we campaigned for him actively because we believed in him," the Houston Negro businessman Hobart Taylor would come to recall of Johnson. Taylor realized the importance of discretion when it came to political activities surrounding the Johnson candidacy. "There were times when it wasn't so expedient for us to have large Negro gatherings developed from the political situations, and we wouldn't show up so that we wouldn't hurt Lyndon. But anyway he understood what we were doing and it finally got to the place where we could sit down and break bread together." The Johnson-Stevenson Senate race was bitter and controversial. There were charges of vote fraud on both sides.

Who knows how many Negroes—from San Antonio to Dallas, from Corpus Christi to Abilene to Houston, from little nowhere prairie hamlets dotted with falling-apart shacks—turned out to vote for Lyndon Johnson in that 1948 election? How many Negro men had pushed back their cowboy hats and wiped their brows and whispered something jubilant beneath their breath as they dropped their creased and papery ballots—with the power of the law supporting them—into the box? How many Negro women stood on tired feet—scrubbing and ironing the clothes of white families—with their precious ballots in the palms of their hands? Lyndon Johnson would need every one of those votes—cotton picker, street sweeper, maid, butler, schoolteacher, shoe-shine man, lawyer, librarian, taxi driver, barber. Each vote was powerful, as powerful as all the blood that had been spilled from Brownsville to Houston and beyond to make those votes felt. Johnson would win that roiling election by a mere eighty-seven votes. His critics would claim he stole it, would mock him by referring to him as "Landslide Lyndon." But he won, and the Negroes of Texas were happy he won. And he soon began vowing that he would do big things in Washington, big things for America. He was as ambitious as the Negro attorney Thurgood Marshall had been as he rode across Texas, determined to change the fortunes of the Negro voter, fortunes that would come to haunt every demagogic southern senator, including those on the Senate Judiciary Committee, for years to come. The *Smith* ruling, Marshall predicted, would, in time, change "the whole complexion of the South."

In 1940, there were 30,000 Negroes registered to vote in Texas. By 1947, three years after *Smith*, there were 100,000. By 1956, there would be 214,000 registered Negroes. Those were improvements, but the numbers were still painfully small. Before 1964, only 22 percent of Negroes were registered to vote throughout the American South. Yes, there was the *Smith* decision, but fear remained; voting rights activists still fell dead from gunfire.

IN WASHINGTON, during the 1950s, Senator Johnson's driver, Gene, sometimes drove Johnson's car back and forth between Washington and his home in Texas when there were things that needed to be transported by land. On occasion Helen, Gene's kindly wife, went along with him on the ride. One day, Gene, a Negro, looked perplexed when Johnson asked him yet again to drive to Texas. Actually, Gene finally confessed to Johnson, it all went deeper; it went to the respect a Negro man was trying to keep for his wife out on the road: "We drive all day but when we want to go to the bathroom just like you all do, we have to go out a side road and our women have to get behind a tree because we can't go into a filling station like you do. We get hungry and we've got to eat just like you do, but we have to go across the tracks to a grocery store and get some cheese and crackers because we can't go in a café. Or if some hamburger stand would take a chance on being insulted and try to get by them, we have to go around to the back and wait till everybody else is served to get something to eat. We drive hard all day long and it comes to 10 or 11 o'clock and Helen and I want to go to sleep." Johnson sat listening as Gene continued: "We can't go in a motel or hotel. We have to drive across the tracks and find some boarding house way down there where they'll take us in for the night because we're not allowed in the hotels or motels in the country." Lyndon Johnson would never forget that conversation.

WHAT THURGOOD MARSHALL had done in the Texas *Smith* case was lay a blueprint. It was a map, a direction. And what Lyndon Johnson had done by winning his Senate election was take an important step toward his ultimate goal—the White House. And once there, he could pick that map up. Then, through legislative willpower, he could grant his Negro driver the same rights that anyone had out on the American roadway—to sleep and eat in a place of decency wherever he wished.

Thurgood Marshall and Lyndon Johnson had emerged across the hard plains of Texas with victories. These were not total victories, as both knew, but they were the kinds of successes that set them on a certain trajectory, one that would lead to the proceedings in room 2228 of the Senate Office Building in Washington, D.C.

POST-HEARING

JULY 25—AUGUST 30, 1967

16

A Nominee in Limbo

Thurgood Marshall graces the cover of *Time* magazine in 1955.

I N ITS ULTIMATE DUTY of "advice and consent," the Senate Judiciary Committee, having concluded its hearings on Thurgood Marshall, now had to go about the work of passing judgment on his fitness for the high court and presenting those findings to the full Senate. The Judiciary Committee was—as those who arrived at room 2228 had seen—a committee of stark contrasts, polarized by political party, philosophy, and age. The committee had been described as "the crossroads of action in the process of selection of Justices." Now that action would be done in private.

And in private, Senators Phil Hart and Joseph Tydings knew what they had to do to secure Marshall's confirmation. They had to rally the U.S. senators from the northern and western parts of the country. Tydings liked the challenge. It certainly gave him an extra bit of adrenaline that Marshall hailed from his native Maryland. But it was also something else: Tydings—well educated, son of a U.S. senator himself—had seen the bitter effects of segregation and never forgot them. When he was in the sixth grade, his mother hired a driver to take her to fetch her son, who was away at military school. Mother and young Joe were quite happy to see each other. On the drive back, they stopped to get something to eat. The proprietor announced to Mrs. Tydings that the Negro, the driver, could not eat in the restaurant. "My mother blew up," Tydings would recall years later. Tydings became a lawyer, and it burned him up when Negro acquaintances, in the 1950s, were denied the right to eat at restaurants in and around Baltimore. He thought it was such grace on their part when they would urge him to not cause a scene.

Tydings and Phil Hart had felt that they could only imagine the challenges Thurgood Marshall had faced in his life. "We had geared up for the voting rights bill fight," Tydings says about himself and fellow senators Hart, Ted Kennedy, and Birch Bayh—the Young Turks now willing to take on the Old Bulls when it came to Marshall. "And now we had to do it again for Marshall's nomination. The voting rights bill indicated it all was a new ball game." The Young Turks—guided by Phil Hart—needed an Old Bull on their side, and they found him in the Illinois senator Everett Dirksen. Dirksen would have them all to his suite of offices, and the cigar smoke would waft and the drinks would be poured and they'd talk about Thurgood Marshall. "He'd hold court Thursday afternoons," Tydings says of Dirksen, who would talk about Senate strategy. "He'd tell war stories and anecdotes about political campaigns. You'd roar with laughter."

Dirksen knew it was important to get the support of northern and western senators to aid Marshall's cause because those senators often had relations back in their home districts with labor leaders, blacks, and liberals—the very constituencies that supported the Marshall nomination. The senators he focused on were, among others, Charles Percy, Republican of Illinois, just elected in 1966; Warren Magnuson, a powerful senator who rode the rails, Woody Guthrie–like, in his youth and who had been in office since 1944, elected from the state of

Washington. There was William Proxmire of Wisconsin, elected in 1957 when Senator Joseph McCarthy died in office; and Frank Church of Idaho, who had helped LBJ pass the 1957 Civil Rights Act. There were wild-card senators like Stephen Young, from the conservative state of Ohio. But Young had a streak of independence, and he was reminded of all the black voters in his Cleveland district. There was a stalwart, Vice President Hubert Humphrey, who, like LBJ, still had many friends in the Senate and had been battling with Dixiecrats for years, shaming them and their policy statements before the public.

Every move and consideration about Marshall's fate would have, as a backdrop, the agony playing out on the urban landscape of America. The news bulletins—be they on mainstream radio, on TV, on black radio stations, or in the daily newspapers—were omnipresent. There were city streets engulfed in flames with dead bodies sprawled on sidewalks. In the Deep South, there was a rise in attacks on blacks commonly thought to be a result of civil rights legislation. "Realization of Dr. King's 'dream,' drifted away in the fires of discontent in the urban ghettos," the *Baltimore Afro-American* wrote in an editorial. "Congress, stirred by peaceful protest, was moved to pass meaningful legislation, but quickly slipped back into a state of resistance to most legislation designed to aid and improve the lot of the downtrodden dwellers of the ghetto."

In 1964 when there was much worry among southern citizens about the planned Civil Rights Act, Senator McClellan reassured all southerners of his strategy. "There is no real need for the people of Arkansas," he would tell them, "to contact Southern Senators for the purpose of urging their opposition to the civil rights bill, since the Southern Senators are leading the opposition to the bill." He went on: "However, it would help greatly if the people . . . would contact friends, relatives and business associates elsewhere in the nation for the purposes of advising them of the serious danger posed by this legislation." And that is what Senator McClellan and Senator Thurmond advised their constituents who opposed Marshall to do: write to their friends, senators, and law enforcement sources to voice their opposition.

Members of the House of Representatives, of course, could not vote on Supreme Court nominees. So it was unique and nearly unprecedented when some U.S. representatives took to the floor of the House to expound on their feelings about the nomination of Thurgood Marshall. Many would say they took to the floor because they recognized the historical weight of the moment. Congressman Samuel Friedel, from Marshall's own Baltimore, praised President Johnson for the nomination and said that Marshall "has earned and deserved a place on the Supreme Court and is the best man qualified for this important position by reason of his training and wide experience." Congressman William Ryan of New York likewise heaped admiration on Marshall while expressing his personal thoughts: "His race should not be a relevant consideration. When this country has reached the point where only a man's excellence is cause for the celebration of his appointment, we will have achieved racial justice."

John Rarick had been in office less than a year, elected to Congress in 1966 from Louisiana. He had escaped from a German prisoner-of-war camp during World War II. He held such distasteful racial views—becoming a member of the White Citizens' Council and howling before the John Birch Society that integration was linked to Communism—that some wondered if he had suffered a brain injury while in captivity. Black voters charged he had courted support of the Ku Klux Klan to reach Congress. "Already subject to racial riots, civil disorders, and an ever-increasing national crime wave," Rarick said, "the American people are now forced to tolerate more salt in their despairing wounds by suffering one of the originators and activists of the problem that now plagues America—the attorney who had to 'get by those boys down there' to upset 180 years of law and order in the nonlegal decision known as *Brown* against the Board of Education, by the use of intentionally misrepresented facts and suppressed truth—all to the knowledge and approval of Thurgood Marshall." With his horn-rimmed glasses, Rarick had the look of a college professor. "Thurgood Marshall's contempt, open ridicule, and hatred of white southerners," he went on, "should immediately disqualify him from sitting on any suit or controversy involving white southerners. Marshall, himself, if honest will have to admit that in such cases he could not render fair and impartial, unbiased justice and would or should be excused."

Days and days began to pass with the Senate Judiciary Committee still behind closed doors. Chairman Eastland sent word that the committee needed more time to go over the transcript of the hearings. President Johnson knew the U.S. Senate as well as anyone ever had, having once been Senate majority leader. He knew all the southerners on the Judiciary Committee. And he loathed being unaware of what was happening behind the scenes. "A liberal Senator has said that the Texan [LBJ] . . . ran 'a little F.B.I.' on Capitol Hill," *Esquire* magazine would report in the summer of 1967, "using his big staff, wide acquaintanceship and his own sensitive antennae to accumulate a vast store of political secrets and gossip." But the only news that Johnson received from Senator Phil Hart was that southern Democrats were digging in their heels against Marshall—and imagining that the burning cities would play to their line of argument about liberals and crime.

During the interim of the Marshall hearings, the voice of Adam Clayton Powell Jr. emerged anew. He was down in Bimini, lolling on his small boat, *Adam's Fancy*, and predicting more mayhem for the nation—"a necessary phase of the black revolution." Fidel Castro, sensing camaraderie with the provocateurs of America's urban unrest, invited Stokely Carmichael to Cuba. "We are preparing groups of urban guerillas for our defense in the cities," Carmichael threatened while taking in the breezes of Havana. President Johnson had cause for deep concern in every direction he looked. American poverty shamed the country before the eyes of the world; racism appeared as intractable now as it had in 1920. And the Vietnam War remained a lethal and political albatross. Johnson announced he was sending fifty-five thousand more troops into Vietnam. The college kids hanged him in effigy. Drafts cards were burned.

Muhammad Ali was sentenced in 1967 to five years in prison for refusing to be inducted into the army. The college kids and hippies fell in love with him. "Why should they ask me to put on a uniform," he said, "and go ten thousand miles from home and drop bombs and bullets on brown people in Vietnam while so-called Negro people in Louisville are treated like dogs?" The prizefighter was a native of Louisville. The Kentucky State Senate issued a proclamation denouncing their native son. The fighter remained resolute: "We've been in jail for four hundred years." (Ali appealed his conviction and sentence all the way to the U.S. Supreme Court, where, in 1971, he was vindicated when they were overturned.)

.   .   .

ON AUGUST 2, *In the Heat of the Night*, a major motion picture drama directed by Norman Jewison, opened in theaters. The premise was a fascinating and fictional tale that might well have been drawn from the dangerous currents in Senator Eastland's Mississippi: A Negro detective, Virgil Tibbs—played by Sidney Poitier—misses a train at night and gets stranded in Sparta, a small Mississippi town. On that same night, the body of a white man—a business leader in the community—is found murdered in an alley. Deputies quickly patrol the town in search of the killer. A deputy comes across the suit-and-tie-wearing Tibbs sitting in the train station. The deputy calls him "boy," orders him to stand up, roughly pats him down, finds cash in his wallet, and is immediately convinced he has found the killer, who obviously committed an act of robbery while doing the deed. The deputy, confident and cocky that he has found the murderer, marches his suspect into the office of Chief Gillespie. Everyone in the office, the entire staff, is white. The chief—barrel-chested and played beautifully by Rod Steiger—looks the Negro suspect up and down, looks at the stack of bills the deputy has pulled from the suspect's wallet now splayed on the chief's desk. It takes the chief just seconds to assume guilt as well.

Voices are raised when the suspect explains that he's a Philadelphia detective, that he was waiting on a train—just then a train whistle is heard in the background—that he has a badge to prove it. The chief feels a pang of embarrassment, gets on the phone with the detective's superior in Philadelphia, who confirms the identity of his detective and praises him as one of the best on the force. When Detective Tibbs gets on the phone, his supervisor suggests he remain in Mississippi to help solve the case. The police chief, realizing the detective wants to get the hell out of this town, taunts him: perhaps he isn't so smart after all; perhaps he doesn't have the brainpower to help them solve the case. Thereupon which the drama unfolds. The Negro detective—coming up against racism, hooligans, black fear—solves the case. The chief has found the semblance of a friendship across the racial divide. American audiences had rarely seen black-white friendship on the big screen with this depth and nuance. The filming itself, however, had not been a calm experience for Sidney Poitier. Poitier had steadfastly told the filmmakers he would not film the movie in Mississippi. It was too dangerous, he said. So the production was filmed mostly in southern Illinois.

And even there, Poitier kept a gun in his hotel room for protection as slurs had been hurled at members of the interracial cast. Poitier had befriended Dr. Martin Luther King Jr. and had his life threatened several times while appearing in the South on behalf of civil rights workers. (The actor told close friends he felt somewhat bewildered by so much personal success, as he could not ignore the everyday woes and hardships that haunted daily existence for the Negro in America.)

Richard Schickel, the *Life* magazine film critic, sensed something unique about Norman Jewison's Mississippi-set film. "Poitier and Steiger may eventually come to respect one another, even to find a certain amusement in one another's company. But they do not suddenly become brothers under the skin, put down their old prejudices or vow to be better men," he wrote. "They have gained only a little more knowledge of themselves and of each other, perhaps a capacity to work with the strangers of the future on a slightly less suspicious basis."

WHILE THURGOOD MARSHALL'S NOMINATION remained in limbo, a photograph appeared on the cover of the Sunday *New York Times Magazine* that—in a cultural sense—fairly stunned the nation. It was a photograph of a beautiful and dazzling fashion model. Her name was Naomi Sims. She hailed from Mississippi, from James Eastland's Mississippi. It was her racial identity that garnered all the attention: Naomi Sims was a Negro. She was the first Negro fashion model to appear on the cover of the magazine. It was a "black is beautiful" moment that sent waves of curiosity and intrigue up and down Madison Avenue. Sometimes politicians and their laws were simply no match for cultural momentum.

As the Senate Judiciary Committee pondered Marshall's nomination, another riot broke out on July 30, this one in Milwaukee. There were four deaths and more than seventeen hundred arrests. President Johnson's Kerner Commission—set up following the Detroit riots—would later issue a report about the 1960s racial violence, saying the confrontations left participants with "a giddy sense of release from the oppression of routine, white dominated life in the ghetto."

Finally, on August 11, the Senate Judiciary Committee chairman, James Eastland, announced the committee had completed its hearing process and was ready to issue its report on Thurgood Marshall's nomination. This was welcome news for the White House, inasmuch as now, at least, the report would be placed in the hands of the full Senate, where it could be debated and Marshall voted on. The judiciary vote stacked up 11–5, with all five anti-Marshall votes coming from southern senators. The delay in getting the report into the hands of the Senate had caused much concern and even anger throughout Negro America. The *Baltimore Afro-American*, in an editorial—citing *The New York Times*—called this phase of the hearings "ordeal by committee": "Black boys in the ghettoes, with stones in their fists and fire-bombs stashed in the garage, read the papers. They may not be able to follow the procedural niceties, but they got the message that . . . Marshall was being stymied."

Now the fate of Thurgood Marshall finally entered the phase that mattered the most, a full airing out before the entire Senate. As senators prepared to go to work on the findings from the hearings, they were presented with a bound copy of the detailed conclusions of Judiciary Committee members. Senator Phil Hart had played the major role in shaping the majority report, which, in addition to Hart, had been signed by Senators Thomas Dodd, Edward Long, Edward Kennedy, Birch Bayh, Quentin Burdick, Joseph Tydings, Everett Dirksen, Roman Hruska, Hiram Fong, and Hugh Scott. Dirksen, the powerful Republican, was the coup and was evidence that Lyndon Johnson had been working behind the scenes with his practiced determination. Johnson, the former majority leader, had a gift for communicating with senators on either side of the aisle, and he would remind them that his willingness to do so now was even more important because he was the president of the United States. Johnson's natural brethren were southerners, and he knew how to flatter them and charm their wives. He remembered the names of their sons and daughters. He'd get them down on the big LBJ Ranch in Texas and feed them barbecue and pork and beans, then tell them he used to live on pork and beans because he was so poor. And he didn't blanch when they used the word "nigger," because he could throw it right back at them because his heart was in a different place from theirs. Johnson once needed to talk to Senator John McClellan, the Judiciary Committee member, the segregationist, and got him on the phone. Johnson planned to appoint Carl Rowan, a

Negro, to be the head of the U.S. Information Agency. The nomination had to go through the Appropriations Committee, and McClellan was head of that committee. Johnson knew it could be trouble.

The conversation:

JOHNSON: John, I've got a little problem. I don't want to embarrass you in any way and the best way to avoid it is to talk to you about [it] beforehand so you know what the problem is. Ed Murrow is dying with cancer of the lung. I've got to get another man. I've got a good solid man that's gone around the world with me and spent a good deal of time working with me and writing stuff for me and helping me and he's a good administrator and he'll listen to me, but he's a Negro. His name is Carl Rowan. He's the Ambassador to Finland. USIA is in your department under Appropriations and I don't want you to cut his guts out because he's a Negro. I've seen you operate with a knife.

MCCLELLAN: I wouldn't say that. I wouldn't put it on that account . . . On things like this, when you tell me, I always show every leverage. I appreciate your calling me and I know you have problems and you're going to do a lot of things I wouldn't do—unless I was president.

Rowan was confirmed.

That little conversation was LBJ's way of warning McClellan that he knew how to wheel and deal. More than a few people over the years had seen LBJ operating with a knife.

President Johnson—in angling Senator Everett Dirksen's hoped-for support of Thurgood Marshall—had reminded Dirksen about their coming together on the 1964 Civil Rights Act, that when Dirksen had thundered to his Senate colleagues—"No army is stronger than an idea whose time has come"—he had gained Negro followers and by extension Negro voters, and he'd likely have those voters for as long as he remained in office. And Johnson reminded him—as if he needed reminding—that the streets were on fire, and he reminded Dirksen of Thurgood Marshall's great legal victories, and he told Dirksen that Illinois had plenty of Negro voters and they were growing by the year.

The name of the Republican Everett Dirksen—along with Hruska, Fong, and Scott—was written right there on the majority report with the names of all the Democrats.

In their majority report, those senators favoring Marshall talked of his "impressive professional record of participation in the civic life of this Nation." They were mindful of the violent demonstrations on American streets and sought to put Marshall's life in perspective against that haunting backdrop. "He has been in the forefront of those who assisted America's Negro citizens in asserting their right to share in our common heritage and to realize their constitutional preroga- tives, yet he has been in the forefront of those who insisted that this progress can and must be achieved within the framework of Ameri- can democracy and of the law." They refuted charges that Marshall's affiliation with the NAACP would impede his judicial impartiality. "We cannot see how this professional connection, formally severed some 7 years ago, can disqualify an otherwise qualified judicial nom- inee any more than prior connections with corporations, law firms, and labor unions could have disqualified prior nominees." So sure of their position, the majority members kept their report to a short—if effusive—three and a half pages. "The Senate," they offered in uni- son, "will do itself honor, the Court will be graced, and the Nation benefited by our confirmation of this nominee to the Supreme Court."

The minority report—signed by Senators Eastland, Ervin, McClel- lan, and Thurmond—was written by Ervin and was six times longer than the majority report. It was also scathing. Ervin's overriding argu- ment was about judicial activism, the subjugation of federal powers, and the sacredness of the Constitution. "It is clearly a disservice to the Constitution and the country to appoint a judicial activist to the Supreme Court at any time," Ervin wrote. "The present composition of the Supreme Court renders the gravity of such disservice greater today than it has ever been." Ervin said he had studied most of Marshall's past decisions with genuine carefulness, and they left him with only one conclusion to make: "Marshall is by practice and philosophy a legal and judicial activist, and if he is elevated to the Supreme Court, he will join other activist Justices in rendering decisions which will substantially impair, if not destroy, the right of Americans for years to come to have the Government of the United States and the several states conducted in accordance with the Constitution." Ervin acknowledged the position he set himself in by opposing a nominee—who happened to be a Negro with stellar and historic credentials—for the high court: "I know that in so doing I lay myself open to the easy, but false, charge that I am a racist. I have no prejudice in my mind or heart against any man because of his race. I love men of all races. After all, they are my fellow travelers to the tomb." President Johnson's powers of persuasion held no power with Senator McClellan this time. In a note of appendix to the minority report, McClellan wished to singularly express his vote. It was clear that Detroit continued to seep into his thoughts. "The crime menace is today the greatest internal threat to our nation's security," he said. "It is reaching astronomical proportions. Accompanying this rising crime rate is a corresponding decline of respect for law and authority." McClellan stated he feared Marshall would join the liberal justices on the court, whose rulings, in his mind, made the country vulnerable to anarchy. "For this reason," he concluded, "and for the well-being and security of our country, I cannot vote for confirmation of Judge Marshall to serve as an Associate Justice of the Supreme Court."

IN 1967, the nation's capital was still very much a segregated city. And while the workforce of the federal government had long been integrated, one could go over to the Government Printing Office (GPO) and see an unusual number of Negroes working there. "The GPO," recalls Jim Flug, an aide to Senator Kennedy during the Marshall hearings, "had more blacks employed than anywhere else. I bet more people in that building knew Thurgood Marshall than anywhere else." And when the printed reports of both the majority and the minority committees began being produced at the GPO, those Negro employees couldn't help but take a look at the findings, reading them line for line, page for page, to see what had been said about Marshall, about their Thurgood Marshall, the lawyer whose name across Negro communities carried the same cachet as Jackie Robinson, Rosa Parks, Martin Luther King Jr.—and Lyndon Baines Johnson. They leaned on windowsills and, with the summer sunlight streaming in, read from page to page. It pained them to read the attacks on Marshall, but they held their emotions in check. After all, they were at work. They packaged the hearings up and had them sent to each member of the U.S. Senate. And then, like the rest of America, these unknown government workers waited.

ON THE MORNING OF AUGUST 30, 1967—more than a month after the Marshall hearings themselves had ended, a delay that only built up more anger and suspicion across black America—the U.S. Senate convened. At the top of its agenda was a vote set on the nomination of Thurgood Marshall to the U.S. Supreme Court. These were the men—and one woman—who shaped the nation's policy, who conferred with the president on the important business of the nation, who brought the emotions and sentiments of their respective constituents to the nation's capital. They were powerful, proud of their ability to bring millions of dollars to their states for roads, bridges, the construction of hospitals. Many were known beyond their state's borders. There were Senators Mike Mansfield of Montana, Everett Dirksen of Illinois, John Sparkman of Alabama, Walter Mondale of Minnesota, Frank Church of Idaho. Gliding about too were Senators William Proxmire of Wisconsin, Ernest Hollings of South Carolina, Wayne Morse of Oregon. On and on they made their way to their seats: Strom Thurmond of South Carolina, Jacob Javits of New York, Hugh Scott of Pennsylvania. They represented nearly 180 million voters. There was one Negro among them, Senator Edward Brooke of Massachusetts. And there was one woman, Margaret Chase Smith of Maine. Their surroundings—oak wood, thick drapes—were full of historic splendor. Southerners had controlled the institution for decades. William S. White, the well-known reporter, would write in 1956 that the Senate represented "the South's unending revenge upon the North for Gettysburg." But those southern senators were realistic. They never expected one of their own to reach the Oval Office. Then came the tragedy of Dallas. But Lyndon—as they had called him in the Senate—presented them with a conundrum: Their Lyndon, whom they could stomach as the Senate majority leader, changed when he became President Lyndon Johnson, with all his social activism and penchant for "Niggra rights"—as Eastland was fond of saying. In the Oval Office, Lyndon Johnson simply bewildered them. They would back him on Vietnam, because they feared Communism too, but this—the push for Negro rights—had upset their voters back in their home districts.

True to form, in the days leading up to the vote on Marshall, Johnson had gotten many of these senators on the telephone. He was urging them, his southern brothers, pleading with them—particularly the ones he already knew were defiant about not voting in favor of Marshall—not to cast their nay votes, because if they didn't cast those nay votes, if they were recorded as "not voting," it would look better for America, the nation, a nation that was on fire and needed, more than ever, a unified front. They could in turn convey to their voters they had actually voted *no* on Marshall. Johnson knew he could not convince all of them, but he had to try.

No one doubted the gravity of the business to take place when the Senate was called to order on the morning of August 30. Mike Mansfield, the Senate majority leader, opened the proceedings.

MANSFIELD: What is the pending business?
THE LEGISLATIVE CLERK: The nomination of Thurgood Marshall, of New York, to be an Associate Justice of the Supreme Court of the United States.

Senators checked their notes one last time. They would rise to give their speeches about Marshall—and the nation—before voting. The press corps was gathered; there were crowds in the Senate gallery. The words spoken on this day would be pinned to the pages of history. Senator Phil Hart—so emotionally invested in the rights of Negroes—opened the testimony in favor of Marshall. He was a northerner, and there was, of course, symbolism in that.

HART: Mr. President, I suspect that the Senate has never had for consideration or approval to serve on the Supreme Court one whose qualifications are so dramatically and compellingly established . . . Thurgood Marshall, as an advocate, won in the Supreme Court on 29 out of 34 occasions. Indeed, I suspect that a part of his troubles in obtaining advice and consent to nominations on earlier occasions is explained by the dramatic success he did achieve in the Supreme Court.

Hart held nothing back and aimed right at the often anguished sweep of American history and its Negro citizenry.

> HART: This is a most appropriate time for an object lesson to a great people who are in such deep travail in our country—the Negro people. It is a time when object lessons are most desirable. These object lessons cannot be synthetically created. However, when God and nature and the process of public policy has produced a situation in which there is an extraordinary breakthrough and object lesson of this kind, we certainly have the right to speak of it and to be thankful that there exists in the United States a Negro who deserves to be a Justice of the U.S. Supreme Court . . . Mr. President, I predict with respect to Thurgood Marshall that he is going to surprise a lot of his critics. He has a rendezvous with history. He is a man of deep conscience. He cannot be taken for granted at all.

Some in the Senate were nodding their heads. He went on.

> HART: Let us remember that the Negro is one of our oldest citizens. He has suffered with the soil of this country. Thurgood Marshall's forebears were slaves. Their sweat and blood and tears have been imbedded in this land for 350 years—more than is true in the case of my ancestors who came over from Europe and took root here in the latter part of the last century. This is a magnificent day. Thurgood Marshall will make a fine judge. There is no question about his fitness to be a judge. And that should be the only question.

They were eloquent and sweeping words about Marshall and his America. Then came the first voice in opposition to Thurgood Marshall. The South—in the person of James Eastland—rose.

> EASTLAND: Mr. President, I rise to speak in opposition to the nomination of Thurgood Marshall as an Associate Justice of the Supreme Court of the United States . . . My opposition to the nominee is based upon my strong and sincere belief that

his elevation to the Supreme Court will have the inevitable result that the Court will truly become not only the keeper of the conscience of the Nation, but will also be the enforcer of the personal views of a majority of its members as to how the people should carry on their daily political, social, and economic lives.

He attacked Marshall's Judiciary Committee testimony, produced documents for the record that he said showed Communist sympathies, and pronounced his deep fear of judicial activism, which he said Marshall practiced.

EASTLAND: I believe that in large areas of our life, especially in the fields of the enforcement of criminal law and court-ordered social change, his philosophy is basically antagonistic to that of the great majority of citizens in this country.

The state of Maryland, haunted by its native son and Supreme Court chief justice Roger B. Taney, who had ruled in favor of the destructive *Dred Scott* ruling denying rights for the Negro, was proud of Thurgood Marshall's legal ascendancy—and the *Brown* case, which had toppled *Plessy*. It was left to the Maryland senator Joseph Tydings to link Marshall's legal accomplishments to the 1964 Civil Rights Act and the 1965 Voting Rights Act.

TYDINGS: [Marshall's] legal victories for equal rights gave renewed strength to the fabric of our democratic society and laid the groundwork for legislative and executive action to make equal rights for all citizens a living reality in this country. That battle has not been fully won yet. But Marshall's legal pioneering remains a fundamental basis of impetus for that battle.

Senator Edward Kennedy had only been on the Judiciary Committee a short while, but he had a reputation for working hard and diligently. The family pedigree certainly did not hurt. He issued a stern and bold warning to his fellow senators.

KENNEDY: I think it is important to realize that every one who votes against Judge Marshall's nomination this afternoon is also suggesting by his vote that the President has not really met his responsibility in making this recommendation and suggestion to the Senate and to the American people.

The South Carolina senator Strom Thurmond had been very eager to speak. And when he did, he launched into nearly an hour-long assault on Marshall.

THURMOND: In opposing confirmation of the nomination of Thurgood Marshall . . . I do not rely solely upon his oft-expressed legal, or political, philosophy that the Constitution is a "living document." To characterize the Constitution as a "living document" is one of the most popular notions of the day, and this is indeed an attractive sounding appellation. When one understands the exact meaning of the phrase, however, one is forced to the stark realization that it is a phrase designed to cover a multitude of sins committed in the name of constitutional interpretation. Indeed, under this theory the Constitution lives more in the imagination of its interpreters than in its original meaning and intent.

He took such pride in his gift of gab. Sometimes—as in 1957, in filibustering against the Civil Rights Act—Thurmond appeared unstoppable. And on this day, he also kept going, inching up on an attack on Marshall's legal knowledge by reciting an episode from the Judiciary Committee hearings that echoed questions and concerns that would have seemed welcome during the poll-tax era.

He was singing "Dixie," but the notes seemed off now.

THURMOND: It was surprising to find that the nominee did not know that the Joint Committee on Reconstruction was the committee that reported out the 14th amendment and that he further did not know any of the members of that committee by name. I then asked the nominee why he thought the framers of the original version of the first section of the 14th amendment added the necessary and proper clause from article I, section 8 of the Constitution to the privileges and immunities clause of article IV, section 2 of the Constitution.

Senator Ted Kennedy had heard enough and cut him off.

KENNEDY: I recall that during the course of the hearing, the Senator from South Carolina asked Mr. Marshall the names of members of the Judiciary Committee who served at [the time] the 14th amendment was established, and the Senator has just referred to it again. I was wondering if we could have that information included in the RECORD at this point. Does the Senator have that information at hand?

THURMOND: I will cover it before I finish.

Kennedy wouldn't relent and insisted that Thurmond—at this very moment—provide the information. Thurmond looked peeved and repeated again that he would provide it before he finished.

KENNEDY: I just raised this question because much was made of Mr. Marshall's knowledge of what many of us thought were extremely complex and complicated and esoteric questions. I noticed that in his remarks, the Senator referred to this question again. I thought it might be helpful, for the record to be complete, that now at least we have those answers.

(An aide was forced to scamper and retrieve the names for Thurmond.)

It went on and on, senators either applauding or assailing the nominee. Senator Hart finally pleaded for a roll call vote on the nomination. But others wanted to speak up and forestall the vote. Senator Robert Byrd of West Virginia stood.

BYRD: Mr. President, the truth of the matter is that I would like to vote for Mr. Marshall, and I am frank to say that I would like to vote for him particularly because he is a Negro. Yet, I consider it my duty as a Senator, under the Constitution, not to let Mr. Marshall's race influence my decision. Having reached the definite conclusion that were Mr. Marshall white, I would vote against him, I cannot, therefore, let the fact that he is a Negro influence me to vote for him when I would not do so otherwise.

White House aides had been tabulating numbers in the days leading up to the vote. While a nominee requires fifty votes to pass, the important number for the White House was sixty votes—the number needed to avoid a filibuster. Told in the days leading up to the vote that they had fifty votes—enough for confirmation—Johnson was focused on the sixty votes needed to stop a filibuster. If the southerners managed to get sixty votes, they could filibuster the nomination into oblivion, and LBJ knew it. With the turmoil in the streets, he simply could not afford a filibuster. And that is what he told those senators on the other end of his phone calls. Strategically, he courted southern senators who listened to him when he urged them to not vote. Because if they did not vote their votes would not show up in the figures to be released to the public. The White House counted a tally of 69–31. Only nine votes beyond a filibuster, and the no-vote count of thirty-one was not a figure Johnson wanted to present to the country. Which is why he kept hammering southern senators *not* to vote. (In the minds of southern senators unbowed and not at all influenced by LBJ yakking in their ear, they needed to reverse a dozen or so votes—and then they would have their filibuster. That was their strategy to bring this drama to a final end.)

After six hours, it was finally agreed that there would be no more delays. The time had come to vote. Senator Mansfield opened the voting. And soon there were the echoes throughout the chamber.

Aiken: Yea
Anderson: Yea
Byrd: Nay
Eastland: Nay
Hill: Nay
Sparkman: Nay
Church: Yea
Lausche: Yea

Pell: Yea
Percy: Yea
Symington: Yea
Thurmond: Nay

Some of the votes were uttered in even monotones, while others soared high in volume, causing necks to crane in the galleries.

Kennedy (Mass.): Yea
Kennedy (N.Y.): Yea
Long: Nay

When it was all over, had every senator cast a vote, the final tally should have shown 69–31. But LBJ and his White House aides had prevailed. LBJ had convinced twenty segregationists simply to refrain from voting. It was known as eleventh-hour horse trading, and the Texan, LBJ, had mastered the art of it. The final tally stood at 69–11. Thurgood Marshall was going to the U.S. Supreme Court. "It was much closer than it looked," Jim Flug, the aide to Senator Kennedy, would say of southern senators who were only nine votes short of a filibuster.

Phil Hart nearly wept. A huge smile crossed his face. All the senators who had fought for Marshall began reaching out to one another to shake hands. They had made history, and they realized it.

HART: Mr. President, I ask unanimous consent that the President be immediately notified of the confirmation of this nomination.

And President Lyndon Johnson was immediately told that his nominee, Thurgood Marshall, would be integrating the U.S. Supreme Court.

Senator Mansfield could not hold back his emotions. He glanced around the Senate, from side to side. They all set their eyes upon him. Then he spoke in a voice clear and strong.

MANSFIELD: Mr. President, the confirmation of the nomination of Thurgood Marshall as an Associate Justice of the Supreme Court is also a confirmation of the vitality of the democratic system. It is a tribute to the good sense of President Johnson who made the nomination, and to the judgment of the Senate which approved it. The confirmation means that a man who loves the law and who has a firm respect and high faith in it moves to the top of his profession by entering the highest judicial body in the United States. Thurgood Marshall's rise to the Supreme Court reaffirms the American ideal that what counts is what you are and not who you are or whom your antecedents may have been . . . This is a shining hour, Mr. President, for Mr. Marshall, for President Johnson, for the Senate, and for the United States of America. We have come a long, long way toward equal access to the Constitution's promise . . . I join my colleagues in the Senate in extending sincere congratulations to Mr. Justice Marshall on this most auspicious day in his life.

The White House quickly got word to Marshall. Then the news echoed around the nation. It went from Washington—those Negroes down in the Government Printing Office, some of whom had already begun to cry—to Marshall's hometown of Baltimore; it flowed into Negro barbershops and hair salons. It reached radios sitting on the edges of still-segregated swimming pools and those public swimming pools that had been integrated. It reached hot housing projects still tender from a summer of unrest that had seen riots and soldiers with rifles and bayonets. It reached small Negro southern towns where too much fear still remained in the air.

It reached the offices of the old NAACP Manhattan headquarters, the building that Marshall used to alight from to go south to try to save weary and frightened souls, the building that had displayed the words "A Man Was Lynched Yesterday" on the flagpole to the world.

When the news reached him, Thurgood Marshall himself was overjoyed. He was also greatly relieved for himself and his family. "I am greatly honored," he said following the vote. "Let me take this opportunity to affirm my deep faith in this Nation and its people, and to pledge that I shall be ever mindful of my obligation to the Constitution and to the goal of equal justice under the law."

A short while later, word reached the newest member of the U.S. Supreme Court that he would have to report to be measured for his judicial robes.

CONFIRMATION

SEPTEMBER 1, 1967

17

Good Evening,
Mr. Justice Marshall

Thurgood Marshall is sworn in as an associate justice
of the U.S. Supreme Court.

FOR SO MANY BLACK AMERICANS in the early part of the twentieth century, it had seemed inconceivable that someone of their own race would reach the U.S. Supreme Court in their lifetimes. But an oppressed people will surely dream. On November 16, 1939, the associate Supreme Court Justice Pierce Butler died. President Roosevelt received plenty of recommendations about a replacement. In Washington, the United Government Employees—which consisted of a group of Negroes who worked for the federal government—sent a missive suggesting Roosevelt appoint Charles H. Houston, the Negro NAACP counsel and Harvard Law School graduate. When they heard news of the communiqué, the editors of *The Cincinnati Enquirer* were so bemused by the suggestion that they wrote a little story about it, with an accompanying headline that must have raised eyebrows, if not guffaws: "Negro Is Suggested for Supreme Court." President Roosevelt appointed Frank Murphy to the seat.

But now the once unimaginable—and high moment of honor—for the Negro populace had come. Thurgood Marshall came to the Supreme Court on September 1 to take the oath of office. He would take a second oath later; this was a private affair attended by family. The oath was given by Justice Hugo Black, the longest-serving member on the court, who had been nominated by President Franklin D. Roosevelt. Marshall thought it was a good thing for the sake of the country to have Justice Black, an Alabama native—a southerner—administer the oath of office. It would show alliance and a kind of camaraderie. But Black's participation in the oath also held tangled threads of history, as well as the power of redemption.

As a young lawyer in Birmingham, Alabama, Hugo Black had joined the Ku Klux Klan, remaining a member from 1923 to 1926. The Klan aided his political rise, and its votes helped send him to the U.S. Senate. When offered a vacant Supreme Court seat, Black told no one in the Roosevelt administration about his past Klan association. William Borah, the Idaho Republican, insisted before the hearings that Black address rumors about himself and the KKK. Black refused, simply saying senators were free to vote against him. He was easily confirmed. But the matter did not end there. The *Pittsburgh Post-Gazette*—its publisher, Paul Block, was a Jewish Republican—put a reporter, Ray Sprigle, on the case. He unearthed evidence of Black's Klan membership. Black had to go on national radio and explain his past. The public rallied behind him in polls, although one can certainly assume those numbers did not include Jewish and black citizens.

Men change, and in time Hugo Black surprised his adversaries. He became a liberal on the court, issuing many rulings that aided the cause of freedom, especially when it came to Negroes. His native South was aghast when he attended the Marian Anderson concert at the Lincoln Memorial after she had been denied the opportunity to sing at Constitution Hall because of her race. By the time the Thurgood Marshall–led *Brown* case came before the court, it was assumed that Black would vote to overturn segregation. He was ferociously intent on doing so. Philip Elman worked at the Department of Justice in the days leading up to the *Brown* arguments. Elman relayed that he had heard "Hugo was telling the brethren that you cannot constitutionally defend *Plessy*, but if and when they overruled it, it would mean the end of Southern liberalism for the time being . . . The guys who talked nigger would be in charge, there would be riots, the Army might have to be called out—he was scaring . . . the Justices, especially Frankfurter and Jackson, who didn't know how the Court could enforce a ruling against *Plessy*. But Hugo was determined to overrule it on principle."

So when Hugo Black administered the oath of a Supreme Court justice to Thurgood Marshall on September 1, it was powerful symbolism that rolled backward across, and beneath, southern history.

A month later, on the morning of October 2, Marshall took his public oath. There were a lot of flashbulbs. The occasion demanded it, but it all heightened quite a bit when President Johnson—grinning, delirious with joy—arrived with Secret Service agents in tow to surprise Marshall and his family. "There is a robe room," explains Lowell Muse, a Supreme Court page who was at the court that day. "They [the justices] have these beautiful wood lockers. They walk through the door and come through these curtains." Muse watched as Cissy Marshall helped her husband with his robe. "He stood there and looked down on her as she was helping. I never seen a woman look up at her husband with such warmth." The oath took just minutes, and then there he stood in his long black robe: the ninety-sixth U.S. Supreme Court justice.

Louis Martin—who had been in the White House the day Marshall was nominated, who had advised presidents on Negro affairs for decades, who had been jawboning with his friend, Thurgood, for years about life in America—was overcome with emotion. As a newspaper executive in Negro publications for years, he really didn't have to tell fellow Negro executives that they must play the Marshall story big. They knew. But he told them anyway.

In an apartment on the East Side of Manhattan, an old judge by the name of J. Waties Waring, Marshall's friend who had been run out of his native South Carolina because of his progressive views on race, received the news. He was overjoyed as he shared it with his wife, Elizabeth. Judge Waring died four months after receiving the news of Marshall's swearing in.

Not long after Marshall became a Supreme Court justice, the doorbell rang in Bowie, Maryland, at the home of Evangeline Moore. It was a package delivery. She wondered what it could be as she had not ordered anything. She signed for it and began taking off the wrapping paper. And when she finished removing the wrapping, she saw a huge picture—four by four feet—of Thurgood Marshall. It was an oil painting, sent to her by relatives down in Florida. They had gotten it for her as a special gift, and it immediately reminded her of her father and Marshall and the days when she was a small girl and they rode together around Florida trying to get Negroes registered for the vote. She hung the picture on her dining room wall.

In looking back over presidential politics, it is highly doubtful that President Kennedy would have had the stomach to nominate Marshall to the high court. The known opposition would likely have frightened him off. Kennedy, of course, had initially wanted Marshall to take a federal trial judgeship. Marshall believed his legal accomplishments demanded a higher position, pointing to the appellate judgeship. And when the time came, President Johnson had a higher and more impressive plateau from which to pluck Marshall to become his solicitor general.

Two days after Marshall's public swearing in, his wife, Cissy, sat down in the couple's home on G Street SW and wrote, in her own hand, a one-page letter to President Johnson.

> *My dear Mr. President:*
> *Thank you so very much for coming to the U.S. Supreme Court on Monday October, 2nd. Again, Thurgood and I are grateful to you, Mr. President, for adding another memorable day in our lives.*
> *God bless you.*
> *Most sincerely,*
>
> *Cecilia S. Marshall*

Two days later, a letter from President Johnson arrived at the Marshall home.

Dear Mrs. Marshall:

I was happy to witness the swearing-in of your distinguished husband. It was an historic occasion that I believe will live as long in America's heart as it will in yours.

Sincerely,

LBJ

To celebrate his rise in salary—Marshall was now making $39,000 a year, more than he had ever made in his life—Thurgood Marshall bought himself a new Cadillac, and he also bought a matching one for his wife. They couldn't help chuckling about their shiny new cars with air-conditioning.

Of all the enduring accomplishments in the area of racial equality during President Johnson's White House years, his nomination of Thurgood Marshall to the Supreme Court carried a special place in his heart. "There was probably not a Negro in America," Johnson would later say, "who didn't know about Thurgood's appointment. All over America that day Negro parents looked at their children a little differently, thousands of mothers looked across the breakfast table and said: 'Now maybe this will happen to my child someday.'"

But the Vietnam War raged on. Johnson's aides began to deliver tight-lipped news: the war was looking unwinnable. All those charts, all those tanks, all those fallen American GIs and marines—and the Vietnamese were hardly ready to surrender. Johnson had been sending troops steadily into Vietnam since 1965, and by 1968 the numbers of committed U.S. soldiers would approach nearly half a million. And despite the best efforts of the administration, racial inequality in America was not going to be doused like candlelight. Martin Luther King Jr. began fearing a spread in violent protest from black militant groups. In early 1968, King launched plans for a poor people's campaign, disheartened by a trip to Memphis to help striking garbage workers that had resulted in civic unrest. Now, boasting twin goals to attack poverty and end the Vietnam War, King appeared in pulpits throughout the nation citing his renewed mission. "I say to you that our goal is freedom," he said that spring from a pulpit in the nation's capital. "And I believe that we're going to get there, because however much she strays from it, the goal of America is freedom."

There was a national campaign looming. Members of LBJ's own party, including Senators Eugene McCarthy and Robert F. Kennedy, were opposing and running against him—nearly unheard of for an incumbent president. Prognosticators thought Johnson could win but never doubted it was going to be a hard-fought election. Then Johnson went on national TV and stunned the nation when he announced he would not seek reelection.

King returned to Memphis and paid with his life. His assassination on a motel balcony on April 4, 1968, unleashed waves of rioting in more than a hundred cities. Congress, its back once again up against the wall, passed a historic housing bill, proving that President Johnson's domestic legislative gains—even if hard to measure with discord on the streets—would go unmatched in modern times. The housing bill was also a tribute to Thurgood Marshall, who, so many years before in his landmark Missouri housing discrimination case, *Shelley v. Kraemer*, had helped lay the groundwork for Johnson's bill.

Richard Nixon—assiduously courting the southern Dixiecrat vote, the beginning of a rapid end of Democratic control of the South—won election with a strategy that partially vowed to end the war in Vietnam. (It would take several more years for a complete withdrawal.)

It deeply pained Justice Thurgood Marshall that President Johnson, whom he considered a dear friend, was leaving the White House. There was an emotional dinner at the White House attended by many of President Johnson's high-level black appointees. Marshall was the spiritual avatar of the group. "The people in this room have just one purpose, to say thank you, Mr. President," Marshall said in a voice full of emotion. "You didn't wait. You took the bull by the horns. You didn't wait for the times, you made them." The president appeared deeply moved.

As the highest-ranking black man in America—and with black anger still in the streets and on college campuses—Justice Marshall was looked to by many people to interpret the times. Other justices might have steered clear of publicly declaring their feelings about national issues, but Marshall, a black man, hardly had such luxury. He bemoaned black militancy. "Black separatism will breed nothing," he said during a New Orleans appearance. "I know of a group of people that said we should have rigid separation, from cradle to grave. And do you know who that group was? The Ku Klux Klan." As he neared the end of his remarks, Marshall offered high praise to those who practiced nonviolence. "It takes no courage to get in the back of a crowd and throw a rock. Rather, it takes courage to stand up on your two feet and look anyone straight in the eye and say, 'I will not be beaten.'" On an earlier occasion, Marshall had been asked about his contributions to Alabama, particularly antipoverty work in the dangerous city of Selma. He reminded the reporter—his voice a bit testy—that he had been working in the Black Belt and throughout Alabama "before you were born." In another one of Marshall's renowned cases, in 1955 he went to the Supreme Court on behalf of Autherine Lucy, a Negro who was admitted to the all-white University of Alabama. The school didn't realize she was a Negro, and she was abruptly suspended when white students began rioting against her presence. Marshall sued to have her reinstated. While he was in Birmingham working on her case, a car screeched by the house where he was staying. Local Negroes had provided Marshall with armed guards. A man inside the car prepared to toss a bomb in the direction of the house, but it went off prematurely, ripping a part of the man's arm off. The occupants inside the house— outside with weapons raised—summoned medical help. The board of the University of Alabama finally decided to permanently suspend Lucy, claiming she had defamed the school. For Marshall and the NAACP, their clashes with Alabama hardly ended there. State officials were so angry at Marshall and the civil rights group that they began a series of legal measures, first trying to gain the names of NAACP members in the state, then trying to shut the organization down. The state maneuvers led the NAACP to exhaust funds, and time, all during the late 1950s as it sought to thwart Alabama's efforts to weaken the organization and taint it with charges of being affiliated with Communist groups.

Lyndon Johnson was the first president to appoint a black to his cabinet, naming Robert Weaver secretary of housing and urban development. Black Americans watched keenly as President Nixon assembled his cabinet, hoping it would not be all white. No blacks were named to Nixon's cabinet, and black Americans were hurt and sensed an undeniable shift in tone at the White House.

On May 22, 1971, a ceremony was held for the groundbreaking of

Lyndon Johnson's Presidential Library in Austin, Texas. The library site sat on fourteen acres. LBJ: big in life, big in monument. A large contingent of his former Senate and White House aides came. Johnson looked relaxed in a tan suit. Why, he was even letting his hair grow out in the back. He chatted up President Nixon and most everyone in sight. As soon as Johnson spotted Justice Marshall and his wife, he let out a roar of delight.

When he returned to Washington, Marshall wrote the president a letter telling him how pleased he and his wife, Cissy, were at being invited to the ceremony. Johnson wrote back. "There wasn't anyone we were happier to see," he confided to the justice about him and Lady Bird.

DURING HIS TWENTY-FOUR YEARS on the Supreme Court, Thurgood Marshall remained unerringly true to his principles. His concurring opinions and dissents echoed his beliefs about the First Amendment and equality. His opinions were often marked with a sly combination of earthiness and erudition. In *Mobile v. Bolden*, about redrawn districts for municipal elections that were harmful to blacks, he dissented, assailing the majority justices for "indifference to the plight of minorities." In *Beal v. Doe*, in which the majority wrote an opinion upholding the denial of state funds under Medicaid for abortion, he again dissented, allowing that the decision had "the practical effect of preventing nearly all poor women from obtaining safe and legal abortions." In *Caldwell v. Mississippi*—a death penalty case in which the prosecutor told the members of the jury if they voted on the death penalty for the accused, it should not haunt them, because it would be reviewed by a higher court—Marshall, writing for the majority, wrote that "to rest a death sentence on a determination made by a sentencer who has been led to believe that the responsibility for determining the appropriateness of the defendant's death rests elsewhere" violated the rights of the accused. In yet another case with death penalty implications, Marshall once wrote a dissent in which a judicial decision overrode a jury's recommendation of life imprisonment for the defendant. "The death penalty's cruel and unusual nature is made all the more arbitrary and freakish," Marshall wrote, "when it is imposed by a [Alabama] judge in the face of a jury determination that the appropriate penalty is life imprisonment." He wrote the majority opinion for *Stanley v. Georgia* that upheld an individual's right to own pornography in the privacy of his home. In the 1978 *Regents of the University of California v. Bakke* case, the high court issued a mixed ruling in which it upheld the affirmative action policy of the medical school at the University of California, Davis. But it also outlawed quotas set aside for minority school students. Allan Bakke, thirty-five years old, had sued the school, proclaiming he was denied admittance because he was white; the school pointed to his age as the overwhelming factor for which he was denied. It angered Thurgood Marshall when federal court rulings overturned remedies such as affirmative action. "Face the simple fact that there are groups in every community," he said in a 1986 speech, "which are daily paying the cost of the history of American injustice. The argument against affirmative action is . . . an argument in favor of leaving that cost to lie where it falls."

His was a singular and sweeping career. Thurgood Marshall wrote 322 majority opinions while on the high court. They delved from freedom of speech to the death penalty, from issues of segregation and discrimination to housing. There were also 363 dissents, giving evidence of a justice who would not bend when he felt the law was against the aggrieved and the dispossessed. No justice had come to the high court with the background he possessed in traveling the land and fighting from courthouse to courthouse and devising national strategies that would alter American law. He was an evangelist on behalf of the law. A potent example of a Marshall dissent lay in the 1973 case of *United States v. Kras*. Robert William Kras was ordered to pay a $50 filing fee to file for bankruptcy. Kras proclaimed he was simply too impoverished to pay the fee. Kras held no job and also had children, one of whom suffered from cystic fibrosis. Kras argued that the Constitution protected him from the filing fee. The justices ruled otherwise, suggesting that surely Kras could save a little money each week toward the filing fee. Marshall—always worried about the self-righteousness of some of his brethren—dissented:

It may be easy for some people to think that weekly savings of less than $2 are no burden. But no one who has had close contact with poor people can fail to understand how close to the margin of survival many of them are . . . A pack or two of cigarettes may be, for them, not a routine purchase but a luxury indulged in only rarely. The desperately poor almost never go to see a movie, which the majority seems to believe is an almost weekly activity. They have more important things to do with what little money they have—like attempting to provide some comforts for a gravely ill child, as Kras must do. It is perfectly proper for judges to disagree about what the Constitution requires. But it is disgraceful for an interpretation of the Constitution to be premised upon unfounded assumptions about how people live.

His were the eyes that had seen, up close, men and women grasping for freedom. He had seen shack-like structures masquerading as Negro schoolhouses. He had heard the wails of Negro mothers crying for their sons who had been sentenced on suspicious rape charges. He had seen how poverty could scar both Negro and white alike. His were the eyes that had seen what very few Ivy League–trained lawyers had seen and he knew it, and he wanted them to know he knew it. Marshall's pen—in speeches he wrote and delivered throughout the 1940s and 1950s—was sharp, weighing in on matters of white supremacy, governmental inaction toward lynching, and police brutality. His pen was aimed at upholding the Constitution and the tenets of American democracy.

In his hearings before the Senate, those who opposed Marshall knew he represented a colossal figure in American jurisprudence, which is why they worked so hard to harm his nomination. It becomes rather myopic to compare Marshall's pre–Supreme Court career with his career on the high court. Dwight Eisenhower's World War II role as Allied commander was far different from his role as president of the United States. Thurgood Marshall was scaling the same mountain—dispensing justice—once he reached the high court, but he was suddenly on a different side of that mountain. While his conscience remained unaltered, the view was undeniably from a different angle. Once on the court, Marshall battled from within, not without.

LYNDON JOHNSON's health deteriorated after he left the White House and retreated to his Texas ranch. His wife and daughters couldn't get him to eat right, to quit smoking. He made few public appearances. He'd drive around the wide open spaces of his ranch and contemplate his legacy. He would brood late into the night. He'd ring up Thurgood Marshall, a Supreme Court justice whom he felt comfortable chatting with—two men who had been hurtled into history.

Johnson and Marshall spoke fairly often. They'd reminisce, talk about the wives and children. Shortly after New Year's Day 1973, Lyndon Johnson again got Thurgood Marshall on the phone. On this particular call, LBJ surprised Marshall when he told him he was going to write a book, and it was going to be about his efforts to get Marshall onto the Supreme Court. The former president confided to Marshall he had been thinking a lot about that episode, about the hatred it unleashed, about all the people who told him it would be suicidal, that he couldn't get it done, that he should wait until his next term when the fires stopped raging on the streets. But Johnson wanted Marshall to know he had no intentions at all in 1967 of waiting. "More and more I'm sure I'm right," the former president told Marshall about fighting to get him to the Supreme Court, about all that eleventh-hour horse trading that took place, "and I'm going to write about it." Marshall himself was intrigued with the idea. "I'll help you, best I can do," he told Johnson. They both knew what had been at stake during those hearings. They "used the Vietnam War as the excuse," Marshall said Johnson told him about his downfall, revealing to him, for the first time, just how much of an effort it took—and how much of a gamble it was—to get him onto the high court. There was pain in LBJ's voice in Marshall's mind, but not regrets. "Well, congratulations," LBJ said before he hung up, "but the hell you caused me, goddamnit, I never went through so much hell to get that—and all that you caused me—."

Lyndon Johnson died at his Texas ranch on January 22, 1973. He never had a chance to write the book he planned to write about the Marshall confirmation hearings. During those long days in the summer of 1967, he had made promises to certain senators about his next term, about what all "they" could accomplish, and they took that to mean they'd be in favor with the president in the next term, after 1968. Only there was no next term. "He died," Marshall believed of Lyndon Johnson, "of a broken heart. What a lovely guy."

· · ·

NOT UNTIL FIFTY YEARS LATER would a national reassessment of LBJ's contributions to civil rights take place. On the fiftieth anniversary of the Civil Rights Act of 1964, men and women, joined by President Barack Obama, gathered in Austin, Texas. Some, like Congressman John Lewis, had been beaten bloody in Selma, Alabama, and other places on the American map where the journey to justice often ended in bloodshed and death. And sometimes, as in the emotional summer of 1967, a part of it ended in a Senate hearing room in the nation's capital.

In June 1991, only two justices remained on the U.S. Supreme Court who had been appointed by Democratic presidents, Byron White and Thurgood Marshall. Marshall was the sole true liberal who remained on the court following the 1990 retirement of Justice William Brennan. He began to feel lonely. The work grew more and more wearying for the now eighty-two-year-old justice. He informed potential law clerks who were interviewing that if they were selected, they should be ready to write *dissents*—and plenty of them. The aging justice had been holding up the barricades, but the opposition clearly outnumbered him.

In the summer of 1991, Marshall made a call to his friend the former justice Brennan and told him he was going to step down from the court. He then shared the news with the other justices. Sandra Day O'Connor, the first woman nominated to the high court—by President Ronald Reagan—began to weep.

On June 28 came the news: Thurgood Marshall was stepping down from the Supreme Court.

The justice walked into the next day's press conference wearing a dark-colored suit, white shirt, and striped red tie. His shirt collar was unloosened and his tie slightly askew. He was leaning on a shiny wooden brown cane. He was an old, gruff man, and his clerks were known to love and cherish him. Television cameras and journalists were arrayed before him. Flashbulbs went off, and he squinted through thick bifocals. There was spreading applause, which he hushed with a wave of the arm. He took a seat in a chair on a makeshift stage. When he sat down, he crossed his legs. He was wearing black shoes and thick woolen white socks. He looked, for all the world to see—the event was televised—like a rumpled Negro one might see sitting in a park on a warm Sunday afternoon. But he was the giant who had made the

Constitution come alive for so many millions, had truly turned it into a living document. His wife, Cissy, took a seat behind him. Next to her sat William Coleman, the attorney who had been LBJ's backup choice had the Marshall nomination to the high court in 1967 failed. "I'm getting old and coming apart," he said when asked why he was retiring from the court. There were chuckles. Many wondered if the court would revert to being all white again or if a minority would be named. Marshall knew about the rising influence of black conservatives in the country, men and women who attacked affirmative action and other social remedies put into place to address the vestiges of discrimination. He mistrusted them. His father, he said, had told him that there was no difference between "a white snake and a black snake. Both bite." After it was over, he ambled out the door and away from public life.

President George H. W. Bush nominated Clarence Thomas to take Marshall's seat. Once on the court, the selection of Thomas—born in Georgia, educated at Holy Cross and Yale Law School—seemed a particularly cruel irony. Thomas, like Thurgood Marshall, was black, but the comparison could go no further. Thomas's legal philosophy and opinions were the polar opposite of Marshall's. An extreme conservative, he concurred with decisions that limited minority rights and freedom of speech. He seemed so utterly unprepared for the high court—having won confirmation following hearings that revolved around sexual harassment allegations lodged against him—that he uttered not a word during his first few years as an associate justice. Later, when he did talk from the bench, his comments were unremarkable and without resonance.

SHORTLY AFTER HE ASCENDED to the Supreme Court, Thurgood Marshall and his wife, Cissy, had integrated a community in Virginia known as Lake Barcroft. They enjoyed the serenity of being fifty miles outside Washington. They enjoyed quiet dinners together. His sons dropped by. Friends would call and check up on him after he left the court. They'd try to get him to come out of the house. Berl Bernhard had been appointed staff director of the U.S. Commission on Civil Rights in 1960 by President Kennedy. Bernhard met Marshall during his early years working for Kennedy. Not long after they first met, Marshall and Bernhard went to Kenya together, where Marshall was helping that country form its own constitution. The plane landed, and when both reached the doorway, they looked down onto a massive crowd of Kenyans. Bernhard was stunned. He asked Marshall why there were so many people. "They ain't looking for no white man," Marshall assured him in his booming voice. "They're looking for Thurgood." While Marshall waded into the throngs, Bernhard's eyes grew wide with awe. "I later said, 'Thurgood, you're acting like the emperor Jones.' He said, 'When I am in East Africa, I am the emperor Jones.'"

Now, all these years later, Bernhard found himself worrying about Marshall. He began calling him throughout 1992, wanting to get him out of the house. He'd suggest outings—dinners, theater, sporting events. "I don't want to do that!" the retired justice would snap.

He'd putter around the house, take long naps. Mail reached him via the Supreme Court—men, women, and school-age children thanking him for his service. He could hardly respond to all of the mail.

He found himself at the Bethesda Naval Hospital in early January 1993. There were heart problems; he was having trouble breathing. Security was assigned to him. They were quite respectful, and didn't want to bother him, but a few members of the security detail told the former justice their wives would surely like to meet him if there was an opportunity while he was there. One day John Warnock brought his wife, Shannon, in to meet Marshall.

"Where are you from?" Marshall asked her.

She told him Mississippi, where she had attended law school.

"So you know of Senator Eastland?" he asked, referring to the Judiciary Committee chairman.

"Yes, sir."

"He was the meanest son of a bitch that ever walked the earth," Thurgood Marshall told her.

THE GREAT JUSTICE drew his last breath on January 24, 1993, less than two years removed from the high court.

WHAT HAD HAPPENED in room 2228 in the summer of 1967 had, in so many ways, changed the country. Fred Graham, the respected legal reporter for *The New York Times*, would write after those hearings that

Marshall had been put through an "ordeal by committee" and that it would change the nation forever. The *Baltimore Afro-American*, in the days after those 1967 hearings, came to the same conclusion. "In an article for his newspaper, *New York Times* writer Fred P. Graham," wrote *The Afro-American*, "notes that hearings on the nomination of Thurgood Marshall as a Justice of the U.S. Supreme Court revealed that the present procedures serve only as a punishment to a future justice by political enemies." Marshall was the first nominee to undergo such an extensive grilling face-to-face, and his hearings created a new level of senatorial inquiry. And once those senators smelled blood, it only pushed them deeper and deeper. A year after the Marshall hearings, the Senate blocked Justice Abe Fortas from ascending to the position of chief justice. Democrats circled a Nixon nominee, Clement Haynsworth, and kept him off the court because of ethical violations and comments deemed racist. Nixon's next appointee, G. Harrold Carswell, had shown an attraction to white supremacy in his younger days. He too was rejected. It could be argued that the nation—Marshall's stinging dissents surely proved it—had lurched to the right during the Reagan years. One of the archconservatives of those years was the federal appeals court judge Robert H. Bork. Among many things he had written, the one that most galled so many was his objection to the 1964 Civil Rights Act. Democrats, liberals, and some Republicans joined to thwart the Bork nomination, and he was defeated.

President Lyndon Johnson had famously said the Democratic Party would lose the South for the foreseeable future after passage of the 1964 civil rights bill. He was referring to the white voters who would abandon the party. It was a prescient statement: the South has been ruled by Republican officeholders since the Reagan years in the early 1980s, when Democrats began having difficulties winning statewide elections. "He told friends that we'd never get Democrats in the South back," the former senator and vice president Walter Mondale said of Johnson.

The Dixiecrat party all but saw its rebirth in the form of the Tea Party, an overwhelmingly white political offshoot of the Republican Party that has gone on to bedevil the basic political process and anger many in the Republican Party mainstream. "They say Obama has got to deal with the Tea Party. That's like playing Ping-Pong," said Joseph Califano, the LBJ aide. "We had a much tougher world."

President Lyndon Johnson believed in the 1964 civil rights bill, and he believed in Thurgood Marshall, and he threw his presidency behind both. "Johnson had, for all his problems, a feel for poor people," added Mondale. "And most blacks were poor. People on Johnson's staff would be humiliated when they took trips home" to the South.

In looking back at the Marshall nomination—and the hearings that took place following 1967—it cannot be overstated how narrow a window Lyndon Johnson had to accomplish his feat of getting Marshall onto the court. The configuration of the U.S. Senate after 1967—and its hard partisanship battles that would show an acknowledged rightward tilt—would likely not have allowed for the likes of a Thurgood Marshall to reach the high court. With his civil rights legislation in the mid-1960s, Johnson had bruised the conscience of the Senate; he had, for a moment at least, weakened the obstructionists who were now being crowded out by Negro voters who no longer had to worry about a poll tax or about being tested to see how many bubbles were in a bar of soap. Johnson acted as if such a time would not be allowed to come again, at least in his lifetime.

Perhaps the most resonant aftereffect of the Marshall hearings was that black law school enrollments increased. The law—jurisprudence—was considered the bedrock of the nation, and now the law had a black face, as LBJ himself had imagined, indelibly linked to it. As well, it cannot be underestimated the extent to which Thurgood Marshall introduced white America to Negro America. Others who championed the cause of equal justice—Booker T. Washington, W. E. B. DuBois, Martin Luther King Jr.—did not go through the federal courthouse and the U.S. Supreme Court. The law—unlike sports or entertainment—was a different and deeper concern for the nation. It was what was discussed in the households up and down Main Street, U.S.A.; families could not escape the law. A law, once passed—no matter the effort unruly groups went through to undermine it—was sacrosanct.

One need only look back to the morning of January 27, 1993, in Washington, D.C.—to the public viewing of Thurgood Marshall—to appreciate the hard rock of American history that played out against the backdrop of his life.

It began with his body, in a plain wooden coffin, placed atop a bier and carried inside the Supreme Court. Mourners strolled by all day long. Some had to wait outside longer than they planned. But they stood and inched forward. It was cold and only grew colder as the sun crawled and dipped from the sky. Twelve hours passed; nearly twenty thousand people would pay respects until ten o'clock in the evening. The next day, at the National Cathedral in Washington, the funeral of Thurgood Marshall took place. The president and the vice president were there, so too were many of his former law clerks. Powerful words were spoken.

For days and weeks afterward, in Negro pulpits all across the country, ministers—so many of them had supported him and his cause during the 1950s and 1960s—paid handsome and long tribute to Thurgood Marshall. (He had a special affinity for the word "Negro," believing it held a special sturdiness throughout his life. He would never stop using it.) Those ministers had marched with him. They had shielded him in their safe homes in times of danger. They had eaten meals with him in houses and shacks at the end of dirt roadways as he plotted his opening remarks the next morning in the local federal courthouse. "Eighty percent of the branches of the NAACP when I went there," Marshall once said, "were run by ministers, in churches. Ninety-eight percent of the meetings were held in Negro churches. The Negro church support was beautiful, from one end of the country to the other." They had prayed for him during those five days of confirmation hearings in Washington, D.C. Their words of mighty praise floated out and over their congregations, from southern hamlet to big city, from one-room church to those with two levels and overhanging balconies. And a single word would come flowing back from their throats in honor of the life of Thurgood Marshall. The congregations would send that one word back to the ministers, back up to their pulpits, and it would be the best way they could thank Thurgood Marshall. The word seemed to melt into their voices until all of their voices merged as one with the sweetness of a singsong moment. It brightened their eyes—especially the eyes of the frail Negro men and women who remembered the walls of segregation tumbling down—even as they closed them and swayed their heads as the word came out. They were somehow convinced Thurgood could hear them: "Amen."

That is what they said—and kept saying—about Thurgood Marshall. "Amen."

EPILOGUE

Requiem for Thurgood

The funeral procession stretched as far as the eye could see.
The justice lying in state in the Great Hall of the United States Supreme Court
building. Marshall was later laid to rest in Arlington National Cemetery,
near the site where former slaves are buried.

I N THE LATE SPRING OF 2010, Thurgood Marshall's name hopped
back on the front pages of American newspapers. It had been seventeen years since his death.

On May 10, 2010, President Barack Obama nominated the Harvard
law professor Elena Kagan for a seat on the Supreme Court. Justice
John Paul Stevens had announced his retirement. Within minutes of
the Kagan announcement, Democrats and Republicans began gird-
ing for battle. Confirmation hearings, for years of course, had evolved
beyond mere confirmation hearings. Now they were partisan battles,
televised and constantly looped around the clock on news outlets for
the world to see.

The Kagan hearings opened on Monday, June 28. Within minutes, the Republicans on the Senate Judiciary Committee went after Kagan by denouncing the Supreme Court justice she had once clerked for—Thurgood Marshall. Kagan began working for Marshall in 1987. "Justice Marshall's judicial philosophy is not what I would consider to be mainstream," said Arizona's senator Jon Kyl. Senator Jeff Sessions of Alabama weighed in, assailing Marshall as a "well-known activist." Then Senator John Cornyn of Texas insisted to the millions watching and listening that Thurgood Marshall practiced a "judicial philosophy that concerns me." Inasmuch as the hearings were supposed to be about Kagan, the attacks on Marshall—an iconic figure in American jurisprudence—seemed quite bizarre. Marshall's name and career were cited more than two dozen times that first day, and mostly in unflattering terms. Many were outraged, and not just black Americans, though the attacks on Marshall—who led the fight to legally dismantle separate but equal—perhaps struck a rawer nerve among them than in other corners. Those at the hearings who held Marshall in highest esteem did not let the attacks go unanswered. "America is a better nation because of the tenacity, integrity and values of Thurgood Marshall," said Senator Richard Durbin, an Illinois Democrat. Durbin was quick to point out that Marshall had successfully argued a multitude of cases before the Supreme Court, winning twenty-nine of them. And Durbin lauded Marshall's legal acumen in the epochal *Brown* desegregation decision: "If that is an activist mind at work, we should be grateful as a nation."

The full Senate eventually confirmed Kagan in a 63–37 vote.

But Thurgood Marshall hardly needed public verbal attacks from Republican officeholders to redeem his judicial standing. It was already matchless. Schools had been named after him. The international airport in his hometown of Baltimore had been renamed in his honor.

Cissy Marshall, always quite shy, would be persuaded now and then to appear in front of some civic group in Virginia or Washington. She would share memories of her husband. She seemed to especially enjoy reminding schoolchildren of what her husband had accomplished and the ongoing struggle for equal rights. Then, as quietly as she had arrived, she'd slip away.

Artists and organizations had long been taking note of Marshall's historical import. In 2008, the gifted actor Laurence Fishburne opened on Broadway at the Booth Theatre in *Thurgood*, a one-man play, which told of the justice's sweeping life. It was a much-lauded performance and was later telecast on HBO. Visitors to San Francisco's Grace Cathedral could look up at the Human Endeavor windows and see all the windows that were named in honor of heroic figures and their craft. Albert Einstein (Natural Science) had a window. So did Jane Addams (Social Work) and Robert Frost (Letters). Thurgood Marshall's window (Law), like the others, sat up high in the cathedral nave. The church would only grant you a window if it had accepted you into the realm of sainthood.

On its editorial page on March 6, 2011, *The New York Times* penned an editorial, simply titled "Thurgood Marshall." It was unusual on that page to have a life revisited after the passage of so much time. It was a lovely and tender tribute about the ongoing artistic homage being paid to Marshall's life. "On the Supreme Court today," the editorial stated, "there is no justice who seems similarly placed there to speak for the powerless by such a sweeping tide of history. There is no one whose life translates so magisterially into art." (In 2014, Bill Keller, the former executive editor of *The New York Times*, left the newspaper and became editor-in-chief of the Marshall Project, a nonpartisan news-gathering organization devoted to covering and exposing the inequities in the American criminal justice system. The project was named in honor of the career of Thurgood Marshall.)

All of the attention gained Marshall new admirers. Tourists would troop out to Arlington National Cemetery to visit his grave site. The cemetery sat on land once owned by a prominent Confederate family. After the Civil War and the South's defeat, the land would be sold to the federal government. Old and bent and jubilee-singing Negroes, fresh from the slave plantations, would trudge into Washington without places to stay, hoping their government would help them. Many, who were penniless, were reduced to foraging for food. They were often given housing on the site of the cemetery itself, a part of which was called Freedman's Village. These were the very people whom Secretary of War Edwin Stanton had appealed to for help during the massive manhunt to bring President Lincoln's assassin to justice. And when the final gust of breath had left the former plantation residents, they would be placed in spare wooden coffins and lowered into the earth on the same grounds where Thurgood Marshall—who had worked to free their descendants—would be laid to rest years later, allowing the wind to blow eternally over their gathered and quiet souls.

ACKNOWLEDGMENTS

For years, the life of Thurgood Marshall intrigued me. My challenge as a biographer, however, was finding the proper Marshall story that would satisfy my nonlinear narrative hunger.

In 2009, I began delving into Marshall's Supreme Court confirmation hearings and quickly became convinced it was a story so complex, so rich in drama, that it demanded telling, especially given that it took place against the backdrop of the Vietnam War, the 1960s racial unrest, widespread political upheaval, and the shaping of President Lyndon Johnson's legacy. Then, in 2010, during the Elena Kagan Supreme Court confirmation hearings, the name Thurgood Marshall was uttered yet again in a committee hearing room: Kagan had once clerked for Marshall, and certain senators assailed her for it. The episode only reinforced my belief that I was on the right journey and that Marshall's impress upon the American landscape remained indomitable.

I like to think that, taken together, the quartet of biographies I've written—on Adam Clayton Powell Jr., Sammy Davis Jr., Sugar Ray Robinson, now Thurgood Marshall—serve, through their subjects' respective lives, to sharply illuminate epochal periods in the shaping of the American story. They represent a politician, an entertainer, a prizefighter, and a lawyer, all gliding along unique tightropes in those mid-twentieth-century pre-civil-rights years.

I'm grateful to my publisher, Alfred A. Knopf, for giving me a home for the Marshall, Robinson, and Davis books. My editors, Peter Gethers and Claudia Herr, always understood I was trying to pull history from the shadows to fashion these quintessential sagas. As editors, they are simply remarkable. They not only inspired and encouraged but offered sharp insights and, thank goodness, patience. I also wish to thank, at Knopf, Sonny Mehta, Victoria Pearson, Maggie Hinders, Abby Weintraub (book jacket designer extraordinaire), and Jenna Brickley. I wish to thank Ingrid Sterner for her keen reading of this book, which made it better. Benjamin Hamilton and Susan VanOmmeren also gave the book a final reading, and I thank them for their sharp professionalism.

My giant of a literary agent, Esther Newberg—wonderful and loyal—was familiar with some of the terrain covered in this book. It was very heartening to see her champion it along the way.

The John Simon Guggenheim Memorial Foundation supported the research of this book with a fellowship, and I am extremely grateful. At the foundation, I wish to thank Edward Hirsch and André Bernard. When my finances later became scarce, the National Endowment for the Humanities granted me a fellowship, and for that I wish to express my thanks to the former chairman James A. Leach, as well as to Judith Havemann and Russell Wyland.

This book is dedicated to Michael B. Coleman and Larry James, two men, like Thurgood, trained in the law. Coleman—mayor of Columbus, Ohio—offered some crucial insights during early conversations about my approach to the confirmation hearings covered in these pages. "It's really a thriller, isn't it," he said to me one day about this book. James, of Crabbe, Brown & James (his name is on the building), never let me forget that history, in the end, is indeed personal.

Others offered unforgettable kindnesses along the way. Steve Flannigan, Aimee Sanders, Lucy Shackelford, Bill Orrico, Professor Serena Williams, David Lieber, Dick Rhodes, Peter Cimbolic, Rick Momeyer, Carol Tyler, Sue Momeyer, Connie Higgins, Tina Moody, Lynda Huey, Tom Brockman, Kristi Cimbolic, Lee Daniels, Charles (Nick) Nichols, Peter Guralnick, Sheila Johnson, the Moores (Greg, Nina, Jasmin, Jaden), Bob Miller, Paul and Ceil Hendrickson, Tony Stigger, Pam Williams, Donna James, Keith Alexander, Krissah Thompson, Josie Freedman, Larry Leigh and the Brandywine team, and the crew of Politics and Prose all have my deep gratitude. As do Lynn Peterson, Mary Jo Green, Warren Tyler, Mark Cardwell, Steve Reiss, Valerie Hodge, Demetries Neely, Mark Corna, Mindy Graney, Shirley

Carswell, David Jones, Jill Grisco, Eric Grant, Darryl Fears, and Marty Anderson. Alex Shumate, Eugene Smith, Sheila Smith, René Shumate, and Jennifer McNally all have my appreciation for caring about this book before its publication. Kevin Merida, managing editor of *The Washington Post;* Katharine Weymouth, former publisher of *The Washington Post;* and Alma Gill, also of the *Post,* will always be special. David Hodge, Phyllis Callahan, and Richard Campbell gave me a new home at my alma mater, Miami University, Oxford, Ohio, by inviting me to join the Department of Media, Journalism, and Film. I thank them very much.

NOTES

This book involved personal interviews and extended trips to libraries and research institutions around the country across a four-and-a-half-year period. To those librarians and archivists who aided my quest in unraveling the Marshall confirmation hearings and his interactions with various U.S. senators, I am extremely grateful inasmuch as the hearings constitute a significant spine of the book.

Tamara Elliott, reference librarian at the U.S. Senate, helped me on numerous occasions during my visits there. Aside from the materials I requested, she often retrieved other documents that only heightened my curiosity about Marshall and the U.S. Senate. Also in the Senate, Erica J. Chabot, press secretary to the Senate Judiciary Committee chairman, Patrick Leahy, took time out from her busy schedule to usher me into room 2228—where the Marshall hearings were conducted—to see it for myself. I remember not quite wanting to vacate the room.

At the Lyndon Baines Johnson Library and Museum, Allen Fisher and Margaret Harman were tireless in their efforts to make sure I saw everything I needed to see during my trip to Austin. The John L. McClellan Papers—only available to the public since late 2011, shortly after I began my research—are housed in the Riley-Hickingbotham Library's Special Collections on the campus of Ouachita Baptist University in Arkadelphia, Arkansas. I spent a fruitful week at the library. The McClellan Papers have been assembled with great care, and my gratitude goes to Jacynda Ammons, Janice Ford, Phyllis Kinnison, Margaret Reed, Sherry Laymon, Wendy Richter, and Ray Granade.

James Eastland's papers are at the University of Mississippi, in Oxford. Leigh McWhite, the political papers archivist there, assisted me during my trip to the library and even took me to a fine lunch.

I found more than a few difficult-to-locate books at the main library of the University of the District of Columbia. I thank the staff there for their courtesies.

In 2011, which marked the sixtieth anniversary of the *Briggs v. Elliott* case in South Carolina that led to the *Brown* decision, the Supreme Court of South Carolina's Historical Society hosted a colloquium in Charleston celebrating the occasion. It was called "J. Waties Waring and the Dissent That Changed America." Richard M. Gergel, U.S. district judge for the Charleston Division, District of South Carolina, invited me to the event, and it was extraordinarily memorable. Not only did I meet the late jurist Matthew Perry, but I also sat in the very courtroom where the *Briggs* case had been tried by Marshall and heard by Waring. The occasion also allowed me the opportunity to meet several of Waring's relatives. Beth Warren, a South Carolina attorney, was gracious enough to answer some follow-up legal questions.

It was also a poignant reminder for me of the sweep of Thurgood Marshall's life on the day in 2013 when I found myself sitting in a law office in downtown Washington, D.C., talking to Marshall's longtime ally and friend William Coleman. He was dressed in a beautiful suit and tie. His cuff links shone. He was a wealth of information. He had recently celebrated his ninety-third birthday.

There are some great southern universities in this nation, but upon his death none of those schools wanted the papers of J. Waties Waring. He had apparently been too controversial. The Waring Papers—a treasure trove given my angle—wound up in the Moorland-Spingarn Research Center at Howard University, the historically black institution in Washington. Given Waring's life and times, it seems poetic justice that they landed there. I am profoundly grateful to the staff at Moorland-Spingarn, especially Joellen ElBashir and Richard Jenkins. When collections are cited, the following notations are given:

> CH—*Hearings Before the Committee on the Judiciary, United States Senate, Ninetieth Congress, First Session on Nomination of Thurgood Marshall, of New York, to Be Associate Justice of the Supreme Court of the United States, July 13, 14, 18, 19, and 24, 1967* (Washington, D.C.: U.S. Government Printing Office, 1967). (In the Notes, this document will be cited as "CH" for Committee Hearings.)

JEP—James Eastland Papers
JMP—John McClellan Papers
JWWP—J. Waties Waring Papers
LBJL—Lyndon Baines Johnson Library

Anyone studying President Johnson is greatly indebted, as I am, to Robert Caro's epic and ongoing study.

As to those who took time to meet with me—to invite me into their homes—to talk about Thurgood Marshall, his hearings, the 1960s, those times, each one has my enduring gratitude. Among them were Stetson Kennedy, Beth Warren, James Nabrit, Joseph Califano, Clifford Alexander, Lowell Muse, Birch Bayh, Joseph Tydings, William Winter, Evangeline Moore, Louis Pollak, William Coleman, John Doar, Mimi Clark Gronlund, David Lambert, Roger Wilkins, Louis Sullivan, Nick Katzenbach, Walter Mondale, Kate Harris, Clarence Pierce, Berl Bernhard, Jack Weinstein, Jack Greenberg, Billie Allen, Anthony Lewis, Patrick Leahy, and Jim Flug.

PROLOGUE

BOUND FOR ROOM 2228
The White House aides Clifford Alexander and Joseph Califano shared with me their memories of the day inside the White House that President Johnson nominated Thurgood Marshall to the Supreme Court.

3 "Let the South have": Goodheart, *1861*, 315.
3 "fraught with consequences": Goodwin, *Team of Rivals*, 465.
5 "the Negro support": Marshall Oral History, 1, LBJL.
6 "The nastiest mail": Califano, interview by author.
6 "I want to do": CNN.com, Feb. 25, 2011.
6 "Thurgood, I'm nominating": Alexander, interview by author.
7 "He really had": Tushnet, *Thurgood Marshall*, 496.

DAY ONE: Thursday, July 13, 1967

I THE GHOSTS OF LITTLE ROCK
12 "I'm fond of Joe McCarthy": Laymon, *Fearless*, 118.
13 "steely mask of Old Testament": Ibid., 169.
13 "Virtually every speech": McPherson, *Political Education*, 45.
14 "A friendship developed": Gronlund, interview by author.

15 "I knew him": Tushnet, Thurgood Marshall, 456.

15 "He talked to Tom Clark": Califano, interview by author.

16 "great adventure": Gronlund, *Supreme Court Justice Clark*, 231.

16 "He'd just call Senator Eastland": Califano, interview by author.

16 "At one stroke": Morris, *Theodore Rex*, 55.

17 "There was clear knowledge": Alexander, interview by author.

19 "Marshall was considered": Tydings, interview by author.

19 "Marshall had no idea": Williams, interview by author.

20 "Eastland didn't care for the press": Flug, interview by author.

20 "He is one of the most": *CH*, 1, 2.

21 "a man whose work": Ibid., 2.

21 "While thus engaged": JMP, box 392, file 12a.

22 "The scene was becoming": *Washington Post*, June 14, 1967.

23 "Please do not confirm": JMP, box 490, file 15.

23 "Marshall Appointment Must": Ibid.

23 "No amount of Federal": Ibid.

23 "Please, sir, no nigger": Ibid.

23 "a Negro, an American": Ibid.

24 "legal ability or training": *CH*, 3.

24 "Now back to the line": Ibid., 4.

25 "If we—and now I mean": Baldwin, *Fire Next Time*, 104–5.

26 "I say in answer": *CH*, 6.

26 "The nine men meet": Ibid., 7.

27 "Do you subscribe": Ibid., 14.

27 "reliable Old Bulls": Kennedy, *True Compass*, 192, 194.

28 "Just yesterday . . . in Boston": Ibid., 15.

2 WILLIE AND NORMA MARSHALL'S BRAVE SON

Three valuable books aided my effort to understand Thurgood Marshall's early years: Mark V. Tushnet's *Thurgood Marshall: His Speeches, Writings, Arguments, Opinions, and Reminiscences;* Juan Williams's estimable *Thurgood Marshall: American Revolutionary;* and Larry S. Gibson's unsung *Young Thurgood: The Making of a Supreme Court Justice.*

32 "his career in trade": Gibson, *Young Thurgood*, 38.

33 "The escape of": Swanson, *Manhunt*, 170.

33 "I struck boldly": Ibid., 206.

33 "To the colored people": Ibid., 260.

35 "No Niggers and Dogs": Williams, *Thurgood Marshall*, 44.

35 "In Baltimore, where": *New Yorker*, March 17, 1956.

35 "I can see her now": Gibson, *Young Thurgood*, 47.

35 "She worked like": Tushnet, *Thurgood Marshall*, 417.

36 "Anyone calls you a nigger": Kluger, *Simple Justice*, 177.

36 "Thurgood was restless": Gibson, *Young Thurgood*, 59.

37 "In the department stores": Tushnet, *Thurgood Marshall*, 413.

37 "I remember one day": Ibid., 414–15.

37 "Once a week": Gibson, *Young Thurgood*, 68.

38 "Many times during the term": Ibid., 61.

38 "I was getting in a trolley": Tushnet, *Thurgood Marshall*, 414.

39 "Forget about them": Ibid.

39 "What do you plan": Gibson, *Young Thurgood*, 84.

40 "do good enough": Tushnet, *Thurgood Marshall*, 415.

40 "I like the school": Bernard, *Remember Me to Harlem*, 39.

41 "February of our Freshman year": Lincoln University 1929 yearbook, 9.

41 "rough and ready": Williams, *Thurgood Marshall*, 48.

41 "My first payment": Gibson, *Young Thurgood*, 93.

41 "Norma, how much money": Tushnet, *Thurgood Marshall*, 417.

42 "Penn State . . . has been": Gibson, *Young Thurgood*, 96.

43 "the history of the Anglo-Saxon races": Ibid., 97.

44 "The fact that Marshall": Ibid., 99.

44 "the Wrathful Marshall": Ibid., 100.

44 "So the only money": Tushnet, *Thurgood Marshall*, 415.

44 "a forty-year-old": Williams, *Thurgood Marshall*, 44.

45 "Thurgood was the funniest looking man": Gibson, *Young Thurgood*, 101.

45 "Son of Mr. and Mrs. William Marshall": Ibid., 104.

45 "Most Popular": Lincoln University 1929 yearbook, 3.

46 "The time has come": Ibid., 2.

47 "That was one of the nicest": Tushnet, *Thurgood Marshall*, 272.

47 "the participation of the Negro": Sullivan, *Lift Every Voice*, 138–39.

48 "shameless flouting": Ibid., 139.

48 "niggras vote freely": Kluger, *Simple Justice*, 142.

48 "could have nothing less": Sullivan, *Lift Every Voice*, 140.

48 "conducted with a snap": Ibid.

48 "the first national demonstration": Ibid., 141.

49 "there are not more than": Charles Hamilton Houston, "The Need for Negro Lawyers," MS-CH (Moorland-Spingarn-Charles Houston), box 163-17, folder 12.

49 "This was what I wanted": Kluger, *Simple Justice*, 179.

50 "I'll never be satisfied": Tushnet, *Thurgood Marshall*, 273.

50 "He had come down here": Kluger, *Simple Justice*, 179.

50 "I got through simply": Ibid., 180.

51 "Their brief": Ibid.

51 "lanky, brash young senior": Williams, *Thurgood Marshall*, 58.

52 "It would follow": Houston, "Need for Negro Lawyers."

53 "without parallel in the history": Appiah and Gates, *Africana*, 1681.

54 "I'd got the horsin' around": *Collier's*, Feb. 23, 1952.

54 "Charlie Houston was training lawyers": Tushnet, *Thurgood Marshall*, 273.

54 "Unfortunately, there is in the South": Morris, *Theodore Rex*, 246.

54 "a large-scale, widespread": Kluger, *Simple Justice*, 132.

54 "because the forces that keep": Ibid.

55 "If we boldly challenge": Ibid., 134.

55 "applied and administered": Ibid., 135.

57 "That's why we carried": Williams, *Thurgood Marshall*, 60.

57 "spent $331,932.00": Kluger, *Simple Justice*, 165.

58 "I have had quite a job": Gibson, *Young Thurgood*, 125.

58 "He had a genius": *Collier's*, Feb. 23, 1952.

59 "Old-timers had the feeling": Kluger, *Simple Justice*, 185.

59 "There's never a dull": *Collier's*, Feb. 23, 1952.

59 "get even with Maryland": Long, *Marshalling Justice*, 7.

60 "there will be an Ethiop": Kluger, *Simple Justice*, 192.

60 "I have never sent": Long, *Marshalling Justice*, 8.

60 "I don't know of anybody": Ibid., 18.

61 "tush-tush": Ibid., 19.

61 "School situation is terrible": Kluger, *Simple Justice*, 199.

61 "Charlie Houston passed through": Ibid., 205.

62 "render legal aid gratuitously": Greenberg, *Crusaders in the Courts*, xvii.

62 "I changed things": *Reporting Civil Rights, 1941–1963*, 143.

62 "It's very important": Ibid.

62 "He was a very courageous": Kluger, *Simple Justice*, 223.

63 "When Marshall would come": Louis Sullivan, interview by author.

63 "and hear that culled lawyer": *Reporting Civil Rights, 1941–1963*, 144.

64 "get expert advice": Ibid., 148.

64 "Honey, I am so hurt": Goodwin, *No Ordinary Time*, 522.

64 "Lights out": Sheinkin, *Port Chicago 50*, 57.

65 "Fellows were cut": Ibid., 62.

65 "As was to be expected": Ibid., 69.

66 "Now, the slightest provocation": Ibid., 88.

66 "solely because of their race": Ibid., 122.

66 "As a matter of fact": Tushnet, *Making Civil Rights Law*, 32.

66 "Negroes in the Navy": Sheinkin, *Port Chicago 50*, 138.

67 "I want to know": Ibid., 139.

67 "one of the worst frame-ups": Ibid., 144, 150.

68 "a group of sadistic": Cagin and Dray, *We Are Not Afraid*, 369.

68 "Look, just two sets": *Collier's*, Feb. 23, 1952.

69 "There can be no equality": Long, *Marshalling Justice*, 205.

69 "I can testify": *Collier's*, Feb. 23, 1952.

70 "The hate-ridden orgy": Williams, *Thurgood Marshall*, 134.

70 "The white people of the South": Ibid., 135.

70 "NIGGER, READ AND RUN": White, *Man Called White*, 313.

71 "best example of what happens": Sullivan: *Lift Every Voice*, 314.

71 "Mr. Marshall's condition": Williams, *Thurgood Marshall*, 137.

71 "Open threats": White, *Man Called White*, 314.

72 "We have got to arrest you": Ibid., 320.

73 "I told them that if we": Ibid.

73 "Had Looby and Weaver": Ibid., 321.

73 "Thurgood Marshall's supposed to be": *New Yorker*, March 17, 1956.

73 "What's goin' on here?": Ibid.

74 "Thurgood was this young lawyer": Allen, interview by author.

74 "Dear Mr. Marshall": *New Yorker*, March 17, 1956.

75 "In the glove compartment": Tushnet, *Speeches*, 509.

76 "One day I plowed": Litwack, *Trouble in Mind*, 66.

76 "Yessir, we got good nigras": Kluger, *Simple Justice*, 7.

77 "A very few got seats": Long, *Marshalling Justice*, 290–91.

77 "Segregation of white and colored": Friedman, *Brown v. Board*, 330.

79 "the Court insisted on equality": Branch, *Parting the Waters*, 113.

79 "You can say all you want": Kluger, *Simple Justice*, 747.

79 "Thurgood's wonderful to behold": *Reporting Civil Rights, 1941–1963*, 156.

79 "He's aged so": Ibid.

80 "Brother Rogers": *Look*, Oct. 17, 1967.

81 "He stayed by her bedside": Juan Williams, *Thurgood Marshall*, 234.

82 "I have wanted most": Ibid.

82 "During this period": Greenberg, *Crusaders in the Courts*, 202.

82 "For the purpose of": Ibid.

85 "Her family was not particularly": Williams, *Thurgood Marshall*, 250.

86 "Just read your recent column": Long, *Marshalling Justice*, 353.

86 "I think he had an extra sense": Bernhard, interview by author.

DAY TWO: Friday, July 14, 1967

3 BATTLING WITH A LEGENDARY COUNTRY LAWYER

90 "The Supreme Court will abide": Clancy, *Just a Country Lawyer*, 32.

91 "I think that every Senator": *CH*, 25.

92 "As good citizens": Clancy, *Just a Country Lawyer*, 153.

92 "I love the South": Ibid., 174.

92 "Under the leadership": *Reporting Civil Rights, 1941–1963*, 383, 384.

93 "a tragic day": Clancy, *Just a Country Lawyer*, 178.

93 "I'm sorry but we don't": *Reporting Civil Rights, 1941–1963*, 434.

93 "regrettable that some": Ibid., 437.

94 "If one race be inferior": Litwack, *Trouble in Mind*, 243–44.

94 "The time had come": Clancy, *Just a Country Lawyer*, 181.

94 "a great man": Ibid.

95 "the virtue of judicial self-restraint": *CH*, 27.

95 "represented unwarranted encroachments": Ibid.

95 "Good intentions": Ibid., 48.

95 "I would not disagree": Ibid.

95 "Mr. Webster has deliberately": Goodwin, *Team of Rivals*, 145.

96 "Does it not necessarily": *CH*, 49.

97 "But has it not been established": Ibid., 50.

97 "I would like to invite": Ibid., 51.

98 "Can you tell me": Ibid., 52.

99 " 'Compelled.' Does not the word": Ibid., 53.

100 "How can the words": Ibid., 54.

101 "I think this is a very simple": Ibid., 57.

101 "No, sir. I agreed": Ibid., 58.

103 "That is an arguable point": Ibid., 59.

103 "who had been imbibing": Ibid., 61–62.

103 "Did not the Supreme Court": Ibid., 62.

104 *"Brown versus Mississippi"*: Ibid., 63.

105 "This spring certain Negro": *Life*, June 2, 1967.

105 "overlooking the burning turmoil": Ibid.

106 "Southern senators": *Washington Post*, July 15, 1967.

4 A "PHILADELPHIA NEGRO" SUDDENLY ON STANDBY

108 "he was exemplar": McPherson, *Political Education*, 349.

108 "He could become agitated": Ibid., 31.

108 "where he was at once judge": Ibid., 45–46.

109 "They had been DA's": Ibid., 32.

109 "Whitney, what you're saying": Kotz, *Judgment Days*, 372.

109 "When I see our country": Branch, *At Canaan's Edge*, 580.

109 "By the time of the Thurgood": Katzenbach, interview by author.

110 "I used to have a lot of fights": Tushnet, *Thurgood Marshall*, 471.

111 "McClellan was a motherfucker": Wilkins, interview by author.

111 "The attraction of Coleman": Califano, interview by author.

112 "Our legislative people": Coleman, *Counsel for the Situation*, 180.

113 "Mother introduced us": Ibid., 12.

113 "I said, 'Someday' ": Coleman, interview by author.

114 "My professors presided over": Coleman, *Counsel for the Situation*, 45.

115 "personal commitment": Ibid., 76.

115 "heart leaped to the skies": Ibid., 77.

115 "What I can say of you": Ibid., 92.

115 "I would like to invite you": Ibid., 104.

116 "We'd ask for integration": Kluger, *Simple Justice*, 293.

116 "We respected him": Coleman, *Counsel for the Situation*, 106.

116 "if we can't get Marshall": Ibid., 180.

117 "I said the pay was lousy": Coleman, interview by author.

117 "The southerners knew": Ibid.

118 "a cultivated moderate": McPherson, *Political Education*, 179.

5 THURGOOD MARSHALL AND HIS SOUTHERN HERO

120 "fine, decent slaveholders": Kluger, *Simple Justice*, 295.

120 "Negroes in long lines": Alpert, *Life and Times of Porgy and Bess*, 22.

121 "The whole thing": Kluger, *Simple Justice*, 297–98.

122 "When a mayor": McCullough, *Truman*, 589.

122 "I was shocked": Kluger, *Simple Justice*, 298.

123 "It is time for South Carolina": Ibid., 299.

123 "Why, he'd never shown": *Collier's*, April 29, 1950.

123 "I think you are slow": *Congressional Record Quarterly*, April 6, 1950.

123 "Unless he is removed": *New York Times*, Jan. 12, 1968.

124 "We ought to have": *Congressional Record Quarterly*, April 6, 1950.

124 "Negro parents as a whole": *Harper's*, Jan. 3, 1956.

125 "We'd get in our car": *Collier's*, April 29, 1950.

125 "the guy who let": Kluger, *Simple Justice*, 300.

125 "My opponents are the most": *Collier's*, April 29, 1950.

125 "This was no ordinary": *Reporting Civil Rights, 1941–1963*, 149.

125 "It's going to be hard": Ibid.

126 "The technical witnesses": JWWP, box 110–3, folder 14.

127 "The abolishment of segregation": *Wythe County News*, May 20, 1954.

127 "a sign that America": *New Brunswick Home News*, May 19, 1954. This is also the source for the other quotations from foreign newspapers in this paragraph.

127 "Waties and Elizabeth": JWWP, box 110–1, folder 2.

128 "Negroes have thanked me": *New York Times*, Jan. 12, 1968.

128 "I forgot to tell": JWWP, box 110–24, folder 733.

6 THE CHAIRMAN GOES AWOL, AND THE HUNT IS ON
FOR ANTI-MARSHALL VOTES

131 "Walter, I was amazed": Asch, *The Senator and the Sharecropper*, 92.

132 "bruising": Greenberg, *Crusaders in the Courts*, 365.

132 "the Negro race": *Time*, March 26, 1956.

132 "subversion just as real": Ibid.

133 "If it came to fighting": Ibid.

134 "Holbert is a ginger-cake": Asch, *The Senator and the Sharecropper*, 25.

135 "The most excruciating form": Ibid., 28.

136 "These barbarous scenes": Ibid., 29.

136 "The only plea": Ibid.

136 "A white man": Ibid., 31.

137 "It was a fun place": Ibid., 43.

137 "I know that they desire": Ibid., 92.

138 "I found they were running": *New York Post*, Feb. 15, 1956.

138 "The Negro soldier": *Pittsburgh Courier*, July 7, 1945.

138 "to be a damn good soldier": Ibid.

138 "Senator Eastland is trying to paint": *Philadelphia Independent*, July 7, 1945.

139 "there is no more cowardly": *Louisville Courier-Journal*, July 3, 1945.

139 "irresponsible and fantastic": *PM* (a daily newspaper published in New York City, 1940–48), July 10, 1945.

139 "You gave freely": JEP, series 1, subseries 18, box 10.

140 "Maybe there is no easy": Caro, *Master of the Senate*, 783.

140 "I had special pockets": Ibid.

140 "A mad dog is loose": Ibid., 784.

140 "The Negro voter": Ibid., 842.

140 "Herman Talmadge ably exposes": JEP, series 1, subseries 18, box 10.

141 "People are starting": *New Orleans Item*, June 18, 1956.

141 "He thought we were not": Pierce, interview by author.

142 "Most Congressmen realize": *Monroe News-Star*, Jan. 14, 1957.

142 "Due north of Eastland": *Memphis Commercial-Appeal*, Feb. 5, 1956.

142 "the rebirth of the Ku Klux Klan": Ibid.

142 "My mission was to destroy": *Washington Post*, Sept. 29, 2002.

143 "U.S. Is Prepared": Reeves, *President Kennedy*, 355.

143 "Dear Miss Brower": *Washington Post*, Sept. 29, 2002.

143 "GOD IS GOOD": Ibid.

144 "I'd already brought up": Wilkie, *Dixie*, 25.

144 "We all knew": Ibid.

145 "Please ask them": Branch, *Parting the Waters*, 363.

145 "I didn't pull any punches": Marshall Oral History, 6, LBJL.

145 "I thought you were a man": Haygood, *King of the Cats*, 104.

145 "bigots in the pulpit": Ibid., 271.

146 "There may be a couple": Ibid., 273.

146 "He spent all his time": Marshall Oral History, 5, LBJL.

147 "Well, why?": Tushnet, *Thurgood Marshall*, 484.

147 "Bobby was like his father": Ibid.

148 "Well . . .about how many": Ibid., 487.

148 "Of course Thurgood hadn't been": Greenberg, *Crusaders in the Courts*, 295.

149 "You'd think he was the nicest": Tushnet, *Thurgood Marshall*, 485.

149 "a clear abuse": Caro, *Master of the Senate*, 785.

149 "I'm going to sing": Reeves, *President Kennedy*, 466.

149 "I think that the men": Ibid., 465–66.

150 "For 986,000 Mississippi Negroes": Ibid., 466.

150 "A bunch of niggers": Ibid.

150 "Look, do you understand": Tushnet, *Thurgood Marshall*, 485.

150 "my good friend": Ibid., 486.

151 "Luce just said": Ibid., 487.

151 "If you were on the plantation": Asch, *The Senator and the Sharecropper*, 208.

151 "You have been slaves": Kotz, *Judgment Days*, 158.

152 "There's just nothing": Ibid., 168.

152 "Hey, why don't you hold": Cagin and Dray, *We Are Not Afraid*, 365.

152 "The student volunteers": Ibid., 371.

153 "We lost the Voting Rights Bill": JEP, file series 3, subseries 1, box 45.

153 "Jim Eastland is a dreary figure": *New York Post*, Feb. 13, 1956.

154 "I remember when I was six": Lambert, interview by author.

7 "THE JEW"

157 "I consider Brandeis": Todd, *Justice on Trial*, 42.

158 "typical young libertine Jew": Dray, *At the Hands of Persons Unknown*, 209–10, 211.

159 "I understand that I am": Oney, *And the Dead Shall Rise*, 449.

159 "Let him hang!": Ibid., 485.

160 "I would rather be the widow": Dray, *At the Hands of Persons Unknown*, 212.

160 "I can endure": Oney, *And the Dead Shall Rise*, 502.

160 "Had Georgia sent Frank": Ibid., 506.

160 "Georgia is reaping": Dray, *At the Hands of Persons Unknown*, 213–14.

161 "President Wilson sent a bomb": Todd, *Justice on Trial*, 69.

161 "Of all the Americans": Ibid., 73.

161 "He is a muckraker": Ibid., 78.

161 "A man ought": Ibid., 85.

162 "Mr. Brandeis' mind": Ibid., 107.

162 "I have kept myself": Ibid., 120.

162 "The undersigned": Ibid., 159.

162 "There is probably no man": Ibid., 175.

163 "I am not willing": Ibid., 188.

163 "The real crime": Ibid., 189.

163 "It was sufficiently trying": Ibid., 202.

163 "The prospects for the confirmation": *Wall Street Journal*, May 4, 1916.

163 "In every matter": Todd, *Justice on Trial*, 213–14.

164 "All we need do": Ibid., 218.

164 "To place upon the Supreme Bench": Ibid., 242–43.

164 "Good evening": Ibid., 245.

8 THE LONG MEMORY OF EVANGELINE MOORE

168 "Our kitchen table": Moore, interview by author.

168 "Most of our killed": McGovern, *Anatomy of a Lynching*, 18.

170 "One of the men": Ibid., 65.

170 "Florida to Burn": Ibid., 74.

171 "This bill does not deprive": Long, *Marshalling Justice*, 2.

173 "no jurisdiction": Green, *Before His Time*, 57.

174 "anxious for action": Ibid., 59.

174 "My parents were fired": Moore, interview by author.

174 "remind[s] one very much": Green, *Before His Time*, 74.

175 "Do you think I'm going": King, *Devil in the Grove*, 38.

176 "That is him": Ibid., 117.

176 "The resources of the association": Ibid., 134.

176 "Mrs. Padgett didn't have any idea": Ibid., 193.

176 "Won new trial": Ibid., 219.

176 "any civilized conception": Ibid., 220.

177 "I heard him say": Ibid., 243.

177 "I just wish we could": Green, *Before His Time*, 111.

178 "They had just started": Moore, interview by author.

179 "I'll take a few of them": Green, *Before His Time*, 155.

179 "We seek no special favors": Ibid., 163.

179 "We'll hold the presents": Moore, interview by author.

180 "I got in the backseat": Ibid.

181 "a point of no return": Green, *Before His Time*, 177.

181 "unless they can be secure": Ibid.

182 "worried that physical harm": The Florida Department of Law Enforcement (FDLE) Report (2006), 315. (One of the most intensive civil rights murder investigations in the history of America was launched by the Florida attorney general, Charlie Crist, in 2004 into the Moore bombing. The probe, completed and released in 2006, was led by the Florida attorney general's Office of Civil Rights with the assistance of the FDLE. The NAACP and the FBI also assisted. No one reading the 335-page report, as I did, can doubt the sincerity of its mission. The report is available online at http:myfloridalegal.com.)

182 "booked solid": Ibid.

182 "There isn't much left": Green, *Before His Time*, 180.

183 "bank robbers dividing": FDLE Report, 41.

184 "The house was in shambles": Ibid., 12.

185 "Since Christmas Day": Green, *Before His Time*, 189–90.

185 "did not develop any evidence": Ibid., 240.

186 "lit a fire in Washington": FDLE Report, 316.

187 "It is very likely": Ibid., 335.

188 "I am determined": Moore, interview by author.

189 "not since the Reconstruction Period": Clark, *Red Pepper and Gorgeous George*, 130.

189 "Doesn't this make": Ibid., 140.

190 "This vicious legislation": Ibid., 132.

190 "some Negroes had received": Ibid., 139–40.

190 "with an appeal to ignorance": Ibid., 143.

190 "The defeat of Claude Pepper": Ibid., 154.

190 "spent much of his considerable": Ibid.

191 "How nice it is": Branch, *Pillar of Fire*, 278.

192 "every inch the Boston blueblood": Ibid., 281.

192 "You look just like": Ibid.

DAY THREE: Tuesday, July 18, 1967

9 RETURN OF THE PROSECUTORS

196 "My attitude and outlook": Bronner, *Battle for Justice*, 220.

197 "So, go right ahead": *CH*, 65.

197 "Did not the Court": Ibid., 65–66.

198 "the blight of racial discrimination": Hall, *Oxford Companion to the Supreme Court*, 328.

198 "Do not those two provisions": *CH*, 67.

199 "If as the Supreme Court": Ibid., 69–70.

203 "The *Miranda* decision is based": Ibid., 86–88.

204 "Do you not know": Ibid., 90.

205 "Do you recall": Ibid., 93.

207 "This [Friendly's] opinion": Ibid., 96–99.

210 "The reason I am conducting": Ibid., 155–58.

215 "He had culture": O'Brien, *Philip Hart*, 8.

216 "the failure of leadership": Ibid., 73.

216 "hideous failure": Ibid., 71.

216 "We have to face the facts": Ibid., 93.

216 "Lifelong Democrats": Ibid., 91.

217 "And I do say": Ibid., 104.

217 "We would have to fight": Tydings, interview by author.

218 "They thought Johnson": Califano, interview by author.

10 PAINFUL INTERRUPTIONS FOR A PRESIDENT AND HIS NOMINEE

220 "I hope you will vote no": JMP, box 490, file 15.

220 "The United States isn't ready": Ibid.

221 "The people have purged": Haygood, *King of the Cats*, 103.

221 "We're just waiting": Ibid., 113.

221 "a little kike": Ibid., 118.

222 "the last lady": Ibid., 129.

222 "Walk out": Ibid., 133.

222 "You'd sit with him": Ibid., 191.

223 "democracy's shining hour": Ibid., 194.

223 "fighting for the same thing": Ibid., 241.

223 "The greatest showman": Tushnet, *Thurgood Marshall*, 475.

224 "Any Negro who automatically": Powell, *Keep the Faith, Baby!* 79.

225 "Now Adam": Haygood, *King of the Cats*, 313.

225 "The hell with the bitch": Ibid., 320.

225 "There are those who scream": Powell, *Keep the Faith, Baby!*, 11.

226 "The deep southerners hated": Haygood, *King of the Cats*, 328.

227 "We feel that this": Branch, *At Canaan's Edge*, 623.

228 "Once the Communists know": Ibid., 268.

228 "better prepared than ever": Caro, *Path to Power*, 548.

228 "President Johnson says": *Life*, April 7, 1967.

228 "I don't see that we can": Evans, *American Century*, 526.

229 "the old man": Haygood, *King of the Cats*, 369.

11 DEAR MR. PRESIDENT

232 "worked hard every day": Goodwin, *Lyndon Johnson and the American Dream*, 306.

233 "Now even the Supreme Court": Branch, *At Canaan's Edge*, 623.

233 "was broke": Voter Registration Project paper, Executive Files, LBJL.

234 "I will not give up": Voting Rights speech, same folder, LBJL.

234 "The real hero": Ibid.

234 "that bitch of a war": Evans, *American Century*, 527.

235 "You have in the Supreme Court": Name file, box 112, WHCF, LBJL.

235 "I believe in these very emotional times": Ibid.

235 "Recalling the conditions": This and all of the letters quoted in this paragraph are in ibid.

236 "It will naturally": Ibid.

236 "His legal prowess": Name file, box 113, WHCF, LBJL.

237 "I have written you once before": Ibid.

237 "He was a creature of war": Caro, *Master of the Senate*, 306.

237 "Apart from the history-book": John Macy, Office files, LBJL.

237 "I don't have a fence": Name file, box 112, WHCF, LBJL.

238 "Your recommendation of one": This and the rest of the letters quoted in this paragraph are in Executive Files, FG535, A, LBJL.

DAY FOUR: Wednesday, July 19, 1967

12 A REBEL'S LAST ROAR

242 "It was the equivalent of": Weinstein, interview by author.

243 "low, dirty scoundrel": Bass and Thompson, *Ol' Strom*, 27.

243 "I didn't know what color": Ibid., 61.

243 "I want to tell you": Ibid., 112.

244 "Now, the *American Bar News*": CH, 159–65.

252 "In 1862, the laws of Ohio": Ibid., 168.

253 "Do you think that the Supreme Court": Ibid., 172, 173.

254 "Do you know of any specific": Ibid., 175.

255 "Ever since I was a child": Bass and Thompson, *Ol' Strom*, 286.

256 "Well, now, of course": *CH*, 176.

256 "No, sir": Ibid., 178.

257 "record of success": Ibid., 179.

257 "I think that in passing": Ibid., 180.

257 "Liberty Lobby is strongly opposed": Ibid., 181.

258 "Now, Mr. Marshall's associations": Ibid., 183, 184.

258 "It may be worth observing": Ibid., 186.

259 "I cannot answer": Ibid.

13 FLAMES

261 "Before the very gates": McWhirter, *Red Summer*, 103.

261 "He had a hell": Williams, *Thurgood Marshall*, 33.

261 "Your prophecies of serious race": McWhirter, *Red Summer*, 149.

261 "Violence is as American": Gates and Higginbotham, *African American Lives*, 106.

262 "persuasion": Fine, *Violence in the Model City*, 1.

262 "dragging people down the stairs": Ibid., 161.

262 "Brutality": Ibid., 160.

263 "Are we going to let": Ibid., 161.

263 "You try to talk": Ibid., 169.

264 "didn't need to throw": Ibid., 33.

264 "The Negroes in Detroit": Ibid., 99.

264 "It looks like Berlin": Ibid., 194.

264 "They have lost all control": Ibid., 213.

264 "Those black son-of-a-bitches": Ibid., 196.

264 "I'm gonna shoot anything": Ibid., 199.

265 "There were dark days": Branch, *At Canaan's Edge*, 631.

266 "I went in the service": Hersey, *Algiers Motel Incident*, 19.

266 "Momma, they don't kill them": Ibid., 59.

266 "The certainty of Negroes": Tushnet, *Thurgood Marshall*, 89.

267 "It could be": *Life*, July 28, 1967.

DAY FIVE: Monday, July 24, 1967

14 THE CONSTITUTION

272 "I am very concerned": *CH*, 187–90.

274 "You are quoted": Ibid., 192–94.

275 "For some reason": Ibid., 196–98.

15 THURGOOD MARSHALL'S STAND IN LBJ'S TEXAS

One of the finest books on the white primary voting battle that took place in Texas is *Black Victory: The Rise and Fall of the White Primary in Texas*, by Darlene Clark Hine.

281 "the really beautiful country": Long, *Marshalling Justice*, 68.

282 "a general revolt": Goodheart, *1861*, 49.

282 "Schoolboys have become so excited": Ibid., 50.

283 "the last great mounted maneuvers": Morris, *Rise of Theodore Roosevelt*, 627.

283 "After firing about 200 shots": Morris, *Theodore Rex*, 453.

284 "CITIZENS OF BROWNSVILLE": Ibid., 454.

284 "That the raiders were soldiers": Ibid., 454, 455.

284 "If you possibly can avoid": Harlan, *Booker T. Washington*, 310.

285 "almost . . . hours": Morris, *Theodore Rex*, 467.

285 "executive lynch law": Harlan, *Booker T. Washington*, 311.

285 "When you turned": Morris, *Theodore Rex*, 474.

285 "Look here": Haynes, *Night of Violence*, 75.

287 "Well, if we die": Ibid., 153.

287 "The negro soldiers resent": Ibid., 199.

288 "I'm coming home": Ibid., 5.

288 "In no event": SoRelle, "Darker Side of 'Heaven,'" 172.

289 "The judges were friends": Hine, *Black Victory*, 75.

289 "We find it unnecessary": Ibid., 80.

289 "The Supreme Court has held": Ibid., 81.

290 "all white Democrats": White, *Man Called White*, 87.

290 "This is a white man's government": Hine, *Black Victory*, 112.

291 "the denial of the negro": Ibid., 161.

292 "We didn't go out and organize": Ibid., 130.

292 "We plan to use reason": Ibid., 133.

293 "immediately . . . test": White, *Man Called White*, 88.

294 "Never before since Negroes": Hine, *Black Victory*, 169.

295 "the privilege of membership": Kluger, *Simple Justice*, 167.

295 "In 1935 the Supreme Court": Hine, *Black Victory*, 172.

295 "It should not be difficult": White, *Man Called White*, 88.

295 "So the Negro is endowed": Hine, *Black Victory*, 173.

296 "nail in the coffin": Kluger, *Simple Justice*, 167.

296 "If you want to know": Long, *Marshalling Justice*, 187.

296 "the ideal circumstances": White, *Man Called White*, 88.

297 "We want you to know": Tushnet, *Thurgood Marshall*, 426.

297 "We raised all that money": Ibid., 427.

297 "at last Negroes will work": Hine, *Black Victory*, 200.

298 "Well, I'm going": Tushnet, *Thurgood Marshall*, 427.

298 "blind themselves as judges": Zelden, *Battle for the Black Ballot*, 48.

299 "All his life": Caro, *Path to Power*, 185.

299 "I never had any bigotry": Goodwin, *Lyndon Johnson and the American Dream*, 230.

300 "In the middle thirties": Ibid., 231.

301 "Somehow, you never forget": Ibid., 230.

301 "election officials who willfully": Kluger, *Simple Justice*, 233.

302 "regulate primaries when state law": Hall, *Oxford Companion to the Supreme Court*, 182.

302 "Whereas the Democratic Party": Zelden, *Battle for the Black Ballot*, 82–83.

302 "We have already assisted": Ibid., 93.

302 "We were a governmental": Kluger, *Simple Justice*, 234–35.

303 "the first real big one": Tushnet, *Thurgood Marshall*, 426.

303 "surprised and baffled": Hine, *Black Victory*, 218.

304 "in the first place": Ibid., 219.

304 "The United States is a constitutional": White, *Man Called White*, 89.

305 "I apologized profusely": Kluger, *Simple Justice*, 237.

305 "great achievement": Hine, *Black Victory*, 222.

305 "one of baffled hopes": Ibid.

305 "There is no reason": Kluger, *Simple Justice*, 237.

305 "new contrivances to bar": Hine, *Black Victory*, 222.

305 "We're not going to submit": Ibid., 224.

306 "an alarming tendency": Ibid.

306 "The Negroes down there": Marshall Oral History, LBJL.

307 "Certain members of the Negro race": *Columbia Journalism Review*, May–June 2002 (a lengthy article in this issue discusses the Texas campaign).

307 "We put money in": Hobart Taylor Sr. Oral History, LBJL.

308 "the whole complexion": Zelden, *Battle for the Black Ballot*, 132.

308 "We drive all day": Updegrove, *Indomitable Will*, 51–52.

POST-HEARING: July 25–August 30, 1967

16 A NOMINEE IN LIMBO

314 "My mother blew up": Tydings, interview with author.

314 "We had geared up": Ibid.

315 "Realization of Dr. King's": *Baltimore Afro-American*, Sept. 2, 1967.

315 "There is no real need": JMP, box 392, file 10.

316 "has earned and deserved": *Congressional Record*, June 14, 1967.

316 "His race should not": Ibid.

316 "Already subject to racial riots": Ibid., June 15, 1967.

317 "A liberal Senator": Hayes, *Smiling Through the Apocalypse*, 277.

317 "a necessary phase": Branch, *At Canaan's Edge*, 633.

317 "We are preparing groups": Ibid., 634.

317 "Why should they ask me": Remnick, *King of the World*, 289, 290.

319 "Poitier and Steiger may eventually": *Life*, July 28, 1967.

319 "a giddy sense of release": Fine, *Violence in the Model City*, 165.

320 "Black boys in the ghettoes": *Baltimore Afro-American*, Aug. 12, 1967.

321 "John, I've got a little problem": Goodwin, *Lyndon Johnson and the American Dream*, 184.

321 "No army is stronger": Whalen and Whalen, *Longest Debate*, 188.

322 "impressive professional record": *CH*, majority report, 2, 3.

322 "It is clearly a disservice": *CH*, minority report, 13.

323 "I know that in so doing": Ibid., 5.

323 "The crime menace": Ibid., 51.

323 "The GPO had more blacks": Flug, interview by author.

324 "the South's unending revenge": Caro, *Master of the Senate*, xxiii.

325 "What is the pending business?": *Congressional Records*, Aug. 30, 1967. (The entire voting process quoted here is taken from the *Congressional Record* of August 30, 1967. The accumulated quotations—interrupted by Jim Flug's quotation, which came in an interview with the author—ends with "I join my colleagues" by Senator Mansfield.)

332 "I am greatly honored": *Washington Post*, Aug. 31, 1967.

CONFIRMATION: September 1, 1967

17 GOOD EVENING, MR. JUSTICE MARSHALL

336 "Negro Is Suggested": *Cincinnati Enquirer,* Nov. 20, 1939.

337 "Hugo was telling the brethren": Kluger, *Simple Justice,* 593–94.

337 "There is a robe room": Muse, interview by author.

338 "My dear Mr. President": FG, box 360, WHCF, LBJL.

338 "Dear Mrs. Marshall": Ibid.

339 "There was probably not a Negro": Goodwin, *Lyndon Johnson and the American Dream,* 306–7.

339 "I say to you": Branch, *At Canann's Edge,* 746.

340 "The people in this room": Williams, *Thurgood Marshall,* 343.

340 "Black separatism will breed nothing": Ibid., 343–44.

341 "before you were born": *Washington Post,* Aug. 31, 1967.

342 "There wasn't anyone": Individual Review Folders, LBJL.

342 "indifference to the plight": Tushnet, *Thurgood Marshall,* 521.

342 "the practical effect": Ibid., 518.

342 "to rest a death sentence": Ibid., 520.

342 "The death penalty": *New York Times,* March 10, 2015.

343 "Face the simple fact": Hall, *Oxford Companion to the Supreme Court,* 612.

343 "It may be easy": Tushnet, *Thurgood Marshall,* 372.

345 "More and more I'm sure": Ibid., 492.

345 "He died of a broken heart": Ibid.

347 "I'm getting old": C-SPAN, June 28, 1967.

348 "They ain't looking": Bernhard, interview by author.

348 "I don't want to": Ibid.

348 "Where are you from?": Shannon Warnock, interview by author.

349 "ordeal by committee": *Baltimore Afro-American,* Aug. 12, 1967.

349 "In an article": Ibid.

349 "He told friends": Mondale, interview by author.

349 "They say Obama has got": Califano, interview by author.

350 "Johnson had, for all his problems": Mondale, interview by author.

351 "Eighty percent of the branches": Tushnet, *Thurgood Marshall,* 509.

EPILOGUE

REQUIEM FOR THURGOOD

353 "Justice Marshall's judicial philosophy": *Washington Post,* June 29, 2010.

353 "America is a better nation": *Washington Wire,* June 28, 2010.

354 "On the Supreme Court today": *New York Times,* March 6, 2011.

SELECTED BIBLIOGRAPHY

Alpert, Hollis. *The Life and Times of "Porgy and Bess": The Story of an American Classic*. New York: Knopf, 1990.

Appiah, Kwame Anthony, and Henry Louis Gates Jr., eds. *Africana: The Encyclopedia of the African and African American Experience*. New York: Basic Civitas Books, 1999.

Asch, Chris Myers. *The Senator and the Sharecropper: The Freedom Struggles of James O. Eastland and Fannie Lou Hamer*. New York: New Press, 2008.

Baldwin, James. *Collected Essays*. New York: Library of America, 1998.

———. *The Fire Next Time*. New York: Modern Library, 1995.

Bass, Jack, and Marilyn W. Thompson. *Ol' Strom: An Unauthorized Biography of Strom Thurmond*. Marietta, Ga.: Longstreet Press, 1998.

Bernard, Emily, ed. *Remember Me to Harlem*. New York: Knopf, 2001.

Branch, Taylor. *At Canaan's Edge: America in the King Years, 1965–68*. New York: Simon & Schuster, 2006.

———. *Parting the Waters: America in the King Years, 1954–63*. New York: Simon & Schuster, 1988.

———. *Pillar of Fire: America in the King Years, 1963–65*. New York: Simon & Schuster, 1998.

Bronner, Ethan. *Battle for Justice: How the Bork Nomination Shook America*. New York: W. W. Norton, 1989.

Burke, Lewis W., and Belinda F. Gergel, eds. *Matthew J. Perry: The Man, His Times, and His Legacy*. Columbia: University of South Carolina Press, 2004.

Cagin, Seth, and Philip Dray. *We Are Not Afraid: The Story of Goodman, Schwerner, and Chaney and the Civil Rights Campaign for Mississippi*. New York: Macmillan, 1988.

Caro, Robert A. *The Years of Lyndon Johnson: Master of the Senate*. New York: Alfred A. Knopf, 2002.

———. *The Years of Lyndon Johnson: The Passage of Power*. New York: Alfred A. Knopf, 2012.

———. *The Years of Lyndon Johnson: The Path to Power*. New York: Alfred A. Knopf, 1982.

Cash, W. J. *The Mind of the South*. New York: Vintage Books, 1991.

Clancy, Paul R. *Just a Country Lawyer: A Biography of Senator Sam Ervin*. Bloomington: Indiana University Press, 1974.

Clark, James C. *Red Pepper and Gorgeous George: Claude Pepper's Epic Defeat in the 1950 Democratic Primary*. Gainesville: University Press of Florida, 2011.

Coleman, William T. *Counsel for the Situation: Shaping the Law to Realize America's Promise*. With Donald T. Bliss. Washington, D.C.: Brookings Institution Press, 2010.

Dray, Philip. *At the Hands of Persons Unknown: The Lynching of Black America*. New York: Random House, 2002.

Evans, Harold. *The American Century*. With Gail Buckland and Kevin Baker. New York: Alfred A. Knopf, 2000.

Feldman, Noah. *Scorpions: The Battles and Triumphs of FDR's Great Supreme Court Justices*. New York: Twelve, 2010.

Fine, Sidney. *Violence in the Model City: The Cavanagh Administration, Race Relations, and the Detroit Riot of 1967*. Ann Arbor: University of Michigan Press, 1989.

Friedman, Leon, ed. *Brown v. Board: The Landmark Oral Argument Before the Supreme Court*. New York: New Press, 2004.

Gates, Henry Louis, and Evelyn Brooks Higginbotham, eds. *African American Lives*. Oxford: Oxford University Press, 2004.

Gibson, Larry S. *Young Thurgood: The Making of a Supreme Court Justice*. Amherst, N.Y.: Prometheus Books, 2012.

Goodheart, Adam. *1861: The Civil War Awakening*. New York: Alfred A. Knopf, 2011.

Goodwin, Doris Kearns. *Lyndon Johnson and the American Dream*. New York: St. Martin's Press, 1976.

———. *Team of Rivals: The Political Genius of Abraham Lincoln*. New York: Simon & Schuster, 2005.

Green, Ben. *Before His Time: The Untold Story of Harry T. Moore, America's First Civil Rights Martyr*. New York: Free Press, 1999.

Greenberg, Jack. *Crusaders in the Courts: How a Dedicated Band of Lawyers Fought for the Civil Rights Revolution*. New York: Basic Books, 1994.

Gronlund, Mimi Clark. *Supreme Court Justice Tom Clark: A Life of Service*. Austin: University of Texas Press, 2010.

Halberstam, David. *The Fifties*. New York: Fawcett Columbine, 1993.

Hall, Kermit L. *The Oxford Companion to the Supreme Court of the United States*. 2nd ed. Oxford: Oxford University Press, 2005.

Harlan, Louis R. *Booker T. Washington: The Wizard of Tuskegee, 1901–1915*. Oxford: Oxford University Press, 1983.

Harris, Mark. *Pictures at a Revolution: Five Movies and the Birth of the New Hollywood*. New York: Penguin Press, 2008.

Hayes, Harold, ed. *Smiling Through the Apocalypse: Esquire's History of the Sixties*. New York: Crown, 1987.

Haygood, Wil. *King of the Cats: The Life and Times of Adam Clayton Powell, Jr.* Boston: Houghton Mifflin, 1993.

Haynes, Robert V. *A Night of Violence: The Houston Riot of 1917.* Baton Rouge: Louisiana State University Press, 1976.

Hersey, John. *The Algiers Motel Incident.* London: Hamish Hamilton, 1968.

Hine, Darlene Clark. *Black Victory: The Rise and Fall of the White Primary in Texas.* Millwood, N.Y.: KTO Press, 1979.

Hulsey, Byron C. *Everett Dirksen and His Presidents: How a Senate Giant Shaped American Politics.* Lawrence: University Press of Kansas, 2000.

Kennedy, Edward M. *True Compass: A Memoir.* New York: Twelve, 2009.

King, Gilbert. *Devil in the Grove: Thurgood Marshall, the Groveland Boys, and the Dawn of a New America.* New York: HarperCollins, 2012.

Kluger, Richard. *Simple Justice: The History of Brown v. Board of Education and Black America's Struggle for Equality.* New York: Alfred A. Knopf, 1976.

Kotz, Nick. *Judgment Days: Lyndon Baines Johnson, Martin Luther King, and the Laws That Changed America.* Boston: Houghton Mifflin, 2005.

Laymon, Sherry. *Fearless: John L. McClellan, United States Senator.* Mustang, Okla.: Tate, 2011.

Lewis, David Levering. *W. E. B. DuBois: The Fight for Equality and the American Century, 1919–1963.* New York: Henry Holt, 2000.

Litwack, Leon F. *Trouble in Mind: Black Southerners in the Age of Jim Crow.* New York: Alfred A. Knopf, 1998.

Long, Michael G. *Marshalling Justice: The Early Civil Rights Letters of Thurgood Marshall.* New York: Amistad, 2011.

McClellan, John L. *Crime Without Punishment.* New York: Popular Library, 1963.

McCullough, David. *Truman.* New York: Simon & Schuster, 1992.

McPherson, Harry. *A Political Education: A Washington Memoir.* Austin: University of Texas Press, 1972.

McWhirter, Cameron. *Red Summer: The Summer of 1919 and the Awakening of Black America.* New York: Henry Holt, 2011.

Morris, Edmund. *The Rise of Theodore Roosevelt.* New York: Coward, McGann & Geoghegan, Inc., 1979.

———. *Theodore Rex.* New York: Random House, 2001.

O'Brien, Michael. *Philip Hart: The Conscience of the Senate.* East Lansing: Michigan State University Press, 1995.

Oney, Steve. *And the Dead Shall Rise: The Murder of Mary Phagan and the Lynching of Leo Frank.* New York: Pantheon, 2003.

Powell, Adam Clayton, Jr. *Keep the Faith, Baby!* New York: Trident Press, 1967.

Reeves, Richard. *President Kennedy: Profile of Power.* New York: Simon & Schuster, 1993.

Reporting Civil Rights: Part One: American Journalism, 1941–1963. New York: Library of America, 2003.

———. *Reporting Civil Rights: Part Two: American Journalism, 1963–1973.* New York: Library of America, 2003.

Roberts, Gene, and Hank Klibanoff. *The Race Beat: The Press, the Civil Rights Struggle, and the Awakening of a Nation.* New York: Alfred A. Knopf, 2006.

Sheinkin, Steve. *The Port Chicago 50: Disaster, Mutiny, and the Fight for Civil Rights.* New York: Roaring Brook Press, 2014.

SoRelle, James M. "The Darker Side of 'Heaven': The Black Community in Houston, Texas, 1917–1945." Ph.D. diss., Kent State University, 1980.

Strum, Philippa. *Louis D. Brandeis: Justice for the People.* New York: Schocken Books, 1984.

Sullivan, Patricia. *Lift Every Voice: The NAACP and the Making of the Civil Rights Movement.* New York: New Press, 2009.

Swanson, James L. *Manhunt: The 12-Day Chase for Lincoln's Killer.* New York: HarperCollins, 2006.

Todd, A. L. *Justice on Trial: The Case of Louis D. Brandeis.* New York: McGraw-Hill, 1964.

Tushnet, Mark V. *Making Civil Rights Law: Thurgood Marshall and the Supreme Court, 1936–1961.* New York: Oxford University Press, 1994.

———. *Thurgood Marshall: His Speeches, Writings, Arguments, Opinions, and Reminiscences.* Chicago: Lawrence Hill Books, 2001.

Updegrove, Mark K. *Indomitable Will: LBJ in the Presidency.* New York: Crown, 2012.

Whalen, Barbara, and Charles Whalen. *The Longest Debate: A Legislative History of the 1964 Civil Rights Act.* New York: New American Library, 1985.

White, Walter. *A Man Called White.* New York: Viking, 1948.

Wilkie, Curtis. *Dixie: A Personal Odyssey Through Events That Shaped the Modern South.* New York: Touchstone, 2001.

Williams, Juan. *Eyes on the Prize: America's Civil Rights Years, 1954–1965.* New York: Penguin Books, 1987.

———. *Thurgood Marshall: American Revolutionary.* New York: Three Rivers Press, 1998.

Zelden, Charles L. *The Battle for the Black Ballot: Smith v. Allwright and the Defeat of the Texas All-White Primary.* Lawrence: University Press of Kansas, 2004.

INDEX

Page numbers in *italics* refer to illustrations.

page 2 Marshall and President Johnson (Courtesy of the Lyndon Baines Johnson Presidential Library)

page 11 The Supreme Court, 1966 (Photograph by Harris and Ewing, Collection of the Supreme Court of the United States)

page 31 Marshall's class at Lincoln University (Courtesy of Langston Hughes Memorial Library of The Lincoln University)

page 89 Sen. John McClellan (Associated Press)

page 107 With William Coleman and Wiley Branton (Associated Press)

page 119 Justice J. Waties Waring (Courtesy of the Moorland-Spingarn Research Center)

page 130 Sen. James Eastland (Associated Press)

page 156 Louis Brandeis and William Howard Taft (Associated Press)

page 166 Destroyed Moore home (Courtesy of the Harry T. & Harriette V. Moore Cultural Center)

page 195 Sen. Sam Ervin (Associated Press)

page 219 Adam Clayton Powell Jr. leading aides (Courtesy of The Library of Congress)

page 232 President Johnson shaking hands with crowd (Courtesy of the Lyndon Baines Johnson Presidential Library)

page 241 Sen. Strom Thurmond (Associated Press)

page 260 Man throwing shoe during Detroit race riots (Associated Press)

page 271 Marshall with wife, Cissy (Associated Press)

page 280 Brownsville shopkeepers (Courtesy of Texas State Library & Archives Commission)

page 313 *Time* magazine cover (Time Inc.)

page 335 Marshall being sworn in (Courtesy of the Lyndon Baines Johnson Presidential Library)

page 352 Marshall's casket lying in state (Associated Press)

A NOTE ABOUT THE AUTHOR

Wil Haygood is currently the Karl and Helen Wiepking Visiting Distinguished Professor in the department of media, journalism, and film at Miami University, Ohio. For nearly three decades he was a journalist, serving as a national and foreign correspondent at *The Boston Globe*, where he was a Pulitzer Prize finalist, and then at *The Washington Post*, where he wrote the story "A Butler Well Served by This Election," which became the basis for the award-winning motion picture *The Butler*, directed by Lee Daniels. For his work researching Thurgood Marshall's confirmation hearings, Haygood won a John Simon Guggenheim Memorial Foundation Fellowship and a National Endowment for the Humanities Fellowship. He is the author of *Two on the River*; *King of the Cats: The Life and Times of Adam Clayton Powell, Jr.* (a *New York Times* Notable Book); *The Haygoods of Columbus: A Family Memoir* (winner of the Great Lakes Great Books Award); *In Black and White: The Life of Sammy Davis, Jr.* (winner of the ASCAP Deems Taylor Award, the Zora Neale Hurston–Richard Wright Legacy Award, and the Nonfiction Book of the Year Award from the Black Caucus of the American Library Association); *Sweet Thunder: The Life and Times of Sugar Ray Robinson* (finalist for the first-ever PEN-ESPN Award for Literary Sports Writing); and *The Butler: A Witness to History*, which has been translated into a dozen languages.

A NOTE ON THE TYPE

This book was set in Janson, a typeface long thought to have been made by the Dutchman Anton Janson, who was a practicing typefounder in Leipzig during the years 1668–1687. However, it has been conclusively demonstrated that these types are actually the work of Nicholas Kis (1650–1702), a Hungarian, who most probably learned his trade from the master Dutch typefounder Dirk Voskens. The type is an excellent example of the influential and sturdy Dutch types that prevailed in England up to the time William Caslon (1692–1766) developed his own incomparable designs from them.

Composed by North Market Street Graphics, Lancaster, Pennsylvania

Printed and bound by Berryville Graphics, Berryville, Virginia

Designed by Maggie Hinders